Strictly Business

STUDIES IN INDUSTRY AND SOCIETY

Philip B. Scranton, General Editor

Published with the assistance of the
Hagley Museum and Library

Strictly Business

WALTER CARPENTER AT DU PONT
AND GENERAL MOTORS

Charles W. Cheape

THE JOHNS HOPKINS UNIVERSITY PRESS

BALTIMORE AND LONDON

The Johns Hopkins University Press
2715 North Charles Street
Baltimore, Maryland 21218-4319
The Johns Hopkins Press Ltd., London

Library of Congress Cataloging-in-Publication Data will be
found at the end of this book. A catalog record for this
book is available from the British Library.
ISBN 0-8018-4941-1

To three outstanding teachers and scholars
Willie Lee Rose, Alfred Chandler, and Morton Keller
with appreciation and gratitude

Contents

Illustrations

Acknowledgments

A N Y P R O J E C T of this scope incurs a variety of obligations—financial, professional and personal, and scholarly and intellectual—and this section serves as a modest recompense. Funding came from a number of sources. Loyola College provided both a senior sabbatical and released time. The Center for the History of Business, Technology, and Society at the Hagley Museum and Library supplied several summer grants as well as housing for an extended stay, and the National Endowment for the Humanities funded a semester's research through its program of fellowships for college teachers.

Many people helped in gathering the data. Irving Shapiro and the late Crawford Greenewalt generously shared their memories of Walter Carpenter in oral interviews. Irénée du Pont Jr. permitted me to read and quote from his father's personal correspondence. At Cornell University Ronald Kline obtained a copy of Walter Carpenter's college transcript. Edmund N. Carpenter II, Walter's son, not only sat for an informative interview but also graciously gave me access to his father's scrapbooks and personal papers and diligently read and commented on the entire manuscript. The staffs for special collections at the Baker Library of Harvard Business School and the University Library of the University of Delaware guided me in using the R. G. Dun records and the John Williams papers respectively. Also very helpful was Bruce Watson, assistant to the archivist of the GMI Alumni Historical Collection at the GMI Engineering and Management Institute. At Du Pont David Hellmann and Kitsey Kiley patiently aided me in working with the minute books of the firm's executive committee, finance committee, and board of directors. The Du Pont Company, however, did not solicit or fund this project and had no control over its content.

The people at the Hagley Museum and Library deserve special recognition for the excellent research center they have created. Director Glenn Porter not only encouraged and commented perceptively on the project, but also cooked several excellent Mexican dinners. Elizabeth Kogen, Patrick Nolan, and Carol Lockman of the Center for the History of Business, Technology, and Society arranged for funding and splendid accommodations, organized talks at brown-bag lunches with the staff and visiting scholars, and generally provided a very supportive environment. Jon Williams and his group in photographic collections prepared the illustrations. Heddy Richter and Susan Hengel and the staff of the imprints division tracked down obscure printed materials. At the manuscripts collection in the Soda House, where the bulk of the work was done, Curator Michael Nash, Reference Archivist Marjorie McNinch, Archivist Chris Baer, and their assistants Gail Pietrzyk and Lynn Catanese patiently answered questions, retrieved thousands of documents, listened to trial formulations of the argument, and suggested useful sources. I am especially indebted to Michael and Marge, two professionals who thoroughly know their craft.

My intellectual obligations extend far beyond the notes listed in the text. Particularly helpful were critiques garnered from the staff and visiting scholars at Hagley in formal and informal talks and from students and colleagues in the student-faculty colloquia at Loyola's history department. The book has also benefited tremendously from trenchant readings by Glenn Porter at Hagley, by Tom Pegram in my department, by Alfred Chandler at Harvard Business School, and by Robert J. Brugger, of the Johns Hopkins University Press, as well as an anonymous reviewer for the press.

To all of these people I say thank you while acknowledging my responsibility for any remaining errors.

Introduction

ALTHOUGH Walter S. Carpenter Jr. was for forty years a top executive at E. I. du Pont de Nemours and Company, the largest chemical
manufacturing firm in the United States, he was neither a chemist nor a
manufacturer. Carpenter eventually became a highly successful president at Du Pont, but he never ran a plant, created a product, or directly
handled large numbers of people. His background was in staff
positions—purchasing, development, and finance—instead of line operations. In his time Carpenter was the most impressive manager at Du
Pont and among the most able corporate executives in the United
States, and yet he had no professional business training. In fact, he
never completed college.

Carpenter rose to success and leadership of one of America's oldest
and largest family firms. In the early twentieth century the Du Pont
Company was revitalized by three du Pont cousins (Coleman, Alfred,
and Pierre) and then diversified under three du Pont brothers (Pierre,
Irénée, and Lammot). Ownership and top management had long been
concentrated in family hands, but Carpenter was unrelated by blood or
marriage to the family (though his brother Ruly married Margaretta, a
sister of Pierre, Irénée, and Lammot).

Walter Carpenter was a transitional figure whose success depended
on the critical interplay of talent and opportunity. He was a salaried,
professional manager who spent his business lifetime administering
and directing an enterprise on behalf of others, for he never owned as
much as one percent of the Du Pont Company. Nevertheless, his special
relationship to the du Pont family helped both to create chances for
wealth, promotion, and authority and to limit his power. Early in Carpenter's career, key du Ponts selected and promoted him as a steward

of their family's essential financial interest—the firm that bore their name.

At the same time he advanced as an extraordinarily gifted business executive who was pushed by the dictates of his profession, his personality, and his training to take an impersonal, extended, and comprehensive view of America's biggest chemical enterprise. He thus had to balance the prerogatives of majority owners to whom he was closely linked with the best interests of a large, bureaucratic firm. Furthermore, his leadership and mediation occurred in a society that prided itself on the ideals of individualism, small enterprise, and egalitarianism while he simultaneously moved from middle-class origins in a small city to great wealth and national prominence. How Walter Carpenter was able to accomplish these feats is the subject of this study.

By focusing on a career that highlights the patterns of management in large-scale American enterprise, this book will answer historical questions about how a manager trained and rose, what he did and how he did it, and what limited his power. In short, it responds to the general question, How did top managers maintain and even increase profits and growth in the big firms that they inherited from entrepreneurs and family operators and that have been at the core of the U.S. economy during the twentieth century?

Walter Carpenter was among the first generation of business leaders to run the decentralized, multi-industry enterprise that Du Pont had pioneered between 1910 and 1921. The new strategy of diversification and the new structure of autonomous product divisions meant that top professional managers no longer headed a plant or a functional department. Instead, they assumed direct responsibility for key decisions about resource allocation and organization in a general office. There they systematically coordinated and appraised operations in all Du Pont lines while planning for expansion and seeking new opportunities for investment. Carpenter's career demonstrates how one pioneer executive did just that for four decades.

His business life merits close attention despite the careful scrutiny already given the Du Pont Company by several scholars. Books covering Du Pont's internal communications, its foreign operations, and its pioneering research and development have recently appeared, and earlier works by Alfred Chandler and Stephen Salsbury have analyzed the course of Du Pont operations and management during the first two decades of the twentieth century.[1] But Chandler's and Salsbury's accounts do not extend past 1921, and the more recent books focus on topics other than high-level management, which was Walter Carpenter's occupation between his promotion to vice president in 1919 and his retirement as chairman of the board in 1962.

This work is therefore a case study of an exemplar of a new generation in American industry and does not aim to be a history of the Du Pont Company. The analysis of Carpenter's managerial experience at Du Pont covers important and largely ignored material and is interesting for both particular and general reasons. Tracking the career of an outstanding professional executive also traces the evolution of management at Du Pont (and to some extent at General Motors, where Carpenter was an important director for many years) as the company shifted away from owner operation and completed its evolution into the modern, diversified chemical giant. We have many biographies of entrepreneurs, (mostly) men who owned major portions of the enterprises they built. There are, however, few studies of individual professional managers, yet such executives run today, as they have for decades, most of the key, large firms in the manufacturing, distribution, financial, transportation, and public utility sectors of the American economy.

Walter Carpenter also merits attention for reasons peculiar to his career. His business papers—on file at the Hagley Library in Wilmington, Delaware—are extensive and rich, as are valuable ancillary collections of the company, its owners, and other executives. Carpenter's letters and memoranda are particularly detailed and articulate, clearly revealing his reasoning, his powerful mind, and his underlying values and assumptions that strongly emphasized the detached, long-term, analytical approach of the professional manager.

In addition, Carpenter was simply the right man in the right place at the right time. Shortly after joining Du Pont in 1909 he moved into the development department when it became a focal point for promoting diversified product lines and a new strategy and structure between 1911 and 1921. He was vice president at age thirty-one in 1919 and became treasurer and a member of the key executive and finance committees by 1921. He was appointed vice president for finance in 1926, vice chairman of the executive committee in 1927, and chairman of the finance committee in 1930. He served as president of Du Pont between 1940 and 1948 and as chairman of the board until his retirement in 1962.

Because Walter Carpenter moved so quickly to the top of the big company and remained there for such an extraordinary number of years, his career provides an inside view of Du Pont when the primary challenge was not creating but rather expanding and administering the already large, successful enterprise. Carpenter played a vital role in determining strategy and in allocating resources as Du Pont completed diversification between the two world wars, introducing moistureproof cellophane, nylon, and other profitable lines. He helped pilot the company successfully and profitably through the nation's worst depression. As Pierre, Irénée, and Lammot du Pont gradually relinquished control, he helped formulate policy toward the chemical firm's many constituencies—the family and other investors, financial analysts, key suppliers and customers, government regulatory agencies, and General Motors, of which Du Pont owned about 23 percent. As president, Carpenter led the concern through World War II, balancing its strategy of diversification against the government's demands on the firm's traditional munitions business. As president and as chairman of the board, he played an active role in determining strategy in two massive antitrust cases involving Imperial Chemical Industries and General Motors.

Finally, while Carpenter's career confirms much of our present picture of professional managers and the big companies they operated, it offers a number of surprises as well. Certainly he was the quintessential professsional manager. He attacked problems in an objective manner and worked industriously for an enterprise largely owned by others. His view was long range and his approach analytical, systematic, and informed by careful use of statistical data. He was extraordinarily polite and went to considerable lengths to resolve problems using the techniques of persuasion, consensus, and cooperation so typical of behavior in elaborate bureaucracies.[2]

On the other hand, Carpenter's experiences also challenge common perceptions. His major traits were those that are now frequently condemned as sources of failure in American management and enterprise.[3] He was a financial man who relied heavily on numbers in making decisions. His career was mainly spent in staff and general executive positions instead of those functions—materials processing, manufacture, and sales—usually assumed to be at the heart of an industrial firm. He, and Du Pont, were major exponents of policy-making by committee. And yet he was generally and correctly acclaimed as the outstanding manager in one of America's largest and most successful companies in the first half of the twentieth century.

Carpenter was long a member of top management, a group accorded tremendous power by leading business analysts.[4] As a key executive at Du Pont for over forty years and as the company's chief representative on General Motors' board of directors for more than three decades, he has to be counted among the most powerful men in America in those years. Yet he frequently experienced surprising and sharp checks to that power. He often had to accommodate and occasionally defer to the concerns of the du Pont family—led by Pierre, Irénée, and Lammot—even though Pierre had already established the company as a modern bureaucratic enterprise by the time Carpenter's managerial career began. And issues of popular politics and public policy frequently intruded where business historians have argued that traditional business concerns for changing markets and technology dominated.[5]

This book is neither a company history nor a biography but combines elements of both in a study of a business career. At Du Pont the focus will be on those issues in which Walter Carpenter was directly involved, omitting or slighting major areas like labor relations and research and development, which were generally tangential to his concerns. Likewise, his personal life and his family will be included only as they relate to his managerial experiences. Centering on his career—the intersection of his life and of Du Pont's history—will permit the development of the two themes listed above: the functions of a top manager and the limits of his power.

The book's six chapters are arranged in rough chronological sequence, but each focuses on some topic or question. The first chapter introduces both Carpenter and the Du Pont Company in order to set the scene, but concentrates on Carpenter's background, training, and experience in the development department in order to identify the central factors in his rapid advance to top management. Of special interest are the relative weights of merit and du Pont family support in his promotion.

Chapter 2 deals with Carpenter's career as vice president between 1919 and 1940, when he served as both a financial and a general executive. The first role included negotiating acquisitions, insuring a steady supply of funds for working capital and for expansion, and appraising opportunities for investment in the U.S. Steel and U.S. Rubber Companies. A particularly revealing challenge was his management of a major refinancing effort in 1939, which clearly demonstrated his emphasis on detachment, statistical analysis, the long-term view, and the maintenance of a balance between the firm's family owners and its outside investors. In his second role Carpenter helped influence the evolution of Du Pont's many diversified lines—the shaping of strategy about what products to make how, where, and when. As a general executive he played an important part in the overall allocation of resources, negotiating important foreign contracts, overseeing development of the rayon and cellophane businesses, and helping articulate research policy.

The public dimension of the big business manager and some of the limits of his power are demonstrated in several episodes in the third chapter. Carpenter's recommendations for Du Pont's responses to the Great Depression, to the munitions or Nye Committee investigation of 1934, and to the New Deal reflected his ambiguous position. The impersonal, reasoned, extended view of the professional manager clashed strongly with the emotional appeal and short-term calculus often found in popular politics and public policy. Furthermore, despite his membership in the American Liberty League (sponsored by Pierre and Irénée), Carpenter was not a reactionary. Although owner-operators like Pierre, Irénée, and Lammot bitterly fought government "interference" in the company they had built, Carpenter's focus on management rather than on ownership caused him to be more conscious of the public dimension of the large corporation in order to assure its long-term success. He recognized the need for collective action, but like most of his business colleagues both inside and outside the firm, he much preferred private initiative and self-regulation to state sponsorship or supervision.

Chapter 4 focuses on an unusual managerial challenge—the oversight of Du Pont's holdings of almost one-quarter of the General Motors Corporation. The scale of Du Pont's investment made it a major concern for the company's top people, and yet they lacked the direct control over resource allocation that general executives usually exercise. Several cases—a crisis in General Motors' bonus plan for its managers between 1932 and 1934, a lengthy debate over reorganization in the 1930s and 1940s, and the choice of Alfred Sloan's successor as chief executive officer—demonstrate the curious nature of "indirect" management, the limits of Carpenter's (and of Du Pont's) power, and the surprising differences in operations between two firms generally considered to be models of modern managerial enterprise at that time.

Walter Carpenter's term as president of Du Pont (1940–48), the focus of the fifth chapter, was ironically as much an anticlimax as it was the high point of his career. Because World War II disrupted both national and international economies, the manager who prized the extended view and diversification was confronted with crisis, short-term projects, and government demands for expansion of Du Pont's traditional munitions business and for its cooperation in another major defense enterprise—the Manhattan Project. As best he could, Carpenter balanced Du Pont's commitment to diversification and its postwar planning with immediate needs and patriotic duty. A similar irony was the selection of Crawford Greenewalt, Irénée's son-in-law, to succeed Carpenter as president. Although Greenewalt was highly qualified and was certainly the best candidate available, Carpenter clearly began his presidency expecting a professional manager as successor instead of the perpetuation of family control.

Chapter 6 concludes the book with a continuation of the theme of limits to power. Du Pont's defeat in a giant antitrust case involving its General Motors' holdings represented a significant setback for Carpenter's detached, long-term approach. Public policy and family control (particularly tax law and Pierre's insistence on retaining the company's investment in General Motors) overrode Carpenter's rational argument for divestment and left the concern vulnerable to prosecution. The overwhelming logic and evidence of Du Pont's inability to "control" GM failed to prevent conviction in a lengthy, sensational case. The defeat was costly, depriving the firm of a large cash flow and foreclosing the strategy of acquisition, which, along with internal development, had been so crucial to diversification and growth in the past. Particularly galling was Carpenter's and Du Pont's inability to persuade Congress to protect the firm's stockholders from unanticipated heavy taxation as a by-product of the divestiture.

Carpenter's legacy, then, is an ambiguous one. He led Du Pont to ever greater size, profits, and reputation, and his career is a model of professional management. His meteoric rise and able administration of a large enterprise typify the values of hard work, corporate loyalty, impartiality, rational analysis, extended planning, and preference for advancement on merit. His years as president and as chairman of the board, however, witnessed the perpetuation of significant family control and serious legal defeat for the company. His successful career in a powerful giant enterprise ironically altered much less than might have been expected.

Strictly Business

1

How to Succeed in Business—Quickly

WALTER CARPENTER rose from inauspicious beginnings to remarkably early success in business. He was born a Carpenter and not a du Pont; grew up in Wilkes-Barre, Pennsylvania, instead of Wilmington, Delaware; and came from a middle-class rather than a wealthy family. Yet in 1919, at the age of thirty-one, less than ten years after joining the Du Pont Company, he was vice president and a member of the executive committee, the key small group of top managers who ran one of America's largest, most profitable industrial enterprises.

How did he accomplish this rapid rise? Carpenter's early life combined four critical factors that explain his meteoric promotion: family background and early training; opportunity based on luck and good timing; extraordinary ability including energy, initiative, even temperament, and penetrating intelligence; and du Pont family ties. An examination of his childhood and initial business career helps clarify the role and impact of those factors as well as their interlinking relationships.

The Carpenters of Wilkes-Barre

In 1888 Walter Carpenter was born into a stable, comfortable family environment typical of old stock America—white, native-born Protestants with British forebears, who dominated the country in the nineteenth century. His Carpenter ancestors had emigrated from England to Massachusetts in the 1630s, moving to New York within a generation and to Pennsylvania in the early 1800s.[1] Carpenter males were part of middling America, freemen and property holders who farmed, served as captains in the local militia, and held minor offices while their religious affiliation shifted gradually from the Puritan to the Presbyterian to the Methodist faith, which Walter practiced at least nominally.

Walter's paternal grandmother, Sally Ann Fell, belonged to one of Wilkes-Barre's prominent families.[2] Her great grandfather, Jesse Fell, was a major in the local militia, associate judge of Luzerne County, in which Wilkes-Barre is located, and president of the Luzerne County Agricultural Society. Of Walter Carpenter's maternal grandparents less is known. Mary Catherine Barnet, his maternal grandmother, was the daughter of an iron founder in Easton, Pennsylvania. Robert Ruliph Morgan, her husband and Carpenter's maternal grandfather, was the son of a sea captain and shipowner in Port Deposit, Maryland. After their marriage the Morgans moved to Luzerne County, where Robert became a mine superintendent.[3]

The Carpenters' economic comfort derived from the work of Walter's paternal grandfather, Benjamin Gardner Carpenter, an entrepreneur in a modest Horatio Alger style.[4] He had moved to Wilkes-Barre in 1847 to apprentice as a tinsmith to Theron Burnet, soon becoming Burnet's partner and then buying in 1857 full ownership of their hardware store with its specialty in sheet metal work.[5] Under his skilled and careful management, the operation thrived. With the help of a series of junior partners, Benjamin Carpenter successfully piloted the store through the panic of 1857, the chaos of the Civil War years, and the major depression of the 1870s. He ran the business shrewdly and extended essential credit generously enough to attract customers (many of whom were local builders) but prudently enough to survive the cash shortages and the unexpected, severe credit crunches so typical of the nineteenth-century American economy. His diligent attention received frequent approbation from the correspondents of R. G. Dun, the credit agency, who variously labeled the business as "good," "safe," "honest," and "reliable" and who in 1881 described B. G. Carpenter and Company as the "best bus[iness] in their line" in Wilkes-Barre.[6]

Growth accompanied success and considerably increased the wealth of the firm and of Walter's grandfather. Nevertheless, cash was always short in the company and in the Carpenter household because of customer financing and thrifty reinvestment of profits. In 1874 Benjamin

Carpenter and his partners completed a new "v[er]y fine store" that "v[er]y much embarrassed them for ready funds" though R. G. Dun's agent thought them quite safe.[7] In 1884 the company's net worth, which had been been about $8,000 in the late 1850s, had grown to an estimated $40,000.[8]

By the 1880s Benjamin Carpenter, "the monied man" of the operation, had firmly established himself as part of a local merchant group that still played a large role in the economic and civic life of American towns and small cities.[9] Besides his share in the store, he had real estate worth about $25,000, held mortgages for some $21,000, and owned stock in a nearby stove works, in a local street railway, and in the Wilkes-Barre Water Company, of which he was president and manager.[10]

His grandfather's position and success defined the world in which Walter Carpenter was reared. His father, Walter S. Carpenter Sr., had made B. G. Carpenter and Company a family enterprise by becoming a partner and, along with his younger brothers and junior partners, Benjamin H. and Edmund N. (Walter's Uncle Harry and Uncle Ed), he had inherited the business at his father's death in 1889. Within a year of his joining the firm in 1875, the income and security of the partnership allowed him to marry Isabella Morgan, daughter of a local mine superintendent. Together they bought a house and land at 69 Union Street (valued at about $2,000) in Wilkes-Barre, where Walter Samuel Carpenter Jr. was born on January 8, 1888, the last of seven children (three of whom died in infancy).[11]

The scanty available evidence indicates that Walter's father as president and half owner of B. G. Carpenter and Company provided his family with a comfortable life from his steady but unspectacular management of the store, whose value in 1910 was approximately $40,000 —just about what it had been twenty-six years earlier.[12] Walter, who was variously called Junior, Sam, or Bulla by his family and playmates, seems to have had a healthy, happy childhood spent mostly in Wilkes-Barre (though there was a glorious visit to Uncle Ed's encampment in Kentucky during the Spanish-American War in the summer of 1898). He attended public schools until entering the Wyoming Seminary, the local private academy, to complete his high school education. The choice was a logical one for a Carpenter. Walter's grandfather had served as a trustee and had named his youngest child Edmund Nelson after Dr. Reuben Nelson, the seminary's first principal. Walter's father and uncles as well as his older brother Ruly had already attended the school. Here he obtained (in his own judgment) an "excellent grounding" in mathematics, developed a taste for sports (football, baseball, and track), in which he was a determined competitor, and foreshadowed his future career when he delivered a talk entitled "Industrial Corporations" for his senior oration.[13]

Carpenter did well enough to be admitted to Cornell University, where he began the study of mechanical engineering in the fall of 1906.[14] As the first of his family to attend college, and an Ivy League school at that, he considered himself among the less privileged at Cornell. Given the opportunity and the energy exemplified by his grandfather and father, he worked hard at both classes and play. He competed on the varsity track team as a sophomore and junior, played intramural football, and was a cheerleader. He later recalled that as a student he "was diligent, perhaps more than average." His course load was challenging, comprised almost entirely of math, science, and engineering classes, and it grew more arduous in his junior and senior years. Walter certainly got full value from his college career though his academic performance was steady and unspectacular. His grades were largely Bs and Cs, perhaps in part because of his work load and in part because he always valued the concrete and practical over the academic and theoretical.

As a college senior Walter Carpenter foreshadowed much of what he would be throughout his business career. He was in excellent physical health with a wiry, slender build to go with his medium height. His avid interest in sports, especially golf and tennis, and his fiercely competitive spirit (the counterpart to a voracious appetite for work in business) would keep him active and in fine shape for decades to come. His penetrating intelligence disciplined by his high school and engineering education made him a quick study. His energy and diligence paired steady, hard work with an able mind.

Complementing these abilities was a calm, even temperament. He was quiet and private but not shy. He enjoyed good times with close friends but to casual acquaintances he was extraordinarily polite and pleasant while maintaining a firm reserve. He readily conceded that he was "temperamentally inclined to avoid outward expressions of feeling," but in a rare personal observation he stoutly denied being "even slightly affected by introversion. I am sure that I do not suffer from it, even though I would not be called an extrovert either."[15]

In sum, Carpenter's family background and training, one of the critical factors in his rapid, early rise, were closely intertwined with opportunity, a second key element. His upbringing not only prepared him for a successful business career, but also helped create the chance for such a career by placing him in the category of people who were the source for most top corporate managers in America in the twentieth century.

Not surprisingly, a substantial majority of executives like Walter Carpenter and such contemporaries as Alfred Sloan at General Motors and Philip Reed at General Electric were native-born, white males of Anglo-Saxon, Protestant ancestry. An excellent study of managerial recruitment, which surveyed the backgrounds of presidents and chairmen of the board of large nonfinancial firms in 1900, 1925, and 1950, also pointed out that while family wealth declined in importance over time, college education, which was always useful, became even more critical.[16] Thirty-nine percent of the 1900 group had college training, which was ten times the figure for the male population of its age. The figure rose to 51 percent in 1925 and to 76 percent in 1950, which was twelve times the average. Almost one-third of this latter group had engineering degrees, by far the most common academic specialty. Furthermore, such managers came disproportionately from the eastern United States, and many had fathers with small or general business backgrounds.

Walter Carpenter's experience made him a virtual model of the managerial type, and he was probably part of the data base for the 1950 sample. Nevertheless, his location in key categories explains only so much. The accident of birth avoided or removed unfair and unnecessary barriers like race, ethnicity, religion, and gender. Higher education provided polish and formal training that others could and did learn on the job. In fact, Carpenter spent most of his career in finance and made little, if any, direct use of his engineering courses, although they may have helped him better understand the numerous technological developments in product and process that were so central to Du Pont's success in the twentieth century.

Furthermore, as a WASP male Carpenter was part of a huge group, for millions of Americans of that description came of age between 1900 and 1920, when large industrial firms evolved and the managerial ranks were especially open. Although college education was certainly uncommon, more than 350,000 attended college in 1910. Yet very few came close to equaling Carpenter's success despite their opportunities.[17] By 1914 at Du Pont alone there were some two thousand salaried administrators and other white-collar personnel, many of whom were competing with Carpenter but who did not match his accomplishments.[18]

Thus, the more significant result of Walter Carpenter's background was the inculcation of traits, skills, and patterns of behavior that were commonly found in American managers and that encouraged him to combine productively his native intelligence with his opportunity.[19] His quiet confidence in his abilities, the by-product of a secure, comfortable upbringing, meant that he could concentrate his attention on the business challenges at hand and avoid distractions like gnawing self-doubt or needless self-promotion. The work ethic—that mixture of discipline, duty, and diligence that had been so obvious in his grandfather's and his father's lives—kept Walter's energies focused on the tasks at hand. He enjoyed work and clearly derived immense satisfaction from solving difficult problems.

His grandfather's and father's careers also led him to value business as a vocation that created wealth and general well-being. Their thrifty handling of money and careful reinvestment of surplus deeply impressed Walter with the value and importance of capital accumulation. Their operation of a small firm in a hands-on, practical manner instinctively disposed him to prefer the empirical over the theoretical, while his engineering training encouraged systematic organization and objective analysis of data in order to identify questions, find patterns, and determine the most effective solutions. In other words, he learned to use his intelligence in a way that produced judgment or wisdom, a critical ability in a top manager.

At the same time his family taught him extraordinary politeness, but not the servility or bland niceness that would have been fatal for long-term success. Objective analysis required independent judgment and decisiveness, and politeness for Carpenter was a form of enlightened self-interest, an awareness of and even a concern for the needs of others. It would become in his career an indispensable ingredient in reaching agreements that achieved his ends while advancing or doing the least feasible damage to the aims of others. His attention to others was gratifying to them and would frequently win cooperation and appreciation not only for the deal at hand but for the many future encounters likely in a large-scale, bureaucratic enterprise.

Finally, while Walter Carpenter's training helped shape a personality and character that made him attractive to others as it prepared him for a business career, it also inculcated initiative. His strong competitiveness in sports suggests that he inherited his grandfather's aggressiveness. That go-ahead spirit encouraged an energetic willingness, desire, and determination to anticipate, to prepare, and to act in advance—a decided advantage over those who simply responded to events. Indeed, such decisiveness in seizing opportunity was not only critical for his eventual career but was also essential for his immediate entry into the Du Pont Company.

Adventure in Chile

In the fall of his senior year Walter Carpenter was doing well at school and certainly should have finished with his class in the spring of 1910, but he never completed his degree. He abruptly withdrew from Cornell in November 1909, and within two months arrived in Valparaiso, Chile, to begin a career with the Du Pont Company that would last the rest of his life.

Carpenter later reminisced about the sudden change as an adventure that unexpectedly intruded into his life. "The thrill of the anticipated experience" enticed him into taking a job in Chile for two years.[20] At first he was in the commercial end of the business, the buying and shipping of nitrate ore for Du Pont. Later he visited the nitrate pampas, where the "hard caliche ore" was mined and refined before shipping.

The adventure was rooted in his part-time jobs at the Du Pont Company as a "cub" engineer during his college years. In the summers of 1907 and 1908 he had worked at the company's Repauno dynamite plant in Gibbstown, New Jersey, under J. L. "Pop" Warner of the engineering department, and in 1909 he moved to the Carney's Point smokeless powder plant at Penns Grove, New Jersey. The summers had been great fun and were not unlike college. He lived away from home in a boarding house with other young engineering students like himself, applying to simple drafting, design, and construction work the principles learned in school.

Carpenter later recalled that while at Repauno he was fascinated by watching the nitrate boats arrive from Chile in a scene far removed from prosaic Wilkes-Barre. "I was . . . witnessing a part of the commerce of the world. These boats had been loaded with ore, brought down from the interior of Chile to the ports of the Pacific Coast, loaded on the ship, taken around the Horn and brought up the Atlantic Coast and were there unloaded. The trip was perhaps 8,000 to 10,000 miles. It was part of the great ocean-born [sic] traffic of the world. To me it was commerce and romance as well."[21]

Joining that world of commerce and romance was part of the adventure itself. In November 1909 Walter traveled from Ithaca to Philadelphia and attended the Cornell-Pennsylvania football game with his oldest brother, Robert Ruliph (Ruly) Carpenter, who headed Du Pont's development department. Ruly told him about a sudden opening for an assistant to the man in charge of the Valparaiso office, but also explained that an immediate decision was necessary for a departure within a month. After a quick family conference during which he decided to seize the opportunity, Carpenter rushed back to Ithaca to leave school so rapidly that his transcript still carries a "W" signifying withdrawal without cancellation.

Departure from his family appropriately became a rite of passage for the twenty-one-year-old. Walter's father gave him one hundred dollars, which Walter Sr. thought was "all that he could afford" because of the scarcity of cash in the Carpenter household.[22] (The ceremony so impressed Walter Jr. that he subsequently made a point of writing a letter of passage and conferring a generous cash gift on each of his three sons on their twenty-first birthdays.)[23] Walter later told his son John that clothes and expenses gobbled up the hundred dollars, and that after spending Christmas and his twenty-second birthday aboard ship, he arrived in Valparaiso on January 21, 1910, without "a cent until the first pay day came around."[24]

Carpenter's colorful account was true as far as it went, and certainly it highlights the importance of story-book opportunity and of his own initiative and decisiveness in the evolution of his career. However, additional evidence introduces or accentuates other factors critical to his start, particularly family background and du Pont family ties.

Ruly Carpenter (who was eleven years older than Walter) was not only his brother and director of Du Pont's development department; he was also married to Margaretta (Peg) du Pont, sister of Pierre du Pont, one of three cousins then running the company.[25] After graduating from Wyoming Seminary, Ruly had worked in the Carpenter family store and with several engineering and manufacturing firms, including the Manufacturer's Contracting Company, a Du Pont subsidiary. In 1906, the year of his marriage to Peg, he joined the Du Pont Company as a district purchasing agent, and in the following year he attended the Massachusetts Institute of Technology (undoubtedly with Pierre's help) to study architecture. After one year he left MIT in 1908 to take a position with the development department, then headed by Irénée du Pont, Pierre's brother and also Ruly's brother-in-law.

Ruly not only helped Walter get summer jobs with Du Pont; he also introduced the entire Carpenter family to Pierre. Probably with Pierre's and Irénée's approval, Ruly arranged for the offer of the position in Chile. Pierre, who constantly watched for bright young talent to staff his rapidly growing firm and who was apparently impressed by Walter Carpenter, listed Walter's college residence in his address book and made a special effort to cheer him up during the long journey to Chile.[26] While at sea on Christmas Day 1909 Walter opened a package from Pierre containing a pin and a handwritten note to "remind you that we are all thinking of you and wishing you all kinds of good luck." Pierre cautioned, "There will be difficulties to overcome as well as new things to see, do and enjoy . . . but if troubles arise don't let two or three thousand miles interfere with calling for help from Pierre."[27] Later he wrote Walter's boss in Valparaiso asking about his progress.[28]

If the colorful account slights the role of family, it also understates Carpenter's use of his own abilities. The decision was not a spur-of-the-moment choice, but a carefully thought-out calculation. Carpenter must have learned of the opportunity in the summer of 1909, because in that fall at Cornell he added courses in Spanish and political economy for which there was no precedent in his previous curriculum.[29] He calmly decided that a promising career opportunity was more important than completing a degree, for after nearly three and one half years he had most of the substance of formal engineering training. The rest could be learned on the job if and when necessary. As he later put it: "While the idea of leaving college in his senior year was not a pleasant one, after all a good job might lead to one's life work, and such things were not always available."[30] The rational balancing, the extended perspective, and the choice of the practical and concrete over the academic and theoretical were typical of his thinking throughout his lengthy business career.

Part of that calculation was the weight assigned to the position and to the firm, and in 1909 E. I. du Pont de Nemours and Company was quite an attractive setting for a business career. Founded in 1802 on the banks of the Brandywine Creek in Wilmington, Delaware, the enterprise had prospered under three generations of family management during the nineteenth century and had dominated the manufacture of gunpowder and explosives in the United States as the leader of an industry cartel.[31]

In 1902 the fourth generation, led by Alfred I., Pierre, and T. Coleman du Pont, had assumed control, and by the time Walter Carpenter joined the company the three cousins had transformed it into a mod-

ern big firm.[32] Led by Coleman as president and Pierre as treasurer
(Alfred concentrated largely on running black powder operations), Du
Pont had bought up competitors and substituted a virtual monopoly
for the old cartel arrangement. The cousins quickly moved their firm
from horizontal combination as a holding company of scattered, autonomous subsidiaries into the consolidation and rationalization of
manufacturing plants to achieve economies of scale and location.
Simultaneously Pierre and Coleman shifted to a strategy of vertical
integration to gain further savings by creating a series of functional
departments in sales, finance, purchasing, development, and engineering to coordinate manufacturing and marketing while obtaining maximum throughput and the lowest possible costs in the organization.

As a pioneer in American big business, Du Pont's success was obvious
to Walter and to the rest of the nation. In 1909 it was the twenty-seventh
largest industrial firm in the United States with assets of $74.8 million
and net earnings of $6.0 million on sales of $30.8 million.[33] It employed 7,800 with sales offices and a full line of black powder, smokeless
powder, and dynamite plants stretching across the country. In order to
administer the operation, the cousins had gone beyond the du Pont
family to hire men like Frank Tallman, Charles Meade, and William
Coyne, who would be Carpenter's contemporaries as salaried, professional managers in the company's lower, middle, and top ranks. To put
it simply, Walter Carpenter was attracted by the opportunity for talented, non-family members to achieve advancement, power, and
wealth in a leading American enterprise. By 1914 there were ninety-
four such positions paying annual salaries of $4,200 or more in the top
and middle executive ranks alone at Du Pont, a figure that omits all of
the lower and many of the middle-level slots with lesser pay.[34]

The position offered to Walter Carpenter resulted directly from Du
Pont's vertical integration and made him one of two key men in a small
and remote but vital and highly visible operation.[35] Nitrate of soda, an
essential ingredient in gunpowder and explosives manufacture, had
long been bought by the company from importers shipping it from
Chile, the world's major source of supply. Prior to combination and
consolidation, such purchases were critical but relatively small and
could be safely left to a New York importing firm. Expansion and the
creation of the large enterprise meant that Du Pont annually bought 30
to 50 percent of all nitrates brought into the United States.

The scale of purchases (which each year totaled over one hundred
million tons), their critical nature (a two-month supply was always kept

on hand to assure the continuous operation of Du Pont plants), the amount of time involved (mining and shipping required many months), and their cost (which sometimes approached $5 million annually, including $380,000 in commissions to New York importers) quickly had the company investigating alternate sources. In 1905 Pierre du Pont himself studied the industry closely and made an extended trip to Chile in hopes of securing the company's own nitrate mine. He soon decided that local conditions—the unreliability of current reports on nitrate fields, a speculative boom that had vastly inflated the cost of mining properties, and the difficulty of insuring good management given the problems of time and distance—precluded any immediate purchase of nitrate property.

As a compromise, Du Pont set up its own purchasing office in Valparaiso to buy direct with lower costs, closer coordination, and better information about a critical raw material. Local conditions required rather complex arrangements for payment. Because Du Pont was new to Chile, nitrate sellers would not accept its notes. There were no American banks in the area, and payments were customarily made in pounds sterling. As a result, Pierre engineered an intricate three-party network involving Du Pont as well as English and U.S. banking houses.

In 1909, after the first such partnership had ended, the National City Bank of New York agreed to create a $2 million credit at two major English banks, the London City and Midland Bank and the Union of London and Smith's Bank Ltd. The Du Pont Company issued ninety-day drafts against these accounts in Wilmington and sent them to the Valparaiso office for signature and endorsement to the sellers of nitrate. The drafts then circulated as money in Chile without paying interest until redeemed at the London banks, which were subsequently reimbursed by the National City Bank. Du Pont in turn repaid National City, which required a permanent $500,000 deposit as collateral for the service. For further protection the New York bank kept title to the nitrate (with the shipping documents as evidence) until Du Pont paid its debts. Meanwhile the purchasing department in Wilmington chartered ships to transport the nitrate, whose loading was overseen by the Valparaiso office.

The large savings and steady, assured supply that resulted more than repaid Pierre's efforts. Direct purchases averaged at least seven cents per hundred pounds below the prices of W. R. Grace and Company, the leading importer. Total annual costs of working capital were nearly halved to about $2 million while a safe two-month supply of nitrate was always maintained in Wilmington and several additional months' needs were being bought ahead and put in transit.

The critical linchpin in the process was the head of the Valparaiso office, who had to have virtual autonomy (given the constraints of time and distance) to negotiate purchases and to arrange payments. For this essential position, Pierre chose Elias Ahuja, a dealer in the nitrate trade who had accompanied him during his 1905 inspection tour. The Spanish-born Ahuja had emigrated to the United States as a boy in the early 1870s and lived in the Boston area before becoming a broker or speculator in the New York nitrate business in the late 1890s. During their journey he impressed Pierre with his rare, essential combination of honesty, judgment, and knowledge, and the two were close friends for many years.[36] Ahuja left his investments and accounts in the hands of Pierre, who in turn let the Spaniard buy and sell on Du Pont's account in Chile in order to supply the firm's long-term needs at the lowest possible cost. Even after the purchasing department under director Frank Tallman began running operations from Wilmington in 1907, Ahuja retained some autonomy until his departure in 1914.[37]

Thus, the chance to be Ahuja's assistant in Valparaiso was an excellent place for Walter Carpenter to begin his career with the Du Pont Company. Though far from Wilmington, nitrate operations were so critical, risky, complex, and expensive that they—and the few key individuals involved—received continual and careful scrutiny from senior officials. In 1910 Pierre wrote William du Pont, his cousin and subsequently a fellow company director, that "the financial arrangements for handling nitrate are very important," that they gave the firm "distinct advances" in the trade, and that they were being handled "in a very advantageous way" in Chile.[38]

Though Elias Ahuja remained in charge, Walter quickly became a very able assistant. He helped complete arrangements for payment, prepared essential documents for shipping and insurance, and oversaw the loading of cargo. Later, after the company acquired its own mine, he visited the site and apparently helped coordinate shipments from the interior to the coast.[39] In his spare time he read diligently about the Du Pont Company and the explosives industry as well as about international banking. Years later he recalled being so impressed with the monthly newsletter of the National City Bank that he became a subscriber and "perused [it] with a great deal of interest as it told of numerous goings on in a world which [was] to me at that time, and perhaps still is, a fairyland."[40]

One observer thought that Walter worked so hard that he was "in rather a rut," but in fact the two-year stay must have been quite an adventure for an unmarried twenty-two-year-old.[41] While in Chile Carpenter experienced an earthquake, fled a scarlet fever epidemic, heard William Jennings Bryan speak, attended balls and races, and helped Santiago celebrate the one-hundredth anniversary of its independence.[42] In a world regulated by the pace of shipments, a young man could both work and play hard.

Nor was he lonely at his Valparaiso outpost. His Uncle Ed was already there, searching for mining properties for Du Pont, and soon there were visits from Ruly (who came to negotiate the purchase of a mine), from his distant cousin Ralph Derr (who was sent to superintend mining operations), and from his college classmate, Belin Mercur (a du Pont relation who also came to work in Chile). Nevertheless, the visits and distractions never threatened to turn him into a playboy (as they did Belin Mercur). His Uncle Ed reported that Walter got bored when he was away from the office.[43]

Carpenter's work so delighted Elias Ahuja that he soon became Walter's mentor and the two established a close friendship for life. Ahuja, who discovered that he and Walter had been born on the same day twenty-five years apart, served as an honorary uncle or surrogate father to the young man. Ahuja actually called himself Walter's uncle and later became godfather to his first son.[44] Carpenter's Uncle Ed wrote Walter's grandmother that Ahuja "looks after Walter like a father," solicitously sending him out of Valparaiso when scarlet fever broke out.[45] Thus Walter Carpenter established an extraordinarily close relationship to the man whom Pierre's biographers labeled "one of Pierre's close personal friends."[46]

Uncle Ed, a mentor who would both teach Walter and report on his progress, gave him a second close link to Pierre. In 1909 the Du Pont Company at Pierre's request had sent Edmund Carpenter to Chile to negotiate the purchase of a nitrate property. As in the case of Ahuja's position, the demanding job entailed considerable risk on the company's part and required someone who possessed honesty, diligence, knowledge, and judgment. Data about the nitrate mines as well as the operators themselves were entirely unreliable. Claims were salted; surveys incorrect or unavailable; intermediaries untrustworthy; and prices ridiculously inflated.[47] The colorful Carpenter, who had served in the Spanish-American War, prospected for gold in Alaska, and hunted and mined in the American West, proved to be an excellent representative.[48] Walter, who frequently saw his uncle either at Ahuja's house in Valparaiso or on visits to the pampas, watched his dealings or heard detailed accounts of them. Edmund Carpenter rejected bribes and spurned fakers as he meticulously inspected and appraised sites, carefully identified attractive candidates, and skillfully negotiated prices.

After several false starts he was soon successful. The Oficina Carolina, capable of supplying about 40 percent of Du Pont's needs, was offered for £205,000. Located about eighty miles by rail from a deepwater port, the mine contained (as Edmund Carpenter had determined) about eight million quintals of proved reserve and an additional seven million quintals of claimed reserve. When the development department sent Ruly Carpenter to complete negotiations, Uncle Ed wrote that the impatient Ruly "rages around like a wild animal" and worried that he would pay too much.[49] Walter observed closely as the protracted haggling defeated his anxious brother and was eventually completed by his more patient Uncle Ed (with Ahuja's help) at £160,000, which was £25,000 below the price Du Pont was willing to pay. Pierre wrote Edmund Carpenter that he "much appreciate[d]" the acquisition of the mine (which the company renamed Oficina Delaware), and he arranged for Walter's uncle to receive a bonus of fifty shares of Du Pont stock.[50]

His two years in Chile gave Walter Carpenter a fine start at Du Pont. He acquired expert knowledge about the nature and supply of a critical raw material. He demonstrated genuine promise as he soon mastered the instruments and intricacies of the financing of international trade. And he developed important links to key men in the firm's operations, who in turn reported his progress directly to the top.

He also had gained education of a broader nature that was critical to his understanding of and rise in large-scale enterprise. Although the scanty evidence offers no direct proof that he inculcated such understandings at this time, his mastery of them within a few years as a very young executive suggests that this experience was critical. Walter's lessons included the value of carefully judging people, of patient bargaining, and of establishing good men with full authority as close to operations as possible. He learned the importance of extended horizons in a company in which high fixed costs imposed rigid demands, for Du Pont's big investment in explosives plants required a steady supply of nitrate for efficient operation. His exposure to purchasing, shipping, finance, and raw material processing provided critical comprehension of the potential benefits of large scale in enterprise. Given the proper markets and the right product and process technology, vertical integration of several functions in a single firm offered real savings through lowered transaction costs and closer coordination of supply and demand.[51]

The Investigator

After two years in Chile, Walter Carpenter returned to Wilmington in January 1912 to become an investigator in the development department, and the familiar factors of opportunity, du Pont family ties, and superior performance continued to advance his career swiftly. Eventually labeled one of the four major divisions of the company, the department served as the investigating arm of the executive committee, the small group of high-level managers who ran Du Pont.[52] It made commercial studies of new products and processes, raw material sources, and potential acquisitions while the laboratory, with which it worked closely, did the chemical research required for such problems. The development department, for example, oversaw Edmund Carpenter's search and negotiation for a nitrate mine in Chile.

As the crossroads of Du Pont activities, it was an excellent place for a young employee to gain broad experience and to get attention. Though small (it employed only nineteen people in 1914, six of whom were at a Georgetown alcohol plant), its investigators analyzed and reported on vital questions directly to top management.[53] In addition to Walter Carpenter, a number of future Du Pont executives began their careers in the department during this period, including Leonard Yerkes, later vice president and general manager of the rayon department; Walter Beadle, future vice president, treasurer, and member of the executive committee; Charles A. Meade, eventually vice president of the miscellaneous manufacturing department and member of the executive committee; and Fin Sparre, subsequently vice president and director of the development department.

Although the department was a logical place for new young men with college experience to start their service, Carpenter and du Pont family ties also played a role in Walter's assignment. Ruly Carpenter had become (in Pierre's words) "the right-hand man" to his brother-in-law Irénée when the latter headed the department, and in 1911 succeeded him as director.[54] Walter's appointment in 1912 was hardly a surprise, though his training and performance in Chile certainly merited the position.

Carpenter's assignments quickly involved him in the department's wide-ranging tasks. His reports to and appearances before the executive committee, which began in 1912 when he was twenty-four, soon won the attention of Pierre and Irénée du Pont, John Raskob, and other top managers at Du Pont for their clarity, conciseness, thorough research, and incisive analysis. The subjects varied, given the episodic nature of the challenges sent to the department, but Walter's work in two major areas was essential in establishing his credentials and in bringing further, rapid promotions.

The first issue centered on a series of questions and investigations over several years about Du Pont's nitrate supply and built naturally on the expertise Carpenter had developed in Chile. Within months of joining the department, Walter was asked to arrange for explorations by his Uncle Ed in Peru for additional nitrate lands.[55] He quickly and smoothly concluded a joint agreement with the Peruvian government that demonstrated his negotiating abilities even though the search (like so many) was unsuccessful. Du Pont's expenses were only $40,000 because the government agreed to pay half the costs of the work and to grant the company a twenty-five year monopoly on any nitrate beds discovered. Walter soon learned that a program, no matter how well planned, could nevertheless be at the mercy of events beyond his control—a lesson that would be repeated many times in his career.

The advent of World War I again raised the nitrate issue, but in far more urgent fashion. The war created a double burden by requiring a tremendous jump in the production of gunpowder with a concomitant leap in the amount of nitrate needed while at the same time raising serious questions about the availability of nitrate supplies and shipping from Chile. Pierre remembered years later that "there was a great deal of anxiety concerning nitrate during World War I" and that at the war's outbreak Du Pont bought all the nitrate needed for existing orders and sought to fill its storehouses as well. The purchasing department was unsuccessful, for exploding demand consumed supplies as fast as they arrived and the storehouses never reached the level of guaranteeing a comfortable surplus.[56]

The development department, and Walter Carpenter in particular, scrambled to find additional sources of nitrates, preferably in mines that Du Pont could purchase and operate for itself. By chance he already had in view a potential property in June 1914, when the assassination of Austrian Archduke Francis Ferdinand triggered a series of events that led to war in less than two months. The Sud America Nitrate Mine was being offered on behalf of its owners by W. R. Grace and Company, a major exporter of nitrate from Chile, but how valid was the asking price of £103,000? Could Du Pont expect to make a reasonable return, or was it being held up in a seller's market? Would the asking price allow the mine to meet the minimum 20 percent rate of return set by the executive committee for all nitrate properties?

In several reports and appearances before the committee, Carpenter quickly, thoughtfully, and incisively answered the questions and persuaded it to act in violation of its 20 percent rule.[57] Adopting a technique based on careful quantitative and financial analysis, first developed by Pierre as treasurer and by 1914 a hallmark of decision making by top company executives, Walter demonstrated both his own skill and the soundness of a purchase. Drawing on his experience in Chile, he prudently discounted claims of reserves of ten million Spanish quintals as inflated and grounded his calculations on two-thirds to three-quarters of that figure. By his estimate the property would return 15 percent to 19 percent on the purchase price, and he succcessfully urged Du Pont to continue negotiations on that basis.

In early July the threat of war prolonged negotiations and moved Pierre to request more precise, comprehensive data on what additional investment was needed to expand the Oficina Delaware and to buy and expand the Sud America property so that Du Pont could supply all of its nitrate requirements.[58] Walter quickly responded with a detailed report demonstrating that £609,000 would be required, including £165,000 to double the Delaware operation's capacity and £444,000 to buy, repair, and expand the Sud America oficina so that the two mines could produce annually the 2,520,000 quintals of nitrate needed by Du Pont. The report also drew on his expertise to judge just how much the firm could recover by sale of the lands after depletion (£201,000) with the residue (£408,000) as the net investment against which earnings would have to be calculated. Assuming a profit per unit of 18d, Du Pont would realize a return of 18.3 percent on its total investment in the Grace property if it bought the mine for £90,000. As a result the executive committee not only had a benchmark from which to judge its risk; it also had a sensible counteroffer for W. R. Grace.

Once again circumstances intervened and negated some very fine work. There is some evidence to suggest that W. R. Grace was using the Du Pont negotiations to improve its own position, in which case Walter

Carpenter was a pawn in a larger game of which he was ignorant.[59] Far more critical was the outbreak of World War I, which quickly improved expectations for nitrate lands. Once war began in August 1914, the owners decided to retain their holdings and halted negotiations.

Throughout the war Walter Carpenter continued to search vigorously but unsuccessfully for a mine. When in 1916 Folsh and Company of Berlin sought a conference with Du Pont to discuss the sale of its Chilean nitrate lands (which it could not operate because of the British naval blockade), Carpenter resisted the tempting opportunity and insisted first that the approval of the British be sought. As he wrote to his Uncle Ed, then Du Pont's liaison to the British government in London, "it is our opinion that we should be just as open and above-board as possible with the English authorities on this matter and not do anything for which they could take exception."[60] When the government objected, talks were cancelled. In 1916 he also reopened discussions with W. R. Grace and Company, which represented the Tarapaca and Tocopilla Nitrate Company of Chile, but again cancelled negotiations when the price was judged to be excessive, despite criticism from some members of the executive committee about the failure to find new supplies.[61]

Carpenter's "failures" did not tarnish the assessment of his performance. In fact, they helped advance his career by demonstrating his independence, superior knowledge, judgment, and comprehensive, extended view. Though never plentiful, Du Pont's nitrate supplies were always adequate, and there was never a crisis. More important, other considerations outweighed the potential acquisitions. The German lands were never as valuable as maintaining a harmonious relationship with the English government, not only because of the political significance of a nation soon to be allied with the United States but because the British were major Du Pont customers whose munitions orders generated millions of dollars in profits.[62] In the case of the Grace negotiations in 1916, Carpenter explained to the executive committee that the price was unacceptably high because Grace was in the process of acquiring the land for itself and had no desire to see it sold to Du Pont. Furthermore, Walter reminded the committee that Germany's recent development of the Haber-Bosch process for synthetic manufacture of ammonia from the air would certainly produce a glut in the nitrate market as soon as the war ended, destroying all hope of amortizing Du Pont's investment over eleven years as planned.[63]

Although his work on nitrate lands had resulted in correct but negative decisions, Walter Carpenter's work on the celluloid industry, his second big task as an investigator, led to a major acquisition that served as the core of a plastics division and established the Du Pont Company in an entirely new business. Top executives like Pierre and especially Irénée hoped that diversification would use excess resources while putting Du Pont into new lines that shared process technology or intermediate products with the manufacture of explosives. In this case, the obvious link was nitrocellulose or guncotton. This critical ingredient in the making of gunpowder was also the basis for celluloid, a pyroxylin plastic made by nitrating cotton or paper with the addition of camphor as a solvent. A further advantage was Du Pont's recent development of acetaldol, a synthetic compound that it hoped to substitute as an artificial and cheaper form of camphor (which was then expensive and in short supply).[64]

However, except for the company's recent small investment in the artificial leather business, moving from the laboratory into a new and different product line was an experience virtually unknown to Du Pont. The challenge of commercial development clearly belonged to the development department. The firm needed to know about the product; the stages and process of its manufacture; the character of its market and the standard marketing arrangements; the costs, prices, and expected return on investment; and the competitive structure of the business. In short, before entering the industry, the company had to know what the business was as well as how and where to get in it. As the investigator assigned to the project in 1913, Walter Carpenter skillfully undertook a tortuous, two-year process that culminated successfully for Du Pont and for himself.

Because American makers of celluloid were suspicious and secretive, the company had to go to Germany for information. Pierre and Ruly established the initial link during a European trip in 1913, when they offered Du Pont's patent rights on acetaldol to Dr. Paul Mueller of Vereinigt-Koln-Rottweiller-Pulver-Fabriken, a German chemical enterprise, in exchange for his firm's information and rights to celluloid manufacture in the United States.[65] When Walter Carpenter visited Mueller in Germany in late 1913, he quickly got the promised data on commercial operations, including profits, prices, and trade conditions.

However, his knowledge and interest as well as his candor and polite charm also brought a good deal more. Although Mueller was not expected to divulge detailed technical or proprietary data, he twice took Carpenter through his plant at Troisdorf and arranged for his access to two factories producing celluloid articles, an opportunity not available in the United States. Mueller also shared information about the competitiveness of German and U.S. output, which was quite important given a recent sharp reduction of American tariffs on celluloid, as well as technical information on cellulose grades, types of camphor, and the comparative advantages of using pure and denatured alcohol in the process.[66]

With the information gleaned from Mueller and supplemented by interviews with domestic producers and marketers and with informed census officials, Carpenter wrote in February 1914 a comprehensive report that supplied the knowledge base for the company's ultimately successful efforts to enter the celluloid business.[67] The young investigator's report was a masterpiece of thorough, thoughtful, and focused analysis. He explained that the industry fell into three groups: producers of celluloid plastic in semifinished form such as sheets, tubes, blocks, and other basic shapes; manufacturers who fashioned the forms into finished articles; and marketers.

The four firms that comprised the entire producer group dominated the industry.[68] The Arlington and Celluloid companies led with roughly equal market shares, followed by the Fiberloid Company; the Viscoloid Company was a poor fourth. Together they produced about 8.4 million pounds of plastic annually, roughly half of which they fashioned into finished articles (collars and cuffs, combs and hair ornaments, and novelty items) or into transparent sheets for automobile windows, while selling the remainder to other manufacturers of finished goods. Marketing arrangements were mixed. The producers sold directly to the article manufacturers; finished goods were largely handled by jobbers except for branch houses operated by the producers in big cities. Carpenter's remarkably well-informed study of a closely controlled, secretive industry also included valuable data on minimum efficient plant size and total investment required.

Just as important was his exposition on the courses of action open to Du Pont. Most preferable was the sale of nitrocellulose to the celluloid producers not just because it was the simplest and cheapest of the alternatives, but also because, as Carpenter perceptively noted, it fit "the purpose of [the] investigation, viz: to find an outlet for our present nitro-cellulose plants rather than a field for investment."[69] Sensing potential resistance from uncooperative producers who already made their own nitrocellulose, he noted that the next best choice was a $1 million investment to build a plant of minimal efficient size (about 1.6

million pounds annual capacity) to produce raw cellulose plastic for sale to article manufacturers. Figured conservatively, such a plant should return about 10 percent on investment, but cost and competition were serious obstacles. The third alternative, engaging in production and manufacture, was even less attractive, for it was more expensive and complicated than simple production of sheets, and it necessitated marketing and competition in consumer trades with which Du Pont had little experience. Finally, purchase of an existing concern would require the largest amount of capital and would do little to solve the basic problem of the company's excess nitrocellulose capacity.

The analysis was both accurate and perceptive, but successful action would require almost two years. Carpenter's subsequent investigations deepened but largely confirmed his initial work. His careful study of tariff policy, for example, demonstrated its remarkably slight impact. Six months after the two-thirds reduction in duties that resulted from the implementation of the Underwood-Simmons Act in late 1913, imports of celluloid items had grown to less than 2 percent of U.S. output.[70] Unfortunately, although Du Pont was ready to sell excess nitrocellulose and even to expand its plant capacity if necessary, celluloid producers refused to buy, preferring to control their own supply, to protect their own investment, and to avoid sharing their proprietary specifications with an outsider whom they mistrusted.

The problem, then, as Walter had implied in his prediction of that refusal, was the strategic assumption underlying the investigation. Du Pont had to shift its aim from developing sales of a by-product, which would increase return on existing capacity, to genuine diversification, which required full-scale entry into an unknown industry, a strategy virtually untried in American industry at that time.[71] As an integral part of this major innovation, Walter Carpenter quickly mastered it, and, as we shall see, his subsequent role in full-scale diversification at Du Pont rapidly accelerated his rise.

The challenge was not only the risk of investing several million dollars in a new business, but also the choice about how and where to take the risk, a difficulty compounded by rapidly changing events. The decisions rested with the executive committee, but Walter's investigations and assessments strongly affected the eventual course of action. Once the sale of nitrocellulose was eliminated, Du Pont's alternatives lay with the second and fourth choices that Carpenter had originally outlined: building a cellulose plant or buying a going concern.

Irénée, who oversaw and urged diversification, and Pierre apparently wanted an acquisition, but neither the timing nor the candidates were favorable.[72] Carpenter's research demonstrated that the Viscoloid Company was too small and unattractive; the Celluloid Company was unavailable; and the Arlington Company, perhaps the best choice, was both probably unavailable and too expensive.[73] At Irénée's request, in the spring of 1914, Walter negotiated the purchase of the Fiberloid Company, but a temporary shortage of cash, the outbreak of war, and Irénée's own uncertainty about the proper strategy (he was still intrigued by the chance to sell nitrocellulose) terminated negotiations. The abrupt break angered Fiberloid's owners, who firmly refused when Du Pont later attempted to reopen discussions.[74]

Construction remained the company's only option and quickly became the executive committee's formal choice, but Walter's well-informed reports, the outbreak of World War I (which effectively removed a joint venture with Mueller's firm from the picture), and the continuing uncertainty of the committee about full-scale diversification delayed any action. The war absorbed attention, capital, and energy as well as the excess capacity that was still the major purpose for action in the minds of some top managers.[75] When Irénée and Pierre urged reconsideration of internal development in November 1914, Walter, who had judged construction "highly inadvisable" six months earlier, again pointed out that another plant would increase industry capacity by 15 percent and depress returns. Nevertheless, he thought that economies of scope—Du Pont's carefully coordinated supply of its own alcohols, acids, and nitrocellulose as well as its superior technology in the manufacture of those intermediates—along with some economies of scale in production might permit the building of a plant that would return 20 percent on total start-up costs of $1.1 million.[76]

But in addition to his excellent grasp of the economics of diversification, Carpenter also added special knowledge. His research indicated considerable variation in the processes of celluloid production among the major firms. Given this critical uncertainty and the war's disruptions, he reminded the committee of another alternative mentioned in the previous spring: the building of a small pilot or experimental plant under the development department's direction to obtain the essential information cheaply.[77] Impressed with the pitfalls of internal development suggested in Walter's report, the executive committee voted $26,300 for a pilot operation and in addition reversed its previous direction, voting unanimously that the development department again search for a profitable acquisition.[78] Given the unfavorable circumstances, the committee simply decided to keep both options open.

Once again Carpenter's report reminded the executive committee of his thorough research, his perceptive formulation of questions, and his astute analysis of evidence. As a junior investigator he properly did not tell the committee what to do. He did make it clear that plastics was indeed a suitable and attractive business for Du Pont and that acquisition was the best means of entry, but he left the final decisions and the data on which to make them to the executive committee, which was charged with determining policy. In short, for a twenty-six-year-old he had a remarkable understanding of bureaucratic protocol as well as business strategy.

Chance and Walter Carpenter's skillful use of unexpected opportunity eventually resolved the dilemma. Carpenter had always been interested in the Arlington Company, perhaps the leading firm in the field, but it was thought to be unavailable. Its attractions were several. Incorporated in 1886, Arlington was an established, steadily growing concern with average annual earnings of nearly $600,000 on sales of about $4 million, which gave it about 40 percent of the market. It was also fully integrated with small subsidiaries supplying raw cellulose; with a main plant in Arlington, New Jersey, producing celluloid sheets; with article manufacture at Arlington, in Poughkeepsie, New York, and in Toronto, Canada; and with sales offices in New York City, Cleveland, and Chicago.[79]

In 1915 age and internal dissention suddenly made the company available.[80] Henry Chapman, whose family holdings were a majority of the stock, was seventy-eight, and his son Brewster, though president, was uninterested in the business. A minority faction, which included treasurer J. E. Ellsworth, was so worried about its own future, that it secretly arranged for a third party, New York stockbroker Norman Peters, to negotiate with Henry Chapman for an option to sell at $165 a share. When the deal collapsed, a friend of Peters asked Du Pont director Henry F. du Pont if his company was interested.

With his skills in financial analysis and negotiation and with his industry expertise, Walter Carpenter quickly seized the opportunity. Within a week of learning about the incident, he identified the two factions, opened discussions with both groups, tailored an offer on which the actual purchase would be based, and arranged to retain capable members of the management in order to assure operating knowledge and continuity.[81]

The details of the process offered impressive evidence of Carpenter's abilities. He persuaded the sellers to define an initial proposal based on average annual earnings for 1911–14, which allowed Du Pont to negotiate on the basis of return on investment. The Arlington people offered all forty thousand shares at $173.50 per share (which was twelve times annual earnings per share or an 8 percent return on Du Pont's investment) for a total cost of $6.94 million. Walter fashioned a counteroffer approved by Pierre, Irénée, and Ruly based on ten times earnings subject to verification of Arlington's financial data. In any event, the projected share price was fixed between $130 and $170 in order to protect both parties. The sticking point was Arlington's insistence that earnings for 1913 be increased $75,000 to compensate for a strike, which it had included in its original calculation and which Du Pont resisted.[82]

Carpenter smoothly arranged a compromise. He persuaded the Arlington group to accept a share price based on ten times verified earnings in exchange for the adjusted 1913 figure. Pierre, Irénée, and the executive committee agreed to the proposal when Walter demonstrated that $75,000 was probably less than half the actual loss so that Du Pont's purchase price was at least $300,000 below one based on fully adjusted earnings.[83] At any rate, Arlington's acceptance of the ten-times-earnings formula meant a final purchase price of $5.36 million (again assuming that its calculation of returns was correct), a savings of more than $1.5 million on the original asking price and well below the firm's $6.45 million in assets.

The jubilant Carpenter must have been somewhat sobered when at the deal's closing in December 1915 the actual purchase price turned out to be $6.7 million, much nearer Arlington's figure and slightly in excess of the company's assets.[84] Chance intervened to skew his carefully drawn compromise. Careful review of Arlington's figures apparently revealed a significant understatement in the company's 1914 earnings, which raised the price. Furthermore, the firm reneged on its tentative agreement to the formula because Francis Gudger, vice president and chairman of the selling committee, persuaded Brewster Chapman to hold out for more.[85]

Nevertheless, both Walter and Du Pont were quite pleased, because the company had completed its first major acquisition for diversification. (The 1910 purchase of Fabrikoid, the artificial leather company, had cost only $1.2 million.)[86] Despite the high price Du Pont had bought an industry leader with proprietary information, expertise, and experience critical to successful entry into a new business. Pierre, Irénée, and the executive committee readily approved the deal, expecting that their firm's experience with nitrocellulose and other intermediates along with its excellent financial and managerial techniques would soon improve return on investment to 15 percent, which had become Du Pont's target. Arlington served as the core of a plastics business that remains an important part of Du Pont operations to this day, and though profits were initially disappointing until reorganization in 1921, the division was earning almost 15 percent by 1928.[87]

For Carpenter the purchase was a watershed in his career. Years later, after his retirement, he told a friend that "my greatest personal satisfaction came from our purchase of Arlington. There was a seven million dollar investment at stake—a lot of money for a young man to be handling. When the purchase worked out well, both for us and for the people in Arlington, it was a great thrill for me."[88] His work on the celluloid business and the acquisition had clearly demonstrated Walter's skills as an investigator, his success as a negotiator, and his understanding of the complexities of the new strategy of diversification. To key executives the deal also marked him as a potential star in Du Pont management and assured his continued rapid rise.

Middle Manager

Promotion to middle management came quickly, even before the Arlington deal was made. Walter Carpenter became acting assistant director of the development department in May 1915, assistant director five months later, and director in April 1917. His rapid rise through the ranks again resulted from the combination of Carpenter and du Pont family ties, chance, and, most important of all, performance. As he had since joining Du Pont, Walter continued to follow his brother Ruly. (Ruly had arranged Walter's first job with the company, and when he had become head of the development department he had brought Walter along with him.) In 1914 Ruly became a member of the executive committee and joined the board of directors, and in the following year Walter became his assistant in the department. In 1916 Ruly was appointed vice president, and in the next year Walter was promoted to head of development reporting to his brother.[89]

Chance and family ties were interlinked when Pierre, Ruly's brother-in-law, seized an opportunity to buy control of the company in 1915. By late 1914 Coleman du Pont, Pierre's cousin and the firm's president, wanted to resign his position to devote his energies to his operations in New York City real estate.[90] In order to finance his speculations, he also needed to sell at least some of his stock. (He had about 63,000 shares or 22 percent of the total common stock and almost 14,000 shares of the nonvoting preferred stock.) When Coleman offered part of his holdings to Du Pont at $160 per share, his cousin Alfred, the third member of the triumvirate that had taken control of the company in 1902, persuaded the board of directors to refuse, arguing that the price was too high.

After several weeks of fruitless deliberation, Pierre stepped in. Organizing a syndicate that included his brothers, Irénée and Lammot; his cousin, A. Felix du Pont; his brother-in-law, Ruly Carpenter; and his close confidant and company treasurer, John Raskob, Pierre and his associates bought all of Coleman's stock. Alfred fought back angrily, but after losing a prolonged, bitter suit, he left Pierre and his allies in charge. Pierre's victory clearly advanced Ruly's wealth and career and indirectly benefited Walter.

A second opportunity came with the outbreak of World War I, which directly affected the Du Pont Company and all those associated with it. All facets of the firm grew at a previously unimaginable pace. By 1918 assets had almost quadrupled the 1914 level and profits were seven times the prewar annual high.[91] To handle the construction and expand the operations necessary for the production of 1.4 billion pounds of explosives for the United States and its allies, the workforce grew from 5,300 in 1914 to 85,000 in 1918 while the number of salaried personnel jumped from 2,000 in 1914 to 6,600 in 1919.[92]

Ruly and Walter Carpenter rose rapidly because of the huge expansion of top and middle-level management as the number of Du Pont executives earning at least $4,200 annually almost tripled from 94 in 1914 to 259 in 1918.[93] Ruly Carpenter was promoted to the executive committee as part of the creation of a "wartime cabinet," and Walter's first job in middle management as assistant director of the development department was a new position established to help cope with that department's wartime burdens.

In Walter's case the war played an even more direct role, for it vastly accelerated diversification. Although it had a long, tortuous path at Du Pont and was not the product of any single event or person, nevertheless diversification was a major responsibility for Carpenter during his years as an executive in the development department. The company first began to consider moving into new businesses in 1909 after a serious recession and the threat of government production of munitions as a remedy in an antitrust suit against Du Pont's monopoly.[94] As noted earlier, its first investigations focused on industries using nitrocellulose technology such as celluloid plastics, artificial silk, and artificial leather, but a small investment in the Fabrikoid Company and the manufacture of artificial leather in 1910 was the only significant consequence. In 1913 and 1914 excess capacity resulting from an economic slump renewed interest, and Walter's celluloid investigation and the Arlington acquisition resulted.

As that assignment ended in 1915, the firm's huge growth in gunpowder manufacture for World War I made excess capacity an urgent consideration. Even though Pierre carefully provided for full amortization of new plant construction as part of wartime contracts, there remained the question of how to employ those sites after the war. The development department accepted the assignment, and its specially created excess plant utilization committee began investigating a wide variety of products, including dyes, paints, and photographic film. However, it soon found itself unable to make diversification fit a procrustean bed defined by nitrocellulose-based technology and the special location and characteristics of Du Pont plants.

In early 1917 the department persuaded the executive committee to remove the shackles. Henceforth it could pursue opportunities for growth in areas with related products or technologies that used Du Pont's excess resources in the broadest possible sense, including (in the words of the historian of Du Pont's strategic innovations) its "talents, equipment, and capital."[95] The particular targets were to be industries dependent on cellulose and cotton purification such as artificial leather and pyroxylin (celluloid) plastics; dyes and related organic chemicals; paints and varnishes; vegetable oils; and water-soluble chemicals and acids.

In addition to excess capacity, related technologies, and corporate resources, Du Pont's experiment with diversification was also driven by chance and excess funds. In 1917 it also made a $25 million investment to buy 23.8 percent of the combined, outstanding stock of the General Motors Corporation and the Chevrolet Motor Company.[96] Personal investments had tied first John Raskob and then Pierre du Pont to William C. Durant and GM, and when that company needed funds in late 1917 it naturally turned to Du Pont.

In persuading the executive and finance committees to make the investment, John Raskob argued that the war had generated a great deal of money that the company was not using. According to his figures, the concern had $150 million in capital of which $60 million was in the explosives business and $40 million was in diversified lines. Unless the company found an outlet for the remaining $50 million, it would see a terrible shrinkage in profits and dividends when the war's end cut off its extraordinary returns from gunpowder manufacture. With Pierre's support, Raskob pointed out that unless the GM investment was made, "the earnings of our Company after the war will be insufficient to support the dividend policy and the matter of properly employing this money in a way that will result in a proper return to our Company is one of most serious consequence."[97]

Finally, Du Pont also experimented with diversification by marketing the expertise of some of its functional departments. During the war and until 1921 the development and the engineering departments sold their services by outside contracting, principally to the U.S. government and to General Motors. The engineering department built government powder plants, two GM automobile factories in Michigan, the Tower Hill School in Wilmington, and some local public works, while the development department performed contract research for General Motors in such areas as plate glass, storage battery, and aluminum production.[98] High overhead costs with little comparative advantage, GM's wish for independence, and a major recession and reorganization in 1920 and 1921 ended the experiment and the period of innovation in diversification methods. In the future, Du Pont would concentrate on the development of its chemical lines and on the oversight of its GM investment via the finance committee.

In the tangled course of the company's diversification, several key people played an important part in events. Pierre and Raskob were the architects of the General Motors investment. Irénée du Pont oversaw and pushed much of the work at the Du Pont Company, first as director of the development department from 1908 to 1911, then as vice president and chairman of the executive committee, and finally as president after 1919. As Irénée put it in the midst of the process, he was "convinced that we should make a special effort to extend the operations of the Development Department, looking into new industry which we might profitably enter, as an offshoot from our present business, and to find an outlet for the probable surplus products after the war is over."[99] Fin Sparre, who worked in the laboratory and in the development department and who chaired the excess plant utilization committee, played a primary role as researcher and investigator and shaped the strategy of diversification based on Du Pont's broad talents that was adopted in 1917.[100]

Finally, Walter Carpenter was also a leader in the company's diversification, which occupied much of his time and energy as a manager in or head of the development department between 1915 and 1921. While Sparre helped set the course of diversification as an expert in technology, Walter's impact resulted from his expertise in business analysis and management and took several forms. As we have just seen, his research and articulation of choices in the celluloid case led to Du Pont's commitment to full-scale diversification and to its first major acquisition in pursuit of the new strategy.

In the development of Du Pont's dyes business, Carpenter helped determine the pace and course of diversification that originated externally. The outbreak of World War I and the British blockade had severely restricted America's access to synthetic organic chemicals, including the artificial dyes that the Germans had developed in the previous half-century.[101] When Du Pont started to manufacture its own toluene and diphenylamine, organic intermediates critical to both explosives and dye manufacture, it began consideration of dye production. In late 1915 the company was first forced to make a decision when Morris Poucher approached it on behalf of American textile enterprises suffering from the severe shortage. Poucher asked that the firm manufacture and sell dye intermediates to a trading concern owned jointly by Du Pont and himself. The trading company would in turn sell its output to British dye makers, provided that half of the dyes would be sent to the United States for sale by the trading firm.

When asked by the executive committee to analyze the proposition, Carpenter produced a report so clear, balanced, and well argued that it persuaded the committee to refuse the proposal against the inclinations of Pierre du Pont.[102] Walter carefully noted that rejection could compromise a major postwar opportunity and provoke a public outcry over the company's use of scarce raw materials for production of military explosives for export (since the United States was not yet in the war) instead of making dyes badly needed for domestic manufacture. Nevertheless, he opposed the suggestion because the company's explosives contracts fully committed its available plant capacity, technical personnel, and critical supplies of scarce raw materials through 1916. He wondered "whether we [should] forego sure present profits on all the crude material we could possibly buy [for military explosives] for a problematic profit on the production of intermediates in which we are, up to the present time, inexperienced." In addition, the postwar possibilities were certain to be compromised by the return of German competition and "a tremendous excess capacity."[103]

Impressed by the cogency and independence of the young manager's case, the executive committee voted to accept it. Carefully read, Carpenter's argument was not against dye production, but only rejected a proposal requiring major disruption for the risky manufacture of intermediates. Ultimately, however, Walter's strong skepticism did not prevail. Some months later, when an opportunity surfaced for full-scale entry into the dyes industry with the help of Levinstein, Limited of Great Britain, Du Pont went into the business. Walter Carpenter readily accepted his superiors' decision, helping negotiate the acquisitions of the Federal Dyestuff and Chemical Corporation and the dye manufacturing department of the United Piece Dye Works as part of that diversification.[104] As he had foreseen, entry was "problematic." Trial and error learning, high capital requirements, and postwar competition despite generous tariff support meant an investment of $22 million while incurring losses of $18 million before the first profit appeared in 1923.[105]

In addition to his work in plastics, Carpenter's major contribution to diversification came through his role in development department management between 1915 and 1921. Frank MacGregor, who worked in the department from 1916 and helped create the paint division, thought that while Fin Sparre led the excess plant utilization committee, "Walter was the driving force" in executing diversification.[106] Carpenter reviewed the work and the recommendations of Sparre's committee, and he was directly involved as investigator, negotiator, and analyst in acquisitions for the artificial leather, paint, plastics, and dyes lines as well as for areas like photographic film that were not developed at this time. In the case of rayon (then called artificial silk), he made the first contacts with Albert and Henry Blum, the American representatives of the Comptoir des Textiles Artificiels (the French patent holders) in 1916, and then strongly supported the work of Leonard Yerkes, who negotiated the acquisition of patent rights for Du Pont in 1920.[107]

When the paint acquisitions failed to perform as expected, Carpenter quickly appreciated and vigorously supported Frank MacGregor's recognition of the strategic problem.[108] Profits lay in varnishes, which had a high value-added in their manufacture, and in specialized paints for big industrial accounts—not in simpler mixed paints, which generated low returns through trade sales and small industrial accounts in a fragmented, competitive business. Neverthless, William Coyne, vice president of the sales department, and Lammot du Pont, vice president of the miscellaneous manufacturing department, continued to insist on more mergers in the name of increasing volume. When they proposed the purchase of the Chicago Varnish Company in 1920, Carpenter wrote the executive committee about the urgent need to establish a clear policy based on competitive advantage. As for the acquisition, he firmly stated that he was "very much opposed to it" unless it could be consolidated with operations and fitted to MacGregor's strategy.[109]

Diversification was only part of Walter Carpenter's work as head of the development department. In late 1917 he persuaded the executive committee to limit the addition of more new lines because the press of war work and the problems of overseeing the new businesses already in hand had strained the department to its limits.[110] During the war Carpenter led a small group of fifteen investigators and two assistant directors who annually researched at least one hundred subjects ranging from plant locations and deposits of raw materials to joint ventures and corporate acquisitions and wrote over six hundred reports for Du Pont and for the U.S. government as part of rapidly growing contract work. In 1918 a motors development section was added to handle work for General Motors. In addition, the department also managed pilot plant operations for new lines until they were assigned to the company's main operating departments or were set up as separate product divisions.[111]

As director Carpenter assigned projects and personnnel, oversaw operations, and appraised performance in addition to carrying out his own investigations. He personally reviewed all of the reports and probably helped rewrite a considerable number, for questions about them from the executive committee reflected on the director. One of his successors recalled that even in more stable times the department "had some men . . . that just never could learn to write reports[. Y]ou have to give [th]em a chance to do something, assemble information, but then it was always a chore to sit down and whip it in shape."[112]

Under great stress and without much experience, Walter did an extraordinary job. In the company's annual report for 1918 that summarized the firm's war contributions, Pierre concluded that the development department "has handled its work in a masterful manner and deserves great credit for [the] results obtained."[113] In short, its director had clearly demonstrated his executive capacity.

Promotion and Assessment

In April 1919 Walter Carpenter was promoted to the office of vice president for development and appointed to the executive committee and to the board of directors of the Du Pont Company. These positions, which included major policy-making as well as administrative duties, moved him into top management after less than a decade with the firm. As in his previous career, an analysis of his experience reveals several familiar, key factors in that extraordinary advancement.

Chance, especially the impact of an unusual external event like World War I, which raged for nearly half of his early career, had a considerable role. Growth stimulated by the war created numerous managerial posts and accelerated promotions. Huge profits and excess capacity from the war brought major diversification, which became Walter's special focus.

The war's end also meant new top management, for neither Pierre nor Irénée was entirely happy with the wartime executive committee. Pierre simply said that the company had reached "another turning point" and that it was time to move to the next line of men. Irénée, who succeeded Pierre as president at this point, was more critical. He remembered years later that the old committee "had developed too much of a 'touch and go' attitude" as a result of wartime pressures. The new group (which retained only three of ten men) "would be more careful in accumulating fuller information before taking action."[114] Walter Carpenter's penchant for well-informed, independent analysis made him an early and certain choice as the previous members moved to the finance committee to watch the company's investments. He later remarked modestly that "like a number of others, I happened to be in the right place at the right time. The combination of good fortune and circumstance was simply overwhelming."[115]

Opportunity was also closely linked with ties to the du Pont family, a second key factor. Carpenter's first two mentors, Elias Ahuja and his Uncle Ed, not only promoted him to the family but to the right part of it. As a result, Pierre du Pont, who became president and who won the battle for control of the firm, closely watched Walter's career from its beginning. Even more important was his close association with Irénée du Pont, Pierre's successor as president.

Perhaps because of their shared interest in diversification and in the development department, Irénée soon became Carpenter's new mentor. Walter first met the woman who would become his wife at Irénée's house. Mary Wootten, reared in Laurel, Delaware, as the daughter of a retired army sutler, had come to Wilmington to be governess to Irénée's children. At Walter and Mary's wedding in 1914, Constance and Eleanor du Pont, Irénée's youngest daughters, were flower girls. Irénée served as usher, and the reception was held at his house.[116] The Carpenters' three children grew up calling Irénée "Uncle Bus," and each reflected the sponsoring Walter had received. Irénée was godfather to John, the second boy, and Ahuja was godfather to Sam, the eldest son, while Ned, the youngest, was properly named Edmund Nelson after Walter's uncle. The house they grew up in was Irénée's home at Eighteenth Street and Rising Sun Lane in Wilmington, which Walter bought in the mid-1920s.

The strong personal relationship was matched by ties at the company. In 1917 Irénée and Pierre each privately sold Walter five hundred shares of Du Pont common stock at $149 a share, a price calculated on the basis of net tangible assets per share instead of the current market value, which was $261. Because the young man could not begin to pay the $149,000 cost, Irénée arranged for finance through the Fourth Street National Bank of Philadelphia, of which he was a director.[117]

Like other Du Pont managers Carpenter had received generous compensation from the company, but this windfall was a separate, private arrangement with the two owners. His salary had more than doubled from $2,400 in 1914 to $5,700 in 1916, when his total income was $38,000 as a result of regular bonuses in cash and stock.[118] Irénée explained that the special, personal gift of the $122,000 difference between the stock's purchase and market prices was made "in order to interest you 'as a partner.'" Like merchants in previous centuries, Pierre and Irénée acted to assure loyalty and diligence in a key man by making him part owner when ties of blood or marriage were not available. When Walter hesitated because he thought the transaction "too one sided" in his favor, Irénée explained that Carpenter was bound to stay with Du Pont and hold the stock for at least four years. "Securing your prime financial interest in the company will safeguard the value of our residual stock to an extent that will well warrant [our] apparent sacrifice."[119]

Two years later Irénée again began arrangements outside the firm that foreshadowed the elevation of Carpenter's status from small partner to eventual successor as head of the company. He asked the owners of the Christiana Securities Company, the family holding company that effectively controlled Du Pont through its ownership of the stock acquired from Coleman as well as Pierre's own shares, to distribute blocks of 1,250 shares to Walter Carpenter and to Donaldson Brown, the treasurer of the Du Pont Company. Irénée worried about the absence of qualified du Pont family members to lead the enterprise after his generation and urged that Christiana owners select "from the important men, because of their knowledge of the business, such individuals as seem desirable to become trustees of a large part of our estates, . . . men intimately known by us and in whose integrity we have full confidence, who are exceptionally able, and who have a deep financial interest in the same investment."[120]

Since youth was essential, he recommended Carpenter and Brown (who was three years older than Walter) from among all those on the new executive committee. "The one who is younger is much more desirable for the purpose, because of his increased likelihood of surviving the present partners with expectation of a reasonably long business life thereafter."[121] The deal was never completed because other arrangements were eventually made that covered the entire committee, but the selection of Carpenter as a nonfamily successor in top management was obvious, especially since Brown left Du Pont shortly thereafter to join Pierre in the management of General Motors.

Family favoritism undeniably played a part in Walter's rapid rise to top management, but in his case being a Carpenter was as important as being a du Pont. Not only did the accident of birth provide excellent training and permit him to avoid the discrimination against women, immigrants, and nonwhites; it also meant that he benefited from his brother, who presented him with the opportunities to demonstrate his talents to the du Ponts. Ruly got him the summer jobs and the position in Chile, appointed him to the development department, promoted him into middle management as assistant director, and probably arranged that Walter succeed him as director.

Ruly's use of his family was not limited to his brother nor was it rare. He nominated Uncle Ed for the mining acquisition in Chile; selected Ralph Derr, a distant cousin, to superintend the mine; and appointed Olin Derr, another cousin, as an investigator in the development department. Nor was the reliance on kinship in the enterprise confined to the du Ponts and the Carpenters. Donaldson Brown, who became vice president and treasurer, was the son-in-law of Hamilton Barksdale, who had been the firm's general manager, and his brother, J. Thompson Brown, became vice president in explosives operations. J. Amory Haskell, a vice president and early member of the executive committee, was the older brother of Harry G. Haskell, who also became a vice president and member of the executive committee. John Raskob was vice president and treasurer, and his brother Will became assistant treasurer and secretary of the company.

Despite the importance of family in Walter Carpenter's rapid rise, performance was far more critical as Irénée's statements implied and as Ruly's own case demonstrated. Walter was entirely unrelated to the du Ponts while Ruly's marriage to Margaretta made him a brother-in-law to Pierre, Irénée, and Lammot. Yet Ruly was shunted aside from the executive to the finance committee in 1919 just as Walter's career blossomed. Ruly would briefly serve as a general manager in two smaller divisions and would rejoin the executive committee in the 1920s. However, lacking Walter's wide-ranging comprehension, analytical detachment, and patience, he would never again return to the inner circle in which he had participated as a member of the wartime executive committee.

Walter Carpenter's mastery and understanding of big business were amply demonstrated in "Development—The Strategy of Industry," the article he wrote for a special issue on modern manufacturing published by the prestigious *Annals of the American Academy of Political and Social Science* in 1919, the year of his promotion.[122] The essay reflected a professional manager's proud participation in an important breakthrough in his field and his understandable desire to report it to his colleagues outside the enterprise. Comparable to Donaldson Brown's subsequent, more famous pieces on decentralization and capital accounting,[123] Carpenter's article alerted the business community, probably for the first time, to Du Pont's adoption of the new strategy of diversification and its use of a functional department to oversee broad innovation in the firm by serving as "a clearing house for business ideas" from both internal and external sources.[124]

In effect, the piece simultaneously demonstrated both Walter's abilities as an executive and Du Pont's leadership in American enterprise. Carpenter was clearly immersed in his profession and committed to his company. He enthusiastically reminded his audience that new ideas for growth were especially timely since the return of peace offered American businessmen "the greatest opportunity in the world's history." His perceptive forecasting of the 1920s boom in the United States rested on the nation's enormous human and natural resources, its wealthy and rapidly growing market, and a system of government and public policy very supportive of private enterprise.

Taking full advantage of that opportunity required a comprehensive strategy, and Carpenter briefly revealed to his readers his appreciation of the Du Pont Company's recent innovative use of what analysts now call economies of scope, meaning the economies of joint production and distribution.[125] A firm could grow rapidly by moving outside its existing industry to "untried, though related, lines of business." By developing "new lines of activity radiating from a common centre," the enterprise could find "profitable outlets for by-products, capital and energy." Carpenter clearly meant not just sidelines, but "the taking over of allied industries," which could be "incorporated into an established business" so that "its output increased vastly, at a saving in overhead and administrative costs which makes a decided difference in the balance sheet."

To implement the new strategy a company needed to institutionalize innovation in a development department. It would not only become responsible for finding the opportunities for diversification, but would also search out "new ideas to be applied to lines already established"; research "new processes of manufacture"; locate substitutes or "new sources of supply for materials vitally necessary"; and investigate the firm's processing of such critical substances in lieu of purchase.

Carpenter was also careful to advise the use of a comprehensive, long-term view in making calculations. After reminding his readers of the importance of measuring return on investment as well as return on sales in appraising performance and of selecting carefully among potential projects, he warned against the simplistic application of a formula. A businessman had to look at his entire enterprise. Securing supply and assuring quality and quantity of output essential for a large fixed investment "may often warrant a substantial investment, even though the saving in . . . actual manufacture does not represent a very great return."

Finally, Walter offered a few guides on operation. In order to avoid duplicated effort, the development department should take full control of its projects until they were ready for release. At the same time, the department needed to work closely with the rest of the organization. Consultation was vital—with the production department to determine the feasibility of manufacture, with the sales department to estimate the nature and scale of market opportunity, with the transportation department to learn critical costs, and with the accounting department to calculate profit.

The influence of Carpenter's article is uncertain, given its brevity, matter-of-fact tone, and odd place of publication for business readers. Nevertheless, at an early age Walter Carpenter had demonstrated to his bosses and to discerning readers an extraordinary grasp of the principles and opportunities of big business. He was among the few who appreciated Du Pont's innovative strategy of diversification by related product lines, which would be duplicated by an increasing number of leading American companies in the next two decades.[126] He fully understood the critical importance of maintaining innovation in a big, bureaucratic enterprise. He knew that large, fixed assets required careful calculation of return on investment for accurate appraisal and for guidance, but he also realized that management always demanded judgment, the balancing of benefits and costs to achieve the solutions most consistent with maximum long-term growth of fixed investment. Just as important, management also required clarity of authority and responsibility as well as consultation and cooperation.

Despite the *Annals* article and his many other accomplishments, Walter Carpenter's rapid advancement was also remarkable for what he had not done. He had been neither infallible nor irreversible. The Arlington Company did not initially perform well after its purchase by Du Pont, and Pierre had overruled Walter when the company entered the dyes industry. Nevertheless, his positions had been forceful and sound given the data available when his recommendations were made. Arlington was a profitable firm prior to its acquisition; Du Pont had yet to learn how to operate in a new field. And entering the dyes business was a long, costly process.[127] Even when Carpenter did not "win," he demonstrated the thoughtfulness, independence, and judgment so criticial in a top manager.

Likewise, Walter had not stood out as a major innovator. He had not invented a new product or developed a significant breakthrough in a manufacturing process. He alone was not responsible for any primary strategic change. Du Pont's decision to diversify had begun before he arrived, involved several key people, and was vastly accelerated and expanded by World War I's impact on the American economy. Furthermore, Walter was not committed to the entire diversfication program. As we have seen, he disapproved of the firm's move into dye production, and he also joined his brother Ruly in opposing the company's investment in General Motors.[128]

In short, Walter Carpenter was not an entrepreneur in the mold of an Andrew Carnegie or a Henry Ford, men who allocated the means of production in fresh directions or did old things in radically new ways.

Carpenter entered an enterprise already created by entrepreneurs. E. I. du Pont had originally established the Du Pont Company and the three cousins, Coleman, Pierre, and Alfred, had revitalized it. Walter arrived as part of a cadre of salaried managers employed to administer an existing concern. As a member of a team he was involved in a collective instead of a heroic process of decision making. The replacement of individual actors by group decision making was not unusual, for such groups of managers were rapidly coming to run the big firms in manufacturing, transportation, distribution, and finance that have dominated the core of the U.S. economy for much of the twentieth century.[129]

While still in his twenties Carpenter played an extraordinary role in a large, established enterprise and began making his contribution as a manager by becoming a key player in the continuing process of collective innovation at Du Pont. He alone did not take the company into plastics, but he did help shape that decision and the purchase of the Arlington Company as the core of Du Pont's new business. He did not develop new dyes or new means of producing synthetic organic intermediates, but at a critical point early in the process he correctly interpreted the fragmentary available data to provide an appreciation of the risks of entering an unknown yet very important business. Furthermore, he played a central part in identifying and forcing the implementation of a rational strategy for Du Pont's chaotic, unprofitable paint business.

At the time of his appointment to the executive committee in 1919, Walter Carpenter had demonstrated an unusual combination of skills, experience, and understanding. In less than a decade he had clearly shown the abilities to act energetically, to research thoroughly, to analyze perceptively, to negotiate effectively, and to judge soundly and independently. He already had training or service in several areas of business, including engineering, purchasing, development, and finance, which equipped him with the broad general background essential for a senior executive. As a researcher who saw things in fresh ways, as an analyst with rare insight and even rarer judgment, as a negotiator with the gift of persuasion, and as an executive with a remarkably comprehensive, extended view, Carpenter was well qualified to seize the uncommon opportunity at Du Pont in 1919 to move into top management while still a very young man. In the next two decades as a vice president at Du Pont, he would amply demonstrate the wisdom of that promotion.

2

Top Manager

WALTER CARPENTER'S promotion came at the end of a crucial transition period in the U.S. economy. Between the 1880s and World War I, much of American business shifted from small, owner-operated companies often linked in pools or federations to big, integrated concerns each rooted in a single industry with an oligopolistic structure. At the top, salaried managers who owned little if any of their firms worked with and increasingly began to replace entrepreneurs and owners. In addition to heading daily operations, such executives started to assume responsibility for resource allocation, policy-making, and the basic direction of their enterprises. Their development, implementation, and administration of techniques for coordinating, appraising, and planning were critical for achieving economies and for maintaining the growth of the new, large firms. Carpenter's experiences as a high-level manager at Du Pont in the two decades after World War I provide concrete illustration of just what such people did.

Getting Established

Carpenter's appointment as vice president coincided with a major reexamination and reorganization of Du Pont operations, which fundamentally reshaped both the company and Walter's career and also served as a model for numerous big American concerns in the next several decades.[1] A new, decentralized structure proved a critical complement to the company's recent, innovative strategy of diversification. By making possible the profitable operation of recently acquired product lines, it provided both the funds and the opportunity for further expansion.

Like most of America's newly integrated industrial enterprises, Du Pont had originally been organized around functional departments. In the century's first decade under the leadership of Pierre, Coleman, and Alfred, the company had established departments for each of its key operations, including production, sales, finance, development, and purchasing. Each department had two heads: a director who administered daily operations, and a vice president who oversaw them and served on the executive committee.

This committee, all of whose members were on the board of directors and whose numbers varied between seven and ten, was the company's most important body. Charged by the board with responsibility for all matters except finance, it met weekly to review operations, appraise performance, and set policy. As one member said succinctly, it "ran the show."[2] Because the executive committee contained all of the top operating people—the president and the major departmental vice presidents—and allowed them to act as one, Walter frequently likened it to a "synthetic superman."[3] As a subsequent member explained, "Everyone expresses his point of view freely so that a decision . . . reflects those many points of view and . . . is a sounder one than one made by a single individual or indeed a smaller group of people."[4] Collective policy-making by capable people helped avoid the biases and idiosyncrasies of a single, powerful leader, be he owner or manager.

The finance committee, whose members also served on the board of directors, met twice a month and had several functions. It oversaw finances through its supervision of the treasurer's department; it monitored the company's investment in General Motors; and, as one member explained, it had indirect responsibility for general company policy "exercized [sic] through potential veto power over Executive Committee actions."[5] Its members included holders of major blocks of stock (or their surrogates) to represent the owners' point of view. Although this group sometimes included owner-operators like Pierre, Irénée, and Lammot du Pont, it frequently contained du Ponts who were "outside directors," men like William and Colonel Henry A. du Pont, who had significant holdings but no connection with actual administration. In addition to owner-operators, "inside directors" also encompassed top financial executives like the vice president for finance or the treasurer who provided data, expertise, and guidance.

Both the finance and the executive committees reported to the board of directors, from which they received their charge and which represented the stockholders. Although nominally the top body in the organization chart, the board normally rubber stamped the recommendations of its two main committees at its monthly meetings. As Lammot du Pont noted when he was president of the company, "It is rarely the case that the Board is required to take action on anything that has not already been carefully considered and acted upon by the Executive Committee and/or the Finance Committee."[6] This pattern existed in most large American firms because of the knowledge and expertise of the inside directors who dominated the major committees, but it came more swiftly at Du Pont, where for many years top executives like Pierre, Irénée, and Lammot du Pont were also major shareholders, thus delaying the split between ownership and management.[7]

Although Du Pont's structure, with its functional departments overseen by a central office including the president and the vice presidents, was standard for large American industrials and successfully carried the firm through the tremendous challenges of World War I, diversification soon demonstrated its limitations. Separating the enterprise into functional departments worked only as long as the company's concentration on a single industry provided a countervailing integrative force. New lines like dyes, paints, and plastics fitted poorly into an organization established for explosives, for they put Du Pont into several businesses and eroded its unified focus. They also destroyed the logic of the departments themselves; functional executives in manufacturing, sales, and purchasing were no longer handling related products and markets with which they were fully familiar, and economies of scale were lost.

The evidence of failure mounted quickly. The celluloid operation, which was built on Du Pont's purchase of the Arlington Company's successfully integrated plastics business, suffered rapidly declining profits as its components were divided among the explosives firm's functional departments. Return on investment fell from an estimated 21.06 percent in 1916 (the first year of acquisition) to 10.95 percent in 1917 and 6.60 percent in 1918 while other plastics companies continued to do well.[8] Du Pont's paint products did just as poorly despite several acquisitions to develop a full line and to achieve a critical minimum volume. As one report observed, "The more paint and varnish we sold, the more money we lost."[9] The fledgling dye operation, which continued to absorb millions of dollars in investment while losing money, proved so difficult that the company made no attempt to fit it into the functional departmental structure, and it remained an entirely separate unit.

The business cycle soon made bad results even worse when the short depression of 1920–22 brought terrible returns. In the first six months of 1921 Du Pont lost more than $2.4 million, probably the worst record in its history at that time. Although explosives generated profits of almost $2.5 million, diversified products lost more than $3.8 million (with interest and miscellaneous items accounting for the rest of the red ink).[10] Clearly, structural reorganization was essential to accommodate the new strategy of diversification; otherwise the new lines would destroy what had been a remarkably profitable explosives company.

Du Pont's response was confused and tortuous for several reasons.[11] First, hindsight has made the analysis of the problem as an organizational issue artificially clear, but at the time some executives quickly and logically pointed to the costs of learning and developing new businesses and to the recession's impact as the causes of their problems. Second, because the company was pioneering diversification among American firms, it had no model. Reorganization around product divisions (the eventual solution) challenged the tenets of functional departmental structure that prevailed overwhelmingly in American practice and theory.[12]

Finally, heritage blocked change. Owner-operators like Pierre, Irénée, and Lammot du Pont who had the final say resisted the reform efforts by their middle- and upper-level executives. Led by Irénée as company president, they were naturally reluctant to exchange what they had so successfully built for a radical, untested solution. When Pierre surrendered the presidency to Irénée in 1919, the three brothers typically thought in terms of rebuilding the postwar firm around new, talented people instead of systematic restructuring. If anything, the fresh team of able top managers (including Walter Carpenter) who composed the new executive committee of 1919 made the functional organization, which focused on four departments (production, sales, finance, and development), even stronger than before.

Nevertheless, reorganization did come, stimulated by the efforts of those managers who had to face directly the problems of diversification and by the repeated failure of the existing structure. A 1919 subcommittee appointed by the executive committee to study the problem of disappointing sales results in diversified products highlighted the differences between marketing standard commodities sold in bulk to industrial producers (like explosives) and the handling of packaged goods distributed to the retail trade (like household paints and celluloid combs, cuffs, and novelties). Its distinction implied different sales organizations for different products.

More important, in 1920 a special sub-subcommittee perceptively diagnosed the problem and offered the eventual solution. Composed of representatives from sales, production, finance, and development along with a spokesman for the president, it blamed "divided control" for the company's distress. Du Pont, which handled so many products, in effect separated oversight of sales and manufacture; its more successful competitors, in contrast, concentrated on a single industry. Critics noted that dyes and artificial silk were each administered as units and recommended the same for paints and varnishes, plastics, and artificial leather.[13]

In short, each group of products would be treated as a separate business. In each case, purchasing, manufacture, sales, and accounting would be removed from the big functional departments and combined under a general manager who reported directly to the executive committee, who had full authority and responsibility for his operation, and who could rely on the functional departments at his discretion. Thus, the development, engineering, chemical (laboratory), and service departments would become auxiliary operations in support of the main product divisions, which Du Pont would call industrial departments. Each business was to return at least 15 percent on investment, and transfers of intermediates between lines would be calculated at market rates in order to measure true costs.[14]

Nearly eighteen months were needed for final acceptance, and Walter Carpenter played a central but ambiguous role in the process. Given his responsibilities in the development department and his role in diversification, he was actively involved in the early recognition of the problem, but he also soon became part of the opposition that delayed implementation of the new structure until late 1921. In early 1919 he served on small subcommittees of the executive committee to study marketing problems in paint and plastics. These bodies first identified and articulated the important differences between selling industrial goods in bulk and packaged consumer products. Their findings served as the basis of the report of the 1919 subcommittee on general merchandising (on which Walter also served) and pointed to the need to disaggregate selling operations.[15] In 1919 Carpenter also helped establish the special sub-subcommittee that first developed the decentralized plan. He then appointed as the development department's representative Frank MacGregor, with whom he had worked closely to analyze the problems of the paint line and to develop a rational strategy for its further acquisitions and its consolidation.

After that group's landmark report was rejected in 1920, Carpenter joined with sales vice president Frederick Pickard to keep the reform movement going. Together they encouraged three departmental executives, one each from manufacturing, sales, and development, to meet (as Pickard put it) "unofficially and without portfolio" to study the problem as it specifically related to the paint business. Walter's appointee, Frank MacGregor, led what was soon called the paint steering committee, which in turn established the decentralized structure by a back-door process. In late 1920 the paint committee's report strongly impressed the executive committee with its concrete suggestions on how to cut costs and earn 10 percent in the paint business with coordinated control by a council composed of a sales director, a production executive, and a neutral member. As a result, the senior executives ratified the proposal and appointed the paint steering committee to implement its own plan. Within a week the executive committee adopted the new division council technique for other areas of the company.[16]

Despite the ad hoc adoption of product-line organization, the Du Pont Company steadfastly and simultaneously refused to accept formal and complete restructuring. The resistance, led by President Irénée du Pont, was strongly seconded by Walter Carpenter, who opposed radical reorganization as unnecessary and apparently somehow hoped to fit the new industrial departments into the existing structure. In the summer of 1920 the executive committee committed itself to product divisions headed by general managers after a subcommittee of its own members (Donaldson Brown of finance, Frederick Pickard of sales, and William Spruance of production) recommended the plan originally proposed by subordinates. In a company in which top management normally operated on consensus, the executive committee was so convinced of its proposed solution that it took the extraordinary step of submitting the reorganization to President Irénée du Pont despite opposition from him and from committee chairman and vice president Lammot du Pont. Given its own certainty, the committee wanted to force the president's formal refusal before abandoning further discussion.

During the debates in the summer and fall of 1920, Walter Carpenter consistently joined with Lammot du Pont and with J. B. D. Edge, the vice president for purchasing, in fighting the proposal. When the committee resolved that product divisions "would" have advantages over functional departments, Carpenter and Edge moved and lost an amendment to substitute "might" for "would." In addition, Carpenter, Edge, and Lammot du Pont twice unsuccessfully opposed resolutions to send the plan to Irénée for his formal rejection.[17]

Irénée's veto only temporarily halted discussion; the company's huge losses in the continuing depression again forced the issue in August 1921. Notes from a special joint meeting of the executive and finance committees indicate considerable tension and testiness among men frustrated by the deadlock and worried about the sustained and deepening failure of diversified operations. They record that Walter Carpenter "questions the plan of divided responsibility by having separate industrial units" and "is not in sympathy with [the] views of the majority of the Executive Committee."[18] Privately he had a bitter, sarcastic debate with his brother Ruly, who supported the reform from his position on the finance committee. Walter, who blamed the crisis on the depression, decried "singing the praises of organizations based on the idea of centralized control [in product divisions] as a panacea for all ills" and abruptly dismissed Ruly's reasoned response. "The shift from earnings to generalities is regretable [sic]. . . . Laborious wading through organization disruption in pursuit of catch phrases and theories is not a substitute for ascertaining and changing the causes of losses."[19]

Carpenter's opposition is puzzling, especially given his work in the development department in acquiring new product lines as separate businesses and his early support of reform and of Frank MacGregor's efforts in particular. MacGregor later explained the anomaly as a conflict in roles. Years afterward, he recalled that "Walter Carpenter was sort of between and betwixt. He agreed with me but he was colliding with them 'upstairs.' "[20] Although MacGregor's statement makes little sense in the face of Carpenter's outspoken disagreements with his colleagues on the executive committee, it is logical if "upstairs" refers to the du Pont family. Walter owed a great debt (including his Du Pont stock) to Pierre and to his mentor, Irénée, who stubbornly opposed and stopped reform until his reluctant capitulation during the crisis of

1921. Certainly Carpenter's votes in 1920 against sending resolutions for restructuring to Irénée can be seen as attempts to avoid embarrassing his friend and sponsor.

Walter's resistance before 1921 was also an attempt to preserve his own department. As of late 1920 organizational reform included a revamped executive committee composed of the heads of the five new industrial departments, the chairman (Lammot), the treasurer, and the vice presidents of sales and production. Carpenter and Edge fought the omission of their development and purchasing departments and the possible fragmentation of their functions among the industrial departments, and they proposed instead separate purchasing and development organizations reporting directly to the executive committee.[21] The defeat of their motion made little difference at this point, for Irénée's veto of reform in 1920 shelved the issue for another year. By the time change did come, Carpenter had been appointed treasurer.

However, Walter's opposition stemmed from more than simple self-interest. Like Irénée, he sincerely believed in the efficacy of Du Pont's functional organization—the dominant form in American enterprise —and distrusted fundamental reform. In a meeting in August 1921, months after he had become treasurer, he still argued insistently that he "had never had his attention called to an item that could not be as well handled by our present organization as by one arranged on other lines."[22]

More significant than Carpenter's caution and his vague suggestion for compromise was his waspish tone, which undoubtedly reflected his youth and inexperience in consensual policy-making at the senior level.[23] He had yet to learn how to combine strong feelings with persuasive argument in a manner calculated to build respect and agreement. His approach indicated that even "detached" professional managers could lose their perspective on issues that vitally concerned them. In a bureaucratic setting that depended on collective action among strong personalities, anger and sarcasm were counterproductive and invited retaliation, as Walter soon discovered.

But if Carpenter was testy and uncertain, so were his colleagues on the executive committee. Although they had correctly selected industrial departments as the core of the enterprise, they, too, had not decided how to integrate the new operating departments with the old structure. In November 1920 they still wished to have both the new bodies and the old sales and manufacturing departments represented on the executive committee.[24] Clarification came only during the August 1921 financial crisis from Vice President Harry Fletcher Brown, who had been head of smokeless operations and a member of the executive committee and then a member of the finance committee. After his reappointment to the executive committee, the frustrated Brown bluntly charged a "failure of administration" and singled out a weak executive committee, hamstrung by each member's loyalty to his own department, corresponding sensitivity about fellow members' self-interests, and the president's refusal to accept reform.[25]

Brown's solution (including minor amendments during its adoption) was to accept formally and switch entirely to the system of product divisions that Du Pont called industrial departments.[26] (See figure.) At the head of each of the five industrial departments a general manager with full responsibility and authority for all the functions of his business would replace the present division council, which suffered from divided authority among the old functional departments. The general managers in turn would answer to what would become the new executive committee, to which they would report monthly. Brown's major new contribution was his suggestion for reorganization at the top. He had hoped to combine the authority of the old finance and executive committees into a single five-man body, but the finance committee retained its functions (probably at Pierre's insistence) so that in effect Brown was redefining the executive committee.

That committee, on which Walter Carpenter would serve for nearly

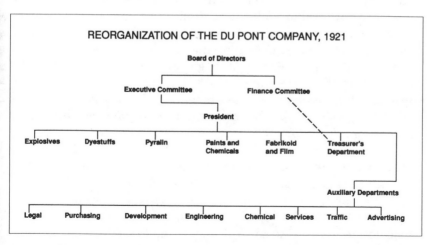

Source: Alfred D. Chandler, *Strategy and Structure: Chapters in the History of the Industrial Enterprise* (Cambridge: MIT Press, 1962), pp. 108–9.

three decades as a central part of his career, would remain in practice Du Pont's most powerful body. Although it was to oversee the administration of the entire company and was ultimately responsible for its performance, its old functional vice presidents were to be replaced by general vice presidents with no operating duties. They were to set policy and plan for, coordinate, and monitor the enterprise without the distractions of daily administration or the biases of special interest. Planning and policy-making established the firm's goals, objectives, and procedures; guided the committee's allocation of such critical resources as funds and managerial talent; and provided for the overall direction of Du Pont for both the near and the long-term future. Monitoring meant the systematic oversight and measurement of performance by studying return on investment and other financial criteria in a specially maintained chart room; by analysis of monthly reports and quarterly presentations from each department; and by review of subjective managerial skills like foresight, judgment, and the handling of people. In other words, the executive committee would tell the managers of the industrial departments what the company's general aims were and then evaluate how well the managers used their entrepreneurial talents to carry out those assignments.

Coordination came from general oversight and common objectives defined collectively by the executive committee, while established procedures like interdepartmental committees also helped unify operations. This device was vital because the traditional, central functions of the business were thoroughly decentralized among the autonomous industrial departments. (Even the employee suggestion plan was to be administered separately in each product line.)[27] Meanwhile, the more specialized functions, like legal, engineering, purchasing, development, and traffic, were transferred to "auxiliary departments" that supplied information and services both to the industrial departments and to the general office that centered around the executive and finance committees. Some functions, like purchasing, auditing and accounting, and research, were located in both the general office and the industrial departments. To better integrate operations, each executive committee member assumed responsibility for the oversight of one or two particular functions. The assignment typically meant heading a committee composed of representatives from the corresponding functional units of the industrial departments and from the relevant auxiliary department, if any.

The reform of the executive committee was just as important as the shift to industrial departments. The latter properly transferred the focus of operations to the businesses that were Du Pont's central purpose and that could be appraised by profit and loss and by return on investment. In addition, the decentralization of key functions moved authority and responsibility down to the level of each industrial department where knowledge was greatest. At the same time, the executive committee's new duties provided for the critical general management and integration of Du Pont's many different businesses.

Put another way, the work of Walter Carpenter and his colleagues in the ensuing decades provided the economies of scope that made the large, diversified firm possible. In effect, their efforts now concentrated on making Du Pont more efficient and profitable than the separate operation of its constituent lines. The innovation of the decentralized structure organized around product divisions was a major watershed in the history of Du Pont and of American business in general.[28]

Adoption of the new structure (which the company still uses in modified form, along with most large U.S. industrials) came quickly and with relatively little disruption at the top. Given the pressure of the financial crisis of 1921 and the overwhelming endorsement of the company's top executives, Irénée (and, of course, the board of directors) accepted the plan in September 1921. Five of the executive committee's nine members stayed on, including Lammot du Pont, its chairman, and Frederick Pickard, William Spruance, and H. F. Brown, who had pushed so hard for reform. Several others, including J. D. B. Edge, Charles Meade, and A. Felix du Pont, became or remained heads of industrial or auxiliary departments. At the same time, the body was expanded from the five originally proposed by H. F. Brown to seven to include Irénée du Pont (who as president succeeded Lammot as chairman of the committee) and the treasurer. The final addition meant that Walter Carpenter, who had opposed the change, remained on the executive committee to help implement the new organization, for he had become treasurer of the Du Pont Company in January 1921.

Although Walter's shift to a new position resulted at least partially from the now familiar factors of opportunity and du Pont family sponsorship, it was also related to the reorganization. Long-term opportunity in the development department was not especially attractive. It would continue to play an important role in diversification, but the exciting period of corporate pioneering had ended. In addition, in 1919 and 1920 Du Pont was fully occupied with its current projects.

Dye manufacture and the newly acquired artificial silk (later renamed rayon) business needed large amounts of money, and the company's investment in General Motors was even more demanding. In March 1919 the finance committee told the executive committee that it preferred not to fund any new lines promising less than a 30 percent return because of better opportunity in the automobile industry.[29] The following year the collapse of the economy made additional acquisitions unlikely until the country and the company recovered.

By contrast, moving into finance as treasurer of the company was quite enticing. The treasurer's department had been one of the firm's four grand units ever since the three cousins' takeover in 1902. In an enterprise that placed financial analysis at the center of its operations and that generated and demanded huge sums of money in its growth, the treasurer had always been a powerful, central figure. Pierre du Pont had occupied the position before becoming president, and his successor, John Raskob, had been Pierre's closest confidant. Raskob's replacement, Donaldson Brown, had quickly moved onto the executive and finance committees and, along with Walter Carpenter, was Irénée's choice in 1919 as future steward of the du Pont family holdings.[30] Furthermore, while discussions about restructuring in 1919 and 1920 threatened to diminish or dismember the development department, the treasurer's department was unchallenged. In fact, that office would emerge even stronger after reorganization as the single remaining powerful functional department.[31]

Because Brown and Carpenter were both extraordinarily able young executives of similar age, they might well have competed for decades for power and influence in the company, but once again chance intervened on Walter's side. In late 1920 Pierre du Pont elected to take Donaldson Brown to General Motors, whose presidency Pierre assumed after the mismanagement of his partner William Durant had left that corporation near collapse. Although Brown remained a member of Du Pont's finance committee and an influential figure at the firm for many years, his career henceforth centered on General Motors.[32] His transfer simultaneously removed a rival and opened a door for Walter.

Once again, Irénée du Pont, as Walter's mentor and president of the company, moved to push him through that opening. In December 1920 he quickly asked the finance committee to select Carpenter as Brown's successor. Irénée argued strenuously that although Walter had not served in the treasurer's office as his predecessors had, he was "the most available man and the most fitting one. . . . Mr. Carpenter's experience in the study of financial statements of companies which we have investigated, as well as in studies of the investments in branches of our own company, and his aptitude in that kind of work, eminently qualify him for the position." He also pointed out significantly that because work in the development department was "at low ebb," a lesser man could handle the position and would not have to be added to the executive committee, which many complained was already too large.[33]

For the first time in his career Walter Carpenter faced serious opposition. Although major personnel decisions were usually settled well in advance and although the president was generally accorded the right to pick his own team, the nomination was first stalled by discussion and doubt in the finance committee for several meetings and then defeated with Donaldson Brown voting against and John Raskob and Harry Fletcher Brown abstaining. The extraordinary process continued as Irénée immediately carried the issue to the board of directors, the formal seat of ultimate authority at Du Pont. The board elected Carpenter, but only after four men, including John Raskob and Donaldson Brown, spoke and voted against him while two other directors including William Spruance, Walter's colleague on the executive committee, abstained.[34]

The remarkable struggle reflected both company politics and Carpenter's qualifications and helped define more precisely the challenges he would face as he moved into senior management. Irénée's own authority was no doubt compromised by his relatively recent rise as president and by his ongoing, stubborn battle with the executive committee over reorganization. In the minds of Du Pont's top men he had not yet fully proved himself a worthy successor to the powerful, dominant Pierre. In fact, the fight between Irénée and the executive committee over decentralization was also a conflict to establish the balance of power between the company's new president and its top operating body as well as a struggle between owner-operators and professional managers. As Irénée's protégé and as an outspoken defender of the status quo, Carpenter had clearly aligned himself with the three du Pont brothers, who so vigorously opposed the reorganization pushed by most of the company's top operating people.

John Raskob (who normally would have sided with Pierre) and Donaldson Brown opposed the appointment for bureaucratic, political reasons. Given the strength of functional departments in Du Pont and other American companies, it was difficult for someone to shift across such units at the top. Only gradually did Du Pont realize that reorganization that exposed administrators to all phases of the business was a better means of training general managers for the executive committee. In 1920 the two financial officers' pride in and fierce loyalty to the department that they had done so much to build demanded that the successor be Angus Echols, one of their own. Raskob wrote Irénée that Echols, who headed a statistical division for forecasting, had "a splendid mathematical and analytical mind." Moreover, Echols' "training in the Department and financial experience" better qualified him. This fact, which was "well understood by the rank and file of the employees in a very large Department[,] must be recognized, otherwise the espirit de corps in the Department will be seriously injured." The appointment of Carpenter would be a "rash" step that would "do much to undermine the espirit de corps in the whole organization."[35]

In fact, Raskob and Brown had a very weak case as Irénée quickly noted. Echols' training consisted of "less than 2 y[ea]rs in a new div[ision] only" and his work in finance was "substantially none."[36] Even Raskob and Brown admitted that Echols' inexperience meant that H. G. Haskell, vice president and member of the finance committee, would have to serve in Echols' stead on the executive committee. Brown even wanted Haskell to become temporary treasurer in order to resolve some unspecified, difficult problem in the department before turning it over to Echols.[37]

The support for Echols' promotion reflected not only bureaucratic considerations but also questions about Walter Carpenter among top managers on the executive and finance committees. Though they respected his basic ability, they apparently doubted both his financial acumen and his maturity and independence. Opponents at the board of directors meeting argued that the position required more financial and executive experience than Walter had.[38] They worried that his rapid rise as the owners' future representative could compromise present operations. Carpenter's youth (he turned thirty-three in January 1921), his prickly refusal to join the managers' campaign against Irénée for structural reform, and his apparently self-interested defense of his own position in the battle raised doubts in the minds of his colleagues.

Their defeat by the family-dominated board of directors perpetuated rather than resolved the issue. Nine months later, during the reconstitution of the executive committee following reorganization, the reformers wanted a five-man body that excluded Walter. At Irénée's insistence the committee was expanded to seven to include

Walter only after the president stated the obvious criticism of the un-precedented omission. "The proposed slate is definitely weak by elim-inating the Treasurer, for through that channel much of the informa-tion will flow."[39] Carpenter not only stayed on the executive committee, but, like his predecessors, as treasurer he was naturally and quickly elected to the finance committee.

Walter Carpenter's first two years in top management were turbulent and ambivalent, for initially his extraordinary early success helped generate opposition to further advancement and power. He had made an important shift to the influential financial department, the area with which he would be most identified for the rest of his career. Except for Irénée and Lammot du Pont, at the end of 1921 Walter was the only man serving on both the powerful executive and finance committees. However, his advance came at the cost of profound doubt and resis-tance from his managerial colleagues that was overcome only by the unusual exercise of prerogative by the du Ponts themselves. In addi-tion, Carpenter had helped initiate major structural reform, but due to inexperience he had misunderstood and misjudged its value and in the end he had aggressively broken ranks with his fellow executives to oppose it.

That break, along with his youthfulness and his extraordinarily rap-id rise, which owed much to luck and to du Pont family support, com-bined to overshadow his remarkable abilities and to raise serious suspi-cion about his independence and judgment. Those developments suggested that high-level management was far more complex and chal-lenging than his previous experiences, and that any further advance would come more slowly.

The Treasurer

As treasurer of the Du Pont Company, Walter Carpenter's major challenges were proving his independence and his financial compe-tence as well as his ability to work within the new structure. His respon-sibilities were to administer the many vital tasks assigned the treasurer's department, which included carrying out or overseeing Du Pont's nu-merous financial transactions, auditing and accounting, preparing sta-tistical data, reports, and forms, forecasting and analysis, and handling credit and collections.[40] Although a strong, able staff performed most of the daily tasks, Walter made impressive contributions over the next

Du Pont's Most Promising Young Executive: Walter Carpenter early in his career (*Hagley Museum and Library*)

five years in administration, in money management, in the provision of important financial advice and commentary to the president and other senior executives, and in such special assignments as getting the company on the New York Stock Exchange and settling a major tax dispute with the federal government.

Carpenter improved administration through a reorganization that made Angus Echols the assistant treasurer with (in Walter's words) "full charge of and responsibility for the affairs of the Treasurer's Department."[41] He thus demonstrated his own confidence and independence by recognizing the talents and promoting the career of his rival for treasurer. Echols, an engineering graduate of the University of Virginia who had joined Du Pont in 1912 and the treasurer's department in 1918, was an able man and an excellent choice who would follow Carpenter as treasurer, vice president for finance, and member of the executive and finance committees.[42] Walter also established a combined salary and administrative division under Will Raskob (the brother of his predecessor and leading critic) and confirmed Echols as head of the forecasting and planning division, J. B. Eliason as comptroller in charge of the accounting division, and E. N. Wead as auditor.

Carpenter also deftly handled the tricky job of decentralizing accounting to fit the needs of the reorganized company. The executive committee's decision to restructure the firm in 1921 had only begun the process of major change. Making the new organization work required numerous, often quite significant adjustments and new routines throughout the enterprise.

In this case Walter had to help create in each of the industrial departments independent accounting divisions that reported to their respective general managers. Nevertheless, he was simultaneously responsible for oversight and maintaining uniform standards. The shift smoothly transferred to the division people the bookkeeping for calculating manufacturing costs and for handling and accounting for raw materials, semifinished goods, and finished products. Their work supplied the general managers of the industrial departments with vital data for measuring costs and for setting prices for outside and interdepartmental markets. To insure consistency and the preservation of standards, Carpenter frequently sent cost auditors to monitor performance with special attention to standards for apportionment of overhead, determination of material prices, and distribution of payroll. He closely watched the gathering and classification of data for reports so that two years later he could confidently report to President Irénée du

Pont that "there has been little tendency to drift away from the 'old landmarks.' " The process had been handled with "entire satisfaction" at his end and "full cooperation" from the industrial departments.[43]

Because of the work of his excellent predecessors, there were few opportunities for innovations in accounting forms and calculations. Nevertheless, in the 1922 annual report to the stockholders Walter offered for the first time a complete consolidation of the earnings and assets of Du Pont and its separately incorporated holdings. Minority interests that owned the shares not held by the company were listed in liabilities on the balance sheet, and earnings owed those holdings were deducted from total earnings in the profit and loss account. The change was important for Du Pont had more than a dozen subsidiaries, some of which represented the operations of industrial departments. Carpenter correctly felt that consolidation gave "the stockholders a more enlightening and comprehensive picture of the results of the activities of all your company's interests."[44]

His actions were also significant for two broader reasons. Walter was demonstrating an appreciation for the importance of external audiences in the extended health of a large firm like Du Pont. This vital quality in a senior executive built on an understanding that he had earlier illustrated in his arguments about dye manufacture and about the purchase of German nitrate mines when he served in the development department. At the same time the reorganized annual reports were a public recognition of the company's gradual evolution away from its long heritage as a family concern. An increasing portion of the enterprise's owners, including many du Ponts as well as nonfamily shareholders, were in effect "outside" investors who knew little or nothing about operations. Walter's efforts kept them better informed while making Du Pont stock more attractive to thousands of similar potential stockholders.

Carpenter continued to be sensitive to shareholders' needs, for as the firm's subsidiaries grew in number and importance, he worried that including their entire earnings and assets in the consolidated statement with an offset line for minority holdings was misleading. In the income account, for example, the amounts owed to other owners were not available for dividends to Du Pont stockholders, but the numbers were too big to omit. Simply consolidating only Du Pont's share of assets and earnings scandalized what Carpenter called "the accounting highlights" because it failed to report all the assets and income available for the company's use, even if not owned by it. His solution was to list as assets Du Pont's investment in its subsidiaries plus its share of the surplus accumulated since acquisition. Since this procedure in effect wrote up the value of company-held securities by stating cost rather than par value, he reduced the good will account correspondingly.[45] As a manager with obligations to shareholders, clarity and accuracy were more important than form.

Carpenter's initiative won attention and tribute and quickly began to dispel doubts about his appointment. When John Raskob wrote to compliment the company's 1922 annual report, Irénée responded (probably with a special sense of satisfaction in this case) that "the praise is due to Walter Carpenter who did most of the work."[46] The treasurer's performance had effectively disarmed a major critic.

The swift proof of Walter's mettle resulted in part from his handling of the 1920–22 depression, which confronted Du Pont when he became treasurer in January 1921. Though brief, the collapse was severe, with a 2.4 percent drop in gross national product in 1921 and a relative decline in national investment worse than the first year of the Great Depression of the 1930s. At Du Pont net sales for 1921 were down more than 40 percent from 1920 and net income fell almost 50 percent, with layoffs of two-thirds of wage earners and one-half of salaried employees in order to cut expenses.[47] As financial head Carpenter led in recognizing the impact and making adjustments. He wrote down inventory losses of $20 million and carefully scrutinized weak areas of operation for elimination. To guide top-level decision making, he joined with Frederick Pickard to draft a report to the executive committee outlining the projected conditions of the industries in which Du Pont was engaged. William Spruance wrote Irénée that the analysis was done in "as comprehensive and definite a way as could be expected at this time."[48] Carpenter had won over a second skeptic, for Spruance had previously abstained in the board of directors' vote for Walter as treasurer.

Walter Carpenter's independence, initiative, and insight were quickly demonstrated in his analysis of the E. I. du Pont de Nemours Export Company, established in 1919 to develop and handle Du Pont's foreign business under Frederick Pickard as the vice president for sales. During a determined search to cut costs and losses in 1921, Irénée wrote Pickard that a *New York Tribune* report showed export business as a source of loss to U.S. firms if there were no special advantages in the particular lines involved. He wondered if it was time to review and trim lines to reduce the "very heavy losses" of the export company.[49]

Irénée's letter was preceded and probably prompted by Walter Carpenter's work nearly three months earlier. His carefully calculated, conservative review of the new subsidiary demonstrated that, even assuming optimistic economies and generous profit margins, the firm would annually have to do $5 million of business just to break even. Since this figure far exceeded present projections and normal prewar volume, he asked Pickard if Du Pont should not "very seriously consider whether we are, or are not, organized on too elaborate a scale for that work."[50] Du Pont liquidated the export company the following March and distributed its business (mostly explosives) to the proper industrial departments. Thanks to Carpenter's perceptive analysis, the firm had reduced expenses in the short run and simultaneously become better organized to achieve future economies of scale within the industrial departments.

Walter's judicious balance of making essential immediate changes while respecting the extended considerations critical for a large firm with high fixed costs was also demonstrated in his handling of adjustments in depreciation rates and reserves. Although wartime inflation and postwar depression had wildly skewed the values of Du Pont's plant and equipment, which were in turn a critical factor in calculating costs and setting prices, Carpenter refused to make panicky changes. The issue was not urgent because for the present the company would have to adjust prices to meet the market and sell off excess inventory. He waited until 1923, when price levels had stabilized, to allow calculations based on more confident projections of the future. He then directed a systematic reappraisal of all Du Pont investment at prices one-third above the prewar level in order to properly measure real expenses on one hand and to avoid the potential inflation of immediate costs on the other hand. The plant account increased $5.8 million, which was credited to depreciation reserve.[51] The results helped set prices that assured a proper return on investment while meeting the competition and maintaining market share.

As treasurer Carpenter also demonstrated his largely self-taught ability to manage money with the necessary mix of prudence, initiative, and imagination. He apparently had only a single home study course on business, but lined his library with textbooks on finance and accounting, which he read voraciously.[52] He also inherited a great deal of wisdom from his predecessors. Pierre in particular had established a conservative tradition of maintaining a high level of cash and liquid assets and of preserving the capacity to borrow for emergencies. At the

Du Pont Company such lessons were based on long experience with volatile explosives markets in the face of war and the unstable capital goods cycle.

In Walter's time deep cash reserves were even more vital. Just as decentralization had required reorganization of the treasurer's department, so diversification necessitated fresh thinking and new routines in money management. He readily appreciated that the newly diversified chemical company depended on products and processes with long lead times, huge costs for development, and high rates of obsolescence. In the 1920s he and Angus Echols regularly maintained cash and marketable securities of $30 million or more so that liquid holdings were in excess of 10 percent of all assets. To obtain high returns on the idle cash while assuring its ready availability, Carpenter began investing large sums in New York's burgeoning call money market, a practice that he may have initiated at Du Pont. By the spring of 1924 Du Pont had placed $12.5 million through the National Bank of Commerce and the Bankers Trust Company to finance brokers' loans (due on demand) for securities transactions. When Irénée fretted over the safety of what was apparently a new arrangement for the firm, Walter reassured him that in order to limit fraud and failure no house received more than $500,000.[53]

To further assure liquidity, Carpenter did all he could to reduce or eliminate Du Pont's reliance on long-term fixed borrowing or bonds. Both he and Pierre wanted to avoid the liability of fixed payments to creditors in a volatile business. As Pierre wrote Elias Ahuja after the company's big wartime expansion, "One of the great features of our development . . . is the fact that in all this enormous expansion the financial strength of the company has been maintained in fact supplemented by the maintenance of very large liquid accounts and reduction of liabilities."[54]

Carpenter demonstrated his commitment to this tradition and the logic that underpinned it as soon as he became treasurer in 1921. In that same year John Raskob arranged for the sale of $35 million in 7.5 percent ten-year bonds in order to finance Du Pont's purchase of William Durant's holdings of General Motors stock in the midst of the depression. Walter immediately began accumulating reserves for annual repurchase of the bonds, all of which were retired within four years. Irénée, who was more aggressive than Pierre, twitted Carpenter that Du Pont should be doing more with its funds than earning 6 percent in a sinking fund or "we will soon go to seed." He properly argued that the firm should be investing in artificial silk, cellophane, and other high-return manufacturing projects.[55]

Walter calmly stood his ground against his mentor and explained to the Du Pont president that his strategy was not caution but the assurance of long-term growth. Redeeming the bonds not only cancelled fixed obligations to creditors and preserved borrowing capacity for more critical times; it also promoted the market for the company's debenture stock, its senior security. Similar instruments had helped finance the firm's consolidation of the explosives industry in 1903, and along with the sale of common stock, Du Pont had relied heavily on debenture or preferred stock ever since as a major source of capital. In the absence of bonds, the debenture issues had first claim on the concern's assets and their fixed annual dividend had first call on net earnings. Given their protected position and net earnings which were several multiples of the guaranteed, fixed dividend, the senior securities were very attractive to estates, trusts, and insurance companies and were readily marketable at relatively low yields for future expansion.

Irénée quickly agreed that since making temporary arrangements to redeem the bonds would "gain strength to do bigger things, I am one hundred per cent with you." In 1925, when Walter retired the last of the bonds, he easily arranged for an issue of $10 million of the company's debenture stock, and in the two decades after 1930 senior securities accounted for about three-quarters of the $200 million raised by Du Pont through the sale of stock.[56]

Carpenter also demonstrated his independence of Pierre and his concern for the Du Pont Company's general well-being through his management of the firm's investments. After the finance committee resolved to dispose of the concern's bank stocks, he began an orderly sale that included a substantial holding in the Irving Trust Company of New York City. Alfred Swayne, an influential banker on Pierre's board of directors at General Motors and a director at Irving Trust, asked Carpenter to continue holding two thousand shares. When Walter sold all of the stock, Swayne complained to Pierre, who accused the treasurer of failing to consult properly and of losing money on the sale. Walter and Irénée responded forthrightly to Pierre that the treasurer had followed company policy and that Swayne had misled the General Motors president. Carpenter had repeatedly consulted with bank officials but made no promise about holding two thousand shares, correctly telling Swayne to make his case through Pierre. In the absence of further instructions, the treasurer sold the stock at a favorable moment after consulting with John Raskob and Donaldson Brown because Pierre was out of touch.

In fact, Pierre, whose loyalties were divided between General Motors and Du Pont, had misjudged the chemical company's best interests. Irénée reaffirmed that both the policy and the sale were good ones, for the bank stock was sluggish. "The handling of the Irving Bank stock matter by our Treasurer's Department does not deserve criticism; in fact, [it] bears marks of care and good judgment." As for losing money, the stock had risen only one point several days after being sold at 230.[57]

In acting as an advisor or commentator on important financial matters, Walter Carpenter evinced not only the careful analysis expected of a treasurer but also the sound judgment and independence essential in a senior manager. Although he knew that both Pierre and Irénée had enthusiastically promoted a generous bonus plan for top executives (of which he was a beneficiary), Carpenter quickly spotlighted its embarrassing financial weakness that reflected on Du Pont finances.

When they established the plan in 1919, Irénée and Pierre arranged that each member of the executive committee receive one thousand shares of Du Pont common stock in exchange for personal notes backed by the stock as collateral. The depression had so eroded the price of the stock by 1921 that Walter had to inform Irénée that the collateral was now "quite insufficient." As treasurer he knew that the finance committee should be notified, but given the delicate situation involving "important employees," he prudently asked Irénée's guidance. Irénée could hardly have been enthusiastic about the call to duty, for seeking additional collateral might embarrass and antagonize the very men who had to lead the company out of its doldrums. He promised to mention the situation orally to the finance committee while dismissing the loans as noncommercial and not a serious problem. However, Pierre as chairman of the finance commitee felt obliged to reorganize the plan and provide additional collateral in order to satisfy the firm's fiduciary responsibility to its shareholders, thus affirming Walter's concerns.[58]

Carpenter also braved Pierre's ire when he quite properly criticized the managers' bonus program that the senior du Pont was establishing at General Motors. At Pierre's request in 1923 John Raskob and Donaldson Brown devised a complex and generous plan to provide General Motors stock as a combination incentive and reward to top company executives. In simple terms, General Motors was to incorporate the Managers Securities Company and offer low-cost shares to eligible top managers. In order to provide the executives with stock in their own concern (what Pierre called owner-management), Managers Securities was to purchase a minority position in the General Motors Securities Corporation, which the Du Pont Company had organized to hold its stock in General Motors. In effect, the Du Pont Company was to sponsor the bonus plan at General Motors by selling control of 2.5 million shares of GM stock for $4.7 million in cash and $32.7 million in notes from Managers Securities.[59]

When asked to comment on the plan on Du Pont's behalf, Walter frankly faulted it as rigid, convoluted, and liable to unnecessary tax penalties. The inflexibility stemmed from granting the individual managers' shares at the outset for a seven-year period instead of making annual awards based on performance. To avoid the complex three-tiered plan, he recommended selling the stock of General Motors Securities directly to the participants. In addition, because he and several others thought that recipients would be taxed, he proposed revisions allowing them to deduct the interest payments on their personal notes used to buy the stock.[60]

Carpenter's cogent commentary brought little adjustment but upset Pierre. Irénée enthusiastically endorsed Walter's suggestions, which avoided the "unusual contract" and which "materially better[ed]" the participants' tax position. "It also definitely enables awards to be made after the fact in proportion to a man's accomplishment. I like it."[61] Donaldson Brown huffily refused to make changes, misunderstanding part of what Carpenter said and claiming that unstated special circumstances at GM required his approach. Pierre sided with Brown and accused Walter and Irénée of opposing the owner-management that he so strongly supported. Irénée responded that he and the treasurer were criticizing the techniques and not the idea of owner-management, which both strongly endorsed at Du Pont. Nevertheless, the plan passed with minor modifications, and Carpenter learned that even the best financial analysis and strongest arguments could not always outweigh owner self-interest.[62]

In addition to his normal duties, Walter Carpenter handled two special tasks as Du Pont's treasurer. Taking the company public by recording its stock on the New York Stock Exchange (NYSE) in 1922 was enormously important, for it gave Du Pont larger recognition and provided access to the organized capital markets that would provide about 16 percent of its funds (about $200 million) between 1930 and 1951.[63] After arranging to sell Raskob's $35 million bond issue on the exchange in 1921, Carpenter appeared before the committee on the stock list of the NYSE in 1922 to register the company's two major sources of funds, $69,521,200 in 6 percent nonvoting debenture stock and $63,378,300 in common stock. In the days before the Securities and Exchange Commission, the process was relatively simple, and Du Pont's response had been relatively unsystematic. It had previously listed one of its debenture issues, but its common stock had traded as an unlisted security. Under Walter's leadership, full registration on May 22, 1922, went so smoothly that it occasioned only a brief note in the annual report.[64]

As chief financial officer of the now public company, Carpenter soon acquired other duties. As we have already seen, he moved quickly to make the annual report clearer and more informative to the firm's growing outside audience. In addition, his previously described efforts to improve the status of Du Pont's senior securities certainly helped increase their attractiveness and their dispersal, thereby expanding the company's pool of potential capital. The total number of shareholders jumped nearly one-half, from 10,579 in 1921 to 15,252 in 1926, Walter's final year as treasurer.[65]

In order to further protect and expand the market for Du Pont's securities, Carpenter risked Pierre's irritation to strike a successful bargain with the family blacksheep, Alfred I. du Pont. Alfred remained a major shareholder, but he was largely isolated from much of the family after his loss to Pierre in their bitter struggle for control of the firm between 1915 and 1919. Part of his wealth was in voting debenture stock (17,385 shares worth about $1.7 million), which he alone had stubbornly refused to exchange for the nonvoting debenture stock held by other senior security owners. Because of their concentrated ownership, the voting debentures could not be listed on the NYSE. When Alfred attempted to sell two hundred shares in June 1922, he found no market except at a considerable discount, and he immediately asked Du Pont for an exchange for nonvoting debentures.[66]

Carpenter cleverly resisted the chance for a cheap triumph in exchange for furthering Du Pont's long-run interests. The exchange period had long since lapsed, and the company had no nonvoting debenture stock available. It would have to spend cash to buy shares in the market or issue new shares after a cumbersome process of charter amendment and stockholder approval. Instead of refusing the troublesome, unpopular Alfred—as he could quite legitimately do—Walter initiated a scheme to accommodate him and to advance the position of the firm's securities. He proposed exchanging all of Alfred's stock on a share-for-share basis (the original ratio) for nonvoting debentures held by the E. I. du Pont de Nemours Powder Company, an inactive, wholly owned subsidiary of the parent company. The deal, which Raskob (on Pierre's behalf), Irénée, and Lammot approved, simultaneously appeased a major shareholder, eliminated the negative reflection of a little-known, unmarketable stock on the company's registered securities, and increased the distribution of the nonvoting debentures.

Carpenter's other special contribution as treasurer was the settlement of a complex, long-running tax battle with the U.S. government. The dispute centered on millions of dollars in taxes for the World War I period (1915–20).[67] It included the definition of large amounts in the categories of net income and invested capital and involved intricate questions about the amortization of wartime plant and equipment, inventory evaluation, the cancellation of contracts at the war's end, a special munitions tax, and the distribution of income and deductions in the proper years. Negotiations were further complicated by several court decisions (pro and con) and by changes in the tax code and its administration as the relatively new corporate tax law (enacted just before the war) evolved.

Donaldson Brown, who went to General Motors in the midst of the battle, described it as a "very complex problem" requiring "very marked ingenuity and resourcefulness" to develop arguments "proving the inaptitude [and]/or fallaciousness of adverse Internal Revenue Department regulations."[68] Du Pont wanted not only a refund of all overpayments in the $50 million in taxes it had paid but also a settlement to end its decade-long battle with the federal tax bureaucracy.

In 1926 Walter Carpenter accomplished those goals with the help of a negotiating team that included Comptroller J. B. Eliason; C. R. Mudge, head of the legal department; John W. Davis of Davis, Polk, a prominent corporate law firm; and F. S. Bright from the accounting house of Price, Waterhouse and Company. The government settled disputed war contracts involving $133 million, made a final agreement fixing Du Pont's tax liability through 1925, and refunded $5.1 million in tax overpayments and about $2 million in interest. With enthusiastic support from a delighted Irénée, Walter received a special bonus of eight hundred shares of Du Pont common stock worth about $160,000 for his work.

Carpenter's successful resolution of the tax problem capped five years of impressive performance in his new position. His management of his department and of Du Pont finances had completely vindicated

Irénée's controversial choice of his protégé as treasurer. Walter's clearly demonstrated ability, judgment, initiative, and independence confirmed him as a worthy successor to a long line of remarkably able and powerful financial men at Du Pont. At age thirty-eight he was truly a senior executive in one of America's most innovative, prosperous firms.

The Financial Executive

In 1926 as a result of his accomplishments Walter Carpenter was promoted to vice president for finance and became the top advisor to a new administration. In that spring Irénée retired to become vice chairman of the board and his brother Lammot succeeded him as president and as chairman of the executive committee. In effect, both Pierre (who remained chairman of the board) and Irénée were now observing —but not managing—owners. Lammot, the new chief executive officer, was hard-working and certainly able but lacked the remarkable ability of his two predecessors. Pierre had directed the evolution of the big company, and Irénée had promoted and overseen diversification. Although Lammot served a long and extraordinarily successful tenure as president, he made no comparable contribution.

Perhaps because they recognized that fact, the two older brothers installed Carpenter, who clearly was an outstanding executive, as Lammot's second in command. Within a year he became vice chairman of the executive committee and held virtually the same position on the finance committee before succeeding Pierre as chairman in 1930. He was a true general executive without operating responsibilities, which he left to Angus Echols, his successor as treasurer. He headed the finance committee, which represented the family's voice in the firm, and was Lammot's alter ego on the top executive body. In these positions his fine performance as a financial and general manager would eventually assure him the presidency.

Although he was a general executive, much of Walter's attention naturally focused on major financial matters, the area of his expertise. His combination of financial and negotiating skills, honed by his work in the treasurer's and development departments, made him particularly useful in major acquisitions, as demonstrated in Du Pont's 1928 merger with the Grasselli Chemical Company, its largest purchase up to that time.

Du Pont wanted Grasselli in order to build its product line in acids and heavy chemicals. Although the firm had quadrupled that business to $4 million in the 1920s, its market share was only 5 percent and was limited to the eastern seaboard by plant location and transportation costs. It needed much larger volume to support a fully integrated product line that included advertising, warehousing and distribution, and research. By contrast, the Allied Chemical and Dye Corporation, the leader in the field, had an estimated 30 percent of the heavy chemicals market.[69]

The Grasselli Chemical Company was a splendid match with Du Pont and the perfect choice to serve as the core of an industrial department for heavy chemicals. Established in Cleveland in the mid-nineteenth century, Grasselli was a family enterprise well known for its manufacture of acids, heavy chemicals, fertilizers, and insecticides. Its sixteen plants, located mainly in Ohio, Indiana, Alabama, and West Virginia, assured excellent access to markets in the Midwest and the south and offered limited direct competition with Du Pont. Its major subidiaries, the Grasselli Powder Company and the Grasselli Dyestuffs Corporation, fitted nicely with Du Pont's explosives and dyes businesses. Grasselli was a substantial, profitable firm with over $40 million in annual sales, more than $50 million in assets, and regular 8 percent dividends on its common stock.[70]

After carefully familiarizing himself with the development department's meticulous study of the concern, Walter Carpenter visited President Thomas S. Grasselli first in Cleveland and then in New York and skillfully laid the groundwork for swift and successful negotiations. Building on a past relationship that had kept the two companies (in Irénée du Pont's words) "in close touch . . . for more than a generation," Carpenter first outlined a tentative proposal to test President Grasselli's interest, and from their ensuing discussion he crafted a concrete proposition that served as the basis for the acquisition. He reassured the president that the plan was more a merger or a consolidation than a sale in order to bolster family pride and to maintain a cordial relationship with those who would continue to run the operation. He explained that the exchange of the Grasselli Company's assets for Du Pont's securities "may appear to be either a sale of an interest in the Grasselli business to du Pont stockholders or a sale of an interest in du Pont to Grasselli stockholders. In fact, it is probably both." Grasselli's representatives were to serve on Du Pont's board of directors "as partners."[71]

As the basis for exchange Carpenter perceptively proposed relative earning power instead of assets. The high fixed investment and low turnover characteristic of the heavy chemical industry meant lower rates of return, and merger on Walter's basis would preserve Du Pont's earning power. To determine the price to be paid in Du Pont stock for Grasselli assets then required figuring the comparable values of the two firms' securities. Walter generously calculated Grasselli's earnings in a way that emphasized the firm's recent 50 percent increase and determined that an exchange of two shares of Du Pont's common stock for eleven shares of Grasselli's common stock would be an equal swap of earning capacity, with the dividend record and market value working in Grasselli's favor by 18 percent and by 10 to 15 percent respectively. Carpenter also figured an equal (one-for-one) transfer of senior securities since their yields were nearly identical and the higher market value (by $6 per share) of Du Pont debentures favored Grasselli.

Walter also made the deal look more attractive by extolling the future value of his company's diversification and economies of scope. Its range of businesses assured balanced prospects for both a safe return on investment and spectacular growth. On one hand many of its businesses served "the basic needs of both industrial and agricultural America and should expect a steady and secure growth with the growth of those fundamental activities." On the other hand there were "those industries, some in operation today and others still in their infancy . . . ,which supply those needs . . . which are alike fundamental but also in step with the constantly elevating standard of living of the populations of this and other countries." Walter could easily impress his counterpart with the understatement that the prospects for Du Pont's future growth matched those of Grasselli.[72]

Carpenter's gracious manner as well as his message persuaded Thomas Grasselli, who later professed "a great admiration for all of the fine characteristics of fairness and honesty of purpose, which you displayed throughout these entire negotiations."[73] Grasselli accepted the deal with only minor modifications—a slightly better common stock ratio (two shares for ten) and the sale of the dyes business to the General Dyestuffs Corporation, which had a prior right to purchase those assets. Thanks to Walter's work, Du Pont now had a new industrial department for acids and heavy chemicals whose market share of about 30 percent made it a stong competitor with Allied Chemical. A euphoric Carpenter wrote with pardonable exaggeration to his old mentor Elias Ahuja that the acquisition was "undoubtedly one of the most constructive moves taken by the du Pont Co. toward the development of its chemical industry."[74]

His simultaneous negotiations with the representatives of the Comptoir des Textiles Artificiels for the purchase of their minority interests in Du Pont's rayon and cellophane businesses were far more tortuous though probably more profitable in the long run. The Comptoir, headed by Edmund Gillet, had provided the American chemical company's original know-how for rayon manufacture, exchanging French technology and some cash for 40 percent of the Du Pont Fibersilk (later Rayon) Company (chartered in 1920). Subsequently, its subsidiary, La Cellophane, had struck a similar deal to obtain 48 percent of the Du Pont Cellophane Company (incorporated in 1923).[75]

By 1928 Du Pont had several reasons to buy out its partners. The company's research and know-how had matured while the Comptoir was no longer sending any significant knowledge. Du Pont, not the French, had recently developed moistureproof cellophane, which would vastly expand the product's market and profits. Significant rayon patents had expired and new developments were being shared by patent pools. Furthermore, although prospects for rayon seemed to be dimming after a very prosperous decade, cellophane needed vigorous investment to exploit its possibilities, and the French were reluctant to supply their portion of the funds required for expansion.[76] Because they had become shareholders rather than operating partners, Du Pont could simplify its management, eliminate troublesome and time-consuming consultation across the Atlantic, and possibly reap a larger share of the profits merited by its enterprise by making the French general investors in the parent company.

In early 1928 Walter Carpenter began negotiating the solution: an exchange of the textile group's shares in the rayon and cellophane subsidiaries for stock in the Du Pont Company. Because he had participated in the original negotiations earlier in the decade and had a friendly relationship with Albert and Henry Blum, the Comptoir's representatives in New York, Carpenter was Du Pont's logical spokesman.

Walter quickly learned the limits of logic, analysis, and charm. Though the French professed to be amenable to the general proposition of exchange, they had unrealistic expectations for the actual ratios involved. Carpenter's response demonstrated considerable maturity and contrasted sharply with his aggressive language during the reorganization debate of 1919–21. He recognized that patience and repetition were as important as reasoned argument in reaching an agreement. In the rayon case, though the two sides could readily agree on a one-for-one transfer of senior securities, they were far apart on the

exchange of common stock. In a manner similar to the Grasselli negotiations (and with some of the same language), Carpenter offered overwhelming evidence based on open calculations that relative earnings,
dividends, and assets indicated a fair exchange of three and one-half or
four rayon shares for one Du Pont share. Nevertheless, the French
insisted on two for one for six months before grudgingly proposing two
and one-half for one, an inadequate concession that threatened to end
discussion.[77]

Because a decline in rayon earnings was expected to weaken French
resolve, Carpenter calmly persisted by appealing to the "spirit of partnership which dictates an equitable appraisal of the respective holdings of the two parties" and by reminding the French that both sides
agreed that "consolidation is to benefit the rayon enterprise." To Albert
Blum he repeated in detail the basic numbers and projections for the
future and concluded more in sorrow than in anger that he did "not
believe they [the French] have recognized the merits in the du Pont
picture." He carefully left the door cracked, by pointing out that agreement "under these circumstances [demanded by Comptoir], I believe,
will be very difficult."[78]

The ploy worked, for the Comptoir soon agreed to a four-to-one
exchange as the performance of the rayon company slipped in late
1928. At the same time Carpenter won only a two and one-half to one
ratio for the exchange of cellophane common for Du Pont common,
despite his evidence that three and one-third was the logical number.
In this case, however, future expectations for the new moistureproof
product far outweighed present earnings. In January 1929 the finance
and executive committees unanimously voted to accept the agreements
Carpenter had negotiated.[79]

In the long term the contribution was considerable. Rayon's return
on investment fell from nearly 24 percent in 1928 to an average of
7 percent during the 1930s, when the depression, overcapacity, and
changing markets eroded profits. At the same time, cellophane simply
took off; sales tripled between 1928 and 1930 and jumped another
60 percent in depression-ridden 1931. Freed of its French partners,
the American company fully implemented a strategy first developed in
the mid-1920s by General Manager Leonard Yerkes. Frequent price
reductions vastly expanded the market while lower profit margins and
excess capacity discouraged competition. In the 1930s Du Pont averaged a better than 27 percent return on investment while retaining
three-quarters of the burgeoning market.[80]

In addition to acquisitions, Carpenter also advised on major financial investments. Company historians have generally argued that Du Pont settled down to "rational" diversification after World War I, that is, the expansion of its chemical businesses by internal development and by the purchase of small or medium-sized firms (like Grasselli) to serve as the cores of new product lines.[81] Nevertheless, under Irénée du Pont's leadership in 1927 and 1928, it twice attempted more speculative and technologically unrelated ventures similar to its stake in General Motors in late 1917.

The abortive movement had several causes. Irénée, who had just retired from the presidency at age fifty, was hale and hearty and looking for new worlds to conquer. More aggressive than either Pierre or Lammot, he saw the bull market and easy credit of the late 1920s as a chance for bold strikes. With large fortunes of their own, his brothers joined in his speculations and the three naturally looked to their own company, which was generating huge profits and big cash surpluses, as an additional source of funds. In addition, they expected to use their concern's advanced strategic, structural, and managerial techniques as well as Du Pont's deep pool of talented executives to reorganize and revitalize large firms in important industries with big potential growth and profits. In other words, they would repeat what the three cousins had done at Du Pont in 1902 and what Pierre, John Raskob, and their associates had done at General Motors after World War I.

Irénée's first choice, the United States Steel Corporation, seemed an ideal candidate. Although U.S. Steel was the biggest firm in a basic industry, its mediocre and aging management left a great deal of room for improvement. Under Judge Elbert Gary, the chief executive selected by J. P. Morgan and the bankers who had assembled the combine in 1901, the company had established a price umbrella to maintain order and stability in the industry. The result was a decline in market share of more than 20 percent in most lines and the rise of several strong competitors like Bethlehem Steel and Youngstown Steel.[82]

With Gary in poor health (he would die in August 1927), the du Pont brothers thought they saw an opportunity for new leadership to use the steel company's cash and underperforming assets for greater returns and increased market share. In 1924, after conversations about the firm's financial policy with George Baker Jr., vice chairman of the First National Bank of New York and a director of both General Motors and U.S. Steel, Pierre's analysis of the steel company, though based on incomplete data, found it to be sound and well positioned for an easy increase in its earnings. In March 1926 Irénée got together with John Raskob, Pierre, and Lammot to discuss making Pierre a director of the steel corporation. By early 1927 the three brothers proposed to use Du Pont Company cash in a stock pool to acquire a position in U.S. Steel. Irénée explained to one of the participants that "the whole theory" of the purchase was more than just a speculative investment. "The earnings would be greatly augmented if they had owner management and especially if they had younger and more aggressive management."[83]

The three brothers then turned to their financial vice president for an analysis that would bless the use of Du Pont Company funds in the pool, but Walter Carpenter surprised them with an independent, perceptive review that refuted their argument. His report to Irénée and the finance committee confirmed that U.S. Steel did not perform well but challenged the popular belief that the cause was "huge assets" that were underperforming. There were no excessive reserves to draw down earnings. In fact, depreciation was "on the low side." The company had declined because its competitors, like Inland Steel, Youngstown Steel, and Jones and Laughlin, operated more efficiently and earned better returns on lower capital investment per unit. U.S. Steel was handicapped because of the large amount of good will (estimated at $500 million) in its capital account.[84]

As in the case of the General Motors bonus plan, Carpenter found himself overruled by Du Pont's owner-operators. They argued that because the steel company's market value ($172 per share) was considerably below its book value ($280 per share), its stock was a good investment for Du Pont's excess cash as an entree for the subsequent implementation of better management. The finance committee authorized $14 million for a stock pool to which the du Ponts recruited Alfred Sloan, president of General Motors, Seward Prosser, a prominent New York banker on GM's board, and H. B. Rust, president of the Koppers Company (which was controlled by the Mellon brothers investment banking house).[85] During operations in May and June 1927 Du Pont spent the $14 million to acquire 114,000 shares of U.S. Steel common stock (including 16,000 shares received from a stock dividend). Its activity accounted for more than one-half of the 201,000 shares (about 3 percent of U.S. Steel) bought by the pool, which stopped in late June when newspaper leaks brought unwanted publicity and an investigation by the Federal Trade Commission.

In November Carpenter again demonstrated his initiative and independence by urging the finance committee to sell its steel holdings. His additional investigation raised the estimate of good will in the capital account to $800 million so that the net asset value of the stock was in fact well below its market value. He also argued that the delay in finding Gary's successor might signal internal promotion and the continuation of Gary policies. In addition, the bigger burden of good will meant that the old management's performance was better than thought, which left even less room for reform and growth. Du Pont should sell, he asserted, for "if today we had our cash reserves invested, for instance, in call loans or in Government or short-time paper and were as familiar with all conditions as we are today, I doubt whether we would feel disposed to liquidate those investments and place our entire cash reserves in Steel common."[86] In Walter's mind, then, inertia born of speculative investment had no place at Du Pont despite the major owners' personal concerns. Clearly, the interests of the firm and all its investors were paramount.

The sale two months later brought mixed results. The company earned a generous profit of $2.29 million and better than 16 percent on its investment, but the return resulted from a fortuitous stock dividend and not from any plan or managerial reform. The foray had also brought the firm negative publicity as a grasping giant, and it produced an intrusive though harmless investigation by the federal government. Furthermore, in the long run the du Ponts would learn that Carpenter was correct: money invested in the chemical industry, where the firm had obvious competitive advantages, performed a lot better than it did in the steel business. In 1939 one calculation determined that profits on Du Pont common stock were twenty times those on U.S. Steel common for the preceding fifteen years.[87]

None of these considerations deterred Irénée, however, who continued his search for speculative investments. One week after steel operations ceased, he and Lammot implemented a pool to buy an influential position in the United States Rubber Company. Both men had long owned substantial personal holdings in the rubber corporation, and by 1927 it looked like U.S. Steel: a large, powerful company in an important industry, which badly needed managerial reform. U.S. Rubber was a pioneer in a business whose major products in the nineteenth century were footwear and general rubber goods. In the 1920s, when automobile tires consumed 80 percent of the rubber manufactured in the United States, the poorly run company remained part of the oligopoly of five concerns that dominated the industry, but U.S. Rubber suffered flat or declining sales while its competitors boomed.[88]

Perhaps because of the public reaction to the steel venture, Irénée and Lammot at first attempted to keep their operations personal and separate from the Du Pont Company. In the last half of 1927, a pool composed largely of du Ponts and their in-laws established an influential position in the rubber company with the purchase of more than 10 percent of its stock for $7.5 million.[89] Although Walter Carpenter did not participate in the investment, his brief, informal investigation at the du Ponts' request revealed some opportunity. Nevertheless, it also questioned perceptively the existence of economies of scale in the firm's mechnical rubber and foot goods businesses and wondered if its large inventories of crude rubber would not always be a weakness.[90] As he commented to his Uncle Ed, there was "a good deal of cleaning up required."[91]

By the summer of 1928 the three brothers were once again ready to involve their firm in their personal ventures. Irénée asked Walter to evaluate the Du Pont Company's investment in a proposed merger of the U.S. Rubber and Goodyear Tire and Rubber companies. When Carpenter's brief "office review" concluded tentatively that there was "a most interesting opportunity for further exploration," Irénée asked him for a full-scale analysis for the finance committee. He urged that the opportunity was especially attractive because crude rubber prices had bottomed out, leaving the two firms with huge, cheap inventories, and because a new rubber trade association promised to bring better tire contracts with the automobile manufacturers.[92]

As a top Du Pont executive Carpenter once again demonstrated his independence, judgment, and remarkable analytical ability as his powerful final report persuasively defeated his mentor's proposal. In a balanced review he acknowledged that the consolidation presented "a very interesting and attractive prospect."[93] The merger would create the world's biggest and most fully integrated rubber company with the best rubber plantations, the largest rubber trading company, the most substantial tire manufacturing facilities, a worldwide distribution network, more than half of the American market for rubber footwear, and valuable mechanical rubber and rubber chemical producing units.

There were also serious problems, for the collapse of crude rubber prices, poor management, and "ruthless competition" had sapped the two firms' reserve strength. Consolidiation was not enough; timing and fixed cost burdens also had to be considered. "A mere joining of the properties and businesses of these two companies would not materially strengthen their financial or credit position for some time to come.

[M]eanwhile the consolidation would rock along with very large outstanding senior securities, part of which are debts maturing at a relatively early date and also borrowings at bank[s] too large in view of [the merger's] general financial position." The new enterprise would require additional capital of at least $50 million, and "stronger and more capable management at the top is badly needed."

Because Du Pont had the funds and the talent, Carpenter felt that "the situation afforded an attractive opportunity for a big and profitable play." Nevertheless, he recommended against investment because two critical reasons made it unsuitable for the chemical company. The necessary control would require buying out banking interests in Goodyear, who did not wish to sell, precipitating an expensive, uncertain battle for control. Equally important was the protection of the Du Pont Company, if necessary, from the du Ponts themselves. In order to avoid draining it of talent and funds, "one or more strong partners" were required, "of which one should certainly be the General Motors Corporation." But Alfred Sloan, who had replaced Pierre as president of GM, had already refused to interest his firm, and no other attractive candidate had surfaced.

Carpenter's overwhelming case carried the day, and he later recalled that the finance committee's acceptance of his argument "ended any further interest of the [Du Pont] Company in that direction." Subsequent events quickly bore out Walter's projections. The merger fell through and U.S. Rubber performed so poorly that Irénée recruited F. B. Davis, general manager of Du Pont's plastics department, as president to revitalize the enterprise. Though his reforms reduced the company's debt burden by nearly three-quarters over the next decade, the firm did not show a profit until 1935 and did not pay dividends on its preferred stock until 1938 and on its common stock until 1941.[94]

The Great Depression of the 1930s, which helped retard U.S. Rubber's recovery, also discouraged further ventures by Irénée, who soon began spending more and more time at Xanadu, his large Cuban estate. Along with Du Pont's commitment to basic reseach and internal development of products like neoprene and nylon, the economic crash also helped slow the pace of the company's acquisitions. By dropping the interest rate for corporate securities, however, it eventually gave Carpenter the chance for his last great contribution as a financial executive: the refinancing of the company's preferred stock.

The successful transaction, which evolved over three years, reflected Walter's astute analysis, meticulous planning, and delicate management of a very complex process. The initial problem, the question of timing, was raised in 1937 when Du Pont sold its first issue of securities since the depression had begun in order to raise $50 million for new construction.[95] The finance committee rejected his request to sell common stock, apparently to avoid further dilution of voting control. Bonds were eliminated because of the company's tradition of avoiding fixed debt, and the debenture stock paid 6 percent though declining interest rates permitted new corporate issues for 4.5 percent. Furthermore, although debenture stock could be sold above par in order to bring its yield in line with prevailing rates, it also required dividends equal to those on common stock should Du Pont fail to earn at least 9 percent on the senior securities. A protection intended twenty years earlier to make the debentures safer and more attractive now seemed burdensome due to falling earnings rates in the depression. The company's solution was the issue of a new security, a preferred stock paying 4.5 percent.

Its enthusiastic reception immediately raised the question of replacing the firm's outstanding debentures (which totaled nearly 1.1 million shares) with a cheaper security. Declining interest rates had pushed the debenture stock's market value past its call price (the $125-per-share minimum the company would have to pay for its redemption), and the recent preferred issue complicated the firm's financial structure with two senior securities. Carpenter quickly resisted efforts to exchange the debentures for the new preferred in 1937, because he agreed with Morgan, Stanley, the firm's investment bankers, that the complex process of conversion should not be confused with fund raising.[96]

In 1938 he ignored urging from President Lammot du Pont and the company's economist, E. E. Lincoln, to make the switch, citing the uncertainty of tax legislation and a growing antimonopoly movement that might force the sale of Du Pont's holdings in General Motors, a critical asset underlying the debentures. More important, he reminded his questioners that the savings had to be at least $1 million in order to be worth the extraordinary effort involved. He estimated economies at about $800,000 at current rates and argued that the company could get better terms in the near future.[97] By the spring of 1939 his gamble paid off. The Republicans' success in the 1938 elections moderated concerns about New Deal policy, and falling interest rates made possible savings of at least $1.2 million.

Perhaps Carpenter's simplest challenge was his choice of the type of security for exchange. Bonds were eliminated because company policy reserved them for emergency borrowing, and the owner-dominated finance committee frowned on the dilution of control that accompanied the use of common stock. Because there was no point in complicating the concern's finances with yet another new security, he opted for an exchange of the 4.5 percent preferred stock for the old debentures.[98] This approach would also avoid the use of more than $136 million in cash needed to redeem all of the old debenture issue at $125 per share.

Walter's greatest difficulty was the determination of the basis for the exchange. Lammot du Pont and E. E. Lincoln both favored the lowest possible rate, with forced redemption at $125 for those who refused the offer. They argued that debenture holders could be compelled to accept a below-market exchange rate because of the tax consequences of cash redemption.[99] Carpenter insisted on an exchange at market rates. Like many professional managers, he saw himself as an owners' surrogate charged with mediating among a number of publics or interest groups.[100] It would be unfair, he thought, for the common stockholders who would benefit from the annual savings to receive an extra advantage at the expense of the debenture owners.

In an approach that reflected the firm's nineteenth-century family heritage, he looked upon the holders of senior securities as partners who had not only supplied funds in the past but who could also be relied on for future capital. As Carpenter explained to Lincoln, the costs of his approach were "of a relatively small amount" and the advantages were considerable. Du Pont "has for a great many years had a reputation of treating its security holders not only with fairness but with generosity," which has "developed a position in the market for du Pont stockholders which is unequalled by any other Company in the country. The prices at which our senior securities are selling confirms that [belief]. . . . In the long run it is profitable to the Company and to the common stockholders even though the terms of the deal at the moment may not appear to have been at the lowest price."[101] Once again the extended view and a concern for outside investor interests dominated over immediate, lesser advantage as befitted a manager committed to a lifetime career in a large firm with high fixed investments and with a continuing need for big infusions of capital.

Setting the actual exchange rate required Carpenter's best financial judgment. As the deadline for issuing the offer approached, he had to calibrate carefully the changing market values of the debenture and the preferred with his desire for balance.[102] The ideal was a high ratio of voluntary compliance at the lowest possible exchange rate and cash redemption for the few who ignored the offer. Too generous an offer would penalize the common stockholders and unnecessarily raise the cost of capital to the firm. Too little would anger debenture holders, and because Du Pont had foregone underwriting by an investment banking firm in order to avoid registering the stock under the Securities Act of 1933, it would have to spend millions of dollars for cash redemption.

Carpenter worked diligently in determining the rate (which he finally set at one and one-eighth preferred shares for one debenture share) and in winning its acceptance. He consulted with investment bankers and the New York Stock Exchange. He corresponded with and even made personal visits to numerous individual shareholders, trustees, and institutional holders like banks and insurance companies. He ordered two careful surveys of stockholder opinion, and he oversaw the clarification of rules with the Securities and Exchange Commission and an agreement certifying the nontaxable nature of the transaction with the Internal Revenue Service.[103]

The result was complete success.[104] Common and preferred stockholders voted overwhelming approval at a special meeting on September 29, 1939, and in October nearly 97 percent of the almost 1.1 million shares of debenture stock were exchanged for more than 1.2 million shares of preferred stock. After redemption of the remaining debentures the following January, dividend charges on Du Pont's senior securities fell $1.2 million annually, and the firm's financial structure was again simplified with one senior and one junior security. Potential imitators like the Sun Oil Company wrote to request details of the plan, and du Pont family owners were especially pleased with the handling of their wealth. Lammot wrote his cousin A. Felix du Pont that "everyone here seems to be very well satisfied with the way the debenture stock exchange went through," and tartly noted that the unexchanged shares were those "which the owners have forgotten they own. They will find that out when they stop getting dividends on it." Felix responded simply that "the plan was admirably conceived and carried out."[105]

Ever the analyst, Walter Carpenter wondered if he might have substituted an exchange rate of one and one-tenth instead of one and one-eighth, but was inclined to accept the results, for the transaction had been made with a yield basis of about 4 percent, which nearly matched other current senior issues. As he explained afterward to investment banker Harold Stanley, the completed job "has resulted in substantial savings to the Company, the elimination of the awkward provisions of the old debenture stock and we land with a simplified and improved capital structure." He did "not think we should complain too much that we did not gain the last cent in savings," for he judged it "far more preferable that we have the minimum of dissatisfied stockholders. . . . From that standpoint the conversion was a great success. We received almost no letters of complaint from the stockholders and those which we did receive were, for the most part, from people who did not understand."[106]

Carpenter could take justifiable pride in his achievement. He could not have accomplished the same thing in another company, where lower earnings and tighter cash flows necessitated bond issues and required every effort to reduce immediate expenses. But as a top financial executive he had helped bring about Du Pont's higher earnings and had insured steady and ample cash flows. Given the particular circumstances of the company for which he worked, with its heritage of family ownership and its cultivation of senior security holders, he had made a substantial contribution by lowering capital costs while balancing competing stockholder interests and preserving markets for future issues.

The General Executive

As Walter Carpenter's experience in top management grew, so did his part in the general oversight of the company. Of course, he had that responsibility from the time of his appointment to the executive committee in 1919, and, like his fellow committee members, he participated actively in discussion, monitoring, and policy-making with questions, advice, and observations. By the late 1920s and the 1930s, however, a more mature and confident Carpenter was increasingly able to influence and even determine important nonfinancial issues. His promotion in 1930 from vice president for finance (where Angus Echols succeeded him) to vice president without portfolio, a position that virtually made him Du Pont's executive vice president, formally reflected that emergence.

One key area of his impact was the encouragement of management in depth, an essential feature of a large, bureaucratic enterprise. As noted earlier, a number of his subordinates rose to positions as general managers of industrial departments and members of the executive committee, including Walter Beadle, Frank MacGregor, Angus Echols, J. B. Eliason, and Leonard Yerkes. Though direct evidence of his role in their careers is lacking, their promotions, continued productive relationships with Carpenter, and lasting respect for him testify to his effectiveness as a boss who got along well with people and who recognized and credited their abilities and accomplishments.

Walter's broader role in managerial development at Du Pont lay in the evolution of the company's bonus plan for stimulating, rewarding, and retaining able people. A basic, corporate-wide program predated his arrival in 1909 and contained two parts. "A" bonuses were awarded annually regardless of the firm's overall performance to any employee who had made a special contribution such as a product or process improvement. "B" awards went only to managers for exceptional work and were made each year when general company performance justified such rewards to its directing team. Carefully determined formulas and procedures governed both the size and the manner of awards.[107]

Special incentives for top management, however, remained the personal prerogative of the owner-operators, who administered them in ad hoc fashion. Because Pierre du Pont felt that his leading executives should be "owner-managers" with substantial portions of their wealth invested in the company, in 1915 he gave each member of the reorganized executive committee 1,250 shares of stock in the Du Pont Securities Company, the family holding company that he created to pool the holdings acquired from Coleman du Pont and which was later renamed the Christiana Securities Company. In 1919 he awarded 1,000 shares of Du Pont common stock to each man on the new postwar committee, and when the 1921 depression threatened the financial underpinnings of that arrangement, he granted each member 400 shares of the Christiana Securities Company. There were also private, individual awards. In 1917 Pierre and Irénée arranged for Walter Carpenter to receive 1,000 shares of Du Pont common stock as noted earlier, and in 1923 Irénée and Lammot made him a similar grant of 1,600 shares of Christiana Securities. Except for the 1915 case (which involved an outright gift), in both the general and the individual cases executives received the stock at below market (usually book value) rates in exchange for personal notes secured by the stock. Payment of principal and interest was made over a period of years by application of the recipient's annual bonus awards and the dividends paid on the stock.[108]

In the mid-1920s, when Walter Carpenter recognized that the personal, informal approach was inadequate, he moved to establish a comprehensive, systematic program to be funded by the company itself. By 1925 Du Pont had forty-six important managers who earned more than $15,000 annually, but its ad hoc plan covered only the executive committee and a handful of others. After considering and discarding a complex program like the General Motors model, Carpenter offered a simple, straightforward plan that combined incentive, reward, and retention in two parts—an agreement for the sale of a predetermined amount of stock to an important executive in exchange for four personal notes and a trust arrangement to which annual special managers' bonuses would be paid for later application to the notes.[109]

The plan had a number of valuable advantages. Fixing the stock's price at the outset avoided taxes on any subsequent appreciation (as long as the recipient held his shares), and the trust arrangement postponed taxes on stock dividends until their actual application to individual accounts. The use of special service bonuses allowed the firm to price the stock at market value while the employee in effect paid book value, which helped reduce the price and keep the plan open for future entrants. The system of four notes, each representing a quarter of the stock to be "earned out" in turn, provided the flexibility to adjust the plan in case stock prices dropped precipitously in the future as they had in 1921. The seven- to ten-year payment schedules on the notes combined with the company's right to terminate the arrangement because of the recipient's poor performance or departure helped insure his continued effort and loyalty.

In addition, the plan carefully tied the manager's interests and rewards to the firm's annual performance. Not only would he receive any subsequent growth in the stock's value; his yearly bonus was directly related both to the level of his effort and to Du Pont's prosperity. Bonuses were to be paid from a pool comprised of one-half of the "B" plan funds and 8 percent of net earnings from businesses managed directly by the executive committee after 6 percent was paid to the stockholders. Carpenter estimated that after the purchase of the additional stock needed for the plan, it would cost the company about $350,000 annually against yearly net earnings of more than $40 million.[110]

The finance and executive committees were so pleased with the plan that they implemented it in 1927 with only minor modifications. They eliminated the service bonus (probably because of Irénée's insistence that the stock be sold at market value), reduced the executives' share of net earnings from 8 to 6 percent, and opened the plan to Du Pont's top thirty managers instead of Carpenter's original target of forty. The plan worked well and easily survived the acid test of the 1930s depression, requiring only the reduction of interest rates on the recipients' notes to match the drop in the firm's dividend rate.[111] As we shall see in chapter 4, it performed far better than the complex General Motors program, which precipitated a crisis in 1932.

Throughout his career Carpenter remained an enthusiastic supporter of the bonus system, whose merits he readily admitted were a matter of judgment rather than overt statistical proof. He acknowledged to the dean of the University of Washington's business school the absence of a "scientific approach" or "formula" to determine executive compensation. Nevertheless, he confidently asserted that "we merely feel, perhaps we can even say that we know, that if you are to be successful in assembling and retaining an organization of highly competent men, you must pay a scale of salaries which will secure their services in competition with others seeking their services, and if the efforts of those men are to be stimulated to continuing and greater efforts, there must be incentive to such further effort in the form of some prospective increase in reward for those efforts."[112]

Carpenter's and other managers' ready, intuitive support and the large rewards received have sparked debates that endure to the present. Critics have complained about business executives' sense of entitlement to overgenerous payments and about the absence of independent review, and the 1926 plan contained some of the seeds of that discontent. When Harry Fletcher Brown, a fellow vice president, requested Walter to prepare a detailed statement justifying the need for the program, neither Carpenter nor other Du Pont executives felt compelled to reply.[113] And much of the complexity and use of deferred payments that led to mismatched timing of company performance and individual reward stemmed from efforts to avoid income taxes, which had become a fact of life for upper-income Americans in the 1920s.

Nevertheless, Walter's plan dodged many pitfalls. It tied bonuses directly to annual company success, and those awards correspondingly held down executive salaries at Du Pont, which were only 52 percent of the comparable cost per share among firms in the National Association of Manufacturers.[114] In addition, because of the tradition of family operation, a significant part of Du Pont ownership participated directly in the creation and approval of the program. Pierre du Pont remained throughout his life an enthusiastic advocate of the bonus plan to establish a sense of ownership among salaried managers.

Pierre was in effect a transition figure between eighteenth- and nineteenth-century merchants, who regularly made important new men partners in their enterprises, and modern corporate owners. He once wrote a skeptical stockholder that "undoubtedly the success of the company in recent years has been due to the activity of the leading men . . . whose leadership and example, devotion to duty and willingness to serve [went] beyond the value of salary paid to them. . . . Our bonus plan has been one of the most powerful instruments in winning out. . . . Had it not been for the bonus plan or some similar method of attracting, holding and rewarding men of merit I should have refused . . . to have undertaken the work which has produced such wonderful results."[115] Pierre, Irénée, and Lammot readily appreciated and supported Carpenter's imaginative plan to expand and institutionalize the program they had initiated.

As a general executive Carpenter also shaped important policies in his roles as advisor and overseer. Although as top confidant to President Lammot du Pont he usually discussed matters of public policy and external relations (as we shall see in the next chapter), he occasionally influenced operating decisions. When an insurance executive importuned the president for the firm's business, Carpenter made Du Pont's powerful, persuasive case to continue self-insurance in a risky industry. His balanced analysis disarmed his opponent by first conceding the expense of self-insurance while carefully and imaginatively noting the trade-offs and advantages that justified it. Certainly the insurance company's volume made its procurement costs low, and unlike Lammot, Walter recognized that it realized a larger return on its professionally managed reserves than Du Pont did on its fund.[116]

But expertise, incentives, and economies of scale tipped the balance. The company's operations necessitated large cash balances in which insurance was included, and control of those balances allowed short-term, flexible adjustment unavailable with outside insurance. Inspection and coverage of losses were less expensive and possibly more thorough because of the chemical concern's knowledge and self-correcting procedures, for its incentive was the continuation of operations as well as the physical protection of its property. In the long run Carpenter found it "quite improbable" that an outsider could be as cheap.[117]

As advisor to the finance committee Walter played a similar role, which was ably demonstrated in his argument for maintaining conservative, regular quarterly dividends to common stockholders with a year-end bonus to pay any surplus instead of varying payments with each quarter's performance. Again he opened his case by admitting his opponents' strong points. Variable dividends more closely reflected performance and made change less remarkable and upsetting. However, past records demonstrated that dividends already "followed rather closely the trend of earnings." Because the resulting fluctuation would be less than $5 million against cash reserves of more than $50 million, the issue was insignificant. Furthermore, few stockholders could intelligently project any swings so that uniformity became for most an added attraction for the stock. In addition, a fluctuating policy committed the firm to cut the dividend just as it might need to seek more funds in the capital markets—hardly an enticing proposition. Finally, in the midst of the 1930s depression, he noted a slight macroeconomic benefit beyond the enterprise's immediate concerns. "It is no doubt of some value in steadying the course of our national economy, over periods of seasonal fluctuation of business or even over some depressions in business, for corporations to continue distributions to its [sic] stockholders out of reserves accumulated during periods of prosperity."[118]

Carpenter's case, which carried the day, was impressive not only for the anticipated expert financial analysis grounded on solid data. Its comprehensive, long-term approach also reflected the broad view essential in a top-level general executive. As a leader in a large, highly visible, and publicly held corporation, Carpenter had to be sensitive to outside concerns like absentee stockholders and national economic stability, which were also important to the firm's well-being. As we shall see in the next chapter, this sensitivity was more readily found in a professional manager like Walter Carpenter than in owner-operators like Pierre, Irénée, and Lammot.

Like most members of the executive committee, Walter also provided oversight and advice by serving on the boards of directors of important subsidiaries. His appointments included first membership on and then chairing the boards of the Du Pont Rayon and Du Pont Cellophane companies from the early 1920s until their consolidation with the parent company in 1936. Because they were in effect the operating divisions of Du Pont's industrial department for synthetic fibers, Carpenter had a chance to influence administration in two important, high-profit areas that accounted for almost 30 percent of total company investment in the fifteen years following World War I. Cellophane, which the company only introduced in 1924, grew to 10 percent of total sales by 1934.[119]

As noted earlier, in this case Carpenter lacked operating authority or responsibility, which rested entirely with Leonard Yerkes, the general manager for the industrial department. The limits of Walter's power were amply demonstrated when Irénée du Pont asked him if the department was researching the use of synthetic resins in making textile fibers. Carpenter carried the very reasonable suggestion to Yerkes, but when the head of the industrial department ignored the hint, there was little that the general executive could do.[120]

The seemingly insignificant issue was in fact related to a larger, more complex challenge. Just as in the earlier cases of reorganization and money management in the treasurer's department, resolving this problem was part of the adjustment and development of routines essential to working out the consequences of diversification and decentralization in a big, bureaucratic enterprise. In this instance the tricky but critical relationship between the industrial departments and the executive committee required direction by indirection. Part of the personal contact was institutionalized with individual quarterly meetings between the head of each industrial unit and the committee in Du Pont's elaborate Chart Room. There charts for individual departments based on components of the company's elaborate formula for computing return on investment served as a basis for monitoring performance and as a starting point for discussing future plans.[121]

In between times, by communicating, advocating, monitoring, consulting, and suggesting, Carpenter provided guidance and expertise to improve performance and to coordinate departmental administration with the general goals and direction of the corporation as defined by the committee. As a conduit carrying information in both directions, he helped stabilize and strengthen the relationship. Thus, he distributed sample cellulose sponges to all members of the executive and finance committees to familiarize them with a new product. When President Lammot du Pont wondered why the department had not persuaded the tobacco companies to substitute cellophane for tin foil in their packaging, Walter quickly explained that "this very subject was a live one" with Yerkes's people while writing the general manager about the discussion.[122]

Carpenter naturally watched financial matters closely. The replacement of a heating duct merited the department's assistant treasurer a full-page lecture on depreciation procedures. On another occasion he warned Yerkes that his five-year plan for construction was based on marginal rates of return, which were below the company's minimum of 15 percent. When Yerkes negotiated the licensing of the Sylvania Industrial Corporation's manufacture of moistureproof cellophane, Carpenter unhesitatingly offered a general formula. At the same time he acknowledged Yerkes's authority by carefully noting that "you are probably a better judge of this than I can be," and that he was "merely passing these thoughts along while I have them in mind for such consideration as you may feel they are worth."[123]

Carpenter's diplomacy, diligent attention, and thoughtful suggestions readily commanded Yerkes's respect, and they wrote one another frankly and comfortably. Walter did not hesitate to push Yerkes to be more aggressive in advertising Du Pont rayon when he thought the American Viscose Company was forging ahead. He also occasionally offered an idea that the operating experts had not considered. In 1930 the explosive growth of moistureproof cellophane sales swamped capacity. Yerkes had to build new plants while he reduced prices because the unexpected volume had boosted return on investment to 52 percent. He wanted lower, "reasonable" returns in order to discourage potential competition and a price cut to further expand the market, but that action conflicted with the shortage of facilities.

Carpenter shrewdly suggested a combined solution that turned on the importance of timing. He recommended announcing the price reduction immediately but implementing it in delayed stages over four months. The apparent drawback—customers' postponed orders to benefit from the later cut—was in fact a double advantage. It would relieve current pressure on the plants and yet keep customers away from competitors. It might also attract more buyers and even discourage new entrants. The head of the cellophane division wrote Carpenter that he was delighted with the "unique" suggestion, which "would affect our immediate position very nicely and . . . would accomplish the end we are seeking" while leaving the return at 32 percent.[124]

Not all of Walter's suggestions fared as well. Five years later Yerkes turned down an attempt to repeat the price-cut procedure because customers would not postpone orders at Christmas time. Carpenter's proposal for licensing moistureproof cellophane depended on royalties unacceptable to Sylvania. And his concern about return on investment in the construction forecast conflicted with Yerkes's policy of temporarily maintaining excess capacity and low returns in exchange for capturing an exploding market and discouraging competition.[125]

Carpenter's lack of detailed knowledge rather than any limited power or intelligence explained the rejections, for he could not possibly match full-time, daily administrators who frequently anticipated his points. The two men's close relationship left Yerkes open to the general executive's suggestions. The sound ones he accepted and the inappropriate ones he frankly refused without fear of reprisal or reversal. All the proposals were appreciated, however, because they provided a solid, independent, and unthreatening check on operations.

Carpenter was also especially helpful as a negotiator in areas outside Yerkes's expertise such as foreign business. Relations were particularly difficult with Canadian Industries Limited (CIL), Du Pont's joint venture in Canada with Imperial Chemical Industries Limited (ICI), the powerful British chemical combine. Arthur Purvis, CIL's prickly president and an ardent Canadian nationalist, jealously guarded his small firm's limited independence, and there was frequent bickering over contracts between his firm and Du Pont's industrial departments. In discussions between Yerkes and Purvis to license the Canadian company to manufacture cellophane, Carpenter initially proposed a 20 percent royalty fee on net profits. When Purvis unexpectedly and quietly accepted the senior executive's offer, Carpenter and Yerkes themselves felt compelled to reduce it to their original 15 percent target. Purvis's compliance may have resulted from Carpenter's earlier elimination of the Canadian's negotiating problems by establishing a flat rate of cost plus 10 percent on all Du Pont sales to CIL. Carpenter knew that the ratio fell below his company's target of 15 percent return on all business but thought that annual business of $350,000 with a subsidiary was hardly worth the constant turmoil.[126]

Walter's value to Yerkes was even greater when his department started to manufacture outside the United States. As expected, the initiative came from the rayon division, where managers saw a chance to expand an export market by substituting local manufacture. Carpenter, however, furnished not only advice but important support at the top, where some executives were indifferent or hostile to foreign manufacture. Because of European leadership in chemical development and because of the emergence of powerful competing firms like ICI in Great Britain and I. G. Farben in Germany, Du Pont was reluctant to enter overseas markets for fear of retaliation in the United States or lost access to new chemical patents. As Pierre put it in 1916, Du Pont should avoid "active business in foreign countries," unless by acquisition or joint venture with major local concerns. "Otherwise we would become known as 'invaders' of the business of others, our business would be less profitable and we would have less opportunity of obtaining information from foreign sources."[127]

Carpenter helped promote the rayon division's attempt to manufacture in Argentina by linking the venture to Du Pont's broader aims so familiar to the executive and finance committees. First he counseled Yerkes to reduce anticipated uncertainties by arranging for free import of construction materials and equipment, for property options, and for advance settlement of water, sewage, tax and exchange rates. Then he successfully argued rayon's case to other senior executives and to representatives of ICI whose participation as Du Pont's partner would reduce the company's risk. Rayon production made sense in Argentina for the same reasons it did in the United States: a strong market and competitive advantages like technological complexity, high fixed cost investment, and prime mover preeminence. Carpenter reminded skeptics that rayon "has the somewhat unique distinction of being a staple product and yet at the same time being one which requires for its production rather exceptional technique and experience. . . . The rather considerable investment required also tends to confine competition to a few responsible competitors. The first to enter this producing field should be somewhat favored."[128] In short, the planned $6 million investment in a plant with three million pounds annual capacity would preempt the field.

Walter also pointed to several strengths of the Argentine market. The nation already consumed five million pounds of rayon annually, all of it by importation. Because local production would be cheaper than the lowest cost imports from Italy and Japan, "this promises a measure of stability for the new industry there." The market also had noneconomic dimensions. As Carpenter put the case in somewhat patronizing tones, the Argentines were "a people of reasonably advanced culture and, what interests us particularly in this connection, a people who take pride in their personal appearance." Though he labeled as "notorious" the "political eccentricities of the South American countries," he thought the risks no greater "than the usual uncertainties of investments in foreign lands."[129] Like many U.S. corporate leaders (but unlike some of his cautious colleagues at Du Pont), Carpenter was willing to accept political instability if markets were attractive enough.

Finally, Carpenter's status as a senior executive and his foreign contacts helped Yerkes deal with the tricky problem of putting together the joint venture, which was named Ducilo S.A. Productora de Rayon (Ducilo). ICI, Du Pont's major international partner, wanted in but worried about antagonizing Courtaulds, the powerful British textile enterprise. So that ICI could remain an indirect partner, Du Pont agreed to sell 72.5 percent of Ducilo to the Duperial Company, a new South American company owned equally by the British and American chemical firms. Carpenter persuaded the Comptoir, which demanded access to the enterprise by virtue of its rayon license to Du Pont, to accept 12.5 percent. At the same time he convinced his company to accept the French request for 15 percent participation for Bunge and Bourne, a local Argentine concern that otherwise threatened to enter rayon manufacture.[130]

Despite the complex arrangements, the project turned out well. Under Frank MacGregor's direction the plant reached full production in December 1937 and first turned a profit in 1940. By 1945 the firm had generated such large earnings that it could expand without investment from Du Pont.[131]

Carpenter's work as advisor and overseer demonstrated his impressive understanding, skill, and breadth as a general executive. He clearly grasped the principles of competitive advantage that underlay Du Pont's diversification and ably applied them to new situations. He artfully passed information, gave advice, anticipated needs, initiated changes, and smoothed potential conflict, all of which helped promote the communication and consensual management so central to the company's diversified and complex operations. Furthermore, his expertise ranged well beyond his financial specialty to encompass negotiation, establishing foreign enterprise, and the expansion of market share.

In his contributions to policy-making, advising, and overseeing, Carpenter's work as a top manager included the development of learned routines, what one analyst has described as "the creation, maintenance and expansion" of organizational capabilities in manufacture, marketing, and management. Such learning was not just facts but empirically acquired understanding about the nature of the enterprise, its technology, and its industry, which gave the firm its competitive advantages. Sustaining those benefits required the initiation and promotion of dynamic techniques, programs, and approaches that not only solved the particular problem at hand but also served as general guides for handling future growth and constant change in a complex, large, diverse enterprise.[132]

Walter's reorganization of the treasurer's department following decentralization, his emphasis on deep, flexible financial resources in the face of diversification, and his bonus plan were just such routines. The compensation program not only resolved the challenge of rewarding top managers in 1926 but also provided an institutional model that was continually renewed with minor modification. Likewise, his promotion of open, candid discussions with Leonard Yerkes helped define the consensual relationship between the executive committee and the general managers of the industrial departments and provided a concrete pattern for what had only existed on paper at the time of decentralization in 1921.

Walter's several contributions to the higher, more abstract, but absolutely critical challenge of developing and enhancing learned routines were additional proof of his extraordinary talents as a top manager. In the late 1920s, when Du Pont attempted to set up formulas to appraise and guide research, Carpenter realized that the numbers measured the wrong things and that direction for research policy had to be broader and more qualitative.[133] A series of reports developed by Research Director Charles Stine and Treasurer Angus Echols categorized research spending into chemical control, product and process improvement, fresh development for established lines, entirely new products, and fundamental research. Although the reports tabulated the different kinds and amounts of research, they provided no guidelines to answer critical questions about how much to spend and where to spend it. The 1930s depression sharpened the problem, for general managers found it all too easy to bolster profits by cutting research expenditures, an immediate solution with disastrous long-term consequences.

As a general rather than a financial executive, Carpenter realized that cash was a raw material for research, that Du Pont had plenty of funds, and that they ought to be committed in a qualitative rather than a quantitative way in order to achieve long-range if elusive results. The company's rough rule of thumb, which allocated 3 percent of sales to research, was inadequate, for as sales dropped the ratio rose with no real increase in research efforts. In addition, the ratio simply did "not make sense." Du Pont needed a measurement of research expenditures "to the value of the research results" in order to appraise outcomes.[134]

Walter quickly enunciated a policy that as long as the firm had plenty of cash and "worth-while research" projects, it would fund all "well conceived" programs that "we are prepared and willing to undertake . . . with perseverance, enthusiasm and ability." Work that generated "commercially exploitable processes and products" was "unique in that there is no possible overproduction."[135] As he later pointed out, the open-ended approach was important because the chemical industry progressed "by finding and producing things that the public doesn't know it wants or needs. This necessity makes it somewhat difficult to forecast, with any degree of certainty, just what opportunities are likely to be opened ten or twenty years hence."[136]

Carpenter's argument established a policy that endured for three decades and that played a critical role in the firm's remarkable success in those years. As the historians of Du Pont's research aptly noted, "Research expenditures would be determined by quality considerations rather than by a simple formula."[137] Furthermore, the focus on quality allowed the enterprise to select among projects if and when funding grew more restricted.

Walter readily recognized the importance of constant variation in a large bureaucracy, but some of his proposed routines were small-scale and not always successful. He argued in 1938 that the company should regularly change its outside auditors in order to challenge the enterprise for the trouble and expense it went to annually. "An audit of accounts involving hundreds of millions of dollars should not be too easy and comfortable. I would rather see it vigorous and aggressive, not merely for the purpose of trying to stir up trouble or to make a show of activity, but rather for the purpose of re-examining at all times what is being done to see that the best practices known in the profession at all times are being employed." At Du Pont he saw "the same faces down here year after year," and sometimes "confused [them] with our own organization." He did not doubt the auditors' honesty but did "question somewhat their capacity for constantly, aggressively, opening and reopening questions about theories and practices which we are following."[138] At Walter's urging the company changed auditors three times in the next decade before his retirement.

In order to obtain more systematic appraisal and reappraisal, Carpenter persuaded the executive committee to institute in 1929 an annual review of each industrial department and subsidiary in addition to the quarterly discussions that were held with each general manager in the Chart Room. Heads of industrial units were to report on their current industry position, their advances in the past year, their objectives for expansion, their activities for the coming year, and the steps needed to accomplish them. The reports would better prepare the committee for long-term planning and help it cope with the growth and spread of its businesses by providing more uniform, focused analyses.[139] Although Walter had perceptively anticipated practices that would become common in American industry thirty years later, this effort failed. The reports quickly became perfunctory and then disappeared because of the depression and apparently because of lack of support among his fellow top executives.

Carpenter's biggest contribution to establishing learned routines was his promotion of broader strategic planning beyond the regular discussions with industrial department heads and the suggestions of Fin Sparre's development department. The process, which developed slowly and in somewhat ad hoc fashion, encouraged the executive committee to assume a more comprehensive view and involved the application of the principles of competitive advantage to a more considered appraisal of long-term opportunities. Despite Du Pont's enormous cash reserves and its large pool of managerial talent, Carpenter thought it important to choose more systematically and intelligently not only where but also where not to invest.

Walter failed in his first effort, an opposition to alcohol manufacture in 1925. On its face the project seemed logical enough. Du Pont was the nation's largest customer for ethyl alcohol, using three million gallons or about 4 percent of annual U.S. consumption. It had not built its own plant in part because it lacked the steady molasses supply needed for alcohol production. In addition, its own needs fell well short of minimal efficient plant size (eight million gallons) and the company did not want the risk and trouble of marketing the excess. The development department proposed a joint venture, the Eastern Alcohol Corporation, with the Kentucky Alcohol Corporation, a subsidiary of the country's second largest producer. Kentucky Alcohol had an excess molasses supply and would benefit from having a modern eastern facility located at Du Pont's Deepwater, New Jersey, works. The department calculated a 35 percent return on capital plus the purchase of alcohol at one cent a gallon below present costs.[140]

Because the project seemed so attractive, Carpenter began an extended argument with first principles. The lessons of competitive advantage indicated that the firm "should have some good reason for entering upon any new line of manufacture." The industry might be "a particularly attractive one to get into from [an] earnings standpoint." Or top executives might feel that Du Pont could "sufficiently excell [sic] in that industry to make the returns attractive." Or "certain collateral benefits" might "accrue to the other industries of the du Pont Company."[141]

Carpenter's concern was not simply the bottom line, for in that case the projected 35 percent return would have been sufficient. He doubted the proposal's profitability because it failed to meet any of the conditions for competitive advantage to Du Pont. The industry was not profitable, nor could the company expect to make it so. One large firm had recently gone bankrupt and another (Kentucky Alcohol's owner) had earned less than 5 percent on its assets over the previous five years. The low returns were understandable because the raw materials, manufacturing technology, and markets were readily available to all. Alcohol was a commodity in which Du Pont had little hope of developing the proprietary advantages essential for large net earnings.

Nor were there benefits to other Du Pont businesses, for "alcohol is available in large quantities through many sources," several of which would happily contract to secure the company a ten-year supply without any investment by the chemical firm. Any savings in marketing costs by the consumption of its own product were offset by the company's "preferred" position as a large consumer. In the previous three years its purchases averaged nearly 20 percent per gallon below the market price and 10 percent below the price paid by other large consumers.

Furthermore, in order to secure the new venture, Du Pont was to pay a premium in the form of ten-year contracts with Kentucky Alcohol for a molasses supply and for the sale of the final product. Given normally fluctuating commercial and industrial conditions, Carpenter thought it "little short of a presumption of the power of prophecy" to expect such contracts to be fair to both sides for their duration, and he listed several specific points where interests diverged. Finally, he closed with the gentle politeness for which he became so famous after the reorganization debates of 1919–21 and which softened his devastating criticisms so that his points were made without producing anger or resentment. He hoped that if his observations had merit, they could be aids in setting up and operating the new company.

Carpenter lost his case, probably because he was still establishing his reputation in 1925, because his arguments were new, and because alcohol was an important intermediate for several Du Pont businesses. Events quickly proved him correct. By 1928 the company's needs had outgrown its allotment, forcing renegotiation of the contract. Costs never permitted transfer prices at one cent below the current level as predicted, and though returns were a healthy 20 percent, they fell far short of the 35 percent target. In the long run, however, Carpenter was wrong for reasons that neither side foresaw. Du Pont's rapidly escalating need for alcohol not only helped generate profits in the subsidiary but soon led it to buy total ownership of Eastern Alcohol so that it could consume its entire output. Nevertheless, Walter had clearly developed a mastery of the complex process of make-or-buy decisions, a critical management skill in large-scale, twentieth-century enterprises.

A decade later, with more experience as a top executive and with the increased familiarity of his arguments, Carpenter was able to use strategic planning to stop the expansion of ammonia production at Du Pont. In the mid-1920s Du Pont had begun to manufacture ammonia by high-pressure synthesis in order to produce nitric acid, a key intermediate in explosives and other lines. Fin Sparre, director of the development department, pushed the complex, high-fixed-cost technology, which required a $27 million investment and ten years' time before it became profitable. Throughout the 1930s, however, substantial overcapacity in the United States kept profits low.[142] Nevertheless, in 1937 and in 1939 Frederick Wardenburg, general manager of the ammonia department, and Willis Harrington, his ally on the executive committee, argued aggressively to expand output in the face of the increasing needs of Du Pont and of the major customers for the chemical firm's excess supply.[143] For both men the aim was the protection of present business and existing sources of supply even at the cost of return on investment.

Carpenter's response was subtle and complex as well as being a significant refinement of his argument for integrated operations in his *Annals* article of 1919. He rejected the simplistic solution of eliminating a business that failed to meet corporate targets for return on investment. He was never attracted to the rigid application of precise financial formulas in the solution of corporate problems for which Robert McNamara, Charles "Tex" Thornton, Edward Lundy, and their associates at the Ford Motor Company became so famous after World War II and which became so important with the rise of conglomerates in the 1960s and later.[144] In this case, ammonia was an important intermediate, and the department's work with high-pressure catalytic techniques had other important links such as the production of vital intermediates for nylon manufacture.

He then asked the executive committee "to consider the problem from a somewhat broader standpoint" in order to achieve a balance. The synthetic ammonia business was competitive, risky, and unattractive. There was excess capacity in plants with high investment costs and low profit margins, and there were cheap alternatives in Chilean nitrates and in the by-products from coke ovens. In addition, Du Pont had already achieved minimum efficient plant size. Given the economics of production and the long-term oversupply there was no advantage in expanding operations to satisfy either company or outside needs, for more output promised no new profits and jeopardized present return on investment.

The solution then was to make a logical strategic choice among the company's businesses. Du Pont should maintain existing ammonia capacity to assure itself a steady supply of an important intermediate at a minimum efficient volume while letting unprofitable market share shrink as others expanded output. At the same time "we should direct our efforts and our investment in the future toward the utilization of our technique, our man-power, our money and our basic products from the ammonia industry in[to] the development of new industries and new products in those areas which will show the greatest reward for the exceptional capacities which we have in research, man-power, technique, etc., rather than using those efforts in the further enlargement of capacities in the highly competitive fields."[145]

After prolonged and heated debate Carpenter won his argument in 1939. During World War II Du Pont did not significantly expand capacity, but operated government-built plants that it made no effort to buy after the conflict ended. It stopped outside sales in 1949, and its market share of ammonia and related products dropped from 35 percent in 1940 to 20 percent in 1945 and to 7 percent in 1954.[146]

More important, Walter Carpenter had pushed the executive committee toward more comprehensive, conscious, and continuing focus on strategic planning at Du Pont. Because of its novelty and the limited number of businesses involved, the general approach would remain a case-by-case method instead of the application of an institutional formula. Nevertheless, Carpenter had developed ways of thinking and a comparative analysis at Du Pont that would not become standard in American industry for two decades or more.[147]

By 1940, after twenty years in the upper echelon at Du Pont, Walter had proved his knowledge and abilities many times. Furthermore, he had helped define the role of a top executive in a large, complex industrial enterprise. In his position in the diversified and decentralized company, general duties like planning, coordinating, and monitoring translated in practice into very specific accomplishments, including major financial counseling, negotiating significant acquisitions, encouraging management in depth, and guiding important strategic decisions. In addition to simply performing tasks in such areas, he also initiated, promoted, and helped implement new techniques, routines, and policies vital to the firm's continued expansion and adaptation. Although Carpenter was not an important owner or even head of his concern, he had clearly illustrated what an upper-level manager was expected to do as an innovator and as a directing participant in a process of collective decision making.

In a variety of ways he had made numerous, important contributions to Du Pont's growth and improvement. A few were measurable, like the millions gained in the 1926 tax settlement and the savings in dividend charges resulting from the 1939 refinancing. Others were concrete additions, like the Grasselli acquisition as the core of a new industrial department. Some were negative, like the savings from avoiding the U.S. Rubber investment. Others were incremental, like the creation of the 1926 bonus plan and the advice to Leonard Yerkes's department. Still others were more abstract, like the reform of research policy and the development of learned routines to achieve essential economies of scale and scope in the newly diversified, decentralized enterprise. In sum, Carpenter had produced a powerful record.

When he became president of Du Pont in 1940, Walter Carpenter was the most able manager in the company and probably among the most talented and accomplished in American industry. His judgment, initiative, independence, and long-term approach had matured to produce a broad, synthetic view while his power of gentle persuasion in combination with frank discussion had evolved to make him a confident, successful leader among his fellow executives. Even before becoming president, however, his breadth and experience forced him to establish relationships with influential audiences outside Du Pont's managerial circle.

3

Beyond the Firm—Personal
and External Audiences

AT THE END of the nineteenth century, as big business emerged from the sweeping technological changes of the industrial revolution, oligopolistic competition in key industries among a few large firms replaced a pattern of self-regulating struggle among many small companies. In the face of imperfect competition, top executives themselves assumed considerable responsibility for the conscious direction of their firms, and they often replaced market forces in the allocation of resources and in the timing and coordination of flows of materials, products, information, and funds.[1] At the same time large size, much of it in fixed investment, brought to the corporation long-term life expectancy and high visibility because of its great potential impact on the society and the polity.

Such changes meant a considerable adjustment in senior operators' outlook. Although small businessmen could continue to focus safely on their companies, the maintenance and growth of big enterprise compelled managers to look beyond the firm's immediate concerns to other audiences—consumers, suppliers, financial intermediaries, and workers as well as growing numbers of absentee owners. In particular, during the first half of the twentieth century, the widening recognition of imperfect competition and of the imbalance of power and wealth increased government regulation so that both popular and political attitudes toward the company became a special concern of top managers like Myron Taylor of U.S. Steel and Walter Teagle of Standard Oil. In addition to efficient performance, then, the executives' role called for attention to various outside groups and mediation among them in the enterprise's best long-term interests.[2] As Alfred Sloan, then chairman of the board at General Motors, noted wryly, "the average stockholder thinks that supplying the money is all there is to a profitable business. The average worker—at least this applies to General Motors—thinks that if it were not for the workers there would be no business. And the management believes that they should have generous compensation. They are all selfish."[3]

Walter Carprenter's experiences at the Du Pont Company provide specific illustration of generalizations about high-level operators' sensitivity to multiple constituencies. The progress of his career required recognizing and dealing with a number of audiences outside the corporation itself, including himself and his family, the du Pont family, the public, and the federal government. Though his business life largely conformed to the behavior patterns attributed to top corporate executives, there were important exceptions resulting from his personality and from the character and particular circumstances of his company.

The Private Audience: Self and Family

Discussions about managerial personality usually emphasize adaptation—to a sensitive consideration of the power and wealth of the large company and their impact on the firm's leaders and on society at large, to the concern's need for rational planning and long-term analysis, and to the process of consensual decision making essential for a lengthy career in a huge, complex bureaucracy. A big enterprise was an institution with a life of its own, and as one analyst argued, "The more effective an executive, the more his own identity and personality blend into the background of his organization. . . . The more able the man, the less he stands out, the greater his relative anonymity outside his immediate circle."[4] Such an approach avoided needless antagonism and demonstrated successful leadership through persuasion and respect rather than by force or threat.[5]

In addition, adaptation helped senior managers cope with a murky ethical situation. Clearly they had tremendous power. In the words of a leading business historian, they ran "an organization permanently employing thousands of men, with a life of its own that could not readily be understood or meddled with by an outsider, even though he might be a member of the board of directors."[6] But as the scope of management's authority widened, guidelines and justification for its behavior disappeared, for the rise of big business eroded the authority of classical economic theory based on autonomy in a self-regulating world and replaced it with uncertainty. Although one of Carpenter's contemporaries called for management "to define its own responsibilities," in fact top executives found it easier to retreat to homilies about competition, consumer sovereignty, public opinion, and stockholder interest.[7] If the institution was dominant, at least they as individuals were not responsible.

Certainly Walter Carpenter's career reflected an abrupt shift in financial well-being and power. In a very few years he moved from a middle-class family in a modest-sized city to the leadership of the nation's biggest chemical company and one of its largest industrials. Furthermore, as we shall see in the next chapter, he also assumed responsibility for oversight of Du Pont's investment in General Motors, ownership of almost one-quarter of the nation's third largest corporation.

His own income and wealth advanced accordingly. After 1926, with the possible exception of Lammot du Pont, he was the best paid member of the executive committee, with an average annual income of more than $200,000 throughout the 1920s and in excess of $300,000 in the 1930s. His yearly salary jumped from $30,000 in the early 1920s to $50,000 in 1926 and subsequently to $60,000, figures that his annual bonuses often matched or surpassed. These awards in turn paid for stock in the company's special program for top executives, which made him even richer. The 1,000 shares of Du Pont common that he received in Pierre's 1919 arrangement with the executive committee became, by virtue of stock splits and dividends, 15,800 shares worth more than $3 million in 1929. And despite the Great Depression, in 1941 that grant (along with the 400 shares of Christiana common added in 1921) was worth more than $4.2 million not including cash dividends. In addition, he also received 1,600 shares of Du Pont common in the 1926 program, 800 shares from his "A" bonus in 1926, 1,000 shares of Du Pont common by private sale from Pierre and Irénée in 1917, and 1,600 shares of Christiana common by private sale from Irénée and Lammot in 1923 along with smaller grants in the 1920s and other awards in the 1930s. He was worth at least $8 million by 1929 and more than $12 million by 1941.[8]

Despite his great affluence and authority, Carpenter showed no serious unease about the responsibilities and consequences and no need to reshape his personality to Du Pont's requirements. He did not have to *become* a "company man," because his native abilities, family training, and early Du Pont experiences naturally fitted him with a personality and character admirably suited for top management of a big corporation. Walter's three criteria for business success simultaneously reflected his own skills and those generally expected of top managers: "the ability and desire to carry assignments through to completion; leadership, those qualities which evoke cooperative effort; and sincerity and honesty in dealing with people and situations."[9]

No one ever doubted that Carpenter's native intelligence and energy met the first standard. As we have seen, his successful analysis of difficult problems amply and repeatedly demonstrated his ability to ask the right questions, to pick out critical facts, and to organize and interpret them in logical and perceptive fashion. Of special value was his practical turn of mind. Thomas Cochran, the historian of nineteenth-century American railroad operators who were the nation's first professional managers, noted that they solved problems "by practical considerations rather than by any systematic body of ideas." "The railroad businessman seem[ed] to have been first and foremost a pragmatist."[10]

Like his predecessors, Walter Carpenter thought and planned ahead. Innovation resulted less from the use of theory and more from anticipating and identifying concrete problems and from the application of intelligence and system to empirical data, just as he had been taught in engineering school. His approach was illustrated in his determined defense of high tariffs into the 1960s long after free-trade principles had triumphed in economic theory and in public policy. Although he was perfectly familiar with arguments about nations concentrating on areas of relative advantage, he argued that lower tariffs meant the surrender of U.S. markets and jobs to others while awaiting for "those so-called new industries which we are all striving so hard to find, but find so elusive." The abstractions of free trade might be correct, but that was not how the nation got where it was. The world into which he was born had a strongly protected domestic market with remarkable economic growth and high standards of living. Despite the new burdens of world leadership assumed by the United States after World War II, Carpenter worried that a shift to low tariffs would mean a massive dislocation. "It is possible that we shouldn't start from where we are. We should have thought of this many years ago, but the fact is that here is where we are and it is from here that we must go."[11]

Walter's pragmatic approach surfaced in numerous little ways. He vigorously urged brevity, clarity, and conciseness in business correspondence, complaining that department heads' reports ran twenty-five to fifty pages when five would have sufficed. "Some of them," Carpenter lamented, "have weighed pounds."[12] In his early career he read voraciously and widely but concentrated on directly relevant current events in newspapers, business journals, company reports, and commercial magazines, finding little pleasure in novels, classical literature, or history.

Nevertheless, as maturity and experience broadened his outlook, he worried that the absence of a traditional liberal arts education had caused him and others like him to miss a lot. By Walter's sixties his youngest son recalls that his father had amassed and read through "a considerable library containing substantial classical literature and history . . . particularly Shakespeare, Montaigne, and Macaulay."[13] He later acknowledged to Alfred Sloan that he had spent his life "in a fairly circumscribed area of business and industry." Despite efforts to acquaint himself "with some of the broader fields of interest," he thought that "the benefits I have derived from my participation in those areas would have been vastly more rewarding if I had had the benefit of a broader interest and education in my earlier years."[14]

Characteristically he derived the case for a liberal arts education not from abstract considerations but from its concrete advantages for the nation's powerful managerial class. "We have all noted over recent years that we have had more than average difficulty with men highly skilled and perhaps somewhat narrowly educated in the scientific fields. Some of the cases have been important. I have wondered sometimes whether they might have been so extreme if their experience both in their education and in their life work had been in a somewhat broader area."[15] Despite his own specialized training in engineering, intelligent and thoughtful observation contributed in this and many other cases to the kind of breadth essential for a leader of a large American enterprise.

Intelligence and scope were not enough, however, for the first part of Carpenter's prescription also called for hard work, thoroughness, and competitiveness in order "to carry assignments through to completion." As we have seen, Walter's childhood provided just the characteristics that railroad leaders and other professional managers valued so highly. He was reared in the Protestant work ethic that such men preached and generally practiced. The rise of big business required not only extraordinary energy but the full-time concentration of its leaders on the concerns of a single enterprise in contrast to the more dispersed interests of earlier general merchants and entrepreneurs.[16]

Carpenter's sense of duty and attention to detail were legendary. When asked to list his boss's outstanding characteristics, George Weth, Walter's personal secretary for thirty-five years, retorted, "His thoroughness, his thoroughness, his thoroughness!"[17] Ned Carpenter, Walter's youngest son, described his father as "devoted" to the firm. "His first life was the Du Pont Company."[18] When he decided to take a special extended vacation without compensation in 1938 to celebrate his fiftieth birthday after a lengthy bout of hard work, Carpenter typically turned the occasion into a policy discussion on the firm's behalf. Such periodic breaks, he argued, could stimulate new interest, relieve "the constant grind of the day to day work," avoid burnout, and increase the service and productivity of critical senior managers.[19]

Carpenter's correspondence was also filled with meticulous explanations and answers to questions from people inside and outside the organization. In 1948 his four-page, single-spaced response to an apparent stockholder inquiry about the size of managers' salaries won special recognition. *Forbes* magazine had secretly sent the original letter as a test of numerous top executives of large American corporations and singled out Walter's reply for its special politeness, concern, and thoughtfulness.[20]

Tenacity and competitiveness were also essential elements of duty, and Carpenter had more than the requisite share as previous discussion of his service with Du Pont has indicated. His battle to get the company into plastics manufacture in 1914 and 1915, his five-year struggle to win a tax settlement with the Internal Revenue Service, and his fight for strategic planning based on competitive advantage in the debate on ammonia production all reflect his persistence and will to win.

However, Walter's second criterion—leadership that induced collective effort—recognized that victory alone was not sufficient. Working with fellow career managers in a complex bureaucratic environment required mutuality, cooperation, and consent for best long-term results. As Thomas Cochran has noted, corporate executives demonstrated leadership "by winning the loyalty and respect of their associates."[21] Such qualities were especially valued at the Du Pont Company, where Pierre had instilled them by precept and by example in building the large, modern firm.

After his lessons in the 1919–21 debate about reorganization, Carpenter's own emphasis on the values of consideration and patience was reflected in private advice to his youngest son on his eighteenth birthday. "We are inclined to be intolerant or impatient over all things or events which do not conform with our convenience at the moment or with the shortcomings or the idiosyncracies of other people. It is quite well to be sufficiently alert to notice these things. On the other hand it is well not to be too much influenced or biased by them[,] to consider them in short as part and parcel of ones [sic] every day life. Matters, let us say, to be taken in our stride. In this way we save ourselves a good deal of annoyance and conflict with the world and other people and also, I believe, make a contribution toward the smoother running of the affairs about us."[22]

The mature Carpenter's reputation and behavior provided ample evidence that his training and personality disposed him to practice regularly what he preached so fervently. The *Wall Street Journal* dubbed him an "industrial diplomat." Among associates his thoughtful consideration of others and gentle but firm statements of his positions were hallmarks of his personality. Crawford Greenewalt, Walter's successor as president and a long-time colleague, believed that he embodied the thought, cooperation, and calm discussion that Pierre made a tradition in management at Du Pont. Greenewalt judged that although Carpenter could be extremely "tough" when necessary, he had "that feel for people" and was "a great listener." He repeatedly marveled at Walter's "superlative good manners in every situation."[23] George Weth noted that Carpenter betrayed his irritation only in his eyes, for he suffered fools patiently but not gladly. The secretary also remarked on his numerous thoughtful letters of congratulation to employees, fellow managers, friends, and acquaintances for promotion, special accomplishment, and long-term service.[24]

Carpenter's correspondence demonstrated the frequency and effectiveness of his polite approach. He won over opponents by listening to their points and by conceding their merit before defeating them with close reasoning and hard evidence. The sting of criticism was usually mitigated by self-effacing phrases indicating that the document was intended only as a suggestion or as a means of clarifying his thoughts. Thus, his arguments carried their own force and persuaded rather than browbeat others to his case.

Although Walter's modesty at times seemed so extreme that it might have annoyed and raised doubts about his sincerity, its pervasiveness in

private moments without apparent advantage suggest that his personality was genuine. When Carpenter turned seventy, he wrote his physi-
cian offering to change doctors because advanced age meant greater
demands. He told the busy Dr. Lewis Flinn that his treatment was
excellent, but "I cannot reasonably expect to find you available for the
care that I should normally expect to require from here on."[25] In old
age he delighted in giving his own birthday parties; guests were forbid-
den to bring gifts but instead received presents from their host. Pierre
du Pont noted the most famous example of Carpenter's politeness
when the senior du Pont hosted a splendid display of fireworks and
colored lights for guests at Longwood, his impressive estate. As the
ceremony began, a late arrival entered the grounds and stopped until
the exhibition ended. Pierre promptly and correctly identified Walter
as the driver because he had thoughtfully doused his headlights to
avoid detracting from the spectacle.[26]

Such politeness would have been valueless if not genuine, for as
Carpenter perceptively noted in his last criterion for success, honesty
was as essential as ability and drive and leadership. Thomas Cochran
has pointed out that beginning with railroad leaders, honesty had real
"business value" and that "cool objectivity of judgment" was highly
prized and essential for successful operation.[27] As we have already
seen, Carpenter repeatedly asserted his forthright disagreement with
his fellow managers and with the du Pont brothers. He differed with
Pierre about expansion into dye manufacture; he refused to support
the brothers' ventures into U.S. Steel and U.S. Rubber; and he argued
with other executives about Du Pont's programs for alcohol and ammonia production.

Walter, along with his colleagues, recognized that policy-making in a
complex modern enterprise was best achieved in a collective process.
No one could expect to be right all of the time, but it was critical that
each executive offer his independent judgment so that the discussion
jointly produced a decision. The necessary balance of intelligence,
frankness, and politeness was typified during Walter's visit to another
firm's factory. When his host arbitrarily ordered two workmen with a
heavy object off the freight elevator so that he and Carpenter could use
it, Walter blurted out, "No wonder you have so many strikes!" In his
subsequent letter of thanks for the tour, he apologized for the bald
comment but still insisted that it was "no wonder you are having labor
troubles."[28]

The listing of Carpenter's virtues does not make him a paragon. His focus on current events, business, and politics was narrowing, his self-effacement could be annoying, and his honesty could be upsetting or irritating. The point is that his virtues—the residue of birth, family training, and his early experience with Du Pont—admirably and naturally suited him for the position he held. In his case at least, the jump from middle-class life in older, small-city America to wealth and power in the modern world of big business was not a large or difficult leap in personal terms.

Carpenter's private and family life also reflected a relatively easy transition. He handled the company and public activities required by his position as a highly visible executive in Wilmington's dominant enterprise while maintaining some personal freedom for himself and his family. He was never a joiner and did not like to go out. His youngest son remembers Walter spending his evenings at home. He also preferred and frequently managed to have lunch at the house, thanks to Wilmington's compactness and his short commute. Walter's family was known as the "quiet Carpenters" to differentiate it from his brother Ruly's more boisterous clan.[29]

Preserving a private self apart from the company gave Walter and his wife Mary personal freedom from the Wilmington social scene as well.[30] Mary, to whom he remained happily married for thirty-five years until her death in 1949, continued charitable and other interests in Laurel, Delaware, her hometown, and although his parents had moved to Wilmington before World War I, Walter maintained strong ties to Wilkes-Barre, his own hometown. Following his parents' deaths in the early 1930s, he (with support from Ruly) donated a pipe organ in their name to Wilkes-Barre's First Methodist Church, where the family had worshiped. He corresponded regularly and visited occasionally with his Uncle Harry and Uncle Ed in Wilkes-Barre until their deaths in 1949 and in 1952.

Although his summer vacation home on Fisher's Island (located off the Connecticut coast and west of Long Island) was near those of Ruly Carpenter and several du Ponts, he and Mary enjoyed vacationing with close friends not related to either family. Tom and Dorothy Russell (he was a vice president at the Hartford Mutual Fire Insurance Company) and Charles and Marjory Parsons (he was president of the American Hardware Company) had nothing to do with the Du Pont Company or Wilmington. In later years the Carpenters established another vacation home at Hobe Sound in Florida, which was also away from the Wilmington crowd.

Carpenter's philanthropy likewise reflected a mix of corporate expectation and private inclination. His firm commitment to public service, a product of the responsibility taught and practiced by his family in Wilkes-Barre, fitted well with similar traditions held by the du Ponts in Wilmington. To Walter such an obligation did not mean public office but the personal donation of time, ability, and funds. These contributions were a duty for those who were able toward those who were not, a kind of stewardship familiar to the Carpenters and the du Ponts and to most Americans in the nineteenth and early twentieth centuries. Though Andrew Carnegie popularized the belief as an elitist Gospel of Wealth, Walter, like many others, saw a broad, general responsibility that increased with the accumulation of means. As he explained to his eldest son when he entered manhood, "You will find that there are a great many activities, let us say charitable activities in a community which are made possible only by a large number of people carrying their full weight. It is possible that one or even more individuals can get on for a while without doing this, but it is certainly not doing one's part. . . . In the long run in all efforts which are worth while, . . . carry your own weight."[31]

As befitted his code Carpenter's own donations were numerous and diverse and grew in size and impact with his wealth and advancing years. Some were clearly company related. Beginning in 1926, for example, he served for twenty years on the board of directors of the Wilmington General Hospital, which Irénée du Pont sponsored. Many other contributions were personal and informal, including loans or gifts to family and friends in need during the Great Depression or financial support for destitute but deserving students in college and medical school. At the same time he assumed formal roles independent of Wilmington. In 1930 he began a thirty-seven-year tenure as trustee of the Wyoming Seminary in his hometown, and in 1939 he started an eight-year term as trustee at Cornell University, where he served as a special advisor to the president for the creation of a school of chemical engineering. In 1938 he joined with his old friend Elias Ahuja to establish Good Samaritan, Incorporated, a kind of personal charitable foundation.[32]

Perhaps Walter Carpenter's greatest concern was rearing productive, responsible children amidst the trappings and snares of great wealth and power that he had never encountered in his own youth. His success in only two of three cases must have been the source of great personal disappointment. John, his second son, never attended college, and struggled through several prep schools as a rebellious, undisciplined student involved in a number of scrapes. He held various lower-level jobs at Du Pont but never advanced. An alcoholic whose marriage ended in divorce, he died in 1955 at age thirty-seven.

Although John exhibited the classic symptoms of the spoiled rich child, the causes of his problems are unknown and cannot be simply attributed to his Wilmington family life, which also produced two successful, well-adjusted brothers. As a teenager at boarding school he felt estranged from his father and criticized Walter for not writing frequently enough. Nevertheless, though Carpenter's commitment to his work at Du Pont may help explain some of his distance from John, he was devoted to his family and home life.

Part of the problem may have been incompatible personalities, which prevented Walter from effectively expressing his love for a son who was so different. When John complained about not hearing from his father, Walter sent letters that reproved his grammar and his behavior and lectured on duty and discipline.[33] In this case Carpenter's parental affection took second place to his obligation to rear his son in a manner calculated to produce a successful life in the long run.

However, Walter was not a cold man and could certainly express emotion, as his letter to his mother at his father's death demonstrated. "I had been granted many years of wonderful relationship with a beautiful character, may have been blessed with the privilege of bringing some satisfaction and contentment to him, but in any event derived from him a sustained inspiration for doing my part in the great scheme of life. He leaves me with my mind full of beautiful memories of a beautiful life. Should I now selfishly grieve because I am not to have more or should I evidence my gratitude for these great privileges which I have received and delight in their memories? This course seems not only most satisfactory to me but to do most justice to him and respect to his memory. Let us have the memories of him bring us great happiness not grief. He would have it so, I know."[34] Although the note clearly expressed Walter's own sense of love and loss, it was also counterbalanced by the expressions of a rational, orderly mind that had to analyze and objectify, imperatives lost on a confused teenaged boy like his son John.

Perhaps, then, it was not the circumstances of family life in Wilmington that separated Walter from his son but the very qualities of analysis, discipline, and rationality that put Carpenter in those circumstances. Walter's oldest and youngest boys, who shared his tempera-

Walter's Family in the Late 1920s. From the left: Sam, Walter, Mary, Ned (seated on the floor), and John. (*Edmund N. Carpenter II*)

ment, responded well. Sam, the eldest, graduated from Princeton University, married happily, had three children, and capped a lengthy, successful career at Du Pont as a vice president and "topflight" (in the words of Crawford Greenewalt, who appointed him) general manager of its international department.[35] Ned, Walter's youngest and favorite son, completed degrees with honors at Princeton University and at Harvard Law School, won a decoration for bravery in World War II, and developed a distinguished career in the public and private practice of law and as a civic leader in Wilmington, where he also reared a family. A proud Walter once said of Ned, "He always does the right thing."[36]

Carpenter left scanty direct evidence of his feelings about the challenges posed by his extraordinary accumulation of power and wealth at Du Pont. Nevertheless, a remarkable letter to his father provides a rare, personally reflective glimpse of the successful young manager at age thirty-seven. Drafted in 1925 when he was a top executive worth more than $1 million, the letter illustrates directly Walter's relative ease in making the big jump from Wilkes-Barre to Wilmington and confirms what the foregoing examination of his behavior has demonstrated indirectly. He was simultaneously candid, thankful, a little puzzled, but generally comfortable. He marveled "at how extraordinarily well matters have gone with me." In typical analytical fashion, he had "often tried to think it out," but admitted that "I have but little better if any better intellect than my associate contemporaries (I often think considerably less) and no overwhelming desire to grind. Surely Dame Fortune has smiled on me far beyond my deserts."[37]

His unexpected wealth and power were troubling, however: "If I had been considered successful I have been gauged from a very superficial and material viewpoint. It is difficult to analyze what life's real object is:—the teaching of the Christian religion comes about as close to it as one can imagine. If measured from those standards though, I find that I, with most of mankind, have as yet made a bad fizzle, [for] we most of us live and strive too much in the interest of ourselves and our nearest friends and families." He was truly discouraged that even for "the best minds of the world," the answer to balancing God and mammon "is today incomprehensible to the human brain. If I were in charge I would order up a Divine Revelation so clear and obvious as to set us all right."

In the absence of such a directive, he adopted the pragmatic response of a manager and a businessman in a capitalist society as the best choice among imperfect alternatives. He quickly rejected radical solutions, for departure from the capitalist system "might be wholly unavailing and idealistic except as a salve to ones [sic] own conscience unless he first develop a practical reconciliation between the Golden Rule and political and social economics." He believed that "the material welfare of mankind is best served by our heartily cursed capitalistic system and yet it deplorably fails to permit each individual to share that measure of real fullness of life which he greatly deserves." He readily acknowledged that he had "horribly confused material and spiritual welfare," but "being quite human however I feel that to a large extent they must go hand in hand," for "we are not all philosophers and one without the other will not bring contentment."

With the exception of his son John, then, Walter Carpenter's relationship to his private audience—himself and his family—was a comfortable one. His satisfaction as a professional manager was reflected in a career of hard work and devotion to Du Pont that lasted into his eighties although Carpenter could have retired a multimillionaire at age forty. In 1928, when he was age forty, he refused Irénée's offer to become president of the U.S. Rubbber Company. In effect, he was rejecting the chance to head immediately a large firm and to pursue a life as the entrepreneurial associate of a big capitalist, as John Raskob had followed Pierre du Pont.[38] In the decade that separated Walter's career from Raskob's experiences, professional management had come of age as an attractive career that promised to lead to the top at Du Pont and many large U.S. industrial firms. The choice was critical for Carpenter and illustrative of a fundamental change in the leadership of American enterprise as ownership and management were separated. Raskob's career focused on an entrepreneur while Walter's business life centered on a corporation.

The choice of professional management was also eased because, like Alfred Sloan of General Motors, Walter Teagle of Standard Oil, and numerous other executives, Carpenter found, as one business historian aptly put it, that "efficiency and economic progress" did much to define good and bad.[39] Though Walter certainly recognized the limitations of that formula, his own circumstances made it particularly beguiling. The enticement was strong because it was more than personal gain. He had great wealth and power because he helped lead a manufacturing firm that directly raised the national standard of living with marvelous products like cellophane, rayon, nylon, and neoprene. For Carpenter, Du Pont truly did bring "better things for better living through chemistry."

"Family" Audience: The du Ponts

Unlike the leaders of most large American firms in the twentieth century, Walter Carpenter's link to ownership had a special focus. Public finance via the stock markets, the growing role of financial intermediaries like investment bankers at the century's turn, and the dispersal of ownership had made family control uncommon in big American industrial corporations by the 1920s.[40] Because most sizable manufacturing companies had only emerged in the United States after the 1890s, those with multiple generations of family operation, like the Du Pont Company, were especially rare. In this particular case a du Pont had been president of the enterprise ever since its founding in 1802, except for a son-in-law who briefly filled that office in the 1820s.

Du Pont's emergence as a large concern had only strengthened the family's leadership. As we have seen, Coleman, Alfred, and Pierre du Pont reorganized, consolidated, and vastly expanded the company after 1902, and following Pierre's seizure of control in 1915, he and his brothers Irénée and Lammot occupied the presidency for the next quarter-century. Furthermore, even after Pierre and then Irénée stepped down in favor of a younger brother, both were involved in the firm and served as heads of its major committees. As presidents, the three served sequentially as chairmen of the executive committee until 1940. Pierre was chairman of the board of directors until 1940, when Lammot succeeded him, and was chairman of the finance committee until 1926, when Irénée replaced him.

Over time this last body, which was (in John Raskob's words) "composed of the owners of the property and the financial brains of the company," became the strongest center of family control as professional management emerged in operations.[41] Du Ponts usually comprised about half of the committee, which numbered between eight and ten in the 1920s and 1930s, and along with close associates like John Raskob, Harry Haskell, and Donaldson Brown, they clearly controlled it. Within that group the three brothers were again the dominant force. All three served long terms—Pierre for a half-century until his death in 1954, Irénée for three decades after 1915, and Lammot for over a quarter-century after 1917. Together they also led the family holding companies, the Christiana Securities Company and the Delaware Realty Company, which in turn owned about 30 percent of all the voting stock in the Du Pont Company.[42]

In theory the finance committee had equal power with the executive committee. The board of directors created the latter to administer the business and the former to oversee the treasurer's department and the company's finances. In fact, because the finance committee did not initiate policy for such key areas as expansion, new business, and pricing, it came to exercise a veto power by deciding whether to make capital available for any significant project. As Donaldson Brown explained in 1945, the executive committee "actually manages the business," making decisions "which it must be admitted include the financial affairs of the company."[43] Prior consultation with the three brothers, one of whom was president of the firm and chairman of the executive committee until 1940, and with other members of the finance committee almost always avoided conflicts between the two bodies.

Du Pont Family and Company Leadership: Irénée, Pierre, and Lammot du Pont in 1947 (*Hagley Museum and Library*)

The du Pont family was present in other ways as well. Large share-holders naturally had to be consulted in any major financial reorganization, as illustrated by Walter Carpenter's careful education and solicitation of opinion during the 1939 refinancing of senior securities.[44] Pierre's and Irénée's large holdings, long experience, and important roles as members and chairmen of major committees even after retirement from active operation assured their continuing interest and involvement. They also occasionally pushed personal projects for company consideration, as demonstrated by Irénée's promotion of Du Pont investment in U.S. Steel and U.S. Rubber in 1927 and 1928.

Pierre was also capable of intervening in management after he no longer had formal authority. When he and John Raskob built the Empire State Building in 1930, Al Smith, president of their Empire State, Incorporated, asked Lammot as president of the Du Pont Company to consolidate the firm's New York City offices in the new skyscraper.[45] Although Du Pont could have provided important revenues as prospective tenants grew scarce during the Great Depression, Lammot refused to order the switch because he thought the quarters too ostentatious and expensive to meet the varied needs of what were after all autonomous industrial departments. However, when John Lee Pratt of General Motors wrote Raskob that the awarding of refrigeration contracts for the Empire State Building to General Electric embarrassed GM's Frigidaire Division and asked him to intervene, the irascible Raskob, who had only two years earlier been forced out of GM management because of his national political activities, exploded. He responded to Pratt (with copies to Lammot and Pierre) that he would not act on General Motors' behalf because Lammot and the Du Pont Company had not given his building corporation "sympathetic support, cooperation and reciprocity."[46]

Pierre quickly overrode Lammot, his brother and the chief executive officer of Du Pont. He explained to Pratt that "largely on John Raskob's urging, I have reopened the office space matter," though he was also acting inescapably as a major investor in the building company.[47] He wrote Raskob (with a copy to Lammot) that while he agreed with his brother "in principle," his own view "coincides exactly with yours," for "we must presume that the Directors of our Corporations are men of strictest integrity and desire to protect the interests of their corporations. Therefore, any request that they might make for consideration of another corporation or interest must be assumed as made not only in the interests of said other corporation but in the interests of the corporation of which they are Director." He concluded that he would be "much chagrined" if Frigidaire failed to get the refrigeration contract.[48]

Pierre could effectively dismiss any conflict of interest among corporations because he persisted in viewing relationships in personal terms though he realized that many disagreed with him. He pointed out to Raskob that at his Longwood estate, "I have made it a practice to use Du Pont and General Motors products without question and generally without even suggesting a competitive bid. I am happy to say that among my numerous employees practically every one [who] can afford a General Motors car owns one . . . without any solicitation on my part. . . . This kind of personal loyalty counts for much in the promotion of company affairs. What is true of individuals is true of corporations." He had not raised the issue of reciprocity earlier because he thought that "a majority of our directors and important stockholders have no sympathy with the idea that corporation affairs can be promoted by extraordinary courtesy or sympathy with those who are personally related to the corporation."[49]

In fact, Pierre was neither realistic nor consistent in his arguments. He and Raskob moved their personal New York offices into the Empire State Building only after repeated importuning and financial compromise by Al Smith. The fallacies of the senior du Pont's assumptions about equality and independence among men of vastly different levels of wealth, power, and obligation were quickly demonstrated at the Du Pont Company. The executive committee acceded to the elder brother, overrode Lammot's arguments, and ordered the consolidation although savings for the enterprise were miniscule if they existed at all and despite the resistance or indifference of the general managers of the industrial departments, who saw more harm than advantage for their operations.[50]

Though such incidents were few, the lesson was clear. At Du Pont the family's role, particularly the influence of Pierre, Irénée, and Lammot, was vital. If a "retired" Pierre could reverse his younger brother, the president, then unrelated professional managers would have to be attentive to, consult with, and persuade or defer to the three brothers, whatever their official status and authority.

Although the du Pont family's role could both confer advantages and restrict power, Walter Carpenter generally benefited, as noted in the previous chapters. Pierre and Irénée encouraged his career almost from its beginning and were later joined in their support by Lammot. Pierre had shown special interest in Walter's hiring in 1909, had united with Irénée to sell him privately one thousand shares of Du Pont common stock at a bargain price, and had approved his promotion to vice president and member of Irénée's executive committee in 1919 at the latter's urging. Irénée had also introduced Carpenter to his future wife, presided at his wedding, and in 1925 sold Walter his former house, which adjoined Lammot's on prestigious Rising Sun Lane in Wilmington. In addition, he had nominated his protégé in 1919, along with Donaldson Brown, as the future steward of du Pont family wealth, and had fought for his promotions to treasurer in 1921 and to vice president for finance in 1926. In 1930, with Pierre's approval, Irénée persuaded Lammot to appoint Carpenter chairman of the finance committee "because he actually is the financial leader of the du Pont Co. and the most appropriate office for that work is Chairman of the Finance Committee."[51] Earlier, in 1923, Irénée and Lammot had cooperated to privately sell Walter 1,600 shares of Christiana Securities Company common stock at a small fraction of its actual value. Carpenter's acquisition of a significant block of stock in the closely owned family holding company was like an invitation to an exclusive private club and became a significant portion of his wealth.

By the 1930s the business press began identifying Walter as the "crown prince" and started recognizing his emergence as Lammot's eventual successor and the first company president unrelated to the du Pont family by blood or marriage. In 1934, for example, *Fortune* magazine labeled him as the "No. 2 Du Pont man and most potent Du Ponter whose name is not Du Pont."[52] In fact, the three brothers probably selected him as their replacement in the mid-1920s. After 1925 Carpenter annually received the highest salary and bonuses of any manager except the president, and his promotion in 1926 to vice president for finance formally acknowledged his stewardship of du Pont family wealth. In March 1927 he became vice chairman of the executive committee, a public signal that he was next in line to head the operation of the enterprise. As chairman of the finance committee in 1930, he was the first non-du Pont to head a major company committee— significantly in this case the one that represented the family's presence in the firm.

At the same time Carpenter made his own choice. His refusal of Irénée's offer of the presidency of the U.S. Rubber Company in 1928 confirmed his commitment to a career in the Du Pont Company. He was no longer Irénée's protégé nor was he simply the future surrogate for the three brothers or for the du Pont family. As a salaried professional manager, his allegiance was to the corporation and all of its shareholders.

The asymmetry between Walter's sponsorship by the three du Ponts and his primary loyalty to the enterprise opened the door for conflict, and disagreements certainly occurred. As noted in chapter 2, in 1927

Carpenter opposed the brothers' wish to use company funds as part of their ventures in U.S. Steel and U.S. Rubber. Although Walter lost in the first case, he was soon able to persuade Du Pont to sell its steel investment when it became clear that its prospects were poor. He won in the second case, perhaps because he had been proved right in the first.

At the same time, he attempted to force formal recognition of the difference between the company's industrial businesses and the brothers' personal ventures by seeking to separate Du Pont's manufacturing and investment assets. The motion failed, apparently because the three brothers did not wish to recognize any potential conflict between themselves and their firm.[53] The issue was soon moot because Irénée, the primary promoter of the investments, became less active in business, because the rubber concern performed poorly, because the Great Depression discouraged such ventures, and because internal development of new products such as refrigerants and moistureproof cellophane rapidly offered better opportunities within the enterprise.

Carpenter also disagreed with the du Ponts on the membership of the company's board of directors, a conflict that reflected his broader view of the big firm and its public dimension. He worried that the board was composed entirely of managers and owners and wondered "whether we do not some times suffer for a lack of a critical, intelligent outside viewpoint, and whether it not would be worth while considering inviting upon our board people who could bring to us this viewpoint." Speaking for the three brothers, Irénée firmly quashed the idea. He conceded the possibility of "some specific man" of outstanding ability as a candidate, but asserted that "in general . . . a company is better run by stockholder managers than by any other class," which accounted for "much of the success in the past of the Du Pont Company."[54]

Several years later, when Lammot contemplated retirement from General Motors' board of directors, Carpenter unsuccessfully urged the retirement of GM President Alfred Sloan from Du Pont's board. At a time when the federal government's Temporary National Economic Committee was launching its investigations into big business, he wished to avoid "a somewhat unnecessary interlocking of Directors."[55] Although Sloan attended few meetings and was precisely the kind of outside director whom Irénée had previously opposed, he remained on the Du Pont board for more than thirty-five years as a symbol of Pierre's personal investment in GM and of the subsequent linking of the two companies.

The disagreements between the three owners and their favorite manager were few and usually unimportant. He and the three du Ponts shared important business values and acknowledged one another as able, independent businessmen who were expected to disagree—reasonably—in their operation. Their mutual respect grew with every additional year of Carpenter's experience and success. His repeatedly sound judgments and his demonstrated commitment to long-term management and to prudent financial practices in the 1920s and 1930s continually deepened the brothers' trust. By the late 1930s that faith was expressed as the finance committee frequently assumed a pro forma role in ratifying the decisions of the executive committee that Walter chaired after 1940.[56]

Ultimately, of course, the manager had to defer to the owners, as the U.S. Steel investment illustrated, but in company operations such cases became fewer and fewer. Of course, such an outcome was not inevitable, as demonstrated at the Ford Motor Company years later, when an increasingly bitter struggle between Henry Ford II and his top manager Lee Iacocca eventually led to the latter's departure to head Chrysler.[57] Pierre and his brothers deserve credit for their sense and sensibility in surrendering control to professional executives when necessary. Nevertheless, the above examples suggest that different viewpoints between owner and manager were more likely to surface over external issues and outside audiences, a pattern that grew increasingly clear as public scrutiny of the Du Pont Company intensified in the 1930s.

Depression and the Private Company

Professional managers as well as owners naturally had a fervent faith in private enterprise and were quick to criticize government interference in business as arbitrary and inefficient. Thomas Cochran's distinguished study of nineteenth-century railroad leaders like Charles Perkins and Henry Ledyard noted that they "had a deep distrust of legislatures and government officials," doubting their "wisdom, honesty, or efficiency." Fear of reaction or misunderstanding made it best to keep their firms "out of openly partisan positions" unless issues like regulation directly affected them. Yet railroad officers also had to recognize that they were "public figures," given their impact on the economic welfare of the communities they served. Long-term consideration for their careers and for the health of their companies required a sensitivity to popular feeling and attendant government activity. The high profile of large corporations in a society that prided itself on egalitarian ideals necessitated the publication of information to educate consumers and shareholders by explaining their firms' actions or positions.[58]

Walter Carpenter's experience at Du Pont partially matched this concern for outside audiences. As his 1925 letter to his father indicated, he felt a sense of public duty and service very common among businessmen in the 1920s. For him and his colleagues, much of this obligation turned on the application of the efficiency and the economic progress resulting from the company's success. He once reproved a colleague's proposed statement for an annual report that profits were "in fact a measure of a corporation's contribution to the public welfare." Walter felt strongly that the message ignored "the doctrine of greater production, lower costs, and lower prices" that Du Pont had long preached.[59]

Beyond that doctrine and the firm's careful support of high tariffs to discourage competition from powerful foreign chemical corporations, company relations with the public and the government went little further. A publicity bureau established in 1916 disseminated dry company handouts, but made no attempt to mold opinion like the Pennsylvania Railroad, American Telephone and Telegraph, and other, more sophisticated firms. In fact, Du Pont exhibited a kind of curious asymmetry. It pioneered in American business with a strategy of diversification, a decentralized structure, and leadership in laboratory-based scientific research and development, but its attitude toward the public and government was narrow and defensive.[60]

Much of the explanation for Du Pont's public relations lay in its long heritage of owner-operation. The du Ponts, like most other entrepreneurs, viewed the company as their creation and possession, and they handled outside relationships in personal rather than corporate terms. Pierre, who did so much to create the large, powerful chemical company between 1902 and 1919, ignored the public consequences and perpetuated a tradition of a personal and simplistic view of the enterprise's place in the larger society.

A case in point was his handling of a major antitrust settlement in 1911 and 1912. The Du Pont Company, which had purchased competitors and created a virtual monopoly of the American explosives industry in the previous decade, was convicted after prosecution by the Taft administration for violation of the Sherman Antitrust Act and was ordered to be split into several competitive units. At first Pierre left the challenge to his cousin Coleman, whose attempted intervention failed to set aside the verdict despite his membership on the Republican National Committee and connections to the Taft regime.

Only then did Pierre begin adversarial negotiations based on a series of increasingly generous company proposals until a settlement was reached. He had not anticipated the conviction and had made no attempt to influence, manage, and shape a decision as Coleman did. Moreover, he never conceded the firm's guilt and bitterly viewed the entire case as a personal attack. He wrote a close friend that

> negotiations with the Government attorneys are far from reassuring as to their desire to see justice is meted out. . . . I and my associates have a profound conviction that our intentions in the conduct of our business are free from adverse criticism. . . . To me this seemingly unwarranted accusation is sufficiently galling and it is the more so when the transactions of the company dating back to 1872 are brought into question and supposed criminal acts of my father, whom you knew personally, and other relatives of equal integrity are brought forward to show that the present generation should be punished. The whole business makes one ashamed of his American citizenship and casts doubt on the sincerity of our Government officials and their friends.[61]

Pierre's bewildered view of business-government relations and of public attitudes also surfaced in his response to the Old Hickory controversy during World War I. When negotiations for Du Pont construction of a government munitions plant near Nashville, Tennessee, broke down because of bureaucratic delay and mutual misunderstanding and suspicion, the company was criticized by the secretary of war and by the press for profiteering and unpatriotic behavior. The incensed Pierre wanted open debate about the entire issue and was only dissuaded by the thoughtful objections of former Secretary of War Elihu Root, who pointed out that feelings of patriotism and anti-big-business sentiment could only harm Du Pont no matter how rational the businessman's argument. As Pierre's biographers observed, after starting life "as a well-off member of America's upper-middle class," he "could not think of himself as a great capitalist or the big businessman. . . . Even when Du Pont became a giant, Pierre continued to view all controversy in the light of the narrow issues at hand; he could not comprehend that he and his company had become to many the very embodiment of the overmighty corporation."[62]

Although Irénée du Pont had a better sense of humor and a more outgoing personality than his older brother, he shared many of Pierre's views of business and politics. In 1916 he firmly believed that "it would take a business man [sic] of the first order to properly run the United States." Eighteen years' experience did not alter his convictions as he wrote his brother in 1934 that "inherently, the Government ought not 'mess' in business—it will just make one more 'racket' and further decrease efficiency and freedom."[63]

The U.S. Steel investment into which Irénée led his brothers and the Du Pont Company in 1927 demonstrated the same limited understanding. Revelation of the venture led to a huge public outcry and an intrusive government investigation that Irénée neither anticipated nor comprehended. The press hysterically headlined a Du Pont conspiracy with General Motors and Wall Street to take over U.S. Steel and to conquer the Ford automobile company by control of steel prices. In the ensuing clamor, even the probusiness Coolidge administration felt compelled to act and the Federal Trade Commission launched a detailed investigation of the transaction, calling this "community of interest . . . among the largest industrial corporations in this country" a "matter of public concern."[64]

The examination compelled Du Pont to reveal detailed sales data and to disclose previously confidential lists of stockholders in the Christiana Securities Company and the Delaware Realty and Investment Company, the secretive family holding companies. Walter Carpenter provided arguments demonstrating that Du Pont transactions with U.S. Steel were less than one-tenth of one percent of its total sales and purchases, and Irénée stated disingenuously that the venture was "purely an investment" of the chemical company's cash reserve, involving only 3 percent of U.S. Steel stock.[65]

In direct conversation in Washington, William Donovan, assistant attorney general in charge of the antitrust division of the Justice Department, had to explain to the startled Irénée that the numbers were irrelevant. The former Du Pont president wrote John Raskob that Donovan indicated that he took the matter seriously because of "a very strong feeling antagonistic to a large concentration of power in a few hands." Irénée snorted that the issue "seems absurd to me," but belatedly acknowledged that Congress might not think so.[66] The publicity and the investigation (which produced only a still-born report) stopped the investment, but the du Ponts seemed to learn little. In that same year Irénée organized the pool to buy a significant portion of U.S. Rubber Company stock.

Lammot du Pont, who participated in both ventures during his first year as president of Du Pont, was even more narrow and unperceptive about business-government relations than his predecessor. He was almost a caricature of the big businessman—abrupt, frank, private, hard-working, and narrowly focused. Although this youngest brother was four years Irénée's junior, Pierre thought that Irénée looked younger than the humorless Lammot, "who has a more serious disposition and an appearance of years that are not real." Lord Harry McGowan, a long-time English business associate and head of Imperial Chemical Industries, thought that "there was never any subtlety about him and one could always expect that when he said a thing he meant it." He "was the soul of integrity . . . and always dependable."[67]

Lammot's attitude toward government aid and regulation was based on the assumption of an atomistic, self-regulating world. He told *Fortune* magazine that "all government regulation of business, as such, and as distinguished from any other forms of activity, should be abolished." After all, he asserted, "business is merely an aggregation of individuals to do something which a single individual can do, but far less efficiently and successfully. Business should be treated as an individual is treated—no better, no worse."[68] As for government aid, he thought it "somewhat like strong medicine. The more you take, the more you have to have to produce an effect, so that, eventually, you cannot do without it at all. If that is true, the best thing to do is to do without Government aid; and, in that event, the population must have the fortitude to stand the consequences."[69] At the same time he remained an enthusiastic high-tariff Republican, apparently undisturbed by any contradiction.

The three owner-operators viewed their individual political interests as they viewed their speculative investments—as matters of personal concern with little regard for any impact on the firm that bore their name. At times they were even willing to involve the company directly. All three along with John Raskob became ardent and highly visible opponents of Prohibition in the late 1920s, and they spearheaded the Association Against the Prohibition Amendment. Pierre chaired the executive committee on which Irénée also served while Lammot headed the finance committee, of which Raskob was also a member. In 1928 the four men contributed more than $130,000 to the organization, and subsequently Lammot persuaded the Du Pont Company to make a $5,000 contribution.[70]

Their activities, which led to a crisis involving both the Du Pont and General Motors companies, demonstrated the different viewpoints between managers and owners about the consequences of personal involvement in highly partisan political activities. Raskob abandoned a life-long affiliation with the Republican Party and became a close associate of New York Governor Al Smith, an outspoken "wet." When the Democratic Party nominated Smith as its presidential candidate in 1928, Raskob agreed to serve as his campaign manager and as chairman of the Democratic National Committee.

At General Motors, where Raskob was chairman of the finance committee, Alfred Sloan insisted that the public implications and their possible impact on the automobile company were unacceptable. Raskob could not be a top executive in a major political party and in one of the nation's largest firms without inevitably identifying General Motors as a major partisan in a highly charged campaign and beyond. Though Raskob offered to take a leave of absence, Sloan termed the arrangement makeshift and demanded his resignation. Pierre sided with his close friend of almost thirty years and resigned as chairman of the board of directors at GM amid sensational newspaper coverage. Once again immediate, personal relationships triumphed over long-term corporate considerations.[71]

At Du Pont Walter Carpenter was appalled about the public consequences for his very large and visible enterprise, but the professional manager's efforts to ameliorate the potential damages were seriously hampered in an owner-dominated firm. Like Sloan, the professional manager believed it was critical for his company and for General Motors (of which Carpenter was a director) to remain aloof from partisan politics for their long-term well-being. Indeed, he thought it even more essential for General Motors because of its dependence on direct consumer sales. He wrote Irénée that the consequences of the flap were "more serious than we have appreciated. I can think of no way in which the duP-GM interests could have dissipated the good will and respect of the country in so short a time as has been done." In addition, there were "dissatisfactions and dissentions [sic] in both organizations" that would "definitely react against our prestige with distributing channels, which our competitors will not hesitate to capitalize."[72]

For this life-long, high-tariff Republican, corporate consequences were far more important than personal politics. Nevertheless, in a family firm like Du Pont Carpenter could not demand resignations as Sloan had, and he certainly could not alter the behavior of the powerful du Ponts. The best he could hope for was a balance in partisan identification. He wrote Irénée with ill-disguised disapproval that Raskob had "become a crusader . . . almost a fanatical evangelist," supporting "the cure of all the evils of the world—Al Smith." In the elder du Pont's combined support for his friend and for repeal, "Pierre has withdrawn, for what seems to him a great work." The burden of maintaining a balance was too great for Lammot alone. Walter asked Irénée to join his younger brother with a public endorsement for Herbert Hoover and the Republican Party.[73]

In the responses of the two younger du Pont brothers, personal considerations were typically as important as corporate interests. Both men, like other top company executives and most of the du Pont family, were staunch Republicans, and absent Pierre's strong affection for John Raskob, the Prohibition issue alone was not enough to make them switch parties in 1928. Lammot's announcement to the press noted that he spoke publicly because "several prominent and staunch Republicans have gone over to the Democratic camp." Nevertheless, he found it easy to endorse Herbert Hoover, the Republican candidate, because he thought that as always the Republicans were sounder on issues of political economy—the tariff, railroad regulation, and farm relief. He acknowledged that Smith would work to alter Prohibition but thought his solution of local option was inadequate.[74]

Irénée chose to follow his own judgment instead of Walter's advice. He wrote Carpenter that he refused "to 'bust out' into print" for fear of "stir[ring] up additional advertising that the du Pont and General Motors organizations are taking an active part in politics." In a careful private summing up, Irénée thought each man "a most satisfactory candidate" but worried about the Democrats' "tariff tinkering." An engineer like Hoover, he also thought the Republican more probable than Smith "to make a scientific study of an economic question so that for future progress in legislation we might hope for improvement." Though he worried that the Republicans were being driven into the hands of the Anti-Saloon League, Irénée concluded that "surely a Republican Congress should be elected" and that "Mr. Hoover would make the better president."[75]

Given the du Ponts' political views and personal preoccupations, their failure to understand what one historian has termed "the crisis of the old order" in the Great Depression after 1929 was not surprising.[76] After all, they were part of that old order. More notable was the inability of the three brothers and their senior executives, some of the most talented businessmen in the nation, to anticipate an economic collapse although the firm itself easily withstood the crisis.

In the late 1920s both Walter Carpenter and Lammot du Pont offered optimistic assessments of the American economy though each was also concerned about the growth of speculation on Wall Street. In early 1929 Walter privately told his Uncle Ed that the market was too high because the costs of brokers' loans exceeded earnings rates, but he thought industrial conditions were sound and did not plan to sell. Lammot was more pessimistic and forecasted a "break" in 1929.[77]

Once the stock market crashed in October 1929, Du Pont's operators, like most other businessmen, did not immediately foresee the advent of the terrible depression that followed. In the next six months weekly billings were down only between 2 percent and 6 percent from the record of the previous year. Not until the summer and early fall did the seriousness of the slide become obvious at the company after weekly billings fell between 19 percent and 27 percent from the prior comparable period. Du Pont's experience paralleled the pattern of the general chemical industry. In the first quarter of 1930 almost as many firms recorded sales increases as decreases in comparison with the previous quarter, but by July and August all concerns reported decreases and an industry analyst noted that "in some cases these were very severe."[78]

The depression's impact on the company was heavy but not critical. Between 1929 and 1932, the lowest point, sales fell almost 42 percent to $118.4 million; net income dropped more than 66 percent to $9.4 million; and the workforce declined over 26 percent to less than 28,000. Recovery began in late 1932 led by the rayon and dyestuffs departments, and by 1935 gross sales and employment exceeded 1929 levels. In 1936 Carpenter reported privately to a close associate that the firm was doing a "quite satisfactory business" and mentioned the erection of a new office building in Wilmington as well as several examples of plant construction or expansion.[79] Because of its careful financial management, close statistical controls, and introduction of popular new products like moistureproof cellophane, refrigerants, quick-drying paints, and later neoprene and nylon, Du Pont profited and grew throughout the 1930s. Even in March 1932, just before its turnaround, total assets were $58 million or 10 percent higher than in 1929, and the company never lost money in any year of the depresssion decade. Operating income as a share of operating investment went below 5.2 percent only in 1932, when it fell to 2.6 percent, and the ratio's average for 1935–39 was higher than for 1925–29. By 1939 sales revenues were up almost 42 percent and earnings had risen over 19 percent compared to 1929.[80]

Although the firm's resources and outstanding expertise easily car-

ried it through the crisis, its relationships to its public audiences continued traditions of secrecy, isolation, and domination by the personal
views of its owner-operators. While Irénée usually relied on bromides
about limited government and individual responsibility, he proposed
the most iconoclastic solution to the depression: inflation by relaxing
the gold standard and by expanded open-market operations by the
Federal Reserve Banks. His suggestion was ignored or condemned by
the financially conservative, sound-money men who controlled Du
Pont, including Pierre, Walter Carpenter, Angus Echols, and company
economist E. E. Lincoln.[81]

Pierre typically rejected drastic suggestions and relied on a self-
adjusting economy despite the misery that accompanied it. He explained to Irénée that "existing commodities" would reach "such a low
point that it will necessitate resumption of manufacture, mining, etc.,
in order to provide the needs of the country." After all, he confidently
asserted, "our population is no less than it was . . . [and] the demands
of the country are so substantial . . . that we must realize that much
contentment can be had through operations at a less rate of speed than
prevailed when everything was booming."[82]

Although he and his brothers made large private donations for relief, Pierre remained reluctant to take collective action. When Alfred
Sloan proposed a committee of twenty-five top industrial leaders to
study the crisis and to recommend economic policies to the voters in the
forthcoming presidential election, Pierre hesitated. He complained
about intrusive government activities like antitrust prosecution, the
imposition of sales taxes, and banking regulation and wanted freedom
from the Sherman and Clayton acts so that industry might forge agreements to stabilize price and production. He offered no support for
Sloan's proposal for a broad-ranging policy group, but piously reminded him that industrialists should pay proper attention to economic issues.[83]

Lammot, the company's president, was the most rigid of the three
brothers. He saw no larger company responsibility in the crisis and
vehemently opposed expanded government activity, condemning the
Bonus Bill for army veterans in 1932 and flatly demanding a balanced
federal budget by slashing expenditures. To U.S. Senator David Reed's
plea in 1932 that an inadequate defense budget, low pay to federal
employees, and rising employment relief necessitated increased expenditures, Lammot responded that "your letter, like the others I have
received, leaves me entirely 'cold' and discouraged that we have not

Congressional representatives who have the courage, the vigor and the intelligence to really set to work and reduce Federal expenditures."[84]

He firmly believed that recovery would come from the private sector and that government could only interfere. In 1931 he rejected a special session of Congress to deal with the depression because "the factor most likely to influence business recovery is public confidence. . . . If, as is anticipated, the special session should turn its hand to many subjects of great importance one way or the other to business, then the uncertainty would be created, with a very detrimental effect on business confidence. We are unanimously opposed to the special session." In fact, he reasoned that workers were better off than businessmen and stockholders, and refused to consider a request to reduce Du Pont's dividend fifty cents a share in order to generate an additional $200 for each worker's wages. Ignoring soaring unemployment, he argued that workers were free to quit and work elsewhere while management had to lose money and wait for people to buy. If a worker could not quit, his status would be "pretty near being slavery, and that is about what common stock capital is."[85]

In contrast, Walter Carpenter was clearly more aware of his powerful corporation's high profile and of its larger potential benefits to American society. As earnings recovered in 1934, he questioned Lammot's reference to an extra ten-cent dividend in the company's annual report, fearing that the term would "suggest a distribution of excess profits." He suggested instead that an "increase in the regular [dividend] will perhaps occasion less comment."[86]

In more substantial fashion he strongly opposed dropping wage and salary rates in 1931 in response to Lammot's quest for lower expenses as commodity prices, profits, and the cost of living declined. Reflecting the Hoover administration's pleas for business to maintain pay levels, he worried that Du Pont's cuts "might precipitate action on the part of a number of others." Such reductions would increase insecurity about income and might raise expectations of price cuts, which would further delay purchases. His thoughtful analysis suggested that the combination of relatively high wages and low commodity prices "would bring about a very sound stimulation to business beneficial to the national economy." Given the benefits and the firm's secure position he thought the experiment well worth trying, for if it failed wages could be dropped later. If it succeeded and wages remained high, it would be because business and employment had improved, which was the desired aim for Du Pont and the nation.[87]

In November 1929, one month after the stock market crash and before the Great Depression was under way, Carpenter proposed a remarkable, sophisticated plan aimed at forestalling the coming depression, which he projected would last from six months to two years. He recognized, as not many others did, that national income was the result of combined national investment and consumption. Thus, in the 1920s high wages had expanded purchasing power and consumption while high profits had increased wealth and investment; the end product was the nation's most prosperous decade. Carpenter worried that market losses would reduce purchasing power and that expenditure of current income would not sustain prosperity "because of individual conservatism."

In order to prevent the ensuing drop in national income, he proposed a special infusion of capital investment, financed by long-term borrowing or by use of idle existing funds, which would compensate for the anticipated decline in consumption and in normal investment. Sound practice demanded the production of useful facilities and the best types would be "those of transportation and communication," such as the "construction of highways, railroad facilities, including equipment, bridges, telephone lines, power plants, etc." Lower interest rates following the stock market crash would hold down the program's cost and would not detract from current investment and income. Within two years confidence would be restored and normal consumption and investment could again sustain the economy.

Inaction would bring contraction, depression, unemployment, and misery and would produce no capital goods. Intervention and management would generate useful infrastructure and "avoid . . . stress and suffering." Although Carpenter was vague about where the coordinated effort was to occur, he urged the du Ponts to use their considerable national reputation to "agitate a huge construction program" at the federal, state, and local levels of government.[88] Carpenter's program was breathtaking in scope for 1929, anticipated the development of the Reconstruction Finance Corporation in 1932 (after the economy had already collapsed), and reflected much of the later scholarly analysis about the depression's causes although it placed a much heavier emphasis on the role of the stock market crash.

Discussion of the plan's potential effectiveness is moot because it was never tested. Although Irénée was inclined to encourage expanded investment, neither he nor Lammot fought for Walter's idea. Pierre thought that the crash had small impact on the national economy and that "the condition of . . . fundamentals seems sound." Although he argued that "we should use every endeavor to give people courage," he pointedly stopped short of endorsing an expensive construction program and urged that Du Pont proceed "with caution but with determination to be numbered among the brave."[89] In other words the du Ponts would not be in the forefront of a movement for economic stimulation by federal or state investment. Except for Irénée, they preferred to depend on individual action and the self-adjusting forces of the market rather than attempt collective support for management of the economy.

Walter Carpenter's recognition of his company's wider public audiences in government and in the general population had only begun with the U.S. Steel venture in 1927, but within five years this manager's differing viewpoint from his owner-operators and the limits of his power to shape company policy were clear. He and his fellow managers had considerable authority to administer the firm, but control of outside relationships stayed with the brothers. They simply did not share his sense of corporate power, obligation, and vulnerability in the larger society but preferred to focus narrowly on property rights and to continue unfettered their personal, private ways. The du Ponts rejected Walter's call for their leadership in collective action to stem the depression in 1929. In 1931 they reduced salaries (but not wage rates) in their firm's quest for economies regardless of possible consequences for the larger society and of the Hoover administration's request.

The company's message in its 1931 annual report, written during the depths of the depression in early 1932, reflected the commitment to traditional pieties.

> Although the going has been hard, more real advance has probably been made during the past two years of adversity than during the immediately preceding years of comparatively easy progress. Yet we must all continue to be more industrious. Both public and private budgets must be balanced. Errors in judgment are largely responsible for creating present economic difficulties, and only by our own efforts can we overcome our past errors.

The homily concluded that the return of confidence was not too distant and that it would "gradually bring back a sounder prosperity based on a recognition of real values and an abandonment of unsound speculative dreams."[90]

Public Face: Shock and Reaction to the New Deal

Walter Carpenter's differences with the du Ponts over public issues widened as the enterprise struggled to accommodate the many changes brought by the New Deal. Readily acceding to the owner-operators' control of the firm and the consequent limits of his own power, he struggled with mixed success to alter by compromise and indirection Du Pont's relationship with the public and the federal government.

The firm's problems with Franklin Roosevelt and the New Deal were foreshadowed by the clear opposition of most family members and of the company's top managers to Roosevelt and the Democratic Party in the 1932 election. Pierre was an exception as he remained loyal to his close friend John Raskob and continued to contribute to the Democratic Party. Subsequently, he served on the Industrial Advisory Board of FDR's National Recovery Administration in the naive hope that it would maintain business dominance of recovery and prevent further expansion of government power. But even in 1932 he thought that the "only positive outcome" of FDR's election was the probable repeal of Prohibition with increased federal revenues from liquor taxes. By the spring of 1934 he had abandoned all faith in the administration.[91]

Irénée was torn, wanting to remain a loyal Republican but upset by the party's failure to push for repeal. He supported a Democratic candidate for the U.S. Senate from Delaware in 1930 and ultimately voted for Roosevelt in 1932. As late as September of that year, however, he favored Herbert Hoover because FDR's "demagogic propaganda" on "the mal-distribution of wealth" appealed "to such envy and greed as there are in the masses when at a time, above all others, discord and uncertainty should be eliminated." His political contributions for 1932–33 favored the Republicans by a three to one margin. Although Irénée continued to admire Roosevelt as a strong leader throughout 1933, he increasingly worried about the president's appeal to class antagonism and about his threats to property rights. By 1934 he had became a bitter enemy.[92]

Lammot du Pont and the rest of the company's directors and senior executives remained strong Republicans. Lammot gave the party $42,300 in 1928, $25,000 in 1930, and $30,050 in 1932. In fact, of the Du Pont directors and officials reporting their political contributions to the U.S. Senate in 1934, only three (Pierre, Irénée, and Raskob) listed donations to the Democratic Party between 1928 and 1934 while at least sixteen gave to the Republicans.[93]

Opposition to the New Deal was almost immediate, focusing on banking legislation, efforts to inflate the money supply, and the NRA. As president of the company, Lammot was especially bitter about the latter. He was angry that the National Association of Manufacturers had not directly opposed the new program's creation in the spring of 1933 and strongly objected to the claim that in the crisis "industry has thrust upon it at this time a duty." To him "industry has but one duty; namely, to manufacture goods and sell them at a profit. . . . Neither industry nor the leaders of industry have upon them any more duty to guide legislation than has any other citizen." Under his leadership the company attempted to avoid compliance or to sabotage the NRA's intent throughout its existence.[94] By the summer of 1934 the three brothers reunited to form the American Liberty League, an organization that was created ostensibly to defend property rights but that in fact became a vocal and highly partisan critic of Roosevelt and the New Deal.[95]

Walter Carpenter shared much of his firm's suspicion of FDR and the New Deal. He remained a devout Republican, with donations to the party of $3,000 in 1928, $1,000 in 1930, and $2,000 in 1932 when he thought that the Democrats would try "to convince the public that the future is practically hopeless without some revolutionary changes and among these proposed changes will be many elements distinctly discouraging to business." After the election he joined others in attacking the New Deal, concentrating particularly on his special interests— money and banking. In November 1933 he sent a frustrated tirade to his close friend Tom Russell condemning currency devaluation, the abandonment of the gold standard, the weakening of bank reserves, and the burgeoning public debt "for more or less worthless purposes." He participated in the organization of the American Liberty League and contributed $2,500 to it in 1934, while describing himself as "heartily in sympathy with the efforts of the League" and believing "that there is new evidence every day of why we should make some effort to meet the current [New Deal] programs."[96]

Despite Carpenter's criticisms, his statements and behavior suggest that his opposition was more balanced and less virulent than the du Ponts' positions. Conceding his skepticism about the NRA, he told Lammot that he thought that Du Pont ought to sign the President's Reemployment Agreement, which was part of the program. At times he seemed resigned that the New Deal was the necessary result of the depression. He wrote his Uncle Ed that "we are going to have a lot of

sweeping up to be done eventually," but that the costs might be acceptable if they provided relief to millions and reduced the federal debt
through a depreciated dollar. At the end of 1933 he privately admitted
to his old mentor Elias Ahuja that "there has been more encouragement than discouragement in this [New Deal] program."[97]

Even Carpenter's enthusiasm for the American Liberty League
waned as he realized what a disastrous failure it was and how badly the
elitist organization reflected on the Du Pont Company. A historian of
the league has noted that this arrogant association of rich men in the
midst of the nation's worst depression "was doomed from the start,"
having been "made to look ridiculous or dangerous, and sometimes
both" by its own efforts and those of the Roosevelt administration.
Though Walter attended early organizational conferences, he apparently and uncharacteristically made no major contributions. His annual donation declined to $1,525 in 1935 and by that fall he avoided its
meetings.[98]

Carpenter's disagreements with the du Ponts about the company's
public face grew out of concrete issues rather than personal, theoretical
views on political economy. He shared many of their concerns about
the New Deal, and as the battle over endorsements in the 1928 presidential campaign revealed, he recognized that he could not curb the
individual interests of owner-operators who never distinguished carefully between personal positions and corporate activity. They were
more likely than he to issue broad statements about the nature of
private enterprise and the role of government in the economy. As their
agitation grew and the Liberty League floundered, they turned increasingly to business organizations like the National Association of
Manufacturers and the U.S. Chamber of Commerce as vehicles for
their messages.[99]

Walter was far more interested in the defense of the Du Pont Company itself than in the general promotion of capitalism and business, as
the battle over Du Pont's production and export of munitions demonstrated. In 1934 the company found itself engulfed in a heated and
damaging popular debate over the production of war materiel. Growing pacifism, the rise and expansion of totalitarian dictatorship around
the globe with the increasing threat of war, the bitter anti-big-business
feelings engendered by the Great Depression, and the publication of
popular attacks like *The Merchants of Death* crystallized in a search for
scapegoats to explain the United States's entry into World War I. Led by
isolationist Senator Gerald Nye from South Dakota, a special commit-

tee of the U.S. Senate launched a dramatic investigation into the links of arms makers, international bankers, and government.

Although it was only one of many firms involved, the Du Pont Company found itself at the center of the inquiry. At the government's request it submitted reams of confidential material about plant construction, munitions manufacture, and military sales practices and profits. Though the public hearings, in which Pierre, Irénée, Lammot, and Walter all testified, were conducted with decorum, the company was widely pilloried in the public press. Nye's popular campaigning in the 1934 elections and misleading, careless, or inaccurate statements from committee members produced sensational and exaggerated charges that the company was a warmonger and an unpatriotic profiteer. In his speeches that fall Nye called the munitions makers "racketeers [who] . . . build up the hates, fears, and suspicions that build wars, that drive people into war, and then getting them there, they keep them there as long as they can." He even urged that the next great conflict be titled a "war to make the world safe for Du Pontcracy."[100]

Du Pont executives were embarrassed, appalled, and outraged. Jasper Crane, a vice president and a member of the executive committee, noted privately that "the Nye Committee hearings have been a tremendous load to carry" and that "we have been hurt, I don't think there is any doubt of that." Walter Carpenter still bridled at the charges years later, and his son recalled that he often spoke of them "bitterly" and was "very sensitive" to what he considered to be "grossly unfair" criticism.[101]

Carpenter led in organizing the Du Pont Company's response. Pierre was inclined to dismiss the episode as a silly waste of time too ridiculous on its face to be believed.[102] The three brothers seemed content to let the issue blow over and to continue munitions production with little change of policy. Walter had no personal stake, for he was not a du Pont, had never been involved in explosives manufacture, and had not been a policy-maker during World War I. Unlike Pierre, however, the professional manager viewed the incident as a serious threat to the company's public image and to its long-term well-being. Moreover, his alarm did not grow out of any larger moral concern about munitions making because he had not opposed Du Pont's acquisition of the Remington Arms Company in 1933 in order to protect its market for sporting powders.

Carpenter's immediate problem was responding to the false charges flying about and to make clear the firm's policy. He had N. P. Wescott of the development department prepare an elaborate statement that meticulously reviewed the record and refuted three charges: that Du Pont disturbed the peace; that it was disloyal; and that it was a profiteer. Carpenter made small additions of his own, carefully reviewed and edited the forty-two-page document, and circulated it to others for comment, including General Motors executive Donaldson Brown and advertising expert Bruce Barton, who had been an effective advisor to GM. The modified piece eventually served as the basis for three public purposes: a letter of explanation to Du Pont stockholders, a lengthy statement to the press, and a comprehensive presentation to the Nye Committee.[103]

At the same time Carpenter began to initiate and encourage longer-term activities that would better explain the company to the American people. Given his own background in the development department and his active role in the corporation's diversification, he was incensed that Du Pont was so widely and mistakenly viewed as a munitions firm and not as a diversifed chemical company that contributed to the American standard of living in so many ways.

The misapprehension was not simply the fault of Du Pont's critics, for the firm itself had failed to be as enterprising in dealing with the public as it had been with other companies. Carpenter noted that "while we bellyache about the other fellows using us as an example of all that is iniquitous," the company kept backing away from action for fear of some nebulous consequences. In a rare moment of frustration and petulance, he asked, "Why in hell don't we do something—Nothing we can do will be . . . 100% right. Doing nothing is 100% wrong."[104] Thus, he strongly supported and promoted Du Pont's new program for institutional advertising, which included sponsorship of the "Cavalcade of America" program on radio and the development of its now famous motto—"Better Things for Better Living through Chemistry."

Carpenter was not interested in the slick phrases of publicists to paper over embarrassments. What he sought was a better understanding of what his firm had done and what he valued. He clearly expressed his message in a speech to dyeworks foremen, which was subsequently published as a four-page pamphlet, *The Challenge That Was Accepted*.[105] In the midst of the Nye Committee debacle, growing New Deal and popular hostility to big business, and rising labor conflict, the normally reserved Carpenter spoke out forthrightly about the value of large-scale enterprise, Du Pont's emergence as a diversified chemical company, its major contributions to national well-being, and the importance of harmonious industrial relations.

The talk effectively used the firm's development of artificial dyes during World War I to demonstrate the big company's costly and lengthy development of complex technology, which had helped free the United States from dependence on Germany and which had promoted America's synthetic organic chemical industry. He then went on to add his political message—the need for analysis and not emotion in assessing the proper role of large corporations for the nation's economic benefit and, less effectively, the virtues of cooperation over conflict in worker-management relations. The labor portion offered homilies rather than solutions, reflecting his own inexperience in that area, and the irony of the dye discussion was his own opposition to its development during World War I. Nevertheless, the presentation accurately reflected the professional manager's concerns about identifying key outside audiences and making certain that important messages were broadcast for the sake of his company's larger, long-term well-being.

After skillfully urging the country to consider rationally its extended best interests, Carpenter appropriately urged Du Pont to do the same thing as it faced the public. Against the background of Japan's invasion of China in 1937 and an impending war in Europe in the late 1930s, he argued powerfully that the firm should stop selling munitions for export. In typical style he systematically examined and defeated the case for an export policy that dated well back to the nineteenth century. Such sales would not keep the firm in contact with munitions developments abroad because they were now being made to technologically backward nations, and they had not supplied the volume to maintain operations for many years.[106]

He quickly dismissed a new argument of a moral obligation to supply small nations, which would otherwise produce for themselves and "increase the aggregate of armament effort throughout the world." He found this point "highly impractical; indeed, almost quixotic." Du Pont had no duty to provide "the Sultan of Sulu" with "a carload of smokeless powder at his wish." To do so created a false dependency because company policy was to furnish to such countries only "their normal requirements," and neutrality legislation would cut off all exports to them in the event of war. Because the 1930s had brought a "renaissance of brigandage among the great nations of the world . . . , what would be more absurd than for us to attempt to persuade ourselves that our remaining in the export of munitions is in the interest of world peace[?]" The argument might seem "to some of us as somewhat loftier or exalted, and may well appear to some others of us as quixotic, and to the public can only appear as sordid."

In this case "good business" was congruent with morality and patriotism. Stopping the trade would not harm U.S. defense capability or the acquisition of knowledge. The monetary gains were "infinitessimal," amounting to "about two-tenths of one percent of the profits of the Company from other sources" over the preceding twelve years. Du Pont needed to square its behavior with its wonderfully successful strategy of diversification. For this tiny reward in its smallest industrial department, the enterprise was "called upon to suffer all of the odium associated with this business."

Because Carpenter's case attacked part of what had been the core business of the family firm for more than a century, it went before the board of directors in September 1937. The board agreed not to sell munitions to Japan or to China but led by Pierre, the chairman of the board, Irénée, the vice chairman of the board, and Lammot, the president of the company, the directors overwhelmingly defeated Walter's motion. In April 1939 the State Department's request that Du Pont change its policy and export smokeless powder to Latin America was also approved by the executive and finance committees despite Carpenter's continued, vigorous opposition.[107] The combination of patriotism, heritage, and stubborn personal independence of public opinion was simply too much for even the most powerful managerial analysis.

Walter had more success in persuading the firm to accept regulation from the New Deal's securities legislation despite strong resistance from the three du Pont brothers. The Securities Act of 1933 and the Securities Exchange Act of 1934 established the first comprehensive federal oversight of American stock trading. The laws created a Securities and Exchange Commission (SEC) to oversee the New York Stock Exchange (NYSE) and similar bodies and to set rules for corporations that traded on the exchange, including the regulation of securities issues, the standardization of voting procedures, and the reporting of salaries, bonuses, holdings, and transactions of top officers and directors.[108]

The legislation, which was a reaction to the stock speculation and abuses of the 1920s, forced the revelation of confidential information and shocked the du Ponts because of its restrictions on their freedom and privacy. Their own stock trading had been scrupulous and Du Pont stock was rightly considered a sound, blue-chip security. Nevertheless, the owners reacted hysterically to their lost liberty amidst their growing conflicts with the administration in 1934 and 1935, including both the munitions investigation and the launching of the American Liberty League. During debate on the 1934 law, Irénée complained that the legislation would restrict the market and depress stock prices, and he urged "every effort" to kill the bill "in this hysterical era."[109]

When passage seemed certain, the du Ponts demanded several radical responses. Led by Lammot, the owners and top officials insisted that the SEC keep confidential the required reports of their income and holdings. Because of confusion about liability in the company's stock bonus plans, Du Pont terminated installment sales of company stock to employees and to the managers' bonus plans. Finally, in their frustration and anger, Pierre and Lammot asked company counsel C. R. Mudge, financial vice president Angus Echols, and economist E. E. Lincoln to consult with other large concerns about their intentions and to prepare plans to withdraw Du Pont stock from public trading on the NYSE in order to avoid complying with the new regulations.[110]

However incredible the threat that one of the nation's ten largest industrials with more than fifty thousand stockholders would cease to trade publicly, the possibility was real. After all, Du Pont had only been fully listed on the NYSE for little more than a decade, much of the stock was in family hands, and in their anger and personal vendetta with FDR the three brothers were certainly serious. Walter Carpenter clearly saw the need to act in order to protect the corporation, for the proposal would hurt stockholders by reducing the liquidity of their securities, lower the value of Du Pont stock, and make it much more difficult to raise funds outside the firm in the future.

He succeeded in preventing the withdrawal by a series of indirect measures that distracted or wearied proponents while avoiding a direct confrontation with the owners that invited probable defeat. The finance committee appointed a special subcommittee, including Walter and Lammot from Du Pont and Alfred Sloan and Donaldson Brown from General Motors, to study the issue. Extended consultation with prominent lawyers, bankers, securities experts, and top executives in other large corporations, particularly at General Motors, consumed time and energy. New York banker George Baker Jr. advised Walter that other firms did not plan to leave the NYSE because they feared that unlisted securities would be regulated as well. Richard Whitney, president of the NYSE, pointed out that Du Pont could test the process with temporary registration for nine months and withdraw before July 1, 1935, the deadline for permanent listing.[111]

Along with expert advice and gradualism, several other factors were persuasive. The rules established to implement the 1934 law were less draconian than had been feared. Protest letters and requests for confidentiality that accompanied the reports to the SEC, though futile, did provide action without damage. In a similar vein the finance committee scrutinized all reports before their filing, a mechanism that quickly became pro forma.[112] Whenever possible the company took extra measures to minimize filing, as when Walter Carpenter agreed to handle the 1939 refinancing of securities without public underwriting.

With mounting evidence that other companies would comply while testing the law's constitutionality in the courts, that withdrawal would harm Du Pont stockholders, that regulation might not be so harsh, and that past abuses in other companies justified action, Carpenter was able to persuade first the du Ponts and then John Raskob to accept registration and to report the necessary data on personal holdings and salaries. As he wrote Raskob, "I think, in this connection we very definitely have public opinion today against us."[113] The finance committee approved registration temporarily in August 1934 and permanently in May 1935 along with the inevitable riders reserving the right to legal challenges and requesting that individual salaries, which were listed as required, be kept confidential.[114]

The episode illustrated just how radical New Deal legislation appeared to big businessmen and just how defensive and reactionary their responses could be, especially in the case of owner-operators like the du Ponts, who often viewed corporate issues in personal terms. Walter Carpenter shared much of their outrage against FDR and the New Deal, protesting bitterly the Wagner Act, progressive income and excess profits taxes, and expanding federal deficits. He conceded that "some good" had been done, including the reduction of dishonesty and public exploitation, but at "a great price in other directions," including "enormous debt" and the destruction of values like thrift and initiative.[115]

Nevertheless, Walter's outlook differed from the du Ponts' as reflected in his desire for outside directors, for compliance with the SEC, and for terminating munitions exports. Because his career had developed in a large firm and depended on its long-term well-being for his own success, he looked beyond the personal view of ownership and had a higher expectation of corporate responsibility and potential. In the case of the Wagner Act and the growing power of organized labor, for example, in order to stop what he called "rear-guard action" he urged that the heads of large concerns cooperate to formulate a desirable national labor relations policy as a basis for bargaining, for demonstrating a constructive approach, and for forcing moderation on the New Deal.[116] When big business failed in the 1930s to supply such collective, positive reform, he recognized that as a highly visible and vulnerable large enterprise Du Pont had to accept the popular will no matter how flawed it appeared to be. In the SEC case his efforts skillfully accommodated the limits of his power, averted a crisis, and preserved Du Pont as a public company in a nice balancing of corporate, owner, public, and governmental concerns.

His differences with the owners were never so critical that they raised fundamental ethical issues and suggested separation. Long friendship, mutual respect for frank expression by able, independent people, and a shared commitment to the well-being of the enterprise mitigated disputes. Furthermore, there were occasions when he was wrong, as in the case of munitions exports in 1939. Because of Japan's surprise attack on Pearl Harbor and the magnitude of Hitler's threat to humanity, there would be no recriminations for Du Pont's cooperation in the prosecution of the "good war." In fact, directing the company's efforts in World War II would be the central challenge of Carpenter's presidency of the firm. Before turning to that experience, however, we need to examine the issue of his relationship with a very unusual and important "outside audience," the General Motors Corporation.

4

The Manager as Outsider—
The General Motors Case

WALTER CARPENTER'S work at the General Motors Corporation was an unusual experience for a professional manager. Because the Du Pont Company's stock holdings made it the largest single owner of the automobile concern by the early 1920s, the chemical firm maintained a substantial and significant presence on its board of directors. In 1927 Carpenter joined Pierre, Irénée, Lammot, and Henry F. du Pont in representing the chemical company on the GM board, where he remained active for more than three decades until his resignation in 1959.

Walter's appointment was both an important recognition and an anomalous assignment. Reflecting his emergence as the obvious successor to the three brothers as Du Pont's leader, he was one of two nonfamily representatives at General Motors along with Hamilton Barksdale, who had served for a few months prior to his death in 1918. Other Du Pont associates—J. Amory Haskell, John Raskob, Donaldson Brown, and John Lee Pratt—were appointed to the board as top GM executives. At the same time Carpenter's role was an ambiguous one. Most directors of large American companies fell into one of two classes. Inside directors were active managers of the firm; outside directors did not administer but might include major owners or their representatives, financial intermediaries, and a few people representing special publics like American industry, education, or public service.

At GM Walter Carpenter was technically an outside director but of a very special kind. As a career executive he did not speak for an individual investor concerned about part of his financial portfolio, but represented a corporation that looked upon its considerable stake as an allocation of resources. He served with and answered to three brothers who themselves were or had been active chief executives at the Du Pont Company. In addition, Pierre identified personally with General Motors, where he had persuaded Du Pont to invest significant funds and talent and where he had been president and chief executive officer until 1923 and then chairman of the board until 1929, when Lammot replaced him.

Carpenter's training and obligation inclined him to participate actively as a kind of absentee manager. He once argued that because General Motors was run "by some of the best men in industrial life in the world today," his task was "but of a most general nature in the way of advisory work on important matters."[1] In fact, he accepted a much greater responsibility to oversee, review, consult, and influence as well as advise. Alfred Sloan, Donaldson Brown, Albert Bradley, and other leading GM executives welcomed his aggressive approach as a talented manager as well as a spokesman for the firm's largest owner. In his prolonged, energetic relationship with this unusual audience outside his own firm, Walter exercised the same skills, knowledge, and judgment that had made him a company leader at Du Pont.

Nevertheless, just as in dealing with the owners and the public in his own enterprise, he found that his involvement reflected serious limits to his power despite his initiative and remarkable ability. Carpenter was more than an outside director but less than an inside director. In effect, he became an outside manager, and his experiences at General Motors clearly demonstrated the restricted influence of boards of directors in large American enterprises. GM's senior leadership obviously ran the corporation despite the availability of able, external executives on its board. Notwithstanding Walter's theoretical authority and considerable efforts at General Motors, he often observed that serving as a corporate director was "like riding on the observation platform of a train: you did not see anything until it was passed."[2]

The Advisor as Mediator

Alfred Sloan, who had succeeded Pierre as president and chief executive officer of GM in 1923, wasted little time in using Walter Carpenter's talents. In 1929, less than two years after Carpenter joined the board of directors, Sloan had Walter appointed to the finance committee which, along with the executive committee, reported directly to the board. Together they constituted the firm's two most powerful bodies, just as they did at Du Pont. Within five years of joining General Motors, Carpenter assumed an active and important role when Sloan charged him with resolving an extraordinary crisis in the corporation's bonus plan for its executive elite.

Carpenter's involvement in the bonus issue was important for several reasons. The struggle revealed the mechanics and the complexity of compensation plans for top management in large concerns as well as their vital place in the thinking of such executives. It reflected in part just how the Great Depression affected corporate leaders and how they viewed the depression. It illustrated the diversity of interests among big businessmen, even those associated with the same firm. The battle for reform also helped define Carpenter's role as a professional manager working from the outside. He not only served as an advisor concerned with the long-term health of the General Motors Corporation and of his bosses' investment; this case also necessitated a more active, direct part in GM affairs.

His energetic efforts on General Motors' behalf were essential because of the scale and importance of the crisis. By 1932 the company's program to compensate its most important people, which was incorporated as the General Motors Management Corporation (GMMC), was in a shambles. The plan was no longer paying bonuses to top managers, although GM was turning a small profit and performing far better than Ford, its chief rival.[3] More critical was the program's inability to meet several million dollars in annual charges for the reduction of interest and principal on its large debt to General Motors.

More serious still was the collapse of the bonus plan's major asset, the more than one million shares of GM common stock for which the debt was originally created and which stood behind the GMMC stock that served as the actual form of the bonus payments. By July 1932 General Motors stock was one-fifth of the value that the managers' firm had paid two years earlier. As a result, the bonus stock was not only worthless, but it also carried an obligation to the parent company that both wiped out the millions of dollars of bonuses already earned and still left the plan with liabilities in excess of assets by several million dollars more. In short, the compensation plan was useless, in default, and bankrupt just as the Great Depression demanded extraordinary efforts of the enterprise's senior people.

The seeds of the problem lay in a predecessor plan, the Managers Securities Company chartered in 1923, which, as noted in chapter 2, Carpenter had criticized unsuccessfully as treasurer of the Du Pont Company before becoming a GM director. The Managers Company was intricate and complex because of its financing, its purposes, and GM's determination to avoid income tax payments on the bonuses. When Pierre du Pont proposed the bonus program after succeeding William C. Durant as president of General Motors, he suggested that the Du Pont Company supply the GM stock needed to support the plan. General Motors was in no position to purchase large quantities of its stock in the open market after the severe depression of 1920–22. In addition, Du Pont had an unexpected surplus of GM stock in its subsidiary, the General Motors Securities Company, after bailing out Durant's disastrous speculations in late 1920. The original investment in 23 percent of the automobile company had risen sharply, which tied up an excessive share of resources and invited political attacks. As a result, Du Pont sold to Managers Securities 30 percent of GM Securities, representing 2,250,000 shares of GM stock owned by the chemical concern, in exchange for $4,950,000 in cash and $28,800,000 of Managers' 7 percent preferred stock. Managers Securities had raised the cash by selling all of its common stock, $4,000,000 in Class A and $1,000,000 in Class B, to General Motors.[4]

The actual operation of the plan was just as complicated. In order to create a bonus pool for top people, GM contracted to pay 5 percent of its net earnings to Managers Securities after deducting taxes and a 7 percent return on its own capital. (This share was half of the 10 percent set aside for all managers of the automobile enterprise. Only eighty executives, the elite, were eligible, and the remainder, numbering in the hundreds, received smaller payments in cash or in stock that was taxable as direct income.) Average annual earnings at 15 percent per share and the dividends paid on the 2,250,000 shares of GM stock behind the plan would pay the $28.8 million debt to Du Pont and cancel the preferred stock. To transfer indirect ownership of the GM stock into its executives' hands over a seven-year period, General Motors tailored individual offerings of Class A and B shares of Managers Securities to eighty high-level people, who paid part in cash and the remainder from their portion of the bonus fund and from dividends on the stock after it was "earned out."

There were several benefits. Because the recipients in effect owned shares in a bonus fund and did not earn extra compensation directly, they avoided income taxes, which exceeded 50 percent in the upper brackets during part of the 1920s. The potentially large rewards provided incentive for extraordinary effort while indirect ownership and the seven-year period of maturation helped insure loyalty, for anyone leaving the firm forfeited membership in the plan. At the same time Du Pont retained voting control of the GM stock underlying the program by virtue of its 70 percent ownership of General Motors Securities, which maintained close ties between Du Pont and GM and prevented Durant's return.

The plan's remarkable success led to its virtual replication in the General Motors Managers Corporation. General Motors' tremendous growth and profitability in the 1920s (both sales and market share more than doubled between 1923 and 1928) produced bonus payments that retired the debt to Du Pont in 1927. By 1930 each $1,000 cash paid in 1923 as a share in the bonus fund had generated an additional $9,800 in bonuses, a total of $10,800 in GM stock at 1923 prices. But the stock had also soared in value and by 1930 was worth $61,218.[5] In short, each participant who remained in the program for its duration received a sixty-fold return on his original cash investment without immediate income tax liability.

In fact, the stock's value by 1927 was too high to make it an affordable bonus instrument, which led General Motors to implement as a successor the GMMC plan that began in March 1930, a year earlier than expected. At the same time the program was tripled to cover 250 top executives in order to accommodate the huge jump in the firm's size.

Edward R. Stettinius, who dealt with employee welfare and benefits as John Lee Pratt's assistant, drew up the new plan with the same assumptions and techniques and with only a few changes from its predecessor: eligibility for only a limited number of senior executives, the expectation of huge potential growth as incentive, a complex structure for tax avoidance, and indirect ownership with graduated payment for loyalty. Because the automobile company no longer had to rely on Du Pont, General Motors bought 1,375,000 shares of its common stock in the open market in 1927 and 1928 at an average price of about $33 per share to serve as the basis for the new bonus fund. It sold the stock, valued at about $45 per share on the open market in 1929, to General Motors Management Corporation, the new management subsidiary, at $40 a share for a total of $55,000,000. It retained the transaction profit of nearly $10,000,000 for the parent company while the sale below the market price gave the managers' firm a subsidy of almost $7,000,000. GMMC exchanged all of its common stock (50,000 shares with a par value of $100) and $50,000,000 in its seven-year, 6 percent bonds for the 1,375,000 shares of GM common.[6]

Once again the automobile company set up a bonus contract on behalf of its executives. To provide bonuses for some 2,750 people, it agreed to pay to GMMC over a period of seven years 10 percent of net income after deducting taxes and 7 percent to capital. Half of this amount (5% of net income) was to go to approximately 2,500 lower- and middle-level administrators in the form of taxable income as cash or its equivalent in Class A stock of GMMC at market value. Because these people had fully paid for their bonus securities, their Class A shares were in effect preferred stock and they had no liability or involvement in the ensuing crisis.

The other half of the bonus (5% of net income) was to go to the corporate elite, some 250 top managers who enjoyed the same tax-free opportunity as before. Their half of the yearly bonus fund was to pay the principal on the bonds in six annual installments of $7 million, with a seventh and final payment of $8 million due on March 15, 1937. Dividends on the GM stock underlying the plan were to meet the interest charges on the bonds and any surplus accrued to the participants. General Motors offered each executive a predetermined allotment of GMMC common stock on the basis of rank and salary. Nearly all subscribed by paying $100 cash (par value) per share. As common stockholders they had voting control of the corporation and were entitled to the growing surplus of the company as the bonus funds gradually redeemed the GM common in the GMMC treasury at $40 a share. Their earnings were paid pro rata annually in the form of GMMC Class B stock. In effect, they had purchased predetermined portions of the annual bonus fund and options for GM common stock at $40, which could be redeemed at the contract's expiration on March 15, 1937.

Hope of repeating the success of the Managers Securities program left the executives and directors of General Motors, including Walter Carpenter, blind to the risks and rigidity incorporated in both plans. They saw no reason to provide for payment of the interest on GMMC bonds in case GM dividends, which were currently at $3.00 per share, fell below the $2.18 level needed to cover that charge. They also forgot Alfred Sloan's warning in 1923: "I believe they [the beneficiaries] should be told frankly that here is an opportunity to go in business; they take the profit and they take the risk."[7] The risk in this case was exacerbated by the desire to avoid income taxes. Instead of taking annual bonus payments in stock at current value, the General Motors

Management Corporation had bought GM stock in advance at $40 per share and agreed to pay that same price for any unredeemed shares when the contract expired seven years hence. Should the stock decline in the meantime, the managers' firm would stand the loss.

Blindness within the firm matched the executives' and directors' misjudgment about conditions in the larger economy. They launched the new plan on March 15, 1930, almost five months after the great stock market crash of 1929. Emboldened by the successes of General Motors and Du Pont and of the rest of the economy in the 1920s, they blithely ignored any warning signs of trouble, easily assumed that any decline would be slight and temporary, and initiated the program without any apparent qualms.

In December 1932 Alfred Sloan asked Walter Carpenter to rescue the General Motors Management Corporation after more than two years of the worst depression in the nation's history had devastated the program. Years later Sloan attempted to put the best possible face on the request. "In urging the Finance Committee to take action, I was guided by concern for the well-being of the General Motors shareholders as much as that of the General Motors executives. One was intimately related to the other. I felt it crucial to the best interests of all concerned in General Motors to restore executive morale."[8] Restoring executive morale was a mild phrase for a bankrupt plan that had created fear and confusion among management ranks, robbed the company of control over its compensation to its most important people, and badly fragmented managers and directors over the proper solution.

Nevertheless, the phrase certainly described both the participants' primary concern and its eventual resolution. Top managers were not only the people affected; they also dominated the ensuing debate and reform. Sloan as president of General Motors, John Smith as GM's general counsel and president of the General Motors Management Corporation, and Donaldson Brown as GM's leading financial officer and chairman of its finance committee were all centrally involved as chief officials and major beneficiaries of the plan. Sloan was the largest investor with 2,250 shares of GMMC stock, while Smith and Brown tied for second with several others, holding 1,500 shares apiece.[9]

GM leadership's bias in favor of the managers helps explain Carpenter's appointment in December 1932 as chairman of a special three-man subcommittee of the finance committee, which had been discussing the problem since September. The new body was to study the failed plan and offer a solution, and certainly Walter's membership was logical enough. Du Pont was the largest single owner of GM and among its contingent on the finance committee he alone had financial expertise, a continuing oversight of GM's affairs, and independence as a director not involved in setting up the plan or in benefiting from it.[10] Irénée, Pierre, and Raskob had ceased active participation in the automobile company, Lammot had little experience in finance, H. F. du Pont had neither interest nor expertise, Donaldson Brown was a beneficiary, and J. Amory Haskell had retired.

On the other hand, Walter was junior in age and service on General Motors' board and in reputation to the other two outsiders appointed to the subcommittee, both of whom were prominent bankers representing the firm's creditors, the financial community, and the stockholders at large. George Whitney, a partner at J. P. Morgan and Company, GM's investment bankers, had joined the board and the finance committee in 1924, and George Fisher Baker Jr., son of the famous investment banker and chairman of the board of the First National Bank of New York, had served since 1920. As Sloan and Brown hoped, Carpenter, himself a professional executive, took a far more sympathetic view of the managers' plight than the money men during the struggle to fix the program.

When Walter assumed his responsibility, the scale and depth of the crisis called for an early solution, and the presence at GM of some of the best financial and managerial talent in America promised the skill and imagination required to reorganize the plan. In fact, Carpenter's task was neither simple nor quick. The urgency, however, was clear enough, for the company's 1932 annual report (which would be published in the spring of 1933) would have to explain fully the mess to the stockholders for the first time.[11]

Because General Motors had reduced the annual dividend on its common stock to $1 as of March 15, 1932, GMMC had been able to pay on September 15, 1932, only $687,500 of the $1,196,250 interest due semiannually on its bonded debt. As long as the dividend rate remained at $1, the managers would annually fall short of their interest charges by more than $1,000,000. Furthermore, because the automobile company's performance had limited the amount paid under the bonus contract, the managers had failed to earn $3,875,000 of the $7,000,000 principal due on the bonds on March 15, 1932. Since GM's low returns meant that there was no bonus compensation in 1932, GMMC would default on the entire $7,000,000 payment due in March 1933 for a total shortage of more than $10,000,000 in the principal account. Even worse, because General Motors common stock was selling for between $12 and $14 in December 1932, GMMC's bonded indebtedness to the parent company exceeded the value of its assets by millions of dollars and would only break even when the stock recovered to $28 per share.[12]

Despite the automobile company's imminent embarrassment, the diversity of potential solutions and of the interests involved precluded a quick settlement. The possibilities ranged from foreclosure to doing nothing to simple termination and starting over again as well as partial reduction of the program and renegotiation with terms more favorable to the beneficiaries. George Baker and George Whitney, Carpenter's two colleagues on the subcommittee, favored foreclosure, which would conclude the plan with the managers losing their original investment in GMMC's common stock as well as the 170,000 bonus shares they had already earned.

As bankers and representatives of the stockholders, "the two Georges" (as they were somewhat disparagingly named by Walter and the GM managers) saw the problem as a debtor-creditor relationship and therefore called for the standard solution: liquidation. Baker in particular was described by Donaldson Brown as being "very much interested in the problem," though he did not agitate for his choice once a means was found to defer the crisis. Whitney thought that Baker assumed "the attitude of a lenient creditor, not pressing for payment and, if necessary, extending the maturity in the expectation that conditions will take care of the matter."[13] The cautious Whitney thought that foreclosure was the simplest escape from a perilous situation. He had opposed the original contract and now fought its revision because he was, in his own words, "always fearful of the result when we attempted to forecast the future for so long."[14]

At the opposite end of the spectrum, John Thomas Smith represented an untroubled, speculative interest and wrote Carpenter that he still had "the firm, if optimistic belief that the ruling price will be above 40" when the program expired in March 1937. As one who had grown wealthy from the 1920s scheme, he could afford to gamble his earnings on the plan's future recovery and adamantly resisted any reorganization that prevented the managers from taking advantage of potential profits if the stock again rose above the original $40 purchase price. Indeed, he insisted that they were entitled to all profits on the *entire* issue of 1,375,000 shares originally involved, regardless of what portion of the bonus fund was actually redeemed.[15]

Though Smith was a major beneficiary and head of GMMC, he apparently saw no conflict of interest in assessing the relationship between the managers and the parent company as general counsel of GM. He readily conceded that the offer placed responsibility "squarely on the shoulders of the managers." Nevertheless, the lawyer urged the reduction of the interest rate on the bonds to 5 percent and argued that General Motors should guarantee to buy back any surplus stock at $40 per share, thus protecting GMMC from any loss of its bonus funds at the end of the program in 1937.[16] In his view, then, reform should insure the managers against any risk while preserving all possible gains.

Donaldson Brown wanted a middle course. He rejected foreclosure as too harsh a penalty because of its burden on managers less wealthy than Smith and because the designers of the plan had some responsibility for its failure. As he explained his case to Carpenter, given "that the responsibility for the creation of the Management Corporation [GMMC] and [the] inauguration of the Management Corporation plan rests more appropriately upon the officers and directors instrumental in having inaugurated such plan (as it seems to me), it would follow as unsuitable to apply the processes of foreclosure." In Brown's view, Smith's hope that GM might guarantee the executives against losses while allowing them to capture all stock profits was excessive, and simply leaving them prey to the present risk was unfair for the reasons listed above. General Motors' chief financial man urged that the automobile company stop the program immediately, protecting what the managers had earned to date and forgiving any debt. A new plan more suitable to current conditions could be developed, and the company could go forward from there.[17]

In his sympathy for the managers, Carpenter's solution came closest to Brown's proposal, but it had significant differences because of important long-term considerations. Foreclosure was unreasonable because of the designers' culpability. As Carpenter put it, the plan was "so extraordinarily complex" that many had joined because of their "confidence in the management," believing that "somehow their interest would be taken care of, or at least that they would not lose by participating." Inaction was unsuitable because the problem would get worse. The stock of men retiring, leaving voluntarily, or being fired was recaptured at $40 per share as required by the original agreement. The result reduced GMMC's already inadequate assets and left a smaller remaining pool of loyal, able executives to share a growing burden.[18]

Walter rejected Brown's call for termination and reorganization suitable to the current market because he felt that General Motors should not admit to the managers charged with the firm's recovery that the present debacle was its view of the future. In addition, even a generous settlement might look "niggardly" if recovery occurred within a few years. He also condemned as excessive Smith's idea that the corporation should in effect underwrite the managers' speculation in GM stock. Instead, he wanted the plan contracted by 25 percent in order to acknowledge the opportunity already lost in 1931 and 1932 and proposed to reduce the interest rate on the bonds to an amount equal to the dividends paid on the 1,375,000 shares of GM stock. At the same time General Motors would agree to purchase at $40 per share all surplus stock (that portion not earned out by the bonus payments) at the contract's expiration in March 1937. Such a move would demonstrate to the managers the firm's faith in its and their future by protecting their expected bonuses while eliminating both the risk and the potential speculative profits on the unearned stock.[19]

Though Carpenter's proposal served as the basis of the subcommittee's discussions in January and February 1933, divided interests prevented its enactment and temporary compromise encouraged delay. At Carpenter's request, the revised plan was sent to outside counsel for independent review. John W. Davis, the prominent corporate lawyer, approved the program but insisted that any revisions had to be submitted to the stockholders of both firms. The finance committee did not take this step because the two Georges, who constituted a majority of the subcommittee, refused to accept the $40 per share guarantee and because Smith, speaking as GMMC's head, insisted on preserving the speculative option. Carpenter then recommended that the $40 guarantee be removed in order to get unanimity and a quick decision that would avoid any embarrassing special meetings of the stockholders because, he argued, the resulting change did "not affect the aggregate participation in the earnings of the corporation appropriated for all bonus purposes."[20] He urged his two banker colleagues that the subcommittee resubmit the plan to Davis and act "rather promptly" if the lawyer agreed that meetings were unnecessary.[21]

Even this desperate attempt at compromise and resolution failed when the two Georges vehemently insisted on stockholder approval regardless of John Davis's decision. The bankers still saw themselves as representing shareholders as creditors in a contractual relationship with delinquent managers as debtors. Baker insisted that he felt "as strongly as ever that any change which affects the corporation should be submitted to the stockholders," while Whitney argued that he did "not think the Directors have the moral authority to change so definitely a plan which has been submitted to the stockholders without their explicit approval." Both men preferred to wait until the next regular meeting of GM's shareholders nearly a year hence.[22]

The bankers could afford to delay because, as John Smith pointed out, the original agreement required that GM loan GMMC the funds necessary to meet the payments of bond principal while interest charges could simply be deferred as before.[23] This temporary and temporizing solution allowed the simplest of all choices—stalemate and inaction—which Carpenter was forced to accept, an ironic commentary on the work of top businessmen who prided themselves on aggressive problem solving.

The passage of time and changing conditions soon exposed the fallacy of decision by indecision and forced Carpenter to tackle the problem again. By the fall of 1933 the bonus company had fallen more than $10 million behind on its payments on bond principal and was over $1.5 million delinquent on interest charges, which were deferred for the third time that September. In addition, the crisis was beginning to promote the opposite of its intended behavior. Walter noted that at least "several individuals" thought that the program's peculiar circumstances would allow them to "make a fortune over night if they leave the corporation."[24] Their gain would be the difference between the $40 per share General Motors would be compelled to pay if they left before the plan expired and the stock's current market value, which fluctuated between the high $20s and low $30s.

Alfred Sloan weighed in with another pressing problem and with all his authority as the company's acknowledged leader. In order to meet the depression he had ordered a major reorganization of operations in Detroit, including the creation of five executive positions, and he complained to Walter that he could "do practically nothing in the way of supplementary compensation with these people." Direct payment of bonuses subjected them to income tax rates above 50 percent and he could not sell them shares in GMMC for "it is nothing that can conscientiously be sold."[25]

GM's chief executive officer then began to pressure Carpenter for a solution, with special pleading on behalf of his managers. He wrote Walter that he "raised the question so aggressively simply because of the responsibility that rests upon me to develop able men to carry the great responsibilities that our men must carry and to give those men a real opportunity" for proper retirement. Because of the heavy pressure of executive work at General Motors, "our men just can not last as long as is the case in other activities—it is too fast an operation. One only needs to look at the picture as it stands at present to have a full appreciation of the fact that that statement is, in truth, a fact." Sloan closed by urging Carpenter to push through a rapid solution without too much concern for embarrassing opposition from stockholders. "We should deal with this subject as we feel it is to the interest of the stockholders to deal with it, without the word 'fear' entering into it as to what action the stockholders will take on any recommendation that we may make with respect to a re-adjustment."[26]

Donaldson Brown argued still another point: the partial recovery in the value of General Motors stock in the past year offered a propitious opportunity for settlement. With the market price at $28 or above, total losses on the approximately one million shares still unearned were less than GMMC's assets. In fact, at present prices GM could guarantee the redemption of all remaining stock at $40 per share, the original price, and the automobile company's loss would be less than its profit on the original open market purchases in 1927 and 1928. Because of the new circumstances the more optimistic Brown no longer favored terminating the plan. He delicately phrased a point that Walter had foreseen from the beginning. If the program were ended at this point and the stock recovered still further, "an unfortunate feeling of resentment might be engendered in the minds of important executives."[27]

On the other hand, should the stock stay at its present price for the rest of the program's term, the managers stood to lose most if not all of their bonuses and their original investment. In his estimation the result would be calamitous, for "in that given period there is the extraordinary need of gaining loyalty and intensity of effort on the part of those upon whom the Corporation is dependent for efficient management." He now firmly supported Carpenter's earlier solution: guaranteed mandatory redemption of any surplus GM shares at $40 in March 1937, which would protect the managers' bonuses but would deny them any speculative profit on unpaid-for shares.[28]

Walter Carpenter readily acceded to the arguments of his fellow professional managers. He would have preferred to reduce the plan's size and the executives' liability by selling six hundred thousand shares of GM stock—almost half the amount originally available for bonus payments—back to the parent company at the original purchase price.

Because of the depression, much of this amount could never be earned, and the shrinkage of the overall bonus pool along with the reduction of any speculative profits on unearned shares would be a concession to the stockholders for their help. Nevertheless, he returned to the $40 guarantee because it eliminated possible losses in 1937. As he wrote Brown, "The damage done the corporation at that time by endeavoring to force its rights would be lost many times over by the reaction from its important individuals."[29] Securing the executives' position was more pressing than adjusting the size of the bonus, which might after all be moot.

In fact, the diversity of interests at GM continued to destroy any possibility of agreement, and the suggested revision, which called for the $40 guarantee and for scaling down interest charges to the level of dividend payments on the General Motors stock, was never formally proposed. The two Georges stubbornly ignored Sloan's case for his own incentive to leave under the plan's current circumstances. He stood to gain much more than his immediate real compensation by resigning and forcing GM to redeem all of his equity in GMMC at $40 per share. The two bankers resolutely refused to ask General Motors stockholders to rescue their manager-debtors from losses, which still exceeded $8 million.[30]

Meanwhile general counsel John Smith was buoyed by the stock's partial recovery into an even more adversarial position on the executives' behalf. As GMMC's head, he again firmly asserted their rights to all bonuses earned out and to any speculative profits on unredeemed stock. He therefore fought both the $40 mandatory recapture in 1937 as well as any reduction of the bonus pool. Smith wrote Sloan that "it would certainly be anomalous to have the Management Corporation placed in a position of ceasing to own General Motors stock for fear of General Motors foreclosing, when the only justification of the plan was to take and keep [as partners] the managers in the enterprise." Arguing that "strictly legal considerations" by GM invited "a similar treatment by the Management Corporation," he offered a new threat. Not only were managers entitled to transaction profits on the bonus stock they earned; they could also speculate on the hundreds of thousands of shares of surplus or unearned stock during the remainder of the contract, a possibility never contemplated in the original plan.[31]

Faced with the deep split and the specter of the bonus company publicly dealing in GM stock, Carpenter and Brown quashed their own proposal, and the subcommittee dissolved in the winter of 1933–34.

Although they flirted briefly with yet another modification that spring, final resolution of the crisis came only in the summer of 1934 when Carpenter, after nearly two years and several futile tries, determined to take "one more shot" at what he called "the Management Corporation enigma."[32]

The stimuli of the previous year had grown even sharper. For two years GM had compromised by redeeming at its original purchase price only the common stock of GMMC held by departing executives. Now it faced the threat of legal action to compel the redemption of the Class B stock at $40 per share as well, which would reward those who left while placing an even greater burden on the more able and loyal who stayed. In addition, the problem of what to do with new hires and promotions grew with each passing month as the economy and GM's operations began to recover in 1933 and 1934. Moreover, the plan now had less than three years to run before an uncertain settlement would be forced on the automobile company in March 1937.[33]

Carpenter's concern for mediation and for problem solving as a professional manager was amply reflected in his frustration with his failure and in his determination to resolve what he termed a "situation [that] cries to Heaven for a solution." As he wrote Donaldson Brown in June 1934, "More correspondence on this subject will never in the world settle it. Its [sic] a bad problem, . . . [and] personally, I am prepared to set [sic] down with you or anyone else and sit it out until some conclusion is reached." He noted that the issue was one of negotiation, not expertise or invention. Experience clearly demonstrated that a feasible plan could be drawn up, and "our difficulty is purely one of having it adopted. We are certainly in an absurd position when ten reasonable men, whose mutuality of interest in this connection is absolutely unquestioned, cannot agree to act."[34]

In the end Carpenter achieved consensus by further compromising with his colleagues, the professional managers. His new proposal once again removed the deferred interest charges by retroactively lowering the interest rate to the dividend level and protected past and future bonuses by guaranteeing to repurchase any surplus stock at $40 per share. To win the support of Smith's contingent, he suggested splitting equally between General Motors and its executives any speculative profit on unearned shares at the contract's end while the managers retained the profits on their earned shares as provided in the original agreement. In other words, as Walter explained it to Donaldson Brown, "the past and future accumulated equities are reserved in exchange for which one-half of the unexpected and unpremeditated speculative opportunity is foregone."[35]

The combination of urgency and generosity led to rapid acceptance. Sloan, Brown, and Smith readily assented as did Pierre, Irénée, Lammot, and other members of the Du Pont group, who had always promoted generous compensation of executives in the name of owner-management and who were glad to settle the troublesome issue. George Whitney capitulated to Carpenter's arguments because of the great embarrassment of the unresolved issue to GM and because of his weariness with it. He wrote Carpenter that he "would like to get rid of the thing and get it out of the way."[36]

Persistence and weariness almost won over George Baker as well, but after promising to accept the revision he abruptly reversed himself and again rejected the amended program. He lamely explained to Walter that "the lawyers are the ones that have made me adopt this other course" and apologized for the trouble he had caused. The imminence of victory and the professional manager's continuing concern for the preservation of collegiality made Carpenter generous and gentle. He wrote Baker that he had "the highest admiration" for the banker's position and that having "submitted a proposed compromise to the principals, . . . we can do no more." The older man was almost pathetically grateful for Walter's kindness toward his vacillation, and wrote him that "I do not see how you could possibly have written a more friendly or more considerate message."[37]

The near unanimity of the finance committee and the board of directors carried over to both parties involved in the issue. GM's top executives readily assented to a very generous offer. Perhaps more surprising was the remarkable support of the shareholders; over 99.9 percent of stockholders and stock represented in the voting favored the amended program. Carpenter had crafted well for General Motors and especially for its senior managers, and fortune favored both sides. When the plan ended in March 1937, GM stock was selling above $65 a share, producing transaction profits of more than $5 million for both the executives and the shareholders. Although not as rewarding as the Managers Securities plan of the 1920s, participation in GMMC paid extraordinarily well. Bonuses raised the value of each $1,000 invested in common stock to $5,988, and dividends and transaction profits increased the final return to $12,595, a jump of more than 1100 percent over seven years in the midst of the Great Depression.[38]

The reorganization of GMMC clearly demonstrated the valuable part Walter Carpenter could play as an outside manager at General Motors in an important, complex issue. Although potential losses were probably never much more than $10 million against GM's net sales of $441 million in 1932, they exceeded the firm's profits after taxes in that dismal year. Even more important, as all the participants agreed, was the need to insure managerial good will, loyalty, and incentive in the face of the arduous challenge of coping with the worst depression in the nation's history while preserving stockholder confidence in the firm and its executives. As advisor, proposer, and mediator Carpenter steered the company to the successful resolution of a problem so complicated that even Owen Young, chairman of the board at the General Electric Company and a member of GM's board of directors, needed special guidance and information before he could vote intelligently on the issue.[39]

Carpenter also learned important lessons about the limits of a manager's power regardless of his authority and ability, for chance, mediation, and compromise were critical factors in the development and outcome of the crisis. Du Pont and General Motors were among the most advanced, most systematically organized, and best run firms in the United States if not in the world in 1930. Yet despite all their economic and managerial sophistication, business experience, and careful analysis, Walter and his colleagues failed to see the extent of the oncoming Great Depression. In the 1920s large companies like Du Pont and General Motors had pioneered elaborate forecasting and budgeting techniques with detailed annual projections and with comprehensive corporate plans extending forward five years and more. The men who launched the General Motors Management Corporation in March 1930 included some of the most able business minds in the country. Their failure vividly demonstrated that businessmen did not understand the threat of the Great Depression before the summer of 1930, nearly nine months after the Great Crash.[40]

Chance or timing was also essential to the solution of the crisis. For two years able problem solvers let a critical issue go unresolved. Not until the economy's recovery and the rise of GM's stock reduced the cost and risk to the stockholders in 1934 was Carpenter able to craft an answer acceptable to all parties. Critical to its success was an agreement that depended as much on the appearance of sacrifice by both sides as it did on any abstract system of logic or equity. In turn, delay and compromise were necessary because of the confusion of voices involved.

Even among big businessmen, often viewed as a relatively homogeneous group, there was a remarkable diversity of positions. The bankers, Baker and Whitney, interpreted the problem as a debtor-creditor relationship while Smith, the lawyer and manager, took a literal and even adversarial approach. Sloan and Brown as managers simply wanted the difficulty removed so that they could tackle more important problems. As a director Carpenter represented owners at least theoretically concerned with maximum return on investment, yet he (and apparently the du Ponts) as long-time executives viewed the two Georges not as shareholders' representatives but as obstructions to be overcome. Clearly, the directors interpreted their roles based on their differing positions and experiences and not on any formal notions of trusteeship on behalf of absent stockholders.

Furthermore, outside directors like Baker, Whitney, and Carpenter certainly had a veto power in a firm generally believed to be dominated by top executives as inside directors. Nevertheless, with Carpenter's aid the operators' views clearly carried the day. From the outset he sided with Sloan, Brown, Smith, and others who automatically assumed that key managers, and not the stockholders, customers, or workers, were the critical factor in GM's success.

Their confidence and even arrogance stemmed in part from assumptions born in the probusiness era and boom economy of the 1920s. Leaders at Du Pont and General Motors and in other large firms, supported by prominent politicians and the popular media, frequently pointed to their contributions of new and better products, jobs, profits, higher wages, and general prosperity, all of which they celebrated as "service" to the nation. In addition, GM executives actually had led a company that significantly outperformed its environment during the decade. Though total annual sales of new cars were generally stagnant after 1923, General Motors had more than doubled its sales and market share and moved from a weak second to a strong first in the industry by 1930, a position it would hold for more than half a century.[41]

To such men a logical corollary was their presumed entitlement to extraordinary compensation that in turn justified complex arrangements producing huge bonuses and avoiding in large part the income taxes paid by normal mortals. In fact, top managers expected a double reward in addition to already high salaries. As Alfred Sloan's discussion of the management plans at GM illustrated, not only were executives to receive generous bonuses based on performance; as the owners' surrogates and the "real" producers of success they were entitled to profits on the stock as well.[42]

Against this background the assumptions, exertions, and solutions of Carpenter and his colleagues during the crisis are more understandable. Despite the depression they expected things to continue as they had been for top managers in the previous decade. As Lammot du Pont, chairman of the board at General Motors, explained the generous compromise of 1934 when asking for the stockholders' approval, "Unfortunately, as is too well known, circumstances did not work out as anticipated—certainly not through any fault of the executive group."[43]

A comparison of the bonus plans at Du Pont and General Motors demonstrates clearly the shift from owner-operation to managerial domination and entitlement.[44] The Du Pont programs were small, owner-controlled, and relatively simple. The 1919 plan included only the nine members of the executive committee, and the 1927 scheme originally covered less than thirty people. Both were carefully approved and overseen by Pierre, Irénée, and Lammot, and the recipients were men whom they knew personally as close colleagues in the operation of the business. Awards were made directly to individual beneficiaries without the intervention of bonus companies and complex tax avoidance devices. Simplicity, flexibility, and careful control made adjustment to the 1930s depression relatively simple.

The program that evolved from Pierre's urging at General Motors during the early 1920s differed significantly. The numbers were much larger, totaling eighty in the Managers Securities Company of 1923 and about 250 in the General Motors Management Corporation in 1930. Although Pierre and two outside directors nominally administered the 1923 plan, in fact, financial executives Raskob and Brown designed a very complex, rigid program in order to avoid tax liability, and they with Sloan determined the nominees and the size of their awards. The 1930 scheme emulated the earlier program in complexity and managerial control. Although Pierre, Lammot, and Walter comprised the Special Allotment Committee, nominations and the size of awards were set by Sloan, Brown, Smith, and Vice President John Lee Pratt together with the general managers of the firm's various product divisions.[45]

The executives' domination left them vulnerable to narrow vision and extraordinary insensitivity. Their culture celebrated power that rested on accountability, detachment, extended analysis, and efficiency, which in turn was determined by the unsparing test of performance. During the crisis of the 1930s, however, major beneficiaries ignored blatant conflict of interest in their determined, successful, and often short-sighted defense not only of the generous bonuses they had earned but also of one-half of the reward they had forfeited because of the company's poor results between 1931 and 1934.

During the Great Depression, when the loss of wages, jobs, and homes was commonplace, most Americans longed for such forgiveness and security. Whatever the General Motors executives gave up, their influence over their own bonus plan successfully minimized the consequences of their firm's performance. Furthermore, with bonuses added to already large salaries their burden was far less than the depression's cost to most of their fellow citizens. The managers' and outside directors' limited (and ultimately accurate) concerns about stockholder reaction demonstrated slight sensitivity to the declining reputation of big businessmen amidst the revelations of negligence, mismanagement, and even criminal activity that followed the crash and the depression. None, however, showed any appreciation for the relative stakes involved or for the irony that their bonus march paralleled a more celebrated and desperate attempt by World War I veterans, which ended in tear gas and abject failure.

Such convenient isolation helps explain the abysmal misunderstanding and maladroitness that characterized Du Pont's encounter with Franklin Roosevelt recounted in chapter 3. Carpenter's work in resolving the executives' bonus crisis at GM indicated that he shared these values and the accompanying insulation. Although he had a more comprehensive view of politics and public policy than the du Pont brothers, Carpenter was typical of the managerial class, and he would provide no new perspective to his colleagues at General Motors in their own battles with the New Deal.

The Advisor as Manager: Structural Reorganization

Walter Carpenter was successful as an outside manager at General Motors in dealing with bonus reform precisely because in that instance company executives highly prized his independent status. In the case of major internal issues like reorganization of top operations, however, his influence was quite circumscribed. In particular, Alfred Sloan repeatedly rejected Walter's advice despite his enormous respect for Carpenter's remarkable talent and for his role as a representative of the automobile company's largest stockholder.

At first glance their disagreement on the issue of organization was surprising because their firms shared so much. At the same time both companies had led American industrial enterprises in pioneering decentralized management with autonomous product divisions and with a general office above them to coordinate overall activity. In the 1920s Du Pont and General Motors were among a handful of corporations that successfully implemented a structure that would become standard in large, diversified companies in the decades after the Second World War.[46] By the early 1930s Walter Carpenter had abandoned his earlier skepticism to become a determined advocate of the new structure Alfred Sloan had helped develop at GM.

There was an important difference, however. Du Pont, like most American industrials, had reached its new organization by moving away from an older centralized structure built around functional departments. Before 1921 General Motors had been essentially a loosely administered holding company to which William C. Durant, a financial entrepreneur, continually added new acquisitions. After taking control in 1921 Pierre du Pont, Alfred Sloan, and their associates had moved in the opposite direction from the chemical company, for their challenge at GM had been to integrate and concentrate control of a poorly run federation of subsidiaries.

By 1930 they had been entirely successful and Sloan had become the dominant force at General Motors as president and chief executive officer. After losing to Sloan on the development of a new cooling system for automobile engines in 1923, Pierre had resigned as president, and when Sloan forced John Raskob's departure from the finance committee during the nation's presidential election of 1928, the elder du Pont had quit as chairman of the board of directors.[47] Although Lammot succeeded him as chairman in 1929, the Du Pont Company's influence at GM was clearly weakened, and Sloan continued to integrate and concentrate managerial (as well as his own) control in the 1930s. To better coordinate line and staff operations he created a series of policy groups for research, engineering, sales, and other key functions, which brought together executives from the product divisions with important counterparts from the staff in the general office.

Against this background a decade-long battle began in 1937 between Alfred Sloan and his fellow managers on one side and the Du Pont contingent at GM led by Walter Carpenter on the other side. The struggle turned on three issues, some of which were more important than others. The problem of keeping top committees free of minutiae troubled both sides, and Carpenter in particular, but that concern, which was considerably exacerbated by the pressures of World War II, was secondary to two other considerations. Sloan wished to extend managerial authority at the expense of the owners' influence while at the same time maintaining and even strengthening the role of high-level operating executives in policy-making. Carpenter, on the other hand, fought to preserve a special place for major owners (or their representatives) in the decision-making process at the top while he simultaneously tried to convince Sloan to limit management's participation to "neutral" executives without line responsibilities, as was done at Du Pont. The fascinating struggle not only highlighted the varying influence and views of owners and managers. It also demonstrated the care taken by both sides in dealing with powerful people with strong personalities, a critical concern in the running of large bureaucratic corporations.

Sloan inaugurated the conflict when he further centralized authority by reorganizing the company's senior committees in 1937.[48] At his urging General Motors abolished its executive and finance committees, the two major bodies of the board of directors, and combined their functions in a new policy committee composed of important inside directors from operations and finance as well as influential outside directors including Lammot du Pont and Walter Carpenter. The policy committee set and reviewed policy for all the major areas at GM, including domestic manufacture and sales, labor and dealer relations, overseas operations, and finance. As the single most important body at General Motors it reported directly to the board of directors. An administration committee received the recommendations from the policy groups, gave detailed scrutiny to operating issues, and reported to the policy committee on broader and long-range concerns. It was also a training ground for its members, operating executives from product divisions in Detroit, as they moved toward the general office and top management. Sloan, now chairman of the board and chief executive officer, headed the policy committee; William S. Knudsen, the new president and in effect the chief operating officer, chaired the administration committee and served on the policy committee.[49]

Sloan was clearly responsible for the entire change. He later testified that the new committee structure "was entirely my idea from beginning to end" with "complete support" from his managerial colleagues. The increasing role for operating executives in Detroit certainly drew their endorsement while Donaldson Brown, the leading financial officer in New York, recalled that he "whole-heartedly and enthusiastically" approved the reform. The issue was never in doubt, for Sloan dominated the firm. As he candidly noted, "The entire time . . . that I was chief executive officer of the corporation, I never had a recommendation turned down or questioned in any way."[50] Careful prior consultation assured agreement before any formal vote.

The automobile executive's most immediate concern was the failure of the old two-committee system to meet GM's needs. In his view the division of authority along executive and financial lines, which Pierre had transplanted from Du Pont, was entirely artificial. Sloan felt strongly that the financial committee, half of whose members were du Ponts or their associates, exceeded its authority and dealt with issues "whether the money was available or not." In his mind the real distinctions were between administration and policy, though he acknowledged that "of course, it is difficult to decide what is broad policy and what is not—it is a matter of interpretation."[51]

Nevertheless, Sloan was certain that determining that difference was much easier than battling the old, false distinctions in the handling of business policy, which should have been united under one high-level committee. He later argued vehemently to Donaldson Brown that GM's "Finance Committee did not deal with finances except incidentally. . . . The question of business policy in relation to finances, was paramount." Thus, when General Motors bought the Adam Opel Company in Germany in 1928, the finance committee reviewed and approved the purchase though "the question of finances did not arise. We all knew that we had the money. We have always had the money in recent years in General Motors to do anything we wanted." What the committee discussed instead at length was the question, "Is it a sound business policy for General Motors to take over a big manufacturing organization in a foreign country?" Clearly the issue was a "policy determination in the Finance Committee as a senior committee rather than it was the pure function of finance." Likewise, in Sloan's eyes the distinction was equally absurd in the case of executive decisions, for "the administration of a business like General Motors" included finance as well as engineering, marketing, and labor relations.[52]

The issues of definition and division of authority were linked in Alfred Sloan's mind to two other broad, important, and interlocking problems: succession and control. At age sixty-two, after fourteen years at the helm of General Motors, he was preparing for his replacement, and he wanted to assure managerial dominance by the operating people in Detroit, his own route to the presidency. Achieving this goal meant moving top manufacturing executives into senior, policy-making positions and shifting power from New York, the firm's financial center, to Detroit, the center of production. It also called for the further decline of the Du Pont Company's influence as major owner, a role that had been exercised by Pierre, John Raskob, Donaldson Brown, Irénée, Lammot, and others through the finance committee and financial operations in the New York office.

From the time of his successful bouts with Pierre in the 1920s, Sloan had strongly felt that the needs of the business, not the owners, should determine organization and policy. In an extraordinary demonstration of the hubris of a professional manager, he later wrote Brown that "the organization ought to be set up on the basis of what is best for the business. The representation of the stockholders should be a second consideration."[53] The reorganization in 1937 not only united policy determination and moved operating executives into policy-making ranks; it also terminated the finance committee, which had been the bastion of the New York bankers and the Du Pont contingent as representatives of the owners. Henceforth they would be fewer and less powerful. Six GM executives, banker George Whitney, Lammot du Pont, and Walter Carpenter comprised the new body, which dealt with a broader range of questions about which the owners' representatives had less knowledge.

Given Alfred Sloan's enthusiasm, power, and support the change was a virtual fait accompli in 1937. After losing to Sloan over the issue of business and politics in 1928, Pierre and Raskob had turned to other ventures and played a small role at General Motors though both men remained on the finance committee and the board of directors. By the 1930s Irénée had withdrawn from active oversight of affairs at both Du Pont and General Motors, and in 1938 he resigned as a director of GM. Lammot replaced Pierre as chairman of the board in 1929 and retained his seat on the finance committee, but he left the executive committee in 1934, the last member of the Du Pont group on that important body, and concentrated his attention on heading the chemical company. Donaldson Brown, who succeeded Raskob as chairman of the finance committee in 1929, had become a career executive with General Motors and a supporter of Sloan as had John Lee Pratt.[54]

The decision to reorganize was reached in the spring of 1937 when Walter Carpenter, one of the two active Du Pont representatives at GM, was on an extended business trip in Europe. Lammot, the other interested member, quickly accepted the main thrust of Sloan's proposal because he had little choice and because he and the rest of the Du Pont group thought it important to speed the process of succession given Sloan's age. Before his departure Carpenter had led Du Pont's finance committee in expressing "a general feeling of misgiving" at the termination of GM's finance committee without providing for "a concentrated representation of stockholders' opinions on important matters." Nevertheless, in the interests of harmony Lammot did not even present Walter's case at the formal discussion. He wrote to Carpenter that "Alfred seems so insistent on this general plan and was generally backed up by the others that I feel your objection, in which I concur, could well be waived, especially in view of the fact that you and some other man of financial experience from the du Pont Company might be named on the Policies [sic] Committee."[55]

Sloan had won the first battle, but the war had only begun. He appeased the Du Pont group by appointing Lammot and Walter to the nine-man policy committee but as expected they were outnumbered by GM executives including Sloan, President William Knudsen and Executive Vice President Charles Wilson from Detroit operations, General Counsel John Thomas Smith, and Vice Presidents Donaldson Brown and Albert Bradley from financial operations in New York. Sloan also reassured the owners by agreeing to continue as chief executive officer during an undefined transition period. As Donaldson Brown later noted, however, Lammot and Walter had reluctantly capitulated with their "tongues in their cheeks" after "many sessions."[56] For the next nine years Carpenter led an unremitting campaign on the Du Pont Company's behalf that eventually helped force Sloan to restore the two-committee format with a body for financial operations representing ownership. Nevertheless, as we shall see, Walter's victory was more apparent than real.

First of all, Carpenter attacked the new organization's structural weaknesses and ambiguity. Because the policy committee tried to deal with all areas, it covered too much. The inclusion of operating men like Knudsen and Wilson soon flooded the committee with mundane detailed material that properly belonged to the administration committee. As a result of its overcrowded agenda, the policy body treated important issues in a perfunctory and hurried manner.[57] Its meetings eventually became so chaotic that Walter resorted to rare harsh (though still tempered) criticism. He told Sloan that "frankly, I think it is the worst behaved committee I ever sat on, and one of the best. When I was younger I used to be highly entertained by what seemed to me to

The Manager as Outsider: Walter Carpenter with the leadership of General Motors in 1928. From the left: front row—George Whitney, Junius S. Morgan, Alfred P. Sloan, Charles E. Wilson, William S. Knudsen, Walter S. Carpenter, and Samuel McLaughlin; back row—Charles F. Kettering, Donaldson Brown, Henry Crane, John L Pratt, Charles S. Mott, and E. F. Johnson. (*Hagley Museum and Library*)

be a continuous floor show, but now that the novelty has worn off I feel that something should be done. Whether we need a traffic cop, or a sergeant-at-arms or just an agreement on the part of the members to try to do a little better I am not sure."[58]

Ever the analyst and problem solver, Carpenter tried to diagnose the causes of the failure and suggest solutions. In this case the most obvious answer was simple self-discipline and civility among a group of aggressive, strong-minded people. He pointed out to Sloan that "the Committee is made up of men pretty well conversant with the subjects under discussion, with pretty positive views on all these subjects, and with an irrepressible desire either to express those viewpoints or to see to it that a contrary viewpoint does not remain uncontested." Although the lively discussion was "definitely for the good," the results would be "excellent" if the group could "be urged to cooperate a little better and coordinate their efforts." In order to soften this remarkable stricture to the head of one of the nation's largest industrial corporations, Walter closed by noting that "on balance" the committee's performance had "been excellent, though perhaps with some unnecessary expenditure of energy."[59] Although Sloan agreed to chair the meetings with more control and to deal with the detail first and preserve the second half of meetings for discussion of broad issues, the sessions improved only slightly.

Carpenter also expressed concern about the personnel on the committee. When President William Knudsen left General Motors in September 1940 for a position as administrator of war production with the Roosevelt administration, Carpenter opposed the promotion of Executive Vice President Charles Wilson. He considered Wilson an inferior leader and clearly feared that a temporary appointment might become permanent. Although he delicately asked Sloan to resume the presidency in order avoid embarrassment when Knudsen returned, Sloan saw through the ploy and selected Wilson.[60] The Du Pont contingent could advise, but it would not be allowed to control major assignments.

Carpenter had a stronger case when he urged that Sloan consider the use of outside counsel to review the policy committee's actions. At the time General Counsel John Thomas Smith simultaneously served on the committee and passed on the legality of its decisions. Sloan uneasily acknowledged Walter's point but was reluctant to antagonize his long-time GM colleague. Two years later he was still temporizing because of Smith's sensitivity but agreed to ask him to select an independent lawyer to handle the job.[61] Even friendship could limit Carpenter's influence, a difficulty that he appreciated while he continued to pursue the issue.

The Second World War significantly increased the burden on General Motors and on its top executive body, a problem that Carpenter quickly turned to his advantage. In 1942 he complained to Sloan that the volume of material, especially the explosion of minutiae, had swamped the committee because of the "inherently difficult" problem of distinguishing between policy and administration. As a result the policy committee was merely repeating the agenda of the war committee that had temporarily replaced the administration committee. Walter's solution was to return to the old system because the distinctions between financial and operating issues were easier to maintain than those between policy and administration. He even took the trouble of suggesting the makeup of each new body. At the same time he and Lammot urged that Sloan relieve the members of regular administrative duties so that each would be less burdened with detail and could assume independent responsibility for some broad function like sales, finance, or engineering in order to provide both expertise and perspective.[62]

Sloan responded that GM's failures were attributable to execution and not to organizational theory, and he agreed to be more discriminating in chairing the meetings. Nevertheless, he flatly refused to return to a system that made General Motors like Du Pont. With some asperity he told Lammot that he opposed the scheme of independent executives, each possessing some functional oversight. "As I have said so many times, . . . that does not apply here," he asserted, due to the use of functional policy groups earlier in the decision-making process. He carefully but firmly wrote Carpenter that "I do not want to be anything but helpful, but I do want to impress upon you, as well as Lammot, the fact that J. T. [Smith], Don [Brown] and I all feel very strongly that we ought to have a Senior Committee with a broader responsibility than a purely financial one."[63]

To Sloan the logic was clear. Finance was secondary to operation and therefore did not merit its own top committee. He argued to Carpenter that "if the operating problems of the Corporation are intelligently, aggressively and effectively dealt with, the financial problems become more or less academic, in that they do not need too much attention. But . . . on the other hand if the operating responsibility is not dealt with in the manner I have just described, then no amount of financial intelligence is going to make the Corporation successful." Moreover, the Du Pont Company's interests as a major owner might well be diminished by its isolation on a purely financial body. It deserved instead "the reflection of the [broader] operating trend and an opportunity to have that discussed so far as major policies are concerned."[64]

Despite his seemingly adamant opposition to Carpenter's suggestions, other forces soon compelled the automobile executive to reconsider his position. By late 1944 he realized that the firm's growth, the increased burden of government regulation, and the expanding challenge of postwar conversion were swamping the top committee at General Motors. In addition, World War II had extended his "temporary" continuation as chief executive officer for more than seven years. Because Sloan turned seventy as the war ended in 1945, he imperatively needed to arrange for his replacement and for the promotion of younger men into top ranks to guide the corporation in the postwar world.[65]

These concerns, in turn, made him still more determined to strengthen the hand of the company's managers against its owners. Sloan's successors would lack the power and respect that he enjoyed as the result of success and long service, and he wanted to protect their independence and the authority of the firm's line management—its operating organization in Detroit—from the influence of the Du Pont group and the New York office. To Donaldson Brown he explained that the administration committee had to become even stronger.

> Can we not arrange [a] corporate structure that more amply delegates to the Administration Committee directly from the Board, the problem of managing the business, financial, technical, distribution and in all other ways? . . . What I am striving for, and always intended to do, is to concentrate the management of the business in the hands of the Administration Committee without restrictions and as I see it now I believe it would be desirable to separate that function from the Policy Committee if it can be properly defined, making the Administration Committee to that degree directly responsible to the Board.[66]

In short, the adminstration committee, composed of the top product group and division executives, would become "the management body in fact, headed by the President, except as to major questions of policy."[67]

In April 1946 Sloan proposed that the administration committee report directly to the board of directors rather than to the policy committee as before. It would have "complete responsibility for the management phase of the business," including all the operating functions and all regular appropriations. The policy committee, to which GM's top financial officer would report, would limit its concerns to major capital appropriations and all financial matters and would continue to report to the board of directors. As president, Charles Wilson would chair the administration committee and serve on the policy committee while the chairman of the board would head the policy committee.[68]

The new plan, which was quickly adopted in 1946, appeared on the surface to be a triumph for Carpenter. The policy committee, which was renamed the financial policy committee (FPC), became the financial and ownership body he wanted with Albert Bradley as chairman and with Walter and later Du Pont Vice President Angus Echols as members. The operations policy committee (OPC), which replaced the administration committee, seemed to be the executive group he had sought, for it paralleled the executive committee at Du Pont. Chaired by Charles Wilson, who succeeded Sloan as chief executive officer, it reported directly to the board of directors like the FPC.[69]

Although Alfred Sloan had originally intended to retire as chairman of the board in favor of Donaldson Brown, he retained that position at the request of both Charles Wilson and the Du Pont group and also served on the FPC along with the new chief executive officer. Wilson and the Detroit executives did not get along with or respect Brown, while Carpenter and Lammot du Pont expected that deference to Sloan would help temper GM's aggressive president. Because Brown intensely disliked Wilson and refused to serve under him, he promptly resigned as an executive officer though he continued to serve on the board of directors and on the FPC.[70]

For Walter Carpenter and the Du Pont group the victory was a pyrrhic one that included the form of high-level management found at the Du Pont Company but not its substance. Carpenter had always insisted on another critical but still missing element: the creation of an executive body independent of operations that could act as a check on top administrative people. In fact, the new setup only strengthened the power of high-level operating people under Charles Wilson's leadership. From Walter's experience at Du Pont he knew that owners and financial people could veto but not guide line management. Only men with operating experience and knowledge but without allegiance or responsibility to administration could offer both the necessary expertise and perspective. He chided Sloan that to expect more was to depend on "supermen."[71] Furthermore, he thought the new structure particularly vulnerable because of Charles Wilson's narrow outlook and dominating, uncooperative approach.

Carpenter tolerated the reorganization, for he had no real alternative. He wrote Lammot du Pont that he acknowledged Sloan's beliefs that "G.M. and du Pont men have been brought up under different ideologies with respect to organization and we find ourselves like the United Nations—unable to appreciate the merits of the other fellow's philosophy." He accepted General Motors' decision "reluctantly as I feel that we are further crystallizing an organization about which I am not very happy, but which, I must admit, has worked with tremendous success."[72] For Walter the 1946 reform capped an unsuccessful ten-year struggle over Alfred Sloan's replacement, control of the company, and preservation of Du Pont's influence at General Motors. It vividly demonstrated Sloan's power as a long-time chief executive, Walter's limited authority as director and outside manager, and the impact of GM's heritage of strong line management in corporate policy-making as opposed to Du Pont's history of family control.

The Advisor as General Executive

In addition to his work on the managers' bonus plan and corporate reorganization, Carpenter participated in a variety of issues and decisions at General Motors, acting in much the same way as he did as a senior executive contributing to the operation of the Du Pont Company. Once again, however, the important difference was the limitation of his power as an outside manager. Not surprisingly, he was most effective when dealing with areas of his own expertise or when offering advice that Alfred Sloan and other General Motors people wanted to hear.

During the 1930s, 1940s, and 1950s the constant stream of letters between Carpenter and Sloan, Brown, and other high-level GM executives dealt with a wide range of internal questions, including employee investment and pension plans, consumer financing of car purchases through GM's subsidiary, the General Motors Acceptance Corporation, refunding of securities, dividend policy, and management of the company's insurance fund. Although the topics naturally clustered around financial issues, as a general executive Carpenter advised on public relationships, personnel, and other larger matters as well.[73]

Thus, he reviewed drafts of annual reports for their potential impact as well as for their presentation of performance. He urged significant rewriting of sections of the 1935 annual report to avoid the mistaken impression that GM received funds from the Reconstruction Finance Corporation in its dealings with failed banks and to emphasize the firm's contributions to higher wage rates and reduction of unemployment. He repeatedly and unsuccessfully advocated brevity in those documents, but Sloan demurred, citing the differences between General Motors and Du Pont. Because of the automobile company's wide dispersal of stock and direct contact with consumers, he thought it important to reach the public and the stockholders with "a comprehensive survey of the business" in a manner "as interesting and informative as possible."[74]

Nevertheless, Sloan highly valued Carpenter's opinion on delicate public issues. When the United States proclaimed neutrality after World II began, he asked Walter's advice about how to handle South American dealers with pro-Nazi sympathies. "Suppose you had a dealer in Santiago, who was doing a fine job for you but who advertised your goods in a newspaper that was definitely anti-American. Would you cancel him?" Carpenter responded with a detached, well-reasoned approach that typically emphasized the long-term importance of popular good will over immediate profits. Under his leadership Du Pont had just resolved not to make new arrangements with firms or people promoting the interests of Germany, Japan, or Italy "outside the territories of those countries." (Everyone was entitled to be loyal in his own nation!) Existing agreements would be carefully reviewed and undesirable ties would be ended "as quickly as is contractually possible."[75]

After characteristically making a systematic weighing of commercial, patriotic, and public-relations concerns, he strongly urged the supremacy of the last two criteria. "We are definitely a part of the nation here and our future is very definitely mingled with the future of this country." There was no excuse "why we should not do our part in connection with the program of agents." In addition, failure to act "might be a very serious matter and the feeling might last for years." Sloan responded that "in principle, I think it is very bad to inject politics into business," but grudgingly acknowledged the soundness of Walter's advice.[76]

Carpenter and Sloan shared a vision that General Motors was more than a large corporation. Its size as the nation's third largest industrial enterprise in 1935, its wealth and success, and its wide range of mechanical products essential to America's well-being and prosperity conferred on the firm a special status and responsibility. Walter once wrote John Lee Pratt that GM's head had to be "an industrial statesman" who pictured "the Corporation in its role as a great industrial enterprise in the American economy," and who realized that its magnitude required "that its general policy must be thought of in terms of national interest." Sloan wrote Carpenter that he, too, looked at GM "somewhat differently than an ordinary unit in industry. I feel that its dominating position in industry in general, and its equally dominating position in the biggest industry of all, puts it more or less in the position of a national institution" with responsibilities not borne by smaller firms.[77]

Although Sloan may have been indulging in private posturing and personal gratification, Carpenter took the position so seriously that he sometimes suggested unlikely proposals for the automobile company. During the 1937–38 recession, when he feared the country's return to the darkest days of the depression, Walter urged that GM seize the initiative to jump-start the stalled economy. It should ask its workforce to take a 20 percent pay cut in order to spur a quick readjustment of prices and wages and thus avoid the prolonged collapse of 1929–33. General Motors would correspondingly reduce its prices and push for similar concessions from its suppliers. The firm's sheer magnitude would lead the automobile industry, which in turn would stimulate the entire economy. Because he judged that organized labor had fallen out of public favor after a wave of sit-down strikes, Carpenter thought that a few labor leaders might see a chance for a public-relations coup and endorse the plan. The entire action would be private because Washington would not approve and should be ignored. In short, "a great unit in industry and its corresponding labor group" would restore confidence, investment, and the economy in general.[78]

The plan was breathtaking for its naivete about organized labor, its blindness to antitrust prosecution, and its overstatement of GM's economic power as well as for its scope and hopefulness. Out of respect to Carpenter and the imagination and sincerity of his suggestion, Sloan temporized, noting that the idea was "charged with dynamite, and that we must be most careful." He asked Walter to visit New York for further discussion with himself and Donaldson Brown, which quietly ended the matter.[79]

Carpenter, however, never abandoned his remarkable expectations for GM's role in the national economy. As America's entry into the Second World War grew imminent in 1941, he worried that the economy would overheat with the predictable postwar contraction and depression that had occurred after World War I. He asked that General Motors voluntarily raise its prices and finance rates and forego some sales and profits in order to slow down general economic activity for the country's long-run well-being. The program might be adopted through industry cooperation or with an agency of the federal government "in order to avoid any illegal activities," but if necessary "in the long run General Motors should adopt its own policy with courage and leadership." Sloan again calmly rejected the idea, pointing out the limits of GM's impact since dealers and customers would go elsewhere.[80]

Carpenter's faith in the power of business planning and the influence of General Motors to smooth the fluctuations in the economy emerged again in the 1950s. By 1955 he was so worried about the inflation that accompanied the decade's prosperity that he again wanted the General Motors Acceptance Corporation (GMAC) to raise its interest rates, slow down consumer credit, and stabilize an overheating economy in order to avoid the inevitable serious contraction and expanded government regulation. He realized that the action would reduce profits.[81]

Nevertheless, he urged Charles Stradella, the president of GMAC, that "when those engaged in private enterprises do not assume the responsibilities designed to keep our economy functioning normally but on the contrary, encourage its overexpansion and perhaps even its explosion, we must expect that somewhere along the line those in authority will take over." General Motors' size and activities were "so influential on the course of our economy that I think we should have an unusual sense of responsibility for the trend of the national economy, even though pursuing that, we appear to prejudice our own interests. In the long run, I am confident that such a course will pay off." Stradella's familiar response about public outcry, antitrust liability, and the limits of his firm's economic power once again terminated the discussion, for Carpenter had long realized the boundaries of his authority as an outside manager at General Motors.[82]

Walter Carpenter clearly recognized that the emergence of big business had forever altered the character of the American economy, and he never stopped trying to link the microeconomic operations of GM as a special, large firm to macroeconomic policy for the nation. He was very much a product of his youth and experience, with a deep faith in private enterprise, expertise, and careful long-term planning. He was a lukewarm believer in Herbert Hoover's "associative state"—the cooperation between government and business, especially big business, in order to promote national well-being and maximum freedom.[83] Except during the early days of the Great Depression, he showed little interest in working with government or in its expanded activity, of which he was profoundly suspicious, for he reasoned that if big business did its rightful duty such expansion was unnecessary.

In addition, Carpenter was not an advocate of a corporate state in which big business dominated government. Beyond voting and campaign contributions he showed little interest in politics. Certainly he did not seek public office, and he never selected or promoted a political candidate as Pierre du Pont and John Raskob did with Al Smith. Nor did he show any concern for institutionalizing a corporate role in public life, as Donaldson Brown did when he proposed a public affairs department at General Motors.[84] Walter's advice to General Motors on public issues was more ambitious than at Du Pont because the automobile company was larger, more powerful, more visible, more publicly (as opposed to family) owned, and more cognizant of its outside audiences. At both companies, however, Carpenter's approach reflected his career as a professional manager who reacted defensively and unsystematically to the growing role of government in America's economy and society.

Not surprisingly, Walter Carpenter found General Motors more receptive to his advice on financial matters, and he made several important contributions that again involved untangling the complicated mechanism for management compensation that John Raskob and Donaldson Brown had inaugurated with the Managers Securities Company in 1923. The challenge was entirely separate from the rescue of 1932–34 discussed earlier, and it eventually involved the consolidation of the automobile firm's various bonus plans as well as their segregation from any links to the chemical company.

Ironically, Carpenter's first mission was the rescue of Raskob himself, who left GM management in 1929 and wanted the General Motors stock underlying his bonus payments. He had earned about $20 million, which he planned to use in his venture with Pierre du Pont to construct the Empire State Building. By the terms of his own plan, Raskob's payments were in Managers Securities stock, which had considerably less market value than the GM securities behind it. The General Motors Corporation naturally did not want to liquidate its entire management program simply to accommodate a single retiring executive.[85]

Walter's challenge was to convert Raskob's Managers Securities stock into the shares of the General Motors Securities Company (controlled and largely owned by the Du Pont Company), which underlay it, and then change those shares into the GM stock that was the asset of the Securities Company—all of this without wrecking the management plan or incurring tax liability for any of the participants. He and Du Pont Treasurer Angus Echols cleverly devised a two-step scheme of conversion and partial liquidation. The General Motors Corporation agreed to exchange an equivalent amount of its holdings of Securities Company stock for Raskob's shares of Managers Securities. Carpenter then arranged for the Securities Company to distribute part of its assets (GM stock) to Raskob in exchange for his newly acquired shares of the Securities Company.[86] The complex, imaginative solution satisfied all parties involved—Raskob, Pierre, General Motors, and Du Pont.

The depression quickly made the cumbersome structure of the bonus plan even more troublesome, as some executives were forced to leave General Motors and many others needed to convert their payments into more liquid assets. Given the dire conditions, General Motors had to find a means of accommodating its managers without creating any tax liability for them, for itself, or for the Du Pont Company. To achieve this larger rescue operation, which Du Pont also supported, the automobile company quickly turned to Carpenter because of his earlier success. The new challenge was greater because he had to devise a more flexible plan to suit dozens of executives with varying needs. Some wished to convert immediately; others wanted the option to exchange in the future; and still others planned to retain their holdings of Managers Securities stock.[87]

Walter's solution was just as creative and satisfactory as his rescue of Raskob. First, the General Motors Securities Company issued 4,509,000 shares of new Class A stock, which represented that portion of its assets (GM stock) owned by the Managers Securities Company; its other assets, the original 23 percent of GM stock owned by the Du Pont Company, remained behind the Securities Company's common stock that Du Pont continued to hold. The Securities Company then exchanged its Class A stock for the assets of the Managers Company, which in turn liquidated and gave the Class A stock to its shareholders, the GM executives, in exchange for their Managers Securities stock. As a result, the Managers Securities Company ceased to exist and GM executives could convert their holdings of the Class A stock of the Securities Company into GM shares as they wished. By 1932 nearly one-quarter of the Class A had been exchanged and the restructuring was a success.[88]

Nevertheless, the solution was only a partial one, for a complex tangle still remained. Executives at General Motors had some of their bonus in securities of the General Motors Management Corporation and some in the shares of the General Motors Securities Company, which the Du Pont Company controlled. Du Pont owned outright a small portion of its GM stock (156,250 shares), but held most of it (9,843,750 shares) indirectly through its Securities Company subsidiary. By 1938 New Deal legislation created yet another problem. A recent intercorporate dividend law taxed 15 percent of GM dividends to the Securities Company before they could be passed on to General

Motors executives who held the Class A stock and to the Du Pont Company, which owned the common stock and which in turn again paid the tax. The GM managers and the Du Pont stockholders also paid income tax when they received their dividends. At the same time the elaborate holding company network, Du Pont's large investment in General Motors, and its control of a significant portion of the automobile executives' bonuses invited the unwelcome scrutiny of the Temporary National Economic Committee and the newly rejuvenated antitrust division of the Justice Department.

Once again Walter Carpenter was asked to rescue Du Pont, General Motors, and the GM managers from the complex legacy created by John Raskob and Donaldson Brown in the early 1920s. The goal was clear enough: the elimination of the General Motors Securities Company and the severance of the link between Du Pont and the GM bonuses. The normal avenues of resolution, however, were closed or unsatisfactory.[89] If Du Pont liquidated the Securities Company, it would avoid one payment of the intercorporate dividend tax, but the assets going to the Class A shareholders, the GM executives, would be taxed, eroding the gains and good will that Du Pont had promoted for fifteen years. A merger with the Securities Company meant that Du Pont would acquire all of the subsidiary's assets—the 9.8 million General Motors shares it owned as well as the approximately 2 million shares belonging to the GM executives. The net effect would increase vulnerability to antitrust by more tightly linking Du Pont and General Motors. The chemical company would control an even greater portion of the automobile company, whose executives would have their bonuses tied up in the stock of the Du Pont Company. Other avenues could have exposed the entire 11.8 million GM shares to capital gains taxes of $200 million.

Carpenter's solution was to take advantage of new tax legislation, which allowed a combination of a tax-free spin-off of some assets and a liquidation of the remainder.[90] With the help of two prominent corporate lawyers, Paul Shorb and Clarence Alvord, he devised a plan and carefully obtained certification of its tax-free character from the Internal Revenue Service. He arranged to move the Class A stock of the Securities Company and the 1,871,961 shares of GM stock it represented to a new firm, GM Shares, Inc. Because this action was a simple transfer with no profit taken, there was no tax liability to the GM executives. At the same time the new company also acquired the holdings of the General Motors Management Corporation, thus uniting for the first time all the bonuses of the GM executives in a single firm under their control. Du Pont then liquidated the remainder of the Securities Company and consolidated for the first time direct ownership of its ten million shares (23%) of General Motors stock.[91]

When the plan was completed in early 1939, Walter Carpenter had significantly aided both the Du Pont Company and the General Motors Corporation. After more than fifteen years of knotty tangle, he had severed an awkward link and simplified financial and corporate structure while avoiding millions of dollars of tax liability for GM executives and significantly reducing the risk of antitrust prosecution to Du Pont. He also had the dubious pleasure of seeing the propriety and legality of his handiwork tested and confirmed when suits were filed by a few minority GM stockholders in the late 1930s, attacking nearly every aspect of the bonus plans of the 1920s and 1930s. Although the court threw out most of the charges, the judge found General Motors guilty of errors in the accelerated termination of the Managers Securities plan in 1929 and in the calculation of the bonus pool. Carpenter's refinancing plans received no criticism, although he contributed $95,625 to the $4,500,000 settlement as a member of the board of directors, which was held collectively responsible along with several major beneficiaries.[92]

Though his work in personnel relations at General Motors lacked the impact of his financial manipulations, Carpenter also made some important contributions during his thirty-two years as a director. An obvious area of interest was the membership of the board of directors itself, which Carpenter thought ought to have a majority who were not managers. Because the stockholders were already well represented, his concern, just as it was at Du Pont, was the appointment of outside directors to help guide the large firm in its public role. As the New Deal and the Second World War increased the federal government's place in the economy, he urged Sloan to consider men "from groups of different political and economic philosophy" and also suggested that he select businessmen outside the automobile industry.[93]

Like so many other cases at General Motors, Walter had modest success. He helped advance Angus Echols and younger du Pont family members to important GM committees, but received no support for outside directors from Lammot and Irénée, who stubbornly pursued the opposing position they had assumed at the Du Pont Company. As Lammot wrote Carpenter, "You know that I feel that the success and growth of the company and the low cost and excellence of its products are of far greater importance than any meeting of the public interest that might be advocated by the so-called representatives of the public."[94]

Sloan himself was at first inclined to think of outside people as bankers or major stockholders and showed little interest in the list of more than two dozen candidates that Walter sent him. He later relented and acknowledged that the board of a "large scale enterprise" had "a high degree of public visibility" and needed to balance "inside" and "outside" directors even if that ratio contributed "little to the strictly commercial or economic progress or stability of the enterprise." Using the broader approach, he appointed Richard Mellon, one of Carpenter's nominees, while he continued to drop those candidates to whom Walter strongly objected.[95]

Carpenter also helped strengthen ties between General Motors and several of its important directors and managers. As the corporation faced the challenges of postwar conversion and uncertain markets in 1946, George Whitney, a Morgan partner and GM director for more than two decades, wrote Carpenter a "personal and confidential" letter "for your eyes alone" to complain about the company's strategy of product diversification. The nervous banker feared that the automobile company owned "too many unrelated businesses as to distribution and the type of markets to believe that any organization can give to them the attention that they need. . . . Am I cockeyed?" Carpenter stopped potential trouble for GM management by calmly and persuasively reassuring Whitney with a review of Du Pont's parallel experience. For over two decades it had successfully managed ten departments in all areas of the chemical industry, and he thought that General Motors could do the same thing across many "branches of the mechanical industry."[96] His letter quietly ended the matter and headed off any banker revolt.

On another important occasion Walter participated in insuring the loyalty of key people. In 1934 Alfred Sloan worried that the Fisher brothers, who headed GM's body division and who had lost most of their company stock during financial distress in 1931, might leave the firm for another manufacturer. He privately asked major General Motors and Du Pont directors to make one hundred thousand shares of GM stock available to the four brothers on a two-year option. Walter joined his brother Ruly, Lammot, and Irénée in supplying the chemical company's half of the pool from personal holdings and open market purchases while Sloan, Brown, Smith, and Pratt provided the remainder. Although the $40 option price covered their costs, they not only bore the risk if the market fell and the option was not exercised, but also forewent considerable profits when the stock's price rose past $70 before the final sale.[97] The successful mission earned Sloan's gratitude and clearly demonstrated Carpenter's special place among General Motors directors.

Carpenter also paid attention to managerial development, pointedly meeting important new men and urging senior executives to bring along younger people. He particularly scrutinized GM's financial managers and was responsible for coaching and promoting at least one important executive. In early 1941, when Albert Bradley left his vice presidency in finance to become group executive of the car and truck division, Walter began importuning Sloan and Donaldson Brown to consider the promotion of Frederic Donner, a thirty-eight-year-old junior executive, as his replacement.[98] They correctly diagnosed the suggestion as Du Pont's self-interested attempt to maintain a strong financial presence in top management, and refused to be rushed.

Nevertheless, after having identified his man, Carpenter continued to question, educate, and push him. He repeatedly and thoroughly analyzed, second-guessed, and edited Donner's reports, urged him to consider larger questions and to take a longer view, and encouraged him to be more aggressive. The able Donner was a diligent pupil who usually pleased Carpenter with sound answers to his questions, for even at this level a better-informed GM executive could withstand the probing of a more experienced outside manager like Carpenter.

Beyond their formal correspondence Walter developed a genuine affection for the talented younger man. On one occasion, after a lengthy series of letters about an arcane concern, a weary Carpenter surrendered and told Donner that if he heard any more about the issue, "I will never let you carry my books to school again." Later the senior executive indirectly acknowledged what a burden his questions must be, writing Donner that "I am quite sure that if you did not get at least one or two complaints from me a month you would feel I was slipping."[99] Carpenter watched with pride as Donner rose to become vice president, then head of GM's financial division, and eventually chairman of the board of directors.

Finally, as a director and outside manager at GM Walter Carpenter maintained general oversight of operations but reserved his most careful and critical scrutiny for Charles Wilson's leadership in the tumultuous years after World War II. There were many pitfalls in such postwar challenges, including conversion to peacetime production of automobiles, growing labor unrest like the United Auto Workers' strike that idled General Motors for several months in 1945 and 1946, and the uncertain supply of key materials like steel. In addition, Carpenter, like so many businessmen, feared a repetition of the nation's experience after World War I, when the economy at first surged forward before abruptly collapsing and leaving many firms badly overextended. The threat was especially severe for big companies with high fixed costs like General Motors, which had suffered cash flow problems and a major contraction in 1921.[100]

Walter Carpenter was even more worried after Charles Wilson succeeded Alfred Sloan in 1946 as the company's chief executive officer. Walter and other key representatives of owners and financial interests like Lammot du Pont, Donaldson Brown, and George Whitney had never been enthusiastic about Wilson. Although the opposition of Carpenter's colleagues continued the long split between ownership and management, his own interests were more general and reflected his concerns about issues of executive leadership. Walter thought that GM's new leader viewed the corporation too narrowly from his training in production at the expense of financial, marketing, and other broad concerns; that he was impetutous; and that his aggressive, dominating personality sacrificed the collective thinking by top managers that had so long characterized both Du Pont and General Motors. For example, in the reorganization battle at GM between 1937 and 1946, Sloan took pains to get consent even when he failed to obtain complete agreement with his policies. As noted earlier, Carpenter had attempted to prevent Wilson's promotion as president when William Knudsen left in 1940.

Wilson's performance during the war years reinforced the Du Pont executive's skepticism. In 1941 he wrote Donaldson Brown that the new president lacked "the same sympathy with and appreciation of the financial aspects of a corporation that Mr. Sloan has." In 1944 he wrote Lammot that Wilson was "very earnest and very insistent and intent in trying to get over his viewpoint and may sometimes use certain arguments which appear to be somewhat overdrawn." This lack of detached, even-handed judgment, a quality essential in a top manager and a hallmark of Carpenter's own career, was the most devastating criticism he could make.[101]

As chief executive officer, Wilson was responsible for several errors and missteps in the turbulent period between 1946 and 1948, which left Carpenter and others lamenting the weakness of Sloan's successor.

In the booming postwar market the men in charge of car manufacture so feared a shortage of automobiles that they asked for capacity to produce 17,500 cars a day. Wilson supported their request though Carpenter and others thought the estimate fantastic and fought to reduce it to 12,500 vehicles daily. A year later, because of materiel shortages and disruption, daily output was only 7,500 vehicles with no sign that the corporation would soon need all of the added capacity. Nevertheless, General Motors raised $225 million in new capital based on Wilson's 1946 budget projections for 1947–49, but in less than a year the president suddenly demanded an additional $600 million, which would exhaust all reserves and require another $250 million from the stock market. At the same time he supported the request of M. E. Coyle, head of the Chevrolet division, to manufacture a small, cheap car. In the process Wilson and Coyle repudiated their arguments of the previous year that the new car should be produced as a separate line, ignored the certain shortage of working capital, and reversed themselves on the adequacy of Chevrolet's capacity.[102]

General Motors was not in serious trouble and Wilson's associates did not expect perfect predictions, especially in the volatile conditions after World War II. Nevertheless, as Sloan, Pierre du Pont, and other top GM people had learned in 1921, the combination of the automobile market's erratic character with the enterprise's extensive lead times and high fixed investment required planning based on even-handed judgment with prudent allowance for risk and uncertainty. Wilson's impetuous recommendations, his cavalier treatment of data, and the unreliability of his judgment not only dismayed critics like Carpenter, Brown, and Whitney, but also shocked colleagues like Sloan and Albert Bradley. In the case of the small car, a puzzled, angry Sloan wrote Carpenter, "I felt very certain that the statements made were not in accordance with the facts." He promised a separate report of his own to the financial policy committee "dealing with the facts and circumstances as I see them, both dealing with the evolution of the postwar program and its present situation."[103]

The breadth of Carpenter's concern demonstrated that he was not simply bleating with the overcaution of a financial man made timid by the depression of the 1930s. As a chief executive he piloted Du Pont skillfully through the tumultuous growth of World War II and led its conversion and and expansion in the postwar world. As a responsible, perceptive director he supported raising new capital to increase needed output and to provide better facilities. He and others on the FPC were charged with the oversight of the finances of the nation's largest company and urgently needed sound, independent judgment—a quality that Wilson was not demonstrating.

The problem was a twofold one of individual weakness compounded by an unsound structure. Wilson's limitations and inexperience were probably unavoidable. No one could readily match Sloan's record as one of America's most able managers, and Carpenter asked Bradley to persuade Sloan to temper his public criticism of Wilson while he privately sent along his own deceptively mild but devastating rebuke.[104] Nevertheless, a top executive committee composed of men free of daily responsibilities was more likely to avoid the pitfalls of immediate interest and could collectively provide broader, better balanced guidance than did Wilson and the group managers on the operations policy committee.

Events bore out Carpenter's judgment, but, as he probably expected, structural reform was hopeless given Sloan's commitment to GM's heritage of strong line management with increasing centralization at the top. The $600 million for additional expansion was cancelled or deferred so that the company did not suffer severe overcapacity when the market softened in 1949 and 1950. The cheap car was mothballed until a market emerged for the compact automobile a decade later. Sloan criticized Wilson for overexpansion in order to increase market share but continued to insist that the OPC contain major operating managers while suggesting the addition of a key marketing man for better balance with the manufacturing executives.[105]

Wilson apologized to Carpenter for his errors and confessed to being "greatly disappointed" in GM's sales volume, explaining that the recent problems lay in using prewar assumptions about the market in a postwar world.[106] As his tone suggested, however, his approach to management continued. When he resigned to become secretary of defense in the Eisenhower administration in 1953, Wilson successfully nominated another manufacturing executive, Harlow Curtice, as his successor. Curtice ran an even more centralized and personalized operation so that the FPC became a virtual cipher.[107]

By this point, however, Walter Carpenter's own interests in GM were flagging with time and with the acceptance of his restricted power. Although Walter remained on GM's board of directors until 1959, he was less active after 1947. Ill health and his wife's death led to his resignation from the FPC in 1949, by which time, as we shall see in chapter 6, his primary concern became the preservation of Du Pont's investment in General Motors in the face of a major antitrust suit.

Carpenter's thirty-two-year career on GM's board of directors not only reflected a number of successful, important contributions; it also demonstrated the limited influence of even this able, energetic, and forceful director. In addition to his regular, attentive oversight, his most significant efforts were consultation on the company's relationship to the public, the reform and refinancing of its management bonus plans, and the retention or development of some key personnel. Such areas were peripheral to the corporation's main functions: the production and marketing of automobiles and other transportation and mechanical equipment. Despite his experience and the similarities between Du Pont and General Motors as pioneers in American business strategy and structure, Walter Carpenter had little impact on GM's organization after repeated efforts.

Certainly no case could better illustrate to the analysts of power elites in America the dominance of top executives and inside directors over the strongest of outside managers. At Du Pont, the long heritage of family enterprise and the still considerable influence of recently retired owner-operators could restrict the authority of senior professional executives. At General Motors, which lacked a tradition of family enterprise (as did most big business in America), managers controlled.

Even if he was not always successful, Carpenter had an appreciative audience for his unusual role at General Motors. Regardless of his frequent disagreements with Sloan and his colleagues, they readily respected Walter's work, as demonstrated by their habitual consultation on important questions and by his appointment to major committees. Their admiration rested in part on his accomplishments on their behalf, on his diligent attention, sharp questions, and perceptive observations, and on his skills as a financial and general executive. In addition, the long relationship generated friendship and affection among able, strong-minded men who were considerate of one another. After one particularly lengthy letter to Brown on the reform of the management plan, Carpenter wryly apologized for "this long drool" that harangued the GM executive about what he already knew.[108]

Also significant was the managers' mutual understanding of their different situations. Long before business analysts invented the label "corporate culture" to identify the "shared values [that] define [the] fundamental character of the organization," Carpenter, Sloan, and Brown understood the concept as indicated in their debate about reorganization in 1946.[109] The corollary was a tolerance for differences as they agreed to disagree, a kind of corporate cultural relativism. However, despite their vigorous debate over and appreciation of alternatives, their analysis did not extend to the character of big business in general. Top executives at Du Pont and General Motors were far more concerned about differences than similarities and appeared to little appreciate how much they shared as pioneers in the strategy of diversification and in the structure of decentralized management.

Finally, Walter Carpenter enjoyed his role at General Motors because Alfred Sloan was pleased to treat him as a peer. In 1940 he had become president and chief executive officer of the Du Pont Company, the nation's biggest chemical firm and one of its ten largest industrial enterprises.

5

Chief Executive

IN MAY 1940 Walter Carpenter became president and chief executive officer of the Du Pont Company, the position that defined the apex of his career. The achievement was especially remarkable because Carpenter was the first man to head the enterprise who was unrelated to the du Ponts by birth or marriage. Indeed, except for the brief tenure of a son-in-law early in the nineteenth century, his was the first presidency of the Du Pont firm without the du Pont name. At last, he was no longer limited to influencing policy as one of several top managers, but could directly shape and guide the firm as its leader and chairman of the executive committee. However, the forces of circumstance and timing conspired to undermine his opportunity even before Walter could seize his main chance. World War II, which started nine months before he became president and which the United States entered in December 1941, covered most of his tenure, and reconversion to peacetime occupied the remainder.

The war severely curtailed the diversified chemical company that he had always championed and revivified Du Pont as the armaments firm that he wished to abandon. It forced the enterprise to sacrifice long-term planning and strategic decision making for the administration of current output and the resolution of immediate problems. It disrupted the familiar domestic and international markets in which Du Pont had operated so well and substituted a far less predictable world. It vastly expanded the role of government and correspondingly restricted the firm's freedom to act. As chief executive officer between 1940 and 1948, Carpenter coped with crises resourcefully, improved performance, and led the company successfully, but he must have always wondered what might have been.

Wartime President

Walter Carpenter was not promoted to Du Pont's presidency to serve as a wartime leader. He became president because Lammot du Pont turned sixty in 1940 and finally decided to resign as head of the company and to succeed Pierre as chairman of the board and titular spokesman for the firm. The change could have come much earlier, for Carpenter had been identified as Lammot's second-in-command and successor when the latter was appointed president in 1926. By the early 1930s Walter was well prepared to replace him. Nor did the absence of the du Pont name or of ties by marriage deter his promotion. There was no serious challenger from the family, and for many years Pierre, Irénée, and Lammot had accepted this able "outsider" as their replacement due to his commitment to the values and practices of the family firm.

Carpenter served as second in command to a less talented man for fourteen years because Lammot simply enjoyed running the enterprise and because the firm continued to do remarkably well despite the Great Depression. In 1934 *Fortune* magazine said of Lammot that "nine-tenths of his life is the Du Pont Co[mpany]," and after the concern's rapid recovery during the early years of the Great Depression, there were no difficult challenges requiring inspired leadership.[1] The industrial departments grew steadily and profitably while the executive committee, where Lammot was one of nine members, oversaw operations. When he eventually retired in 1940, Lammot was Du Pont's oldest president since the three cousins had taken control of the company in 1902. He privately wrote Sir Harry McGowan that the change "sounds like quite an upset" but that "it is nothing of the kind." At age seventy Pierre was happy to surrender the chairmanship to his youngest brother, and Irénée wanted to be relieved of the vice chairmanship so that he could spend even more time at his vacation home in Cuba. Furthermore, Lammot noted modestly, but truthfully, that "Walter is a more able man to fill the position than I am."[2]

Thus, although he had risen to senior management in 1919 at the age of thirty-one, Carpenter served on the executive committee for twenty-one years before becoming president. The delay made him the oldest man ever to assume the position but necessarily reflected Lammot's right in the family firm. Walter never indicated any frustration because of the wait, but after the promotion he quickly and characteristically published a calm, reasoned letter to all employees to define the new administration's tasks and to seek their help. Titled "To My Associates," the piece took a very effective approach—low-key and modest without spurious humility or clichéd appeals to team play. Carpenter skillfully drew on employee pride and on the essential elements of the corporation's past successes to enlist new effort and cooperation in the face of the challenges raised by World War II. A long history of "pioneering spirit," "perseverance," "a thirst for finding better ways," and "cooperation" was reviewed in the record of such modern accomplishments as synthetic ammonia, dyes, and nylon as well as in the commitment to the research that helped spawn them.[3]

Even though the United States was formally neutral in 1940, World War II threatened to divert the enterprise from its many, varied contributions to the American standard of living. It meant a "turn to the less happy but also vital task of national defense. We have not sought this; we see it with regret; but if called upon we will, as in the past, respond with all our perseverance and determination to do everything and more than may be expected of us."[4] The Du Pont Company would willingly accept its duties in wartime, but it would neither seek nor promote them.

The message reflected Walter's attitude as well as that of key executives and family members. Ruly Carpenter urged an America First stance in the company-owned *Wilmington Journal—Every Evening* and circulated copies of its editorial, "America CAN Keep Out," to Lammot, Pierre, Walter, Willis Harrington, and Jasper Crane, saying that "I think it expresses our views as closely as they could be expressed." After war began in September 1939, Lammot proposed that the executive committee send a private statement to Delaware's U.S. senators as a basis on which the firm could defend itself from anticipated attacks as a "merchant of death." The note explained once again that Du Pont's "interests . . . are best served by the continuation of the Company's peace-time operations, as contrasted with what might be done or might have to be done under conditions of war."[5]

For Carpenter, the reluctant switch from diversified, peacetime production to war manufacture as part of democracy's arsenal was a simple, unavoidable decision. He personally disliked Hitler's Nazi Germany and felt a strong sense of patriotic duty to his country. As he wrote Sir Harry McGowan in late 1938, "Much of the political philosophy of Germany is anathema to me."[6] He also understood that any perceived failure to cooperate with a charismatic American president in "waging neutrality" against a detested enemy would have disastrous popular and political consequences. Finally, he readily recognized that big business, which was the core of the country's industrial economy, would have to play a central role in preparing for and waging war when the United States finally entered the conflict. As events soon proved, the government would inevitably rely heavily on those firms that had the capital, the organizational skills, the research and managerial abilities, and the essential experience with large-scale production.[7]

Under Carpenter's guidance, Du Pont moved rapidly to support the U.S. government's anti-Axis policies and to expand its war production and its cooperation with the military, which had begun under Lammot du Pont with the acceptance of government contracts during early rearmament and preparedness efforts in 1939. In October 1940 the executive committee, which Walter now chaired as company president, declared that the corporation would not sell to Germany, Italy, or Japan "any of its products which are connnected with the waging of war by those countries" and would not purchase from them goods "obtainable elsewhere on any reasonable basis." It would not set up "new connections" or extend or renew current contracts with firms or agents promoting the interests of those nations. Existing agreements would be terminated as quickly as was legally possible. Small investments in several I. G. Farben subsidiaries were soon disposed of.[8]

Munitions output mushroomed. By August 1942 Du Pont was supplying more than two-thirds of the nation's daily production of smokeless powder, almost one-fourth of its TNT, and over 90 percent of its tetryl.[9] At full capacity it daily manufactured more than 3.5 million pounds of military explosives. By February 1943 it surpassed total output for World War I as the number of employees making munitions leaped from about 400 to more than 37,000. In addition to expanding Du Pont's own factories, the engineering department built cheaply and rapidly more than fifty plants for the government. In the case of the Indiana Ordnance Works, for example, to meet a contract dated July 17, 1940, the company broke ground on August 28, 1940, began manufacture of nitric acid on April 3, 1941, and produced its first smokeless powder on April 24, 1941, one month before its original ten-month projection. Explosives jumped from 7 percent of sales in 1938 to almost 25 percent during the war years as the company produced over two million tons of military explosives between 1940 and 1945.[10]

In fact, munitions were only part of Du Pont's contribution to World War II, for the diversified company converted almost entirely to military production and manufactured numerous essential products for the war effort. For example, capacity for nylon, the firm's new synthetic fiber, nearly doubled within one year to almost thirty million pounds of yarn, and output was shifted from consumer hosiery to parachutes and other military goods. Fundamental and commercial research was severely restricted while Du Pont laboratories concentrated heavily on government contract work and on adapting existing products for war use. The entire workforce more than tripled, from about 44,000 in 1939 to over 136,000 in Du Pont and government-owned plants by 1942.[11]

Carpenter and the firm quickly appreciated and adeptly handled the burdens of total war. The company's decentralized structure permitted each industrial department to manage efficiently its contracting, material supply, production schedules, and distribution while the executive committee set central guidelines for contract terms and inventory levels, the development department coordinated material priorities, and the chemical department guided research work. Output more than doubled 1939 levels, and average sales prices dropped 5 percent while wholesale prices rose 37 percent.[12]

Because of Du Pont's acceptance of low, fixed-rate fees for government work, massive contract renegotiation by the government to further reduce its costs, and high excess profits taxes, earnings for 1942–45 were 21 percent below the average for 1939–41 and 5 percent below the figure for 1936–38, but the company compensated by increasing reserves and retained earnings in order to maintain liquidity in preparation for postwar conversion. Although profits provided a poor measure of performance in extraordinary circumstances, the enterprise's record of 128 army-navy "E" awards and white stars for excellence testified vividly to its outstanding success.[13]

For Walter Carpenter the irony was all too clear. He was certainly proud of the accomplishments of the firm that he led and to which he had devoted his career. Nonetheless, he continued to downplay a record that directly contradicted the goals and direction for which he had labored for nearly thirty years: Du Pont's successful transformation from a munitions to a diversified chemical company. He acknowl-

Wartime President: Receiving one of 128 Army-Navy "E" Awards won by Du Pont between 1942 and 1945. From the left: Brigadier General Benjamin W. Chidlaw, Assistant Chief of Staff, Headquarters of the Materiel Command, U.S. Army Air Forces; Walter S. Carpenter; Dr. W. W. Heckert, Assistant Director of Nylon Research; and Captain C. A. Bonvillian, Director of the Naval Boiler and Turbine Laboratory of the Philadelphia Navy Yard. (*Hagley Museum and Library*)

edged the public's current positive sentiments, but he resolutely counseled taking the long-term view and sticking to the company's mission as a chemical concern. The searing memory of the Nye Committee investigation made him certain that "the applause" would "turn to condemnation later when the country starts to pay the price of this war."[14]

The irony went even further. In preparation for his presidency, Carpenter had spent two decades as a top manager skillfully analyzing the company's competitive advantages and opportunities in order to assess rationally the firm's long-term best interests and to establish broad general policies for their achievement. The exigencies of world war inevitably focused the company's attention and much of his own energy on immediate crises and administrative detail. The emphasis was on current operation and output, most of which was best handled by the general managers within the industrial departments themselves.

At the top the executive committee met longer and more frequently in order to cope with agendas choked with the detail of contract approval, government oversight and regulation, and short-term policy alterations necessary to accommodate the corporation's conversion to war work. Despite his careful discipline and determination to say no, Carpenter's own schedule was unavoidably filled with proliferating meetings of Du Pont, General Motors, and government committees, with speeches inside and outside the company, with dedications of new plants, and with award ceremonies. The wartime load so ground down the cheerful workaholic that Carpenter even considered resigning from GM's policy committee. After the war's end, Walter wrote his Uncle Ed that he anticipated a vacation like "a kid at school."[15]

Despite the burgeoning of minutiae, Carpenter continued to lead the executive committee in policy-making for war work, the most famous and important example of which was the decision to play a major role in the manufacture of the atomic bomb. After learning that the Germans had accomplished the nuclear fission of uranium in 1941, the U.S. government's Office of Scientific Research and Development began sponsoring investigation into the fission of uranium at the University of Chicago. In 1942 it created the Manhattan Project under the direction of General Leslie Groves and the Army Corps of Engineers to coordinate and direct research and development of a nuclear bomb. The Du Pont Company had first gotten involved by loaning personnel to the work at the University of Chicago in the summer of 1942. The company then agreed that fall to help Stone and Webster build a pilot nuclear reactor and plant to produce and separate plutonium at Clinton, Tennessee.[16] Nevertheless, Du Pont's role remained marginal, and company officials were unaware of the scope of the project until Groves approached Walter Carpenter and the executive committee in November 1942 and requested that the corporation take complete charge of building the pilot facility at Clinton and of erecting and operating a full-scale plant at Hanford, Washington.

Like so many public and military leaders, Groves looked to big business to meet the nation's major production and supply problems during the war. He wrote later that within two months of receiving the Manhattan assignment he realized that it was much larger than he had first expected. The plutonium project, which he thought should get primary attention as the most feasible method of producing an atomic bomb, was too much for Stone and Webster and there was no government agency that could readily build and run such a plant. He told Carpenter and the executive committee that, based on the company's engineering, design, and construction work in erecting army munitions plants, Du Pont was the "only . . . firm . . . capable" of the job. The key was not corporate size per se but the firm's combination of "highly skilled technical management," chemical knowledge, and engineering expertise, which promised the speed and reliability essential to complete a critically important, risky, and expensive task.[17]

Members of the executive committee, including senior vice president Willis Harrington and former director of corporate research Charles Stine, whom Groves had first approached, were quick to point out the major problems. Du Pont, which had no experience in nuclear physics, was being asked to construct a facility and operate a complex process that existed only in theory and in limited laboratory work without the benefit of a pilot-plant study. It was being asked to build the world's first full-scale nuclear reactor to convert uranium into plutonium for an atomic bomb. The work was so unprecedented that the Chicago scientists were only just creating the nation's first chain reaction on a laboratory scale as Du Pont and Groves were deliberating. The reactor project would proceed in addition to the company's existing full commitment to war work, which already strained its resources. If successful, it would produce a bomb so terrible as to dwarf any previous merchants-of-death label attached to the firm.[18]

Although he was not a technical man, as a savvy, experienced executive of a major chemical enterprise Walter Carpenter fully understood the risks. He later wrote privately to his Uncle Ed that "we were given, as a starter, a lot of scientific data and asked, in as short a period as possible, to design a plant, the like of which has never been seen or heard of, to conduct a process which had never been carried out before. This was [to be] done and completed in a period of a little over eighteen months." In the case of the Hanford facility itself, "the data was far less than we would ordinarily start with; the process more complicated, and the plant vastly larger than we have ever done before." Furthermore, he noted laconically, "the process is all carried on by remote control owing to the hazards involved which . . . involve a bit of difficult designing."[19]

As president and chief executive officer, Carpenter quickly provided essential leadership. While a team of Du Pont technical men confirmed the feasibility of plutonium production among the alternative methods of manufacturing a bomb, he asked the critical question of General Groves: Did this informed head of the project share the sense of national urgency expressed by President Franklin Roosevelt, Secretary of War Henry Stimson, and General George Marshall? Groves answered that the Germans were already working on such a bomb, against which there was no defense except possibly deterrence by the threat to use the nation's own weapon. In addition, success might shorten the war and save lives.[20]

The general's telling response carried the day, and, according to at least one source, Carpenter subsequently led the successful argument for acceptance in the executive committee.[21] After signing its first contract in December 1942, Du Pont built the Clinton pilot plant within a year. In less than two years it completed and began running the full-scale Hanford facility, which produced the material for a test bomb at Alamagordo in July 1945 and for the bomb dropped on Nagasaki in August 1945.

Carpenter continued to monitor progress and play an important role in the project. Nevertheless, the actual work at Du Pont was done in a special TNX division of the explosives department, headed by Roger Williams with Monty Evans overseeing engineering and construction and with Crawford Greenewalt serving as technical director and liaison to the physicists at the University of Chicago. In order to reduce Du Pont's risk and to limit another merchants-of-death charge for war profiteering, Walter insisted on a contract that restricted the firm's pay to costs plus one dollar and that explicitly forwent all patents in exchange for the government's complete assumption of liability. His bitter memory of the Nye Committee debacle was reflected in a special, secret letter as part of the contract, specifically stating that the company was acting in the national interests because of its unique qualifications and guaranteeing Du Pont the use of all classified information before any subsequent congressional investigating committee.[22]

During construction and operation Carpenter twice visited the Hanford plant and continued to harry his technical people about limiting the exposure and risk of construction and operating personnel. He carefully attempted to restrict access to information about the project and explicitly admonished directors, department heads, and members of the executive and finance committees to avoid references to the Clinton and Hanford projects. Indeed, Walter was so secretive that

Crawford Greenewalt and Lammot du Pont thought that the board of directors was inadequately informed of the company's risks. At their urging he made a full presentation in support of the project in October 1943, almost a year after he had first won its approval.[23]

The successful use of the bomb and Japan's surrender ending the Second World War in August 1945 brought Carpenter unmistakable relief and release from Du Pont's terrible obligation and from his personal sense of responsibility, which he clearly expressed to Leslie Groves one week later.

> As my thoughts travel back over the last three years, the entire matter seems much like a dream. When you first met with us it seemed almost as if we were being asked to undertake a huge program for the creation of perpetual motion. As the months passed by and the magnitude of the program seemed to grow, the entire scheme seemed to be even more fantastic. And now as it develops that the program was not only a scientific and industrial success, but also achieved all which could possibly have been expected of it in a military way, it still seems impossible to realize.[24]

Carpenter's uncharacteristic awe and emotion reflected a joy shared with the rest of the nation at the war's end and a realization that he and his firm had played a vital part in his country's success.

Chief Executive

As Walter Carpenter's experience at Du Pont during World War II suggests, his role and responsibilities as president and chief executive officer were not easily and clearly defined. As the chief operating officer in most firms, the president directed line operations and was the single leading administrator of the enterprise. At Du Pont, however, decentralization had moved operating responsibilities down to the heads of the industrial departments, and policy-making was the collective duty of the executive committee, which the president chaired. With a few exceptions like steering high-level negotiations with major foreign competitors and serving as company spokesman, Lammot du Pont, Walter's predecessor, had acted as one among equals who served with but did not order his executive colleagues. Given Lammot's rather lax approach, there remained the question of how the president was to continue his traditional function as leader of the enterprise.

Despite Carpenter's skepticism during the organizational reforms two decades earlier, he now fully accepted the decentralized structure that worked so well at Du Pont. When C. Lalor Burdick asked for major administrative duties as part of becoming the president's assistant, Walter firmly refused. He explained that his tasks were many and his decisions important and that he needed "some assistance in ascertaining and appraising them. However, if I were to undertake from this office to administer other duties which would, in turn, be delegated to my Assistant to handle, I feel that, not only would I not be achieving my objective, but, in fact, might be actually adding to the burdens of my own office. That, I distinctly want to avoid, in the interest of directing all of my own capacities to the important decisions which, of necessity, fall to me as President."[25]

If the president's office was not to expand its formal power, neither was the corporate staff. Exports and overseas operations in the new postwar markets, for example, were to remain the province of the industrial departments and not the foreign relations department. As Walter explained it, "I look upon the export business as merely a branch of the total selling problem of the Industrial Departments and I believe that we should leave the responsibility of that problem with them. If they, or any of them, alone or in conjunction with the Foreign Relations Department should like to have the Development Department explore this, I see no reason why that should not be done."[26]

Carpenter also scrupulously accepted the general managers' autonomy in his personal relations with the industrial departments. With no pressure he simply passed on unusual requests from leading businessmen and politicians to the relevant department heads for an independent review and decision. Walter then sent the results, favorable or unfavorable, as company policy to the original inquirer. In 1944, for example, when rayon was scarce, Delaware Governor Walter Bacon wrote Carpenter requesting a special additional allocation for a particular textile firm in the state. Walter in turn sent the letter to Ben May, vice president of the rayon division, who explained that the mill was already getting 21 percent of its normal allocation while the industry average was only 14 percent. Carpenter told Bacon that nothing could be done and included a copy of May's letter as an explanation.[27] The incident was one of many during the materials shortages of the wartime and early postwar years.

The organizational constraints even affected the transmission of Carpenter's own ideas and interests as years of autonomy and success threatened to make the industrial departments virtual fiefdoms. When he read a *Wall Street Journal* article about the Industrial Rayon Company's new process of continuous manufacture, Carpenter wrote Ben May asking if Du Pont would consider a license. He backed off when May replied that the process was only marginally better than Du Pont's method and that inquiries had brought a "prohibitive" response. After the war Carpenter repeatedly importuned the rayon department to build a cellophane plant on the West Coast to protect a fast-growing market there, but eventually accepted May's refusal to act because projections for immediate return on investment were not favorable.[28]

Walter certainly appreciated the need for central oversight by the executive committee, but a final showdown of the sort he had fought with the ammonia department in the late 1930s was averted when antitrust prosecution made inadvisable the further expansion of Du Pont's cellophane capacity. The accidental resolution of the conflict by an external circumstance was unfortunate, for after Walter's retirement as president the excessive freedom assumed by the industrial departments became a serious problem for Du Pont in the 1960s and 1970s.[29]

As the preceding examples suggest, Carpenter saw his role as direction by indirection in order to achieve collective and consensual policymaking at the top. He seldom ordered actions, but identified the firm's major challenges, articulated its direction, and encouraged and built support for solutions. In effect, he led by initiating, guiding, and prompting. Although this approach at times meant suggestions about specific operations to the general managers of the industrial departments, it more frequently encouraged members of the executive committee to consider the larger questions in their areas of special expertise and to develop systematic policies and procedures for issues where change, growth, and complexity had overwhelmed ad hoc practice.

Carpenter saw the firm as a learning organization and attempted to promote expectations, processes, and routines that encouraged continuous thinking about planning and adjustment and the promotion of organizational capabilities—competititve advantages in manufacturing, marketing, and management. Carpenter had first developed such concerns as a general executive in the 1920s and 1930s, and now his major responsibility as president was to revitalize the executive committee and inculcate such expectations throughout top management.[30] He wanted Du Pont's senior people to avoid settling for passive review of the operations of industrial departments, which had become a tendency under Lammot's regime, and to tackle aggressively major problems and to formulate broad, long-range policies, the primary task of upper-level executives.

Such leadership took many forms, but frequently emphasized the creation of general policy, the articulation of learned routines, and the application of system to provide essential guidance in a diverse, decentralized enterprise. Sometimes he suggested new types of data gathering for constant review so that key people could be better informed about critical issues. Thus, he requested a regular report on patent suits from the legal department, explaining and updating major cases whether Du Pont was involved or not. After General Motors was found guilty of several technical violations in the administration of its bonus plan, Walter fired off a two-page letter to Vice President Angus Echols suggesting an examination of Du Pont's plan for similar liabilities.[31]

Carpenter's value of system, the company's increased government contracts after the commencement of World War II, and the bitter memory of profiteering charges after World War I induced him to prompt a broad, public statement of Du Pont's pricing goals and policy in August 1940, a few months after he had become president. The document, which was intended to establish a dynamic framework, carefully defined the firm's purpose as "the continual venture of capital in the manufacture and sale of its products and services for profit." Prices with higher profit margins often associated with new products were expected to fall to lower levels with time, experience, and competition, thus establishing the boundaries of a profit range that gave an overall adequate return on investment.[32]

Management's primary aim was security for capital and the greatest return "consistent with sound legal, ethical, social, economic, and technical principles, based upon a long-term, enlightened self-interest point of view." Thus, prices would change for such specific reasons as protecting sources of supply, seizing opportunities for increased volume, and maintaining leadership and prestige.[33] General though the statement was, it not only provided an important explanation to the public but also served as a continuing corporate guideline to the hundreds of Du Pont managers who made thousands of pricing decisions.

Carpenter also thought that the company, which had grown so much since 1920, needed to pay more careful attention to developing management in depth all along the line in order to maintain a supply of critical talent. He explained to Alfred Sloan that "as you know a subject in which I have always been much interested is the developing of an organization in which we would have [the] promise of men coming along in the organization to take over the burden of responsibility as the older men pass out of the picture."[34]

Because discussion with individual department heads offered only a fuzzy and incomplete picture, he had a special graph developed called the potentiality chart. With its ordinate measuring compensation and its abscissa recording age, a standard curve was plotted based on the careers of past key people. Locating the experiences of present managers against the standard gave a momentary photograph of the firm. Those men on the left of the curve were accelerating and promising; too many careers on the right indicated both inadequacy and a potential clogging of the pathways.[35]

Although the chart provided a crude aggregate picture and was not an accurate measure of the individuals involved, it could be disaggregated by departments to highlight problem areas. Identifying and tracking the important people was assumed first by Thompson Brown and then by E. B. Yancey of the executive committee, although Carpenter continued to fret about the inherent difficulty of balancing the corporation's broad needs with the autonomy of general managers and department heads actually in charge of key talent.[36]

One particular strength in Carpenter's leadership was his development of Du Pont's relationships to its various publics in the outside world. As president, Walter was able to assure more fully the large enterprise's necessary sensitivity to its special audiences in order to promote its long-term well-being. Despite being a financial man, for example, Carpenter was anxious that professional managers answer to their stockholders in clear, accurate fashion without the distraction of abstruse accounting clutter. Thus, he criticized the first annual report issued under his regime because it began with a discussion of accounting details instead of a concise review of Du Pont's performance during the previous year.[37] He also strove to minimize newspaper and military ballyhoo of Du Pont's extraordinaary munitions production which, though understandable, sent the wrong message to the public. As he put it, the problem was that "it is not very feasible or constructive to advertise what you are not; for instance, that we are not munition[s] manufacturers" but a diversified chemical company.[38]

In the midst of world war Carpenter acutely appreciated the need to balance delicately Du Pont's long-term, peacetime interests with its national obligations. When Lammot du Pont urged more recognition of the company's tremendous munitions production, Carpenter explained to the chairman of the board that "we have spent millions of dollars in endeavoring to dissipate the idea that we are a munitions company and it does not seem to me wise now to undo that effort by endeavoring at this time to parade the accomplishments which we are making in the manufacture of munitions." He acknowledged the nation's current prowar sentiment but feared an inevitable reversal as had occurred after World War I. The prudent solution then was to "avoid criticism for not having shirked in this effort, but not [to] endeavor to make capital out of participating in this [war]."[39]

He also urged that the corporation's use of its power and largesse be balanced and fair. When Henrik Shipstead, a U.S. senator from Minnesota and a member of the Senate Foreign Relations Committee, wrote seeking special consideration for a St. Paul engineering firm after Du Pont received a big government contract to build a munitions plant in that city, Carpenter refused to cave in to a special interest. He politely but firmly reminded Shipstead of the Du Pont engineering department's lengthy, outstanding record. Although local workers would be hired and there might be some limited subcontracting, taking "on at this stage a new firm of designers and engineers is a little like asking us to make a drastic shift in our team's line up . . . [in] the most crucial struggle we shall probably ever be in. . . . I hesitate to think that either you or the United States Army authorities would encourage this." On other occasions he had to mediate among the chairmen of various state war bond drives who wanted disproportionate shares of the company's contribution, a tiny example of the challenges to a national firm in a federal polity.[40]

In addition, balance included the prudent avoidance of extreme and marginally relevant political causes and a logical focus on the economic and social consequences of Du Pont's main function as a manufacturer. In the 1930s Carpenter had felt that the company had too often exposed itself to ridicule as it followed the du Pont brothers' personal and sometimes idiosyncratic interests in politics, a practice that Carpenter could now halt as chief executive officer. Thus, he successfully fought Lammot's suggestion that the firm unilaterally double its annual $50,000 contribution to the National Association of Manufacturers in support of its postwar campaign against organized labor. He and the executive committee agreed to increase the corporation's donation only if other major firms did so. Otherwise, he explained to Lammot, "to double our present, already outstanding commitment would put us [so] far out in front as to be somewhat objectionable from the standpoint of the Company and also possibly from the standpoint of NAM."[41]

Carpenter also supported the legal department's objections when Lammot wanted to send a right-wing economic tract to the concern's stockholders. Walter wrote the company's chairman that if such actions did not serve corporate purposes, "then perhaps they are not appropriate matters for management to place before the stockholders." After electing management as a stockholder, "I do not expect that management to write me and advise me that my capital is in jeopardy . . . because the management of the company feels that there are insidious trends abroad in the land. Nor do I expect management to undertake to school me on the philosophy of economics, morals or metophysics [sic]."[42] Carpenter's independence and perceptiveness helped transform Du Pont into a truly public enterprise rather than a simple extension of the du Pont brothers.

Public sensitivity also included correcting damaging misrepresentations and avoiding potential pitfalls. When Walter Winchell baselessly asserted in September 1945 that the State Department was going to give the secret of the atomic bomb to the Du Pont Company, Carpenter's public letter to Secretary of State James Byrnes stoutly refuted Winchell's nonsense while reviewing the firm's full cooperation with the War Department on the Manhattan Project. A similar letter in September 1940 exposed the false and malicious charges by Congressman Adolph Sabath and columnist Guy Richards of the *Chicago Tribune* that Du Pont was exporting monthly $10 million in munitions to the Axis powers. Carpenter calmly noted that total munitions exports to date in 1940 were only $2.5 million, that the bulk went to China, Great Britain, Finland, and France, and that "not one pound of munitions" went to the Axis countries.[43]

Avoiding snares frequently required Carpenter's anticipation of potential conflicts of interest by himself or by Du Pont managers. As the company had done in World War I, Walter asked men in key positions to shun associations with rearmament and preparedness groups in order to head off charges of warmongering. In his own case, after becoming president he astutely refused election as a director of the Christiana Securities Company, the family holding company in which he held a significant block of stock. In an era of vigorous antitrust prosecution, he worried about exacerbating public hostility to interlocking directorates and about the potential, if remote, possibility of conflict of interest. He explained to Lammot that "as President of the

du Pont Company my responsibility is to the du Pont Company itself."
At the same time he softened any implied criticism of his predecessors,
Irénée and Lammot, by pointing out that because they were members
of Christiana's board before becoming president, resignation would
have been an empty gesture. He did accept the position after retiring as
Du Pont's head.[44]

As part of his executive leadership in the company's external affairs
Carpenter modernized public relations at Du Pont. More than two
decades of oversight by his brother Ruly and direction by Charles
Weston and Theodore Joslin had left the firm with little more than
press agentry from its own publicity bureau, which focused on getting
space and free advertising. As noted in chapter 3, Walter Carpenter
had learned in the 1930s that the large firm's needs were far broader
and more complex. He did not want a grist mill. Instead, Du Pont
needed a department that was fully acquainted with the political and
economic aspects of the firm's major problems, could perceptively
sound out public attitudes, and made constructive suggestions to top
executives about the handling of such issues as antitrust suits and major labor contracts.[45]

As might be expected, Carpenter's goals were balanced, rational,
pragmatic, and long-term. He was less interested in a glossy image than
in the accurate portrayal of what occurred. "In the long run," he
thought, the enterprise "usually gets what it deserves[,] and perhaps in
a sounder sense even in the short run, a company will enjoy that will of
the people that it deserves. In the long run its behavior counts, and that
means both in a positive and negative sense." Public relations, then,
were the firm's enjoyment of the public's legitimate good will and the
"avoidance of bad-will."[46]

Nor did he have rosy expectations about elaborate public education.
He had "little confidence in making economists out of the great mass of
people. It just can't be done. You've got to get the message over in some
simpler form not requiring activity of the brain, which is unpleasant."
He was impressed with organized labor's effective proselytizing by pin
up and comic strip while industry had "attempted a forthright reasoning and therefore futile approach."[47]

To achieve more extensive, integrated use of public relations, Carpenter promoted Harold Brayman as director in 1944, had copies of
the executive committee minutes automatically sent to him, and consulted with him frequently and regularly. The talented Cornell graduate, who had extensive experience as a legislative reporter, quickly

hired Glen Perry, an able assistant with a Princeton degree and training as a political correspondent. Together the two men effectively directed public relations at Du Pont for more than two decades.[48]

The publication in 1946 of *The Du Pont Company's Part in the National Security Program,* a sixty-four-page printed account of the enterprise's role in World War II, best illustrated the public dimension that Walter sought for Du Pont and the cooperation between the chief executive and his public relations director. Like many firms, Du Pont wished both to record its wartime accomplishments and to reinforce the renewed prestige that they had brought big business. Carpenter also wanted a document that promoted the broad capabilities and benefits of the diversified chemical company that he had trumpeted for so long and that correspondingly helped downplay the munitions and merchants-of-death legend. Walter worked closely with Brayman and Perry to draft an accurate, dignified statement. It started as a booklet to the stockholders over Carpenter's signature, but eventually became a record of the firm he led throughout the war as well as Du Pont's self-portrait to the public as it entered the postwar world.[49]

In concert with Carpenter's intent, the booklet quickly established the vital and broad nature of Du Pont's contribution, reminding readers that World War II "was a war of science and a war of industries" as much as it was a struggle between armies. "In this race of laboratories and production lines . . . , chemical research and manufacture produced not only elements of ordnance that insured military success, but materials which went into strengthening and husbanding the very economy of the nation itself." Since World War I, "American chemistry and affiliated sciences [had] crossed new frontiers in technological advancement." With Du Pont playing a leading role, "they have created new chemical products, superior in many cases to imported natural and manufactured materials and have ventured successfully into totally new fields of research and development" with "demonstrated" impact on economic and military power.

The publication quietly made Walter's case for big business. The well-managed integration of multiple functions and product lines into a single enterprise allowed Du Pont to do much more than just make goods. Its thirty-five research laboratories and 3,500 research personnel did development work for the company and for many government agencies on items ranging from incendiary bombs to soles for soldiers' boots. The firm's construction department engineered and built quickly and efficiently in thirty-two locations fifty-four plants for the government costing more than $1 billion in addition to the company's own considerable expansion. Du Pont's transportation arm, the International Freighting Corporation, operated fifty-eight ships that made more than 580 voyages to combat zones around the world, carrying over 5.5 million tons of "tanks, planes, fuel oil, guns, jeeps and other vital materials" as well as 17,000 army and navy personnel and over a thousand U.S. and Allied civilians on war missions. Du Pont's exports supplied over $40 million in goods for Lend Lease and more than $14 million annually to the nation's allies in Latin America in addition to the products of Du Pont plants located there.

The company's manufacturing output was, of course, the core of its contribution to the war effort. Despite the normal wartime shortages of raw materials, manpower, and transport, the firm's expansion of production was phenomenal. By 1943 Du Pont-owned plants alone (exclusive of those built and operated for the government) more than doubled the value of 1939 output, and the $686 million of goods manufactured in 1943 grew to $744 million in 1944 and $731 million in 1945.

Naturally the account noted that a big part of this output was military explosives. In fact, Du Pont's program was "the largest ever undertaken" and accounted for almost two-thirds of the nation's munitions output during the war. During World War II Du Pont manufactured about 4.5 billion pounds of military explosives, three times its World War I figure and 20 percent above the entire volume used by all the Allies in the previous conflict. The total included over 2.5 billion pounds of smokeless powder, almost 1.5 billion pounds of TNT, 110 million pounds of tetryl, and nearly 200 million pounds of RDX compositions.

The company's organizational capabilities allowed it to establish its vital military explosives program quickly (by 1943 it was producing over 110 million pounds of military explosives monthly), efficiently (improved production rates saved the government $17 million for nine additional smokeless powder lines), and flexibly (the firm reached separate production peaks in 1943 and again in late 1944 after premature cutbacks ordered by the War Department). Operating costs "declined steadily" between 1942 and 1945, dropping over one-quarter for cannon powder, one-third for rifle powder, TNT blocks, and RDX, and about one-half for TNT, DNT, and tetryl. Part of the decline was due to government supply of raw materials but "in general" lower costs resulted from improved processes, better operating efficiency, and greater volume.

Impressive as this record was, the book proudly emphasized that it obscured the role of the large diversified company whose enduring peacetime accomplishments were rapidly adjusted to contribute far more to the war effort. Although military explosives comprised about 85 percent of Du Pont's wartime production in World War I, in the Second World War they accounted for only one-quarter of output. Much more important were the contributions of the modern chemical company that Walter Carpenter had helped build and administer as a top executive for a quarter-century.

In an appendix organized around the industrial departments, which had been the core of Du Pont since 1921, the book recounted the extraordinary range of the firm's capability. The ammonia department's products went into fertilizers for increased food supplies and resulted in numerous intermediates for goods like nylon and polyethylene plastic. Cellophane protected K rations and perishable products, bandages, drugs, and other medical and surgical supplies, as well as rifles, ammunition, and other military items. It eliminated the thick coats of grease formerly used in rifle shipments and sealed tank vents against dirt. From Du Pont's fabrics and finishes department came coated textiles for hospital sheeting, tents, engine covers, carburetor diaphrams, protective clothing, and life jackets. The finishes division in the same department supplied over forty million gallons of its products, including "a veritable ocean of paint" for the U.S. Navy (since each battleship needed four hundred thousand gallons) in addition to synthetic camouflage enamels (with colors supplied by the pigments department) for airplanes and interior paint for steel artillery shell cases (to prevent the gunpowder from reacting with the metal). Freon 12 from Du Pont's Kinetic Chemicals subsidiary, was employed not only in refrigeration and air conditioning systems throughout the military and in war plants, but also became the "ideal propellant" for the new aerosol insecticides used heavily in tropical war zones. At the same time Du Pont helped adapt DDT as a general insecticide, making over eleven million pounds for military use.

Nylon, the company's spectacular new product, was entirely diverted from commercial purposes after the Japanese shut off the nation's silk supplies. Eighty million pounds of nylon went to critical military or civilian use, including parachute cord and fabric, airplane tire cord, tow and pick-up ropes, and military apparel like armor vests, mechanics' gloves, and gunners' belts as well as jungle hammocks, flak curtains, and medical litters. Rayon went into tire cords (125 million pounds), tow target fabrics, and bomb parachutes. Du Pont dyes helped color synthetic and natural fiber fabrics. Khaki production alone increased 800 percent, while the firm supplied 40 percent of the dyes for cotton uniforms and helped develop a continuous process for applying indigo to wool.

The book further noted that Du Pont made both prosaic and glamorous products for the war. "A thimbleful of [its] tetraethyl lead . . . was in every gallon of gasoline fueling the Allied air attack," and provided the high octane rating essential for high-compression airplane engines. Although military data were secret, commercial planes using new high-octane fuels "experienced an improvement of 16 per cent in take-off and 40 per cent in climb." The less exciting electrochemicals department produced the metallic sodium essential in tetraethyl lead manufacture, supplied silver and potassium cyanide for silver-plating airplane engine bearings, and helped develop a new "hot dip" method of tinning steel plate for the making of tin cans. The heavy chemicals department made sodium silicate used in the production of silica gel, a catalyst in tetraethyl lead production; strontium nitrate employed in tracer bullets and flares; and chlorosulfonic acid used in the making of sulfa drugs.

More exotic products included films and X-ray materials from the photo products department and neoprene, an essential substitute after the Japanese captured the world's natural rubber supplies. Neoprene went into gas masks, life belts and pontoons, helmet liners, protective jacketing for ship cables and airplane wiring, and dozens of other military and critical civilian products. The plastics department, built on Walter Carpenter's acquisition of the Arlington Company, shipped twenty-six million pounds of Lucite resin for making clear plastic bomber noses and gun turrets, as well as PT boat windows, airport landing light covers, artificial eyes, and lenses for surgical flashlights.

Although the book amply communicated the staggering volume and range of nonexplosive Du Pont products critical to the war effort, Carpenter was also at pains to dispel a related part of the merchants-of-death label: profiteering. Earnings per share between 1942 and 1945 dropped 21 percent from the 1939–41 period and 5 percent from the 1936–38 depression era for a variety of reasons. The company freely provided its know-how to the government; in 1944 it granted sixty-five royalty-free licenses on military explosives alone. Like other firms, Du Pont paid huge tax bills, totaling over $650 million between 1939 and 1945. It agreed to low fees for constructing and operating government facilities. Before taxes, charges for construction were 1.2 percent of costs, and fees for operation were 6 percent of costs. After taxes and unreimbursed overhead, fees netted less than 0.4 percent of building and operating costs.

In sum, the book clearly made Carpenter's case for the utility of the large, integrated, diversified company that he had worked to build. Du Pont's strategy and structure allowed it to combine size, breadth, and efficiency to provide a range of services, including research, engineering, and transport as well as production; to manufacture literally thousands of essential goods in many different lines; to employ at peak times over 136,000 workers with an accident rate about one-seventh the level of the U.S. chemical industry and one-tenth the measurement for all U.S. industry, with only .02 percent time lost due to work stoppages and labor conflicts; and to drop average sales prices 5 percent between 1939 and 1945 while national average wholesale prices increased 37 percent, while Du Pont's raw materials costs increased 47 percent, while salaries and wages rose significantly, and while taxes jumped from two to twelve dollars per share. As the book aptly concluded, "The peacetime size and integration of the Company, which provided the technical background, the pool of executive and scientific personnel and the necessary production experience, have determined the effectiveness of its war contribution."

The presentation not only accomplished its purpose, but fully documented Walter's leadership in transforming public relations at Du Pont. As one historian of the company's public relations reported, Walter Carpenter "not only wanted, but searched out, a new approach to the company's relations to the public." Although Harold Brayman thought that the new era officially arrived with Carpenter's successor, he noted that the change was eased because the "concept had been brought so far under way in the preceding administration of Walter S. Carpenter, Jr." Not surprisingly, when he retired as president in favor of Crawford Greenewalt, Walter recommended that oversight of public relations become the chief executive's job, a suggestion that Greenewalt quickly adopted.[50]

Postwar Leadership

Walter Carpenter's direction of the Du Pont Company's development in the postwar world not only started before the Second World War ended but before the United States even entered the conflict. As usual at Du Pont such major adjustment and expansion depended heavily on long-range calculation, and from the time he assumed the presidency in 1940 Carpenter was determined to make the company more conscious about such preparation as part of the inculcation of learned routines.

Strategic planning was simply expected from the executive committee. In accordance with its decentralized structure, Du Pont had no corporate center or staff department for such planning. The development department came closest to such an agency, but it was in fact an investigating arm that awaited direction from the top. Its role depended heavily on the vision, personality, and interests of its director. Fin Sparre, who had succeeded Walter as head of the department, certainly had the aptitude and the energy, but his focus was often technical rather than corporate or managerial and he had no comprehensive authority. The impetus for much of the firm's growth came from the general managers of the industrial departments and from the executive committee on which Sparre never served. Sparre, for example, had not understood Carpenter's broader strategic arguments against Du Pont's manufacture of ethyl alcohol in 1925 and had not been a central figure in the battle over the expansion of ammonia production in the late 1930s.[51]

Walter had no interest in establishing a formal corporate office for strategic development. Such concentration was more common to General Motors, and it contradicted Du Pont's decentralized structure. Thus, he and the executive committee allowed the development department to assume a role emphasizing coordination, review, and monitoring after Sparre's retirement in 1944, for the company's success with nylon and (as we shall see) the impact of antitrust prosecution pointed toward internal sources for the firm's future growth.[52] As president, he revitalized the executive committee's role in strategic planning in order to strike a balance between a corporate bureau for long-term thinking and total abdication of that responsibility to the industrial departments. He encourged individual members like Angus Echols to assume such responsibility both as a way of attacking the serious problems of coping with World War II's disruption and with adjustment to the postwar world and as a means of reawakening and stimulating such constant examination on the part of other executive committee members.

Echols, whose career shadowed Walter's as treasurer, vice president for finance, member of the executive committee, and director of General Motors, firmly believed in long-range planning, eagerly desired to supply his own ideas, and enthusiastically pushed others to do the same. In early 1941 he called upon the development department to do a "comprehensive study" of the war's impact on Du Pont and of the inevitable postwar reconversion. He decried the current piecemeal response to problems, and because he feared a repeat of the depression that followed World War I, Echols asked for special attention to "the Company's commercial position after this chaotic period is over." In a series of continuous studies the development department would deal with immediate problems like the stockpiling of critical materials, the draft and manpower, and transportation, and with longer-term issues like the expansion of research for new products and the projection of capital requirements.[53]

Six months later Echols supplied his own broad analysis of Du Pont's product lines, which developed more systematically the strategic planning Carpenter had first promoted in the battle over expanding ammonia facilities in 1937 and 1939.[54] Echols divided the company into four stages that grouped its businesses by type or character: explosives, which were the firm's origin; the 1910–20 acquisitions in mechanical processing like plastics, paints and varnishes, rayon and cellophane, and later Remington; the purchase of patents and know-how in chemical manufacture during World War I and in the 1920s to develop such lines as dyestuffs, ammonia, and electrochemicals; and the commitment to original research after 1929 to bring out products like nylon and neoprene. Perhaps because of the war and Du Pont's heritage he said nothing about explosives. He condemned many of the mechanical operations as unprofitable or low return and called for their sale or termination while Du Pont expanded basic research and concentrated more carefully on chemical manufacture in the future.[55]

Carpenter kept the process fermenting by asking Echols to distribute the report to the executive committee, where lively debate ensued. Most agreed that Remington had been a mistake and that expanded research was essential, but critics pointed out that Echols' narrow focus on return on investment missed important linkages like rayon to nylon and paints and varnishes to synthetic paints. The war and inertia delayed any serious consideration of divesting product lines, but growth through expanded research did become Du Pont's major strategic tool after 1945.[56]

Planning also went forward in the development department. Even before Echols' first salvo, Carpenter had challenged Fin Sparre in December 1940, almost a year prior to Pearl Harbor, to begin studies of potential competition that might result from wartime tasks. Walter soon broadened the assignment to include the handling of returning employees from military service, the formulation of policy to direct postwar operations, guidelines for balancing commercial expansion and war work, the development of a pharmaceuticals line, and the suggestion of company routines for rationing and stockpiling key materials.[57]

Carpenter readily appreciated the impossibility of precise answers to specific problems in the face of fast-changing conditions in wartime. What he wanted from Sparre were broader proposals for policies that the executive committee could discuss and develop to focus and guide the many specific decisions to come. Although no such series of blueprints ever appeared, Sparre established a specific division for postwar planning in August 1941, and by 1943 Carpenter could report that the subject was getting "quite a good deal of attention." The development department's specific suggestions included further diversification by internal development of thermosetting plastics and the polymerization process and the expansion of Du Pont's research program.[58]

The growing convergence on research and development naturally led Walter to ask Elmer Bolton, the director of Du Pont's research, to develop a comprehensive approach. Although Carpenter continued as always to be an enthusiastic exponent of laboratory work, he explained to Bolton that in order to assure research "in greater quantity, with the greatest effectiveness, at the lowest cost," the director needed to bolster his plan with a general policy. Increased competition in the postwar world would surely compel Du Pont to "require more and more research for new and improved processes and products." But, "if research is done extravagantly, certainly less research can be afforded. Whereas what we want is more research—not less." Because basic research was to be Du Pont's major means of future growth, Bolton needed to answer "the fundamental question—where are we going, and why, and how?"[59]

Bolton never did find the magic formula to guide and discipline research and development, the recipe that has been sought in vain by the heads of all research-based enterprises. Nevertheless, his response did outline what became Du Pont's postwar program. He argued that because public and private research operations in the United States were going to explode, Du Pont had to move aggressively in the more competitive environment to recruit a strong staff. As a corollary, part of that effort had to be a major new facility for corporate-level work where basic research would be concentrated. Du Pont also had to maintain support for applied efforts to improve existing products and processes. Finally, it needed to expand resources for basic research in order to develop new products, to attract good people, and to insure continued growth and leadership.[60]

By 1943 a framework of general plans had matured sufficiently so that Carpenter and the executive committee could insist that the industrial departments assume the burden of their own planning in accordance with Du Pont's decentralized approach. Each department was responsible for establishing a study group and for submitting quarterly reports of its progress to the executive committee. Soon thereafter the finance committee directed the treasurer to provide assistance with analyses of postwar financial challenges like plant appraisal and reevaluation, adjustment in depreciation rates and reserves, and write-off of good will.[61]

Although Walter was not responsible for such plans, he carefully reviewed them to encourage long-range thinking and to assure consistency with broader corporate goals. Thus, when the organic department considered the manufacture of olefines and moving into petrochemicals, General Manager E. G. Robinson proposed to locate the new facility adjacent to the Du Pont's Chambers Works in New Jersey in order to reduce initial costs. Carpenter asked him if such concentration would also increase the risks of fire, labor strikes, and "capricious legislation." In addition, he pointed out that getting into petroleum cracking might become a big investment and in the long run location would assume prime importance. "Our initial plant should be located at a point which will prove fundamentally sound for a long period of years to come, in the face of considerable enlargement."[62]

Such signals from the president and the executive committee helped free general managers from the immediate burden of return-on-investment benchmarks if they thought their plans worthwhile. These guidelines characteristically promoted the extended view and growth that Carpenter so appreciated and that contrasted sharply with the techniques of number-driven, bottom-line management so prized by Robert McNamara, Tex Thornton, and the succeeding generation of American management.[63] As usual with Walter Carpenter and the Du Pont Company, financial and statistical data served as the starting point for deliberations.

Du Pont's reward for Walter's planning process was a rapid and orderly adjustment to the postwar world despite unanticipated challenges and considerable uncertainty. Disengagement from wartime production for the government moved quickly and smoothly. Following the abrupt surrender of Germany in May 1945, only one industrial department suffered any unexpected drop in business. The company quickly refocused on its primary chemical lines by paring its munitions business and abandoning the plants it had built and operated for the government with the exception of an important neoprene facility in Louisville, Kentucky, which it acquired after persistent negotiation. The firm's annual report for 1945 noted serenely that reconversion of commercial operations went forward "with a minimum of disruption."[64]

Despite opposition from the U.S. government, disengagement from work on nuclear weapons also proceeded as planned. General Groves and Secretary of War Robert Patterson strongly pressured Du Pont to continue its operations at Hanford. Patterson viewed withdrawal as a "great material loss to the project and the nation," while Groves urged the company to remain on the job "in the interests of the national welfare."[65] In addition, there was the attraction of the company's pioneering advantage in an unknown but promising field.

Du Pont never wavered as its top executives and technical men united behind the position Walter Carpenter had assumed from the outset. Crawford Greenewalt, Roger Williams, and Elmer Bolton reported that commercial potential lay largely in power generation, an expensive and risky possibility far removed from the company's chemical businesses. To Walter and other members of the executive committee, atomic fission remained unattractive because of its close association with the military and the strong government regulation involved. Carpenter's letter to the stockholders after the dropping of the bomb in August 1945 took a deliberately low-key approach, emphasizing Du Pont's participation as part of the national emergency without profits or patents. Walter led the firm's graceful exit by cooperating in a major conference with the War Department to discuss the timing and feasibility of Soviet development of the bomb and by agreeing to a temporary extension of operations at Hanford until General Electric, Du Pont's successor, was prepared to take over. The company quietly withdrew at the end of 1946 as scheduled.[66]

Postwar expansion also moved quickly if not always smoothly as Du Pont immediately launched a huge construction program to provide new or improved capacity for its promising and high-profit products like nylon, neoprene, and cellophane. To accelerate action the executive and finance committees dropped wartime targets for return on investment from 25 to 20 percent on established lines and from 20 to 15 percent on new products. The 1945 annual report enthusiastically trumpeted the beginning of thirty-five major projects as part of an unprecedented $342 million building campaign (which included about $25 million for a new research station) planned for the next three years. Funding was readily available, largely from Du Pont's careful retention of earnings and maintenance of generous reserve funds throughout the war. The corporation also raised approximately $70 million in 1947 by the sale of 700,000 shares from an authorized issue of one million shares of $3.50 preferred stock that sold out quickly at 102.[67] (The remainder of the issue was used to initiate an employee pension program.)

By the end of 1948 Du Pont's annual report proudly announced that work was "substantially completed" after the expenditure of $299 million. By previous measures the effort was prodigious, almost equaling total construction outlays for the nine years before 1946. The $115.6 million spent in 1947 alone (which was quickly surpassed in 1948) exceeded the entire amount for 1942–45 and more than doubled building outlays for any previous year in the company's history.[68]

Despite the claim of virtual completion, however, much remained to be done, including the erection of the new corporate research facility. Under Carpenter's leadership Du Pont became more cautious by late 1946 and began deferring less essential projects. The executive committee asked the general managers of the industrial departments to defer 25 to 30 percent of the total amount already committed and told them to expect a 20 percent deferral for 1947. The executive and finance committees also agreed to reduce annual dividends from their eighteen-year average of 88 percent to no more than 75 percent of earnings while setting up a special reserve account of 20 percent of all construction outlays.[69]

The sudden caution was triggered by rapid inflation as the federal government removed wartime price controls and by the escalation of wage rates, labor militancy, and strikes. To executives who recalled the nation's experiences after World War I, the apparently wild upheaval was a repetition of the short spurt of 1919–20 that preceded the abysmal depression of 1921–22. Although the alarms were first sounded only by the ultracautious Angus Echols, by late 1946 Carpenter and the entire leadership at Du Pont were alerted as project costs ran way over

budget and reports of slipshod work were widespread. The retrench-
ments implemented in 1947 received the executive committee's unanimous endorsement.[70]

Like his colleagues Walter Carpenter was equally disturbed by growing labor conflict and the increasing power of unions. Unfortunately,
his lack of experience in worker relations meant that he offered no
insight or perceptive leadership. In his few administrative positions
before becoming president he had directed only small numbers of
professional and clerical employees and had almost no contact with
blue-collar wage earners. He was virulently antiunion like the du Pont
brothers and other top company executives, who had succeeded in
limiting membership in national unions represented by the American
Federation of Labor (AFL) and the Congress of Industrial Organization (CIO) to only 9 percent of all du Pont employees.[71]

By 1946 Walter was uncharacteristically bitter and extreme in his
views of unions. In a private letter to his Uncle Ed he compared labor
leaders to Chinese war lords and unions to gangs. In more temperate
language to Irving Ives, a congressman and a former colleague on the
board of trustees at Cornell University, Carpenter suggested that wage
earners were getting too large a share of industrial output and that the
power of organized workers had so pyramided that it could "practically
throttle the industrial activity of this great country for considerable
periods." The nation's laws and their administration had become so
"one-sided" toward labor that he labeled them "un-American." In his
mind the power of unions certainly contributed to rigidity in wage rates
and to inflation.[72]

Carpenter's inexperience precluded empirical evidence to balance
his ideological bias. His characteristic suggestion that Du Pont establish
a systematic, company-wide labor policy was quickly rejected by his
wiser colleagues. Du Pont had avoided heavy inroads by the AFL and
CIO precisely by working on a plant-by-plant basis to encourage less
aggressive independent unions, which currently enrolled about 80 percent of company employees.[73]

Nevertheless, Walter's sound business judgment prevented excessive
financial conservatism, the bitter memories of the 1921 depression,
and the fears of labor power from hamstringing Du Pont's prepara-
tions for the burgeoning postwar market. His broad, long-range approach to business management led him to reject Angus Echols' timid,
bottom-line analysis. As chairman of the executive committee he supported a series of decisions that balanced the firm's commercial needs

with financial prudence. Disaggregating important from less critical projects allowed Du Pont to stretch out its construction program so that building could go forward for facilities vital to securing major new markets and meeting existing demand for proprietary, high-profit items like nylon and cellophane. Less promising items could wait a year or two as the company's financial reserves accumulated and its understanding of the economy's direction grew clearer.

The special reserve account for 20 percent of construction costs was an especially good example of long-range planning. In arguing the case to Pierre in May 1947, Walter readily admitted that high wage rates, inflated materials costs, and inefficient building practices boosted the fixed costs of production in new facilities, which an economic contraction might not sustain. On the other hand, Du Pont could not afford to delay essential construction. The extraordinary reserve assured a supply of funds that could be applied to lower fixed costs on the new facilities if fears of a slump were borne out. If there were no depression, accelerated depreciation would cover the "extra" costs over time and recapture the cash currently being set aside.[74]

The strategy worked. Crawford Greenewalt, who succeeded Walter Carpenter as president of Du Pont in January 1948, later remarked that there was no conflict or problem caused by deferring part of the firm's postwar construction. He reauthorized the postponed projects, including $25 million for the new research station, and the $116.7 million spent in 1948 was little more than the $115.6 million for 1947. Outlays for 1949 dropped about one-quarter as the economy finally cooled off in a weak recession instead of the major depression that Echols, Carpenter, and the older executives had so feared. More to the point, the postwar construction program that Walter had helped plan and implement sustained a decade of extraordinary growth and profits for the enterprise after his retirement.[75]

One area of Du Pont where Walter Carpenter made little contribution was the corporation's foreign business—even though a major expansion of multinational enterprise characterized much of American big business in the years after World War II. As noted in chapter 2, at least part of the explanation lay in the marginal importance of overseas business to the Du Pont Company as well as to Carpenter himself. Du Pont had historically focused on its domestic market because of the power and technological preeminence of European chemical firms dating from the nineteenth century.[76]

In the 1920s two huge combines, I. G. Farben of Germany and

Imperial Chemical Industries (ICI) of Great Britain, had emerged as dominant competitors at home and abroad. Du Pont's exports were never more than 6 percent of total sales before 1950, and with a few minor exceptions the firm had no operations outside the Western Hemisphere. Furthermore, its plants in Canada and South America were usually joint ventures with ICI as a result of a series of patent and process agreements with the British giant and its predecessors that had arranged for the exchange of patents and know-how and for the allocation of international markets since 1897.[77]

In effect, Du Pont agreed informally with I. G. Farben and formally with ICI to stay out of Europe, where the competition was fierce, while the two international giants restricted their stakes in the United States. So marginal were its overseas investments that Du Pont had not developed a true international division as did most U.S. multinationals. The foreign relations department, which dated from 1930, advised on and helped coordinate foreign business, but actual control of operations remained with the general managers of the industrial departments.[78]

Walter Carpenter's approach to overseas business paralleled his firm's experiences. As a matter of general public policy he supported a high tariff, had little interest in expanding the nation's exports, and after 1945 was unenthusiastic about foreign aid. Within Du Pont itself he strongly affirmed the autonomy and control of the industrial departments over foreign operations. He was reluctant to accept local partners in order to facilitate expansion. He supported Du Pont's expansion into Canada and Latin America, but was at times cautious about political instability in the latter region. In 1946, for example, he opposed the extension of Du Pont's business in Argentina partially because of the hostility of Juan Peron's government.[79]

More restrictive was his application of Du Pont's standards for domestic expansion to overseas enterprise. In 1942 he overruled a recommendation by Wendell Swint, head of the firm's foreign relations department, to establish a heavy chemicals facility in Brazil. As he explained the decision, the issue was not local opportunity but his continuing emphasis on a general policy that focused on competitive advantage. The company's chances for "outstanding success" lay "not in undertaking those enterprises which all can enter, but rather to enter those industries which, due to our own peculiar talents or proficiencies or resources, will be less competitive." Du Pont had many expenses uncommon to other firms such as "heavy overhead, research, etc." To compensate for such costs, the concern needed "a larger profit which can be gained only in those industries requiring the exercise of extraordinary capacities. The Heavy Chemicals Industry is at the bottom of the list."[80] The plant was not built.

Carpenter's interests in European markets were equally tenuous. He made just two trips to Europe in the 1920s and 1930s, and had only weak ties to ICI before 1940. In the two decades before World War II, periodic negotiations with the British firm and its forerunners were dominated by technical men and led by each company's chief executive officer, Sir (later Lord) Harry McGowan at ICI and first Irénée and then Lammot du Pont for the Du Pont Company. As a vice president Carpenter participated in the determination of strategy and in conferences held in the United States, but he was not a major figure. Nevertheless, he certainly supported the patents and processes agreements of 1929 and 1939 to obtain the benefits of shared research and to assure stable and profitable market arrangements.

As Du Pont's president Carpenter pursued a policy of general toleration of the status quo in the firm's foreign business while permitting a slow drift toward separation from ICI. In part, external circumstances dictated his approach, for the distractions and disturbances of World War II naturally dampened overseas activities for most American multinationals. In addition, the relationship between the giant American and British firms was shifting. With the Du Pont Company's commitment to basic research in the 1930s, its startling successes with products like nylon and moistureproof cellophane, and its emergence as the United States's leading chemical company between 1920 and 1940, the firm had become a major power and ICI's equal.[81]

Not unnaturally, friction grew between the two giants. At ICI technical men and junior managers resented what they called Du Pont's arrogance in insisting that nylon was an extraordinary invention to be handled on terms more favorable to the American company outside the general agreement on patents and processes. The two companies also disagreed about strategy in Canada and Latin America. As previously noted, Du Pont advocated a selective policy of complete control, heavy reinvestment, and competitive advantage based on the manufacture of proprietary, high value-added products. ICI was more aggressive and expansionist, more willing to accept local partners, and more concerned about keeping prices up and maximizing immediate revenues than about dropping prices for long-run increases in volume and profits.[82]

Further disagreement emerged during World War II over Du Pont's handling of polyethylene plastic, first developed by ICI as polythene. The British felt that the Americans did not properly appreciate its importance, claimed too much credit for their own contributions in its evolution in order to avoid its treatment as a special product comparable to nylon, and were tardy in its promotion. The ICI people had at least some justification for their views. Du Pont had to be pushed by the U.S. government and ICI early in the war to begin production of polyethylene for insulating radar cable. In addition, the American company failed to capitalize on its initial advantages in the U.S. market and let Union Carbide assume leadership in the new field of polyethylene plastics.[83]

As president, Walter Carpenter maintained a cordial relationship with Lord McGowan and helped dampen the disputes among the junior men, but he offered no strategic innovation or leadership as he did in other fields like planning, postwar conversion, and atomic fission. The two chief executives' frequent and lengthy letters inquired anxiously about the fate of family in wartime, and Carpenter and his associates sent informal "care packages" of scarce consumer items to their more straitened British counterparts. He and McGowan also agreed to postpone thorny negotiations about the final determination of polyethylene royalties until more congenial face-to-face meetings were possible after the war.[84]

Meanwhile, Walter urged his own men to take a calmer, long-term view of the polyethylene issue. He wrote Jasper Crane, his colleague on the executive committee who had special oversight of foreign business, that the polyethylene matter had "reached a stage where it is desirable to stop and take stock of the facts and policies involved to insure avoidance of any controversy. The whole matter is at most but an incident in a relationship extending over a half century—a relationship of great importance to both parties. Our position should be one that conforms to the spirit of that relationship and that encourages its perpetuation."[85] Du Pont's subsequent acceptance of the new product's special status and of a temporary sliding scale of royalties beginning at 5 percent allowed full-scale production for the war effort.[86]

The friendship between McGowan and Carpenter helped maintain cooperation whose advantages went far beyond access to a single new product. Each firm worked with the other to cut through the inevitable red tape of wartime regulations. Du Pont, for example, helped expedite the flow of information to ICI, which was provided by the patents and processes agreement of 1939 but was obstructed by the American government's new regulations on the export of technical data.[87]

Carpenter let the uneasy alliance continue to drift along in peacetime. Royalty disputes for 1934–39, which had not been settled because of the war's outbreak, were quickly resolved; disagreements about the 1940–44 period required more protracted negotiation. Du Pont, which had supplied ICI with commercial products that the British company could not manufacture for its own markets in wartime, made no attempt to follow up its advantage and to penetrate European markets opened by the defeat of Germany and desolation of Great Britain. Walter's visit to Europe in 1946 left him so disheartened about conditions that he was not inclined to seize any long-term opportunity.[88]

Nevertheless, the weakening of personal ties due to the impending retirement of Carpenter and McGowan, the shifting relative strengths of the two firms, and the upheaval in world markets caused by the war virtually assured a new relationship between Du Pont and ICI, which Walter made no concerted attempt to tackle. In part this failure was due to his disinterest and to the challenges of conversion to peacetime markets. Equally important, however, was an additional factor unanticipated when he became president: the role of antitrust.

Limits to Power: Public Policy and Age

Walter Carpenter did a fine job of keeping the Du Pont on its course despite the distractions and disruptions of World War II. War, however, was not the only force that affected his leadership at Du Pont; public policy was equally important in restricting and defining his alternatives.

Much of the increased government regulation of business was a direct result of the world war. Although "normal profits" by prewar standards were taxed at 40 percent, the federal government demanded 95 percent of "excess profits" (which reflected in part recovery from depression levels). A postwar credit for 10 percent of the taxes on excess profits softened the blow only slightly, but Carpenter readily conceded that in the case of war-induced gains on existing investment, "a very high tax on such profits seems not unreasonable."[89]

Returns were also significantly reduced by contract renegotiation, the result of 1942 federal legislation based on the premise that the unprecedented volume of war contracts justified much lower profit margins than in peacetime. In Du Pont's case, the adjustment was severe, totaling nearly $100 million. In 1942, for example, renegotiation captured $21.9 million, more than 40 percent of the firm's profits for the year, and return on sales correspondingly dropped from 28.6 percent to 15.3 percent.[90]

By 1944 the company had adjusted to the new regulation with special reserves and estimated interim payments in advance because individual contract prices were paid in full and the degree of rebating was determined only retroactively after considerable calculation and negotiation. Carpenter and Du Pont did not complain, of course, since they recognized that higher tax rates and renegotiation were essential, legitimate means to help assure that business bore its share of the war's costs. Nevertheless, the impact on profits was considerable. Return on operating investment exceeded 9 percent in 1940 and 1941, Carpenter's first two years as president, and surpassed the average for the 1925–29 predepression period. During the war years between 1942 and 1945, it averaged only 5.9 percent.[91]

The burden of government regulation and red tape was not limited to national and state governments in the United States. Because of his firm's agreements with ICI, Carpenter found himself involved in protracted discussions about patent and royalty rights with the British. When W. F. Lutyens of ICI suggested that Du Pont forego all royalties on nylon to the British government during the conflict, Wendell Swint, director of the foreign relations department, angrily rejected what he called "confiscatory action." Carpenter's more reasoned response proposed that ICI and Du Pont follow the American firm's policy with the U.S. government: in both countries rights and royalties would be enforced for operations funded by the chemical companies' own investments, but no charges would be made when public money was being used for the war effort. Thus, each enterprise would be assured of a normal return for its efforts so that its contribution of that profit to the war effort could be subsequently determined by general law and tax policy.[92]

Although McGowan thought the solution "broad and statesmanlike," the British government's reliance on mixed enterprise complicated the case and any calculations because of the simultaneous use of public and private funds in old and new plants with output going both to the government and to third parties for further processing. This particular instance involved a contract between the Ministry of Aircraft Production (MAP) and British Nylon Spinners (BNS), which called for

BNS operation of its own plant on the basis of cost plus a fixed return to capital. The MAP planned to insert a standard clause denying any royalty charges to cost and leaving the calculation of patent rights to later determination by public tribunal. BNS then asked ICI to drop its claims to royalties on nylon and ICI in turn sought relief from Du Pont, suggesting that each firm represent its partner's best interests to its home government but not be intransigent.[93]

Recognizing the need for accommodation of varying government practices, Carpenter accepted the proposal in order to expedite production and to avoid charges of profiteering. ICI negotiated so well on Du Pont's behalf, however, that the MAP tried an end run, and the American company soon received a deceptively simple letter from a ministry bureaucrat blandly requesting a blanket surrender of all royalties for "any Nylon material which is required by the United Kingdom entirely for the purposes of the present war."[94]

Walter patiently restated Du Pont's practice in the United States, which distinguished between public and private capital, and noted that Du Pont treated a patent as part of its capital on which it normally received a return in its own plant. He smoothly ducked any controversy by conceding that he did not wish to be in "the awkward position of having made more favorable arrangements with the British Government than with our own" and by suggesting that the MAP deal with the ICI as Du Pont's representative.[95] Throughout the entire episode he pragmatically and flexibly accepted public constraints on his and Du Pont's power while clearly making his best case and warding off unnecessary and potentially damaging controversy.

Although wartime regulation was intrusive, time-consuming, and costly, the federal government's antitrust attacks on the Du Pont Company during Carpenter's presidency had far more serious, long-term consequences. Between 1939 and 1946 the antitrust division of the U.S. Department of Justice launched fifteen suits against Du Pont; in 1948, the year of Walter's retirement, there were nineteen. The company was a defendant or co-defendant in cases involving a wide variety of industries, including explosives, nitrogen, dyestuffs, titanium pigments, plastics, acids and heavy chemicals, paints, vitamin D, and brake fluid.[96]

As the wave of charges poured in, Carpenter wearily accepted the unwonted burden to the firm's already heavy workload and presided over a mixed strategy of delay, negotiation, resistance, and settlement in order to limit damage. At times, however, a bitter anger boiled to the surface over charges and proceedings he thought unfair, irrational, and politically motivated. A 1952 speech best summarized his hostility:

> With the budget of the Antitrust Division multiplied many times squads of investigators, armed with subpoenas swarmed through the files of our large corporations for ammunition to present to congressional committees, to bleat from [the] platform and to promulgate through the press in [a] demagogic effort to arouse public antagonism. To intensify the virulence of the assaults and frighten the victims criminal indictments were brought even though the alleged offenses were regarded as being of a civil character.[97]

Privately, he described the stream of cases as a "constant persecution from Washington" against Du Pont and as part of a Democratic plot to embarrass big business supporters of the Republican Party.[98]

His accusations were probably correct in some particular instances, but they did not explain the general campaign as he himself admitted in calmer moments. In the explosives case, for example, after a grand jury in Norfolk, Virginia, refused to issue a complaint, the Justice Department took what one authority on antitrust described as "the extraordinary step" of going to a Philadelphia grand jury where it was successful.[99] In addition, two of the most sensational cases, involving Du Pont's relationship with ICI and its holdings in General Motors, were propitiously filed in the election years of 1944 and 1948.

Nevertheless, the charges against Du Pont were not especially targeted but were part of a large-scale resuscitation of antitrust in the late 1930s. After 1936 Franklin's Roosevelt's New Deal shifted away from attempts at economic planning and an associative state to a strategy based on extensive government regulation of a flawed and still failing economy. Under Thurman Arnold the staff of the antitrust division quadrupled and its appropriations quintupled. It launched 177 cases between 1938 and 1942, almost one-half the pre-1938 total. Despite a lull during World War II, 157 new cases were initiated in the five years after the war ended.[100]

At the same time legislation like the Robinson-Patman Act and the Miller-Tydings Act as well as vigorous prosecution led to strengthened antitrust law. Successful attacks on the traditional rule of reason narrowed the behavior permitted under reasonable restraint of trade, and conspiracy became easier to prove. In the case of oligopoly, the definition of workable competition relied increasingly on structural arguments based on the number of firms, their size, and their market share at the expense of defendants' performance-based arguments, which depended on outcomes like lower costs and prices, higher outputs, and new products and processes to legitimate questionable practices. The Justice Department also turned more frequently to criminal suits, the subpoena power, and contempt of court citations, which facilitated investigation and bolstered enforcement with an increase in the personal attacks and indictments that Carpenter so detested.[101]

As a careful observer of changes in law and public policy because of their importance for Du Pont, Carpenter understood the investigations and the charges even if he did not like them. Public officials' irrational posturing, exaggeration, and nitpicking over practices often insignificant or already abandoned certainly irritated a manager who had always depended so heavily on the reasoned, pragmatic, long-term view, but such behavior was part of the democratic process that he firmly supported. He noted that "sometimes it becomes very discouraging; other times I think perhaps we must recognize that such things are to be expected and we should not take them too seriously." Criminal charges against Lammot and himself were "a part of that burden which all of us are called upon to bear in one form or another under present conditions, and we will try to carry on withal." On another occasion, after complaining privately to his son Sam, he admitted that the administration and the Justice Department were "well within their rights" and that Du Pont did not have "any complaint."[102]

The professional executive's conclusions today seem fairly obvious and unremarkable. Nevertheless, they differed sharply from the political extremes pursued by Pierre, Irénée, and Lammot in the previous decade, and they once again demonstrated the manager's willingness to curb personal views because of their potentially harmful consequences for the firm he served.

At the same time, Carpenter realized that precisely because the antitrust movement was so comprehensive, Du Pont was not being singled out. The large and unprecedented number of cases against one firm resulted directly from its successful strategy of diversification. A company located in so many industries was especially vulnerable when Thurman Arnold inaugurated a practice of "industry-wide" prosecutions.[103] Typically, Walter kept an often revised scorecard toting up the results of the cases as a means of maintaining a comprehensive view in the midst of frequent discussions in the executive and finance committees, numerous consultations with corporate and outside counsel, and sometimes detailed preparation for testimony.[104]

Patience, persistence, and the expenditure of the necessary funds for gathering data and employing excellent outside counsel like future Secretary of State Dean Acheson helped Du Pont deal quite effectively with most of its cases. Astute references to its extensive and vital war work for the government quickly persuaded Secretary of War Henry Stimson to arrange for postponement of many of the suits until after the war. Delay dissipated early sensational and inaccurate charges of collaboration with the Germans via agreements with I. G. Farben and allowed the firm to benefit from the considerable public applause for its contributions to victory. Du Pont also understood more clearly the costs of failure to resist when the Internal Revenue Service threatened to stop refunds of overpayments on excess profits taxes because of what it termed illegal profits due to antitrust charges. As a result the firm decided to fight the paint and varnish prosecution even though its co-defendants pleaded nolo contendere.[105] Both postponement and the victory in the paint case helped Carpenter and the company realize that some aspects of the government's expanded role could be used to offset other parts.

In 1946 Carpenter proudly noted that twelve of fifteen suits had been resolved with little damage to the firm. An independent study reported subsequently that in three cases—dyes, explosives, and acids and heavy chemicals—Du Pont pleaded nolo contendere and accepted small fines. In the nitrogen proceedings it accepted a consent decree and in the pigments suit it agreed to minor adjustments in its practices. It won the paints and plastics trials and saw the vitamin D and brake fluid litigation dismissed or dropped. Most of the criminal indictments were also thrown out or abandoned though a few resulted in small fines, none of which involved Carpenter.[106]

Two major charges brought during Walter's presidency remained to be settled after his retirement. In the cellophane case filed in 1947 Du Pont won a resounding victory in 1953, which the U.S. Supreme Court upheld three years later. Accepting the company's performance-based argument, trial judge Paul Leahy ruled that "the facts destroy the charges." The firm's $90 million annual business and its market share of more than 75 percent had come not simply from its original purchase of patent rights but from its innovations and improvements like moistureproof cellophane and from a production and pricing strategy that rapidly increased output and reduced prices. In effect, it had increased competition by developing products that contended with other wrapping materials like wax paper.[107]

The ICI case, which was filed in 1944 and decided in 1951, had a much less happy result and was Du Pont's first major defeat in its antitrust battles since 1911.[108] Walter Carpenter played a major role in the process and was partially responsible for the decision to accept a trial rather than a negotiated settlement. He cajoled Lord McGowan in hopes that compromises in patent and marketing agreements and in joint ventures would win acceptance from the Justice Department. To protect the company's patent and royalty rights on nylon, its major concern in the case, he visited ICI in London in 1946 to push through a more liberalized agreement on the firm's very profitable synthetic fiber. Other adjustments included revised arrangements with Canadian Industries Limited (CIL) and for less restrictive licensing terms for polyethylene plastic. Finally, he closely monitored and assessed the progress of negotiations with the Justice Department in 1946 and 1947.[109]

When discussions stalled in late 1947, Carpenter and the executive committee decided to face a court battle rather than accept the government's demand for royalty-free licenses for nylon. Significantly, their concern was the protection of the domestic market of their very profitable fiber because they were willing to compromise on all aspects of the ICI relationship, including the patents and processes agreement that Crawford Greenewalt renegotiated in 1948 prior to going to trial. By 1946 and 1947 Walter recognized the strong possibility of defeat because of past joint arrangements for control of markets and technology, changing antitrust law, and McGowan's growing intransigence. He predictably took the long-term view and pushed contingency plans for splitting up the cooperative ventures in 1947, though he had to accept the British executive's refusal to discuss the profitable CIL enterprise.[110]

Confirming the expected, the final judgment relied on a structural analysis that emphasized easily proven collusion at the expense of Du Pont's claims of beneficial impact. It found that Du Pont and ICI "were engaged in a combination and conspiracy in restraint of trade and commerce in chemical products, sporting arms and ammunition" in the United States and elsewhere. Judge Sylvester Ryan therefore ordered the breakup of the joint ventures including CIL and abrogated the patents and processes agreement of 1939 as well as its predecessors and the recently renegotiated arrangements for nylon and polyethylene. The harmful defeat meant that Du Pont faced serious competition from foreign firms in its domestic market, lost the advantages of cooperative research with a major partner, and had to build its own international business from scratch.[111]

Nevertheless, Carpenter could find some solace in the verdict and the results. He and other top executives named in the suit were personally vindicated and indictments against them were eventually dropped. Judge Ryan noted that "no charge is made of monopoly, or of unscrupulous practices in dealings with competitors. These individuals committed no acts of personal wrong calling for censure or condemnation."[112] In addition, Walter's pretrial work helped smooth the required breakup of the joint ventures. Furthermore, although the verdict compelled the compulsory licensing of all products involved in the patent agreements, including nylon and neoprene, Du Pont retained the right to charge royalties at market rates. Finally, the historian of ICI argues that the decision only formalized an existing ad hoc policy of drift toward separation.[113] In any event, although Carpenter's last major task before retirement as president resulted in a serious defeat, he had helped Du Pont minimize the penalty of the almost predictable outcome.

However, the impact of the antitrust cases during Carpenter's presidency was much broader than the terms of the ICI decision. Public policy significantly altered Du Pont's behavior and limited its tactical and strategic alternatives. In preparation for existing cases and for fear of future charges Du Pont began terminating its joint enterprises with other large firms, including the production of refrigerants with General Motors in the Kinetic Chemicals Company and the manufacture of tetraethyl lead for gasoline with the Ethyl Corporation as well as the dissolution of its South American ventures with ICI. It also limited expansion of sodium and cellophane capacity for fear of monopoly charges.[114]

For the same reason it made four thousand patents (two-thirds of its holdings) available for license in 1949 and increased the number to five thousand two years later. In addition, Du Pont aggressively sought to establish major competitors such as Olin Industries, Chemstrand, W. R. Grace and Company, and National Distillers Products Corporation in industries like nylon, cellophane, and sodium where it had a large if not a monopoly share of the market. As Carpenter explained the situation in the cellophane case, "We . . . have our choice of monopoly under Government control or freedom of competition without."[115]

The largest impact, however, was the restriction of strategies for future growth. The ICI decision and other cases virtually ruled out joint ventures and mergers as a means of acquiring new products and processes or of establishing new industrial departments. Walter Carpenter, who had helped arrange the Arlington and Grasselli purchases and the rayon and cellophane agreements with the Comptoir, certainly appreciated the historical importance of such techniques as well as their value in providing flexible paths for expansion. Nevertheless, as early as 1941 he remarked publicly that "the trend of political thought in this country over recent years and perhaps for some years to come, may be to discourage the enlargement of our activities by the acquisition of other companies." He thought it important "to attempt to organize our forces and our efforts for the future in anticipation of not having these sources of new developments."[116]

That belief was a critical factor in his support for concentration on primary research and internal development for future growth as part of the long-range planning process that he sponsored during his presidency. By 1945 the strategy was supported by Crawford Greenewalt, Carpenter's eventual successor, who called for expansion of fundamental research because "growth by acquisition seems certain to become a less important factor in the Company's progress." The ironic result was that during the next two decades Du Pont became more inward looking as it grew more conscious of external forces, probably to its ultimate detriment.[117]

After coping with the impact of war and more intrusive public policy during nearly eight years as president, Walter Carpenter confronted passing time and advancing age, which inevitably limited even the most successful business careers. Typically, he started to plan for his retirement and succession at the beginning of his tenure as chief executive, although once again results did not quite evolve as intended.

His timing was nearly perfect. After becoming president in 1940 he reviewed the record of Du Pont's previous four chief executives and noted that they had retired at fifty-one, forty-nine, forty-nine, and fifty-nine. Because he was then fifty-two and because he devoutly believed in turnover and in relative youth at the top, he "planned that, if the Directors should care to bear with me that long, I would turn over the Presidency to my successor in the spring of 1948."[118] In fact, his retirement was moved up four months to January 1948 because of ill health.

However, Carpenter's expectations for a successor did not work out as intended. From the outset Walter saw his appointment as a watershed between leadership by family members and by professional managers. He wrote his brother Ruly in 1942 that the day of owner-operators had passed. Pierre, Irénée, and Lammot were men of "great energy, great industry and great ability" who "not only directed [the company's] affairs in a broad way" as owners but "actually constituted the nucleus of the operating management of the Company." Inevitably they became less active with age but remained "interested and sufficiently informed" to benefit the enterprise with "counsel, advice, influence and great moral strength." Now, he thought, "we are, unfortunately, in the last quarter of that game," and prudence clearly required anticipation.[119]

The solution would be future presidents like himself, men with long experience in the company and with holdings of Du Pont stock that comprised a major portion of their estates, though they were not significant owners of the firm, as the du Ponts were. He referred to the process as "active" or "operating management" as opposed to "owner-management" and obviously based his expectations on the heritage of the company's executive bonus plans for identifying, rewarding, and retaining top people since Pierre became president in 1915. Walter resisted the term "professional management," because in his mind it conjured up images of consulting firms that temporarily operated a bank's acquisitions. In addition, he may have been reacting against the criticism of self-interested salaried executives and of the separation of ownership and operation in large-scale enterprise that had surfaced in the 1930s. Nevertheless, what he meant were professional managers whose experience and stake in the firm assured their knowledge, ability, and commitment.[120]

He certainly did not anticipate succession by a member of the du Pont family, either by blood or by marriage, because although the generation following Pierre, Irénée, and Lammot was large and still closely linked by family ties, none of its members had the "extraordinary capacity" to hold top positions in a large, complex enterprise such as Du Pont had become in the twentieth century. Nevertheless, by virtue of their holdings of Du Pont stock, the most able of such men had the power and the duty to participate in the oversight of the company as members of the board of directors and the finance committee. (Like most other executives of his time, Walter never expected women to be seriously involved in business.) He explained to Ruly that in such positions they could learn the business, make informed judgments, and come to know those "actually in control of the operating management of the Company." He had in mind men like Crawford Greenewalt, a du Pont descendant and Irénée's son-in-law, and Lammot du Pont Copeland, nephew of Pierre, Irénée, and Lammot, who were currently under consideration for just such positions.[121]

Once again the Second World War upset Carpenter's plans and limited his options. Unlike his predecessors Walter apparently had no particular candidate in mind as his successor. Because Lammot had remained as president for so long, most of Walter's contemporaries on the executive committee were already too old or would be elderly when he retired. Thus, he expected that a replacement would come from among the new appointees made early in his administration. However, the press of wartime business kept older senior executives in place until mandatory retirement while it pushed forward Crawford Greenewalt, whom Carpenter had consigned simply to family representation on the finance committee and the board of directors.

Greenewalt, who had begun a promising career in Du Pont's laboratories in 1922 after earning an engineering degree at MIT, was thought by his boss to have "to an unusual degree, a combination of research and executive ability," but was also reputed to be happy with laboratory work. His appointment at the age of forty in 1942 as technical director for Du Pont's work on the Manhattan Project demonstrated his broad view and his ability to handle people and brought him into close, regular contact with Walter Carpenter, who for the first time appreciated the young man's executive talents.[122]

When the project ended in 1945, Carpenter, who faced retirement in three years with no obvious successor, immediately put Greenewalt through a crash course to test his fitness for top management. In short order, he served effectively as assistant director of the development department and as assistant general manager of the pigments department, became director of CIL, and went to London for discussions with Lord McGowan. Walter was so pleased with Crawford's performance that in 1946 he proposed Greenewalt for promotion to vice president and membership on the executive committee, where the president thought "that, with this wider scope for the employment of his talents, he will serve the Company in progressively increased measure."[123]

Within a year Greenewalt's thoughtful contributions in committee discussions and his astute observations in a report to the president on Du Pont's long-range future growth caused Carpenter to urge the younger man's promotion as vice chairman of the executive committee.[124] This informal recognition of Crawford's selection as Du Pont's next president became official at the age of forty-five in the following January, when Walter announced his retirement as chief executive to become chairman of the board after thirty-eight years with the company.

Walter Carpenter's presidency was a microcosm of his entire experience with Du Pont. He had entered a large, thriving firm, and by applying long-term planning and systematic, pragmatic analysis he had succeeded in making it bigger and more prosperous. Typically, his administration was not dramatic, but it was impressive despite war and government attack. Between 1940 and 1948 the company's sales almost tripled to $968.7 million and its total assets jumped almost 70 percent to $1.59 billion. Wartime excess profits taxes and contract renegotiation policies make profits difficult to judge but in 1946 and 1947 average operating income as a share of operating investment again exceeded 9 percent as it had in the first two years of Carpenter's presidency, a level that surpassed the annual average for the last five years of the prosperous 1920s. The firm was so cash rich that retained earnings financed more than three-quarters of its huge postwar expansion and still left reserves one-quarter above the corporation's standard, comfortable margin while generous dividends annually exceeded 70 percent of net income. The product line remained vital and growing, for in 1947 $450 million, 58 percent of sales, resulted from products developed after 1928.[125]

There were questions and areas of uncertainty. Du Pont's leadership was aging, with members of its executive committee averaging in the mid-fifties after 1945, ten years higher than the level after World War I. Although net sales grew an impressive 236 percent between 1939 and 1948, that achievement ranked Du Pont only fifteenth among the growth rates of twenty-seven chemical companies with sales over $20 million in 1948.[126] The restriction of the development department's role in strategic planning properly placed a tremendous burden on the executive committee to maintain a long-term, corporate-wide view and to establish clear, continuous guidelines for the increasingly powerful heads of the industrial departments. Finally, the refusal to enter the new field of nuclear power and the financial conservatism during 1947 at the outset of the nation's tremendous postwar boom raised the issues of growing or excessive caution with age and success.

Nevertheless, Carpenter left Du Pont well positioned for the future. He had successfully piloted the company through the upheavals of World War II, had reaffirmed through extended planning the firm's concentration on its pioneering strategy as a diversified chemical company, and had preserved its extraordinarily effective structure of decentralization. His recognition of the importance of public relations and public policy, unprecedented among Du Pont's chief executives, had helped minimize the intrusions of expanding government regulation. He had selected a vigorous, young successor who was firmly committed to an entrepreneurial strategy of internal growth through large-scale fundamental research and who was supported by an executive committee seven of whose nine members were appointed after 1944. With new leadership, huge resources, and renewed focus on research and development, Du Pont would realize 12.6 percent annual growth in sales in the decade after World War II.[127]

6

The Manager in Active Retirement

W H A T D I D a chief executive do in retirement after nearly thirty years as a senior manager in a large, complex concern like the Du Pont Company? At Du Pont, Walter Carpenter's new position as chairman of the board carried an impressive title but little power in a largely ceremonial role. As might be anticipated, Carpenter dutifully presided at stockholder meetings, offered advice when consulted by active management, served as a company spokesman without authority, and concentrated increasingly on his private life and growing philanthropic activity.

Nevertheless, although retirement usually signaled the virtual end of a vigorous business career, once again events did not evolve as Walter expected. The advent of Du Pont's most important antitrust case after he became chairman soon altered his idyllic role. In 1948 the U.S. Department of Justice began an antitrust battle with Du Pont over the firm's huge investment (ten million shares or 23 percent of common stock) in General Motors, the nation's second largest industrial enterprise. The titanic struggle stretched over fourteen years and involved not only a major trial but two appeals to the U.S. Supreme Court, two rehearings by the original court, and several years' lobbying for tax relief legislation from Congress and the Eisenhower and Kennedy administrations.

Walter Carpenter's past quickly thrust him into an active, central role in the conflict. As a key representative at GM on behalf of Du Pont for a quarter-century, Walter was an important witness, a useful link between the two firms under attack, a valuable advisor, and a significant source of information. After his long sponsorship by Pierre and Irénée, the still vigorous, able manager was now the logical spokesman for the family and other major stockholders as a member of Du Pont's finance committee and of the board of directors of the Christiana Securities Company. In addition, his forty years with the chemical enterprise made him solicitous of its continued well-being. Finally, a career in high-level management conditioned him to enjoy and respond to the challenges of resolving a major problem.

The outcome, however, was disappointing. Du Pont's eventual defeat in the Supreme Court was beyond his control. Toward the end of the battle, however, his advice at key points helped aggravate the consequences of the loss and revealed the limited ability of an aging master of private enterprise to understand and cope with the political process.

A Busy Retirement

Walter Carpenter quickly learned that "promotion" to chairman of the board, a title with great prestige but little power, meant a number of adjustments, some expected and some not. The new chairman was himself a little uncertain about his duties, and just after the change he reported to one correspondent that "I am still a little confused as to just what my responsibilities are as Chairman of the Board. As someone expressed it, perhaps I have returned to a forty-hour week." Nevertheless, as his response indicated, after a vigorous career he was not yet ready for pasture. When one friend referred to Walter's movement into "the eventide of a notable life," the new chairman noted on the edge of the letter: "Don't like accent on this quite yet."[1]

Though much of his work in the new position was of marginal importance, he performed successfully. He presided over monthly meetings of the board of directors and over annual assemblies of the stockholders with skill and aplomb. His performance even earned admiration from professional minority and special-interest stockholders whose personal agendas he easily sidetracked.

Carpenter recalled the days of the intensely private and closely held firm when the arrival of even a single unexpected stockholder upset the routine. Nevertheless, his long sensitivity to Du Pont's public dimension let him adapt comfortably to the open, less orderly air of the

Chairman of the Board: Walter Carpenter, with Crawford
Greenewalt, presiding over the 1959 stockholders' meeting of
the Du Pont Company (*Hagley Museum and Library*)

postwar sessions of the now widely owned company. As attendance surpassed the one thousand figure and forced a change of location in the 1950s, he noted that the gatherings had become a "sort of a cross between a business meeting and a floor show and I am sure that about 90% of those who attend come to see the latter rather than the former." Nonetheless, he found a "certain merit" in the company's new popularity and at times conceded that even "pestering stockholders" were "not a wholly bad institution. They jar Management periodically into a sensibility of their responsibility, not only to the stockholders but to the public at large." The net result was "in the long run . . . a good thing."[2]

Given Crawford Greenewalt's special interest in promoting Du Pont's public dimensions still further, Carpenter was a perfect partner in the new administration. He cheerfully helped host annual conferences of college and university professors in an effort to "educate" representatives from a group who were among the firm's harshest critics. He consulted on the annual report, made speeches, and acted as ambassador from Wilmington at groundbreaking ceremonies and plant openings, all of which freed Greenewalt's time for management while demonstrating headquarters' continuing interest in its far-flung empire.

Nevertheless, there was much that Walter could not do. Despite repeated attempts he did not succeed in bringing outside directors onto the board. He could not stop Greenewalt's decision in 1950 to accept the federal government's request to build and operate a plant for the production of nuclear materials at Savannah River, South Carolina, which reversed Carpenter's earlier extrication of Du Pont from the atomic weapons business. Executive committee member Roger Williams and research director Elmer Bolton dismissed his concern about overconcentration of research efforts on polymers, a natural consequence of the company's success with nylon.[3]

Nor could Walter halt Greenewalt's push to consolidate the ammonia and plastics departments into a new polychemicals department. Although the president made his case based on the ammonia department's production of most of the intermediates used by plastics, Carpenter perceptively pointed out that marketing failures had led to the definition of product divisions in the reorganization of 1921. He argued futilely that the markets for Du Pont plastics depended on a wide variety of specialty users and demanded adaptability, which the ammonia people were ill equipped to supply. The disappointing performance of polychemicals in the 1950s bore out Carpenter's assertions but made little difference in his authority.[4] Top management decisions remained with the president and the executive committee; Walter could advise and recommend but he could no longer decide such major issues.

Declining power and responsibility left Carpenter more time for private affairs, which, along with his now considerable wealth, led to a major expansion of his philanthropic activities. He typically determined to focus his efforts more systematically on libraries and education and made a number of large gifts in the years after 1948. To Wyoming Seminary, his boyhood school, he donated a boys' dormitory and a gymnasium. In his wife's honor he funded the building of a public library in Laurel, Delaware, her hometown. Beginning in 1959 he served on the board of trustees of the University of Delaware for twelve years, including a term as president of the board for the first three years. To his alma mater, Cornell University, he was especially generous, giving $1.25 million for Carpenter Hall, which contained a library for the engineering school; $1.5 million to the Graduate School of Business and Public Administration for a building housing a library and classrooms; and about $1 million to endow professorships in international studies and engineering. With these and other major gifts for hospital construction in Wilkes-Barre and Wilmington, Carpenter's annual contributions ranged between $500,000 and $2 million annually between 1955 and 1971.[5]

Carpenter's expectations for his private and family life in retirement did not go as planned. After enjoying excellent health for almost sixty years, he suffered debilitating illness between 1946 and 1949, when his doctors determined that Walter had emphysema. Its severity forced him to advance his retirement date by four months, compelled him to take a six-month leave of absence in 1948–49, and hospitalized him several times. Although his condition stabilized after 1949, he was a considerably weaker man who was subject to fainting spells and occasionally dependent on oxygen treatments. Even more devastating were the deaths of his wife Mary from cancer and his brother Ruly from a heart attack within a few months of one another in 1949. Although he subsequently enjoyed the company of women, Walter never remarried.

Grief and ill health, however, did not drive him into complete retirement, though he seriously considered that course, for the emergence of a major challenge to Du Pont renewed his concentration on his business career. In August 1948 the antitrust division of the U.S. Department of Justice announced an investigation of Du Pont's relationship with General Motors, which inaugurated the biggest, longest-running antitrust case in the chemical company's history. The Justice Department eventually accused Pierre, his brothers, and his close associates in the Du Pont Company of violating both the Sherman and Clayton Antitrust acts. It further asserted that beginning in 1915, they had conspired to acquire control of General Motors in order to "restrain unreasonably" interstate trade, to reduce competition, and to monopolize markets. Formal charges in the civil case included Du Pont, General Motors, and U.S. Rubber as well as the two family holding companies, Christiana Securities and Delaware Realty, which together owned about 30 percent of Du Pont. In addition, the government formally added Pierre, Irénée, Lammot, and more than one hundred other du Ponts as part of the conspiracy.[6] The fourteen-year battle had Walter Carpenter at its center and kept him on as chairman of the board until its final resolution in 1962.

After almost twenty antitrust charges in less than ten years, Carpenter and his top colleagues at Du Pont were convinced that this attack was part of a political persecution of a firm whose owners had been notorious and virulent critics of the Roosevelt administration and the New Deal. Crawford Greenewalt privately labeled it as "about as flagrant a witch-hunt as we have ever seen" and noted its perfect timing for Harry Truman's flagging fortunes in the upcoming presidential election. Carpenter thought the charges were confused and fuzzy and wrote his son Ned after the election that the prosecutors' "plans theretofore had been rather precipitate, feeling that they had but very little time to create a good deal of mischief before leaving office."[7]

Evidence for political motivation certainly existed. Attorney General Thomas Clark hyped the case as "the breaking up of the largest single concentration of industrial power in the United States" in his press release, while prosecutor Willis Hotchkiss asserted in Churchillian tones that never had "so few had such dominant control over so many." Empaneling a grand jury for criminal charges before the election eventually produced no indictment but did lead to subpoenas and spectacular accusations involving Remington Arms, Bendix Aviation, North American Aviation, and the Ethyl Corporation as well as those defendants eventually named in the subsequent civil suit. Prosecutors based the investigation and held the trial not in Wilmington or Detroit or New York, where Du Pont and GM had headquarters, but in Chicago, where the antitrust division had been particularly active and successful. A historian of the case judged that it was "probably filed with partisan intentions by the Truman administration."[8]

Nevertheless, although partisanship accounted for timing and zeal, there were more substantial, broader issues than Carpenter and Greenewalt were willing to concede. The case had begun not as an attack on Du Pont but as an investigation of General Motors that was expanded as evidence of their links was uncovered. The grand jury process compelled the firms to cooperate and to release documents that they had refused to supply the year before. Finally, the case was part of the reinvigoration of antitrust prosecution and the strengthening of antitrust law which, as noted in the previous chapter, had begun a decade earlier. An important decision against the Aluminum Company of America in 1945 and rising popular and legal attacks after World War II on big business per se only fueled the impetus against the Du Pont investment in General Motors.[9]

Precisely because Walter Carpenter understood the menace in that trend, he fought vigorously and futilely for years to separate his firm from GM. He made repeated efforts, beginning in the late 1930s when he successfully refinanced Du Pont's preferred stock. During his presidency Carpenter and Angus Echols considered at least five major means of divesting the chemical concern's GM stock while working closely with Ellsworth Alvord of Alvord and Alvord, a prominent Washington, D.C. law firm, to explore closely the company's options under existing tax law and to monitor the possibility of new legislation.[10]

Walter had important long-term reasons for getting rid of the firm's ten million shares of General Motors common stock, despite its profitability. The investment required his close oversight but made no real contribution to the company's revenues, for Du Pont had consistently passed on to its own stockholders all the dividends received. In fact, by the mid-1940s the GM holdings comprised about one-third of all Du Pont's assets but were unavailable to its executives for investment in the chemical company's activities. Carpenter even considered some kind of sale or exchange in order to raise funds during the big postwar building program.[11]

Equally significant, his awareness of the rising tide of antitrust regulation left Walter worried about Du Pont's vulnerability. An investment that produced more value for the concern's stockholders than for the enterprise itself exposed the chemical company to ugly charges of monopoly and to protracted, expensive litigation. Finally, at any point new legislation or a fresh court interpretation of existing law might force the sale of a $1 billion holding with tax consequences that could cost half its value.[12]

Although prudence, extended planning, and efficient use of resources counseled divestment, Carpenter's decade-long search for a solution failed for two reasons. Public policy blocked the way because, despite numerous and imaginative explorations of the internal revenue code, no means of sale could be found without, in Walter's words, a "substantially confiscatory" tax burden. Second, Carpenter did not urge any serious effort for relief legislation in this case because once again family ownership tied his hands. Pierre du Pont viewed the investment as a personal achievement and stubbornly refused to part with his legacy, particularly in the face of a government threat. Irénée and Lammot strongly supported his position, and there the situation remained until the attack Carpenter so feared came in 1948.[13]

The Du Pont Company quickly decided to fight the case, which was tried on its merits and without a jury before Judge Walter LaBuy in Federal District Court in Chicago. Although public attention and strong feeling on both sides made prior resolution unlikely, the decision to litigate was not an emotional one. The firm's other options were unattractive, and its lawyers forecasted victory though with some risk. John Harlan, senior partner in Root, Ballantine, Harlan, Bushby and Palmer, one of the nation's preeminent corporate law firms, predicted that he could show on the facts that the company had bought GM stock as an investment and not with the intent to monopolize. Furthermore, having established that position, Du Pont and Christiana did not abuse it by controlling commerce with General Motors. The uncertainty lay in the Supreme Court's interpretation if the government appealed the decision. As Harlan explained, "If there is a case left after that, the Supreme Court has got to make some new law which is something we cannot control."[14]

Walter Carpenter—and not President Crawford Greenewalt—assumed a leading role in directing the case on Du Pont's behalf. Carpenter had over two decades of experience with GM while Greenewalt had none, but the key factor lay in the traditional handling of the chemical firm's stock in General Motors. Because the GM holdings had always been treated as an investment and not as resources for direct management, oversight had remained with the finance committee instead of the executive committee. Although Angus Echols had chaired the finance committee since 1940, on this issue he was (in the words of a close, knowledgeable observer) merely a "spear carrier." The actual leaders who determined strategy after consultation with legal counsel were Pierre and Walter.[15]

Their approaches differed considerably. Pierre, who turned eighty in 1950, had the same emotional attachments he had demonstrated during the big explosives antitrust case of the Taft era and in the Old Hickory debate during World War I. To a man who never really understood or accepted the legitimacy of antitrust, such issues were personal attacks on his integrity, and he devoted a large portion of the last years of his life to researching the GM-Du Pont history and to practicing his answers in court.[16]

As Pierre's top lieutenant and the one executive most capable of reasoning with him, Walter Carpenter offered the broader, perceptive, and extended view that had characterized his entire career at Du Pont. He was "almost a lawyer" himself by virtue of long interest and self-education, according to Irving Shapiro, who had joined the firm after a decade with the Justice Department to counsel on conspiracy law and who met frequently and regularly with Carpenter for consultation and discussion during and after the trial.[17]

Walter assumed many roles in the proceedings. Based on his knowledge and past positions at both Du Pont and GM, he testified forthrightly and effectively after a lengthy review of the historical record. He calmed nervous retired executives like Donaldson Brown, who fretted repeatedly and ineffectually over the handling of the case. He fielded inquiries from stockholders and bankers worried about the financial implications of the case. He read transcripts of all of the testimony and scrutinized the arguments of both sides, which he then analyzed with Shapiro. Although the conduct of the case was in the hands of expert lawyers, he pointed out to Du Pont's counsel flaws in the facts and assumptions of the government's presentation.[18] Through it all, the evidence and the excellent performance of Du Pont's fine lawyers made him confident of victory. In 1954, after testimony had ended, he wrote privately to an early associate at Du Pont that the chance of loss "seems so remote as to be almost absurd."[19]

Judge LaBuy's decision was a complete victory for Du Pont, bearing out Walter's optimism and John Harlan's predictions about the course of the trial. LaBuy found that the record did not demonstrate any conspiracy by Pierre and his associates to control General Motors on behalf of Du Pont but did prove an opportune and profitable investment. The chemical company had made active efforts to garner GM's trade, especially in fabrics and finishes, where it had a major share of

Hallway Huddle and Antitrust Muddle: Irénée du Pont, Walter Carpenter, and Pierre du Pont at the Du Pont–General Motors antitrust trial in Chicago in 1952 (*Hagley Museum and Library*)

the automobile corporation's business, but there was no evidence of secret agreement or dictation of policy. The judge decided that General Motors in fact "exercised complete freedom" in its purchasing practices. The bonus plan that Pierre had sponsored at GM was "a business principle" and not an attempt to control the automobile firm's executives. Du Pont's power as the single largest owner of General Motors declined over time as Alfred Sloan demonstrated vigorous, independent leadership. In short, LaBuy concluded that "the record shows consultation and conference, but not domination."[20]

Managing Appeal and Defeat

Despite the overwhelming victory, Walter Carpenter and his associates at Du Pont, especially those on the finance committee, realized that the proceedings were far from over when Judge LaBuy announced his decision in December 1954. Indeed, they had not yet reached the halfway mark, for nearly eight years remained during which the company would be twice defeated before the United States Supreme Court and would be compelled to accept an unsatisfactory compromise in order to achieve essential tax relief for the compulsory divestment of its GM holdings. Walter Carpenter played a central role in the ongoing process but with declining effectiveness as age and political inexperience weakened his judgment while public policy continued to limit his power as a top executive. The results could have been far worse, but in fact he retired after defeat.

Although many contemporaries and some later historians emphasized the probusiness character of the Eisenhower administration, which took office in the midst of the trial, top people at Du Pont had no illusions of favoritism. Pierre, who died in 1954 before the final judgment was rendered, astutely noted just prior to Eisenhower's election that "in anti-trust matters, the Republicans have not been any better than the Democrats, so that a change in administration will not help us a bit." Shortly after the decision, Carpenter chortled to Lord Harry McGowan about the "sweeping victory" that "completely annihilated" the Justice Department's "reckless charges." Nevertheless, though he doubted the legal grounds for an appeal, he readily admitted that "we all recognize that the political aspects of the situation may prompt a different decision."[21]

Carpenter's foreboding was sound but his reasoning was too limited. Certainly the Republican administration had to anticipate charges of being soft on antitrust if it failed to prosecute, but other important factors helped determine its decision for a successful appeal. Failure to act could hurt other cases. In addition, Eisenhower's Department of

Justice maintained the tradition of antitrust enforcement now well established for more than a decade. Furthermore, it was also encouraged by the Supreme Court's general support for government appeals of antitrust decisions in this period.[22]

In this case, the Supreme Court rewarded the administration's efforts by upholding its assertions. In June 1957 with the abstention of Justice Thomas Clark, the former attorney general in the Truman administration, which had launched the case, and of Justice John Harlan, Du Pont's former counsel, it voted four to two to reverse Judge LaBuy. Writing for the majority, Justice William Brennan ignored the charges under the Sherman Act and focused on those under Section Seven of the Clayton Act, which had been almost an afterthought by the prosecution.

For the first time the Court applied the Clayton Act to vertical acquisitions (the purchase of firms in other stages or functions of the same industry) and shifted its focus away from behavior and intent at the time of the purchase to "whether at the time of suit there is a reasonable probability that the acquisition is likely to result in the condemned restraints [on trade]." The majority conceded that top executives at Du Pont and General Motors had "acted honorably and fairly," but its reading of the record established just such a present-day probability of restraint of trade. Justice Harold Burton dissented vigorously but vainly about the majority's brief, selective treatment of the record to establish its decision that Du Pont dominated GM's fabrics and finishes business, a position that ignored powerful, countervailing patterns of evidence.[23]

The Court remanded the case to Judge LaBuy for "equitable relief" against Du Pont, General Motors, Christiana Securities, and Delaware Realty, the only remaining defendants. Just as John Harlan had feared six years earlier, the Supreme Court made new law at Du Pont's expense. In the meantime the stakes had risen significantly, for stock options and splits had multiplied Du Pont's holdings of GM common stock to sixty-three million shares with a total value of more than 2.5 billion.[24]

Carpenter immediately put aside any thoughts of full retirement and worked even more intensely in an attempt to reduce the cost and disruption of the antitrust decision. Although the increased stakes and Walter's age (sixty-nine) inexorably drew Crawford Greenewalt into the conflict, the chairman remained at the center for at least the next two years. Because of his knowledge of the tax code and finance, he presided over an elaborate effort by teams from the treasurer's and legal departments to determine the company's possible alternatives and their impact if the firm were compelled to dispose of its General Motors stock.

The project exemplified the kind of statistically based, systematic analysis that was Du Pont's and Carpenter's hallmark. It produced some eighteen plans whose surviving records fill more than two dozen archival boxes and which considered divestment by direct sale, dividend, exchange, spin-off, formation of a separate company, and partial liquidation. It included careful and extensive consultation with Morgan, Stanley and Company and other financial analysts and with the Washington, D.C., legal firm, Covington and Burling, on tax law and policy and their possible amendment. Du Pont also hired National Analysts, Incorporated, of Philadelphia to survey nearly 15,000 stockholders in order to measure tax consequences.[25]

Although the firm's legal and financial teams did the work, Walter acted as monitor and critic. He constantly reviewed their proposals, suggested new ones, offered modifications and fresh alternatives, challenged assumptions, posed previously unasked questions, and initiated searches for more information. As a top executive he kept the focus from remaining on the simple amassing of data and channeled it toward more effective strategy and tactics.[26]

Carpenter also worked outside the enterprise. Along with Crawford Greenewalt Walter served as a Du Pont spokesman throughout the proceedings. In order to insure a united front, he helped promote cooperation with General Motors on the technical details of financial plans and legal tactics. He argued the firm's position in numerous speeches to company and outside groups, including engineers, salespeople, chemists, stockholders, top educators, and women's clubs. In addition, between 1957 and 1959 he and Greenewalt visited Secretary of the Treasury Robert Anderson, Attorney General Herbert Brownell, and his successor William Rogers in futile hopes of reaching a settlement or of winning support for relief legislation. Such highly visible public officials were naturally unwilling to promote compromises, no matter how open and how reasonable, in order to end the uncertainty for Du Pont, General Motors, and their stockholders and thus shorten a struggle now more than a decade old.[27] Whatever the probusiness sentiments of the Eisenhower administration, the process would wind through normal channels.

Walter also played an important part in the hearings before Judge

LaBuy to determine the means for implementing the Supreme Court's decision and the severity of Du Pont's penalty. The Justice Department insisted on the company's complete divestment of GM stock in order to prevent the reformation of a potential conspiracy. About two-thirds of the sixty-three million shares would be distributed over ten years to the firm's individual stockholders; a court trustee was to sell the other third, which would otherwise pass to du Pont family members or to Christiana Securities and Delaware Realty. The chemical firm's lawyers strenuously opposed the proposal as too disruptive and argued that simply passing through the voting rights to individual holders would accomplish the same end. Stock owned by individual du Ponts or by the family holding companies would be "sterilized," that is, lose its voting rights.

Judge LaBuy accepted a modified version of the Du Pont Company's proposed judgment. He mandated that General Motors and Du Pont could no longer have common officers or directors. He voided all contracts calling for exclusive patent rights or specifying shares of markets and forbade similar ones in the future. He ordered Du Pont not to buy any General Motors stock in the future and to pass through or to sterilize the voting rights of its existing GM holdings.[28]

LaBuy sided with Du Pont because the tax and financial consequences of complete divestiture were, in his words, "unnecessarily harsh and punitive," an argument that Walter Carpenter had pushed so hard to develop. In frequent consultations with Irving Shapiro, the head of firm's special inside legal team for the case, and with Charles Rittenhouse, the director of the corporation's legal department, Carpenter urged a vigorous challenge to the Justice Department's "rosy picture" of divestiture. The Internal Revenue Service had ruled that such dividends of GM stock were fully taxable as income to individual holders, and Carpenter told Rittenhouse that he wanted "a simple, clear and dramatic picture" of the impact on recipients who would be subject to tax rates ranging from 20 to 91 percent.[29]

Walter commissioned expert studies that determined that the total tax burden would fall between $700 million and $1 billion, or about one-third of the total value of the stock. Outright sale by Du Pont itself would subject the company, and indirectly its stockholders, to a capital gains tax absorbing one-quarter of the stock's worth. In addition, the huge volume of panicked and forced sales of the securities over the ten-year period of separation prescribed by the Court would significantly depress their value, harming thousands of Du Pont and GM shareholders who had nothing to do with the case. According to one authority's estimate, total direct and indirect costs would eventually exceed $4 billion. Carpenter shrewdly anticipated one historian's subsequent conclusion that "the importance of the tax code in this case cannot be overemphasized."[30]

Victory in the LaBuy hearings was Du Pont's last major success in the case, but its subsequent expensive defeats before all three branches of the federal government might have been avoided had not Carpenter's judgment deserted him. Prior to the Justice Department's decision to appeal again to the Supreme Court, it offered an attractive compromise that Du Pont rejected in part at least because of Walter's counsel. Robert Bicks, assistant attorney general and head of the antitrust division, insisted that he had to maintain the principle of divestment for the sake of other prosecutions. At the same time, however, he was skeptical about the possibility of legislation for tax relief and he did not want to compromise future cases because of the revenue code's harsh impact.[31]

Therefore, he asked Du Pont to accept a decree calling for divestment but without any specified plan or period of compliance. In the meantime stockholders would have the option of exchanging some of their Du Pont securities for the GM stock behind it. Otherwise, the voting power would be passed through to them or sterilized as LaBuy had ordered. Bicks reasoned that such a mechanism would become self-enforcing because Du Pont would not want a $3 billion investment that it could not vote and would obtain the necessary tax relief at the earliest possible opportunity, a conclusion that in fact company executives had already reached.[32]

Carpenter's response, confirmed by the finance committee that he once again chaired, was to reject the offer even though the company was prepared to accept a similar order that provided for divestiture *after* satisfactory relief legislation was secured. Quite pleased by the firm's recent success before LaBuy, Carpenter saw no reason to aid the Justice Department's attempt to persuade the judge to reverse himself for the sake of broader antitrust policy that was extraneous to Du Pont. After having won its case, the company's support for a reversal would mean "that we had betrayed the Judge, the public and our stockholders." He conceded the possibility of defeat before the Supreme Court as Bicks predicted, but insisted that "at least we would have avoided any conspiracy on our part with the Department of Justice to persuade Judge LaBuy to reverse his present position."[33]

In the absence of additional evidence, the reasons behind Carpenter's noble and ultimately harmful decision are difficult to assess. His memoranda suggest a more rigid fixation on order and abstract logic in the face of advancing age and growing frustration that compromised his career-long detachment and extended viewpoint.[34]

At seventy-one he was caught up in a seemingly endless and irrational process. The Supreme Court had found no one guilty of wrongdoing. Yet it insisted on separation to avoid possible future misbehavior even though the trial record clearly demonstrated Du Pont's declining influence at General Motors. The Justice Department had lost the hearing before Judge LaBuy because it blithely ignored the serious financial effects of its proposed settlement. Now it asked Du Pont to help replace LaBuy's decision with a cumbersome, impractical redemption scheme that burdened the chemical company with two classes of common stock (one with and one without General Motors stock as assets) for an indefinite period of time, which would certainly complicate future financing.

In Carpenter's thinking, the rational solution was the distribution of Du Pont's GM shares with tax relief to avoid financial disruption and unfair penalties on innocent stockholders. The finance committee's unanimous counterproposal of divestment after tax relief made the terms of resolution more concrete, and it logically if informally committed the government's aid in obtaining that relief in order to gain its own ends.[35]

However, Walter ignored the Justice Department's essential need for unconditional divestment, even if in a symbolic victory that asserted only the principle and ignored the timing of its application. In his old age Carpenter was forgetting the bargaining technique he had used so effectively in the Grasselli acquisition, the 1939 refinancing, and other negotiations: the best agreements were those that accommodated the long-term interests of both parties. At the cost of some uncertainty about the advent of the final resolution, the government's proposal secured the company and its stockholders against tax losses. Simultaneously, Bick's plan predisposed the Eisenhower administration to support relief legislation permitting the divestment that both sides wanted but that was ultimately on the terms Du Pont sought.

The penalty for failure to compromise became apparent in less than two years, when the Supreme Court in a four-to-three vote again sided with the government. The majority opinion written in 1961 by Justice Brennan stated that Du Pont's plea of economic hardship was valid only in selecting among effective remedies and not in determining them. Disfranchisement was not sufficient, for somehow Du Pont's potential influence might reestablish itself. Once more the Court reversed Judge LaBuy and crisply remanded the case to him, ordering a speedy conclusion leading to complete divestiture within a decade.[36]

In the next year, prior to the completion of the second set of hearings before Judge LaBuy, the Du Pont Company swiftly shifted its focus to the United States Congress in order to obtain desperately needed tax relief, an approach that the chemical concern had initiated earlier as prudent insurance. The firm rejected the direct sale of its sixty-three million shares of General Motors, for that option threatened to disrupt the securities markets in addition to creating a huge tax liability. As a result, Du Pont had to seek help for its stockholders who were to receive the GM stock pro rata as dividends, the only viable alternative to complete divestment. Although Crawford Greenewalt assumed greater leadership to lobby and testify on the firm's behalf, Walter Carpenter continued to play an important role.

On the surface their task seemed easy enough, for the company had logic, precedent, and powerful connections in its favor. As Carpenter, Greenewalt, and their advocates never wearied of repeating, no tax was justified because there was no financial gain. Du Pont stockholders were merely exchanging some of their securities for the General Motors shares that stood behind them. Furthermore, because previous orders for compulsory divestiture had sometimes unintentionally exposed shareholders to tax liability, there had been a number of instances exempting them from penalty, beginning in the 1930s with the Public Utility Holding Company Act. None of the previous examples had resulted from an antitrust decision, however, and there was no general law on the subject, so Du Pont had to seek its own legislative relief.[37]

The firm appeared to be well positioned to accomplish that end. The Eisenhower administration was in power, and Du Pont had long been a major contributor to the Republican Party. John Williams, a Republican and the senior U.S. senator from Delaware, was the ranking minority member of the Senate Finance Committee. At the same time the corporation was well represented on the other side of the aisle. Senator Harry Byrd, the powerful chairman of the Finance Committee, was a Virginia Democrat with strong ties to Du Pont. The company was a major employer in his state, and his political machine had previously elected Colgate Darden as Virginia's governor. Like Crawford Greenewalt, Darden was a son-in-law of Irénée du Pont. Allen Frear, the junior Democratic senator from Delaware who was facing a tough battle for reelection in 1960, had already introduced and sponsored a relief bill for Du Pont. In addition, the company had recruited the support of Wilbur Mills, Democratic chairman of the House Ways and Means Committee, and Robert Kerr, an influential Democrat on the Senate Finance Committee, and employed as its advocate Clark Clifford, a former advisor to President Harry Truman and one of the most effective lobbyists in Washington.[38]

At first proceedings moved reasonably well despite several compromises and minor annoyances. Frear, with whom Carpenter had consulted personally in 1956 and 1957, introduced the proposal to the Senate in 1958 and arranged for a companion bill in the House. Although it started too late for action in its first year, in 1959 the measure moved steadily toward passage with approval by Mills' House Ways and Means Committee and with consideration by Byrd's committee in the Senate. Du Pont reluctantly accepted an amendment providing for a small tax on corporate recipients, primarily the Christiana Securities Company, which owned about 30 percent of Du Pont common stock after absorbing the Delaware Realty Company. Carpenter objected on principle, but Frear argued that there would be strong opposition unless the company paid something for the privilege it was receiving and that a tax of about $20 million was a small charge for a transaction involving stock now valued at about $3 billion.[39]

Throughout the summer of 1959 alterations and annoyances mounted as part of the legislative process to accommodate personal and bureaucratic interests. The Hilton hotel chain amended the proposal to resolve its own tax problem, which threatened to bog the bill down in an extraneous debate. The Treasury and Justice Departments carped about details and insisted on adjustments to insure the measure's effectiveness as general law for revenue and antitrust. The administration was apparently fearful of the political fallout for providing a lucrative favor to a wealthy and powerful group, no matter how justified the case. It demonstrated no enthusiasm or advocacy for the proposal and limited itself to cautious approval as a necessary reform of general antitrust law.[40]

The stunning shock, however, came in September when Harry Byrd's Senate Finance Committee voted by eight to seven for a substitute bill to increase the stockholders' tax liability from $20 million to more than $320 million, which defeated Frear's proposal for the session. Byrd and John Williams cast the deciding votes to tell Carpenter and Greenewalt that they were living in a fool's paradise.[41] They and the Du Pont Company were being punished for arrogantly ignoring sound political advice and for flaunting such congressional protocols as party loyalty, seniority, and the authority of a committee chairman.

Senator Williams was the prime mover. When he showed little enthusiasm for the company's original proposal and told the Du Pont leaders what they did not want to hear, Carpenter and Greenewalt had chosen to work with a junior Democrat instead of a senior Republican. Based on Williams' own considerable experience, he had insisted that the bill was too generous to Du Pont to pass Congress and popular scrutiny. At the same time, both he and Byrd were committed budget balancers who labored to close tax loopholes and increase revenues.

In this particular case Williams was upset that existing law heavily taxed individual recipients at then high income tax rates while Christiana, the family holding company, paid only a small intercorporate dividend tax calculated on the original and not the market value of the securities it received. His substitute motion, which Byrd and a bare majority of the committee supported, was intended to create new general law for the Du Pont case and for all such future incidents. It lowered individual liability by defining compulsory dividends as capital gains rather than as income. At the same time Williams redefined the corporate rate on the basis of market value, which would cost the owners of Christiana tens of millions of dollars.[42]

Carpenter and Greenewalt were livid. The Du Pont Company had endured lengthy and expensive judicial proceedings, which they considered unjust and inconsistent, and it now risked a draconian judgment with an unprecedented tax liability. The two executives and their colleagues were in no mood to apologize for their inexperience and clumsiness in the legislative arena or to appreciate the niceties of general tax reform and the nuances of Senate protocol. As we have seen in Du Pont's reorganization debates of 1919–21 and in GM's executive bonus crisis between 1932 and 1934, high-level managers could sometimes get so involved in an issue that they lost their normally balanced viewpoint.

In their anger Du Pont's chairman and president blurred their personal feelings and corporate concerns, just as Pierre and his brothers had in the 1930s, and they soon made a bad situation worse. During the fall and winter of 1959–60, Greenewalt engaged in a public name-calling contest with Williams that was widely covered in the Wilmington newspapers. Carpenter, who thought the senior Republican's presentation "very ingenious and disingenuous," vowed that he would forsake a lifetime of party loyalty to back Frear in the fall 1960 elections instead of the Republican candidate. When Du Pont employees received a mailing from Williams that justified his position with elliptical and misleading statements, Louis Schreiber of Du Pont's legal department wrote a harsh response that not only corrected the senator's errors but attacked him personally. Meanwhile Du Pont backed the reintroduction of Frear's proposal in 1960 and attempted to avoid the Senate Finance Committee by adding it to an obscure Treasury bill late in the session.[43]

In their continuing frustration Greenewalt and Carpenter demonstrated arrogance, poor judgment, and naivete by trying to defeat the veteran John Williams in his own institution. After consultation with Harry Byrd, the crafty Republican senator implemented his own well-planned, secret operation. During a Sunday night meeting in the last week of the 1960 session while Frear was out of town, Williams carefully removed the Treasury's proposal from the original bill and arranged for its separate passage. The Delaware Democrat only belatedly realized that his Du Pont legislation was attached to a now hollow measure that had no hope of enactment, and the session ended before he could recover.[44]

The consequence of Carpenter's and Greenewalt's ill-advised anger and stubbornness was a devastating setback that went far beyond Williams' revenge. During the fall 1960 elections they watched the defeat of Allen Frear, their advocate, while a much less sympathetic Kennedy administration assumed control of the Executive Branch. In the following spring the Supreme Court mandated swift and complete divestment as already noted. A chastened Greenewalt made peace with Senator Williams and a defeated Carpenter withdrew from the legislative process. Less than a year later, in February 1962, President John Kennedy signed a law for Du Pont tax relief in substantially the original form recommended by John Williams. Judge LaBuy quickly embodied the terms of the legislation in a final decree that over a three-year period provided for close government monitoring of the sale of all the General Motors stock held by Du Pont, Christiana Securities, and forty members of the du Pont family.[45] Direct ties between the chemical and automobile firms had been severed in 1959 when Walter Carpenter and other Du Pont representatives resigned from GM's board of directors and Alfred Sloan left Du Pont's board.

After the first Supreme Court decision in 1957, the Du Pont Company and the U.S. government had wanted the same thing—divestment—but a host of factors intervened that seemed extraneous to the increasingly impatient Carpenter and Greenewalt. Tax law, party politics, bureaucratic and public policy issues, personality and pride, and concerns about popular reaction helped shape the separation of Du Pont and General Motors in a process involving complex, protracted, and often futile negotiation, the imposition of a heavy tax penalty, and further close government scrutiny. In the end Du Pont salvaged what it could, but the solution was hardly a triumph for Carpenter, Greenewalt, and Du Pont after the promising beginning of the case. Despite the two executives' concern about popular opinion and public relations, they had little direct experience in the political arena. Their failure again reflected top businessmen's limited expertise and ability in anticipating issues outside the normal course of enterprise that nevertheless clearly impinged on the firm's freedom and well-being.

Though embarrassing and costly, especially for Du Pont's stockholders, the consequences of the General Motors case were not as radical for the chemical enterprise as might have been expected, given the magnitude, duration, and notoriety of the case. Du Pont spent well over $7 million on the unsuccessful litigation, and its stockholders paid a tax bill estimated at over $1 billion after Judge LaBuy extended compulsory divestment to Christiana Securities and forty members of the Du Pont family.[46] Nevertheless, because the company had regularly passed on its GM dividends to the stockholders, there was no impact on annual revenues actually used by the Wilmington firm. Despite a huge reduction in its total investment, the company's assets remained many times its obligations to its preferred stock, as Walter Carpenter had carefully determined beforehand.[47] The continuing soundness of the enterprise was a tribute to the prudent financial policies established by Pierre du Pont and perpetuated by Walter Carpenter.

In other areas the effect was also unspectacular. The Supreme Court's application of Section Seven of the Clayton Antitrust Act to potential monopoly was limited to the Du Pont–General Motors case and did not establish an important precedent for antitrust policy, perhaps because the scale and nature of the two firms' linkage were unique in American business. As one Du Pont lawyer later noted, public policy determined that no matter how harmless and how unusual the tie, it was not desirable. The suit also reinforced Du Pont's lessons gained from its numerous antitrust proceedings during Carpenter's presidency. In the 1960s as in the 1950s, growth would come by internal development—not by the acquisition of companies or by the licensing of others' patent rights.[48]

Finally, resolution brought the release that Walter Carpenter had long wanted. His mismanagement of Robert Bicks's suggested compromise and of John Williams' proposed tax relief indicated that he had stayed too long despite his earlier energetic and shrewd contributions to the case. In August 1962 Crawford Greenewalt resigned as president to become chairman of the board while Walter retired at seventy-four to assume a special status as honorary chairman of the board, a fitting tribute to his long, extraordinary service to Du Pont. His colleagues on the board of directors deferred to Carpenter's restrained personality and dislike of sentimental gush, but proclaimed their appreciation in a remarkably apt summary:

> Whereas, knowing well the simplicity and modesty that mark Mr. Carpenter's character, we have no wish to embarrass him with praise, but regard it as a factual statement that his complete integrity, his penetrating and analytical mind, his great thoroughness, and his utter devotion to any task to which he commits himself, coupled with his kindliness, gentleness, understanding, courtesy to and unfailing consideration for all with whom he comes in contact, make him one of the outstanding industrial statesmen of our time.[49]

As a widower and a workaholic who had spent over half a century with the Du Pont Company, including forty-three years in top management, Carpenter never completely retired. He served on the finance committee and worked in his office regularly until 1970, when he was eighty-two. He did not retire from the board of directors until 1975 at the age of eighty-seven, after being bedridden by a stroke. He actively fulfilled a role as an elder statesman whose career spanned a remarkable portion of Du Pont's history. He could remember Pierre's mother's stories of sewing up burlap bags to hold soda nitrate for the powder company in the mid-nineteenth century, and he debated the company's decision to turn to bonded debt in 1974.[50]

He enjoyed being consulted on important issues. As one younger executive put it, "Walter Carpenter's been around here an awful long time, and . . . a person would be venturesome indeed if he was going to make a terrifically unusual change, and didn't get W. C.'s views, because they're available to you. You could disagree with him, but they're available to you."[51] There was a risk of staying on too long and intimidating younger managers. Nevertheless, like Pierre and Irénée before him, Walter sought not to impinge on but to test the judgment and independence of executives while accepting their ultimate responsibility and authority. After unsuccessfully challenging management's proposal to use bonded debt before the board of directors, for example, he introduced the motion to approve the new issue. Carpenter's special pleasure was mentoring Irving Shapiro, the extraordinarily able young lawyer with whom he worked so closely during the GM case. He watched with pride when Shapiro became Du Pont's chairman and chief executive officer in 1974, but still questioned him sharply when Shapiro visited his bedridden mentor.[52]

Despite emphysema Carpenter had an active old age until his mid-eighties, enjoying the arrival of grandchildren and great-grandchildren. He delighted in organizing his annual birthday celebrations, and he accepted the imminence of death with good humor. When the National Geographic Society mistakenly announced his death in 1966, he quipped that he "always suspected the National Geographic of being forward looking."[53] Ten years later he died on February 2, 1976, at the age of eighty-eight.

Epilogue

A study of Walter Carpenter's long, distinguished career confirms a number of generalizations about managers of American big business while it challenges or offers exception to other conventional beliefs. Although Carpenter was not an entrepreneur in the traditional sense, neither was he simply an administrator or a trustee. Pierre du Pont once remarked that he would not have such trustees in his firm because they were the death of enterprise.[54] Walter's career blossomed precisely because he did much more than simply look after someone else's property even though his concentration in finance meant that he created no new products or processes.

As a top executive charged with making a big, successful company bigger and more successful, Walter Carpenter was responsible for a number of innovations of the kind associated with entrepreneurship.[55] He pushed the acquisition of the Arlington Company as the core of what became Du Pont's plastics business. He pioneered comprehensive strategic planning in order to allocate the firm's capital and human resources more effectively among its various businesses, thus expanding promising lines while maintaining, shrinking, or divesting others. As president he promoted the development of learned routines like strategic thinking and continuous long-term planning in the executive committee and among department managers. He also helped push Du Pont into the modern era of public relations. Henceforth, an awareness of important external issues that had serious potential impact on the firm would be factored into corporate decision making, and in turn the import of the company's larger decisons would be communicated to Du Pont's publics.

Carpenter's career illustrated concretely much of the general demographic picture and standard career patterns of American managers.[56] His white, Anglo-Saxon, Protestant heritage, his college education, and his middle-class background were important factors in his training and opportunity. He rejected the presidency of the U.S. Rubber Company in order to devote his entire working life to a single enterprise, which typified executive stability in American corporations before the 1960s. Like most managers, he earned promotions through extraordinary ability, hard work, and accomplishment. The generous rewards that accompanied his success included investment in Du Pont in order to stir his incentive and to intertwine his outlook and career interests with those of his company. By the age of forty his bonuses had produced millions of dollars in personal wealth represented largely by thousands of shares of Du Pont and Christiana Securities stock. Walter held directly and indirectly less than one percent of Du Pont, but although he was not a significant owner of the company, company ownership was a major part of his estate.

His ties to Du Pont and its heavy reliance on a large fixed investment encouraged in Carpenter a broad, extended approach to management as illustrated by his support for the careful financial policies originally developed by Pierre du Pont. His personality, his engineering training, and Du Pont's heritage promoted a rational, systematic outlook that relied heavily on statistical data to organize, test, and assess information, a preference that became obvious as early as his acquisition of the Arlington Company. As illustrated in his negotiations with the Comptoir and the Grasselli people, he easily developed a personality well suited to life in a large organization. He insisted on clear thinking and the firm assertion of sound conclusions, but learned to do so in a manner calculated to encourage consensus and collective policy-making that in turn emphasized long-term harmony, cooperation, and support. He recognized the critical importance of maintaining good management throughout a large enterprise in order to assure its extended well-being. He not only institutionalized such practices as president, but as an individual he helped identify and boost the careers of such top executives as Angus Echols, Crawford Greenewalt, and Irving Shapiro.

Carpenter's career also demonstrated that nineteenth-century Americans could adapt nimbly to the apparently radical shift from rural or small-town life and personal enterprise to the big city and huge bureaucratic corporations largely owned by others. In Carpenter's case at least, a childhood that underscored family, duty, consideration, and diligence was critical to his adjustment. As his protégé Irving Shapiro noted perceptively, Walter Carpenter was "a nineteenth-century gentleman who could be tough, who could be demanding, who could be warm and gentle, and who never lost his cool."[57]

Despite his similarities to many other executives, Walter's career was unusual in many respects. Unlike the leaders of most big American industrial enterprises, who attained high-level office only in their late forties or fifties, he reached the top early when appointed head of the development department and member of the executive committee at thirty-one in 1919 and remained for a very long time until retirement as chairman of the board at seventy-four in 1962.[58] His business life serves as a reminder that chance, particularly availability near the large firm's beginning, could be a real accelerator. Certainly his early and frequent promotions depended heavily on the rapid expansion of the still-young, big chemical enterprise as it diversified and coped with the tremendous demands of World War I.

Carpenter's experience also illustrated that the first generation of industrial managers may have had considerably different career patterns from those who arrived after size had been achieved and after strategy and structure were in place and who comprised a majority of subsequent management surveys. Walter's precocity, for example, owed a great deal to the persistent impact of family control or influence in the Du Pont Company after historians have generally recorded its shift to managerial enterprise.[59] Certainly Pierre and Irénée sponsored his rapid promotions to the development department, the treasurer's department, and the executive committee because they appreciated the need for outstanding managerial talent. Nevertheless, they were also looking for able, trustworthy men to act as stewards for their family's wealth and heritage. Walter Carpenter, like Donaldson Brown, was to be their special representative at the same time that he labored for all of the owners of the enterprise.

First-generation managers like Carpenter and Brown as well as

Charles Schwab at Carnegie Steel and George Perkins at New York Life and J. P. Morgan and Company were transition figures.[60] They were more likely than their entrepreneurial predecessors to see the corporation as an independent institution and not as a personal extension of its operators. Yet because of close contact with the founders who often continued to serve on boards of directors and finance committees, the separation of ownership and management was incomplete, and early managers found distinctions about allegiances to enterprise and to stockholders more ambiguous than their successors. Issues like the shift of control at General Motors from Pierre and the Du Pont Company to Alfred Sloan and the Detroit office were liable to be central features in the careers of first-generation professional executives.

Furthermore, opportunities for lucrative investment via stock options in still rapidly growing enterprises and close association with remarkably wealthy entrepreneurs helped shape such managers' views of compensation. The owner-management that the du Ponts instilled in their first executives produced not only fortunes but firm belief and definite expectation. In turn, such attitudes became the bridge to far larger, more impersonal and autonomous, and sometimes troublesome management bonus plans in mature enterprises as the 1930s crisis at GM demonstrated.

In financial matters close association with founders could cut two ways. Although it might have led to excessive concern for return on investment and a short-term approach to operation, under Pierre and Irénée at the Du Pont Company the impact was just the opposite. Their extraordinary skills and experience moved them to appreciate the advantages of long-term growth and to encourage general rather than financial management. Thus, while they insisted that Walter Carpenter have a strong grounding in finance, it was his superior abilities in overall administration that earned their appreciation as well as his promotion and success.

Carpenter's career demonstrated a pattern of ownership influence and managerial independence that is currently receiving further study.[61] During the first sixty years of the twentieth century, professional executives could remain generalists and focus on their firms' broad and extended needs while they were closely associated with understanding or influential founders or when ownership became widely dispersed. When holdings became both impersonal and more concentrated with increasing institutional investment after 1960, autonomy and the long-term view were often sacrificed for a harmful bottom-line approach that has contributed to the nation's economic stagnation in recent years.

At Du Pont the family's role in Walter's career continued long after Pierre and Irénée pushed his promotion to the executive committee. Lammot's determination to remain president for fourteen years until 1940 delayed Carpenter's own promotion to chief executive officer until he was fifty-two and in effect counterbalanced his early rise into top management. The three brothers' very public and virulent attacks on the New Deal and their extreme defense of privacy, secrecy, and unregulated individualism frustrated Carpenter's concern about the impact of public opinion and a more active national government on big business in a democratic society.

Nor did the du Ponts' influence end in the 1930s. Pierre continued to refuse to consider the sale of the company's General Motors stock for more than a decade after Walter first raised the question in 1938 until Du Pont's holdings embroiled the firm in a huge antitrust case ending in a major defeat after a lengthy battle. In fact, Carpenter eventually discovered that family influence outlasted even his own long career. His two successors as president, who served from 1948 to 1967, were both family members.

The du Ponts' ongoing participation in company affairs never generated a serious break or conflict with their top manager for reasons that go well beyond deference to ownership and the mutual respect and affection among the personalities involved. Following the brothers' respective retirements as president, they seldom interfered in the direct operation of the chemical firm. They generally confined themselves to suggestions and to the review formally accorded ownership through the finance committee, and eventually that body's actions became more pro forma by the late 1930s and early 1940s. During Carpenter's time Pierre's, Irénée's, and Lammot's most intrusive actions came not in administration but in Du Pont's consideration and oversight of outside investments like U.S. Steel, U.S. Rubber, and General Motors. Though such activities did affect management by absorbing considerable time, funds, and executive talent, they were also the special prerogatives of owners. Likewise, the du Ponts' part in defining the firm's relationships to its numerous publics and to government followed logically even though it sometimes embarrassed or constrained Walter Carpenter. After all, the three brothers' name was synonymous with the company they had once headed. Even the perpetuation of family in the presidency following Walter's retirement was the result of timing and chance—the disruption of World War II—and Carpenter had no ready alternative to the obviously capable Crawford Greenewalt.

Nevertheless, the family's role did demonstrate the limits of Walter's power, a common theme in his career that is seldom noted in the literature on management. As a top executive at Du Pont for forty-three years and an influential director at General Motors for three decades, Walter Carpenter long held major positions in two of America's largest, most successful, and most powerful industrial enterprises. Nevertheless, his record is dotted with a surprising number of important decisions that he did not approve, including reorganization at GM, his lengthy tenure as heir apparent to Lammot du Pont, and the firm's frustrating delay in acknowledging the reality of expanded government power.

These setbacks must have seemed trivial, however, when he finally became Du Pont's leader and was simultaneously hostage to the constraints of world war and the impact of expanded government regulation. Though long committed to minimizing the company's role as a munitions manufacturer, Walter spent most of his presidency coping with the disruption of World War II, overseeing the firm's major part in building the atomic bomb, and fighting off more than a dozen antitrust attacks. The two biggest defeats of his career were the ICI and GM antitrust cases, the latter of which demanded his serious attention and energy until his seventies and compelled him to remain chairman of the board long after he wished to retire.

Furthermore, Walter Carpenter, like all of us, was bound by his own experiences and the inevitability of the aging process. Du Pont matured and its top management and bureaucracy solidified even as his own career progressed. His age on becoming president was evidence of those changes, and a nearly wholesale turnover of the executive committee while he was chief executive officer scarcely modified the age level of the firm's top leadership. In 1948 despite the committee's new membership, seven of nine members were over fifty and the average age was fifty-five, in contrast to a mean that ranged in the low and mid-forties between 1915 and 1920 after Pierre engineered two wholesale reorganizations of top personnel in the still young company.[62] In addition, Carpenter's shrill outcries about organized labor, increasing concern about avoiding bonded debt, and caution in the face of an exploding market after 1945 also suggest a growing tendency to become a prisoner of the past and the growing rigidity that so often accompanies old age.

Carpenter's story forces a reconsideration of the relative importance of key factors in the growth of big business. The prevailing history of large American firms emphasizes the evolution of private enterprise as shaped by changing technology and markets, for which the Du Pont Company has served as an important model.[63] Nevertheless, as Pierre neared eighty, he noted tartly that forty of his previous forty-two years had been spent "in some legal struggle with the federal government," and he was writing as the GM case was only just getting under way.[64]

Carpenter's experience with government in business was equally as impressive. He arrived at Du Pont in 1909, when the firm was in the midst of a major antitrust case that would destroy its explosives monopoly and help accelerate its diversification as a chemical enterprise. As treasurer and financial executive he won plaudits for resolving a multimillion dollar tax dispute that extended over ten years, and he watched the company's investment in U.S. Steel aborted by an antitrust investigation. As a general executive in the 1930s he endured the humiliation of the Nye investigation and helped Du Pont cope with the organization of the chemical industry under the NRA, the regulation of its securities and its refinancing by the SEC, and the promotion of unions in its workforce by the NLRB.

His presidency was even more distracted by government activity. In addition to coping with war and litigation as chief executive officer, Carpenter found that antitrust considerably narrowed Du Pont's options as he directed long-term planning for the company's continued growth. As chairman he watched the government's victory in the GM trial force the sale of more than one-fourth of the firm's assets. More frustrating was his anticipation of the antitrust threat in that case but his inability to avoid it because of federal tax policy as well as Pierre's intransigence. For most of Walter's career, then, the expanded role of public policy played a major part in both the immediate and long-range allocation of resources, the critical function of top management in large-scale enterprise.

At the same time Carpenter never became an enthusiastic supporter of expanded government or of the corporate state, as top executives in the two decades after World War II are often accused of being.[65] He was neither a Keynesian nor an internationalist but remained a devout supporter of personal and public fiscal prudence and of high tariffs to protect America's domestic market. His views and those of many of his associates at Du Pont suggest that postwar managers cannot be viewed in monolithic fashion. Clearly such factors as age, company heritage, industry affiliation, and family background helped differentiate top executives' attitudes toward corporate-state relations.[66]

In addition, Walter Carpenter's career points up the untidiness of American business history. Alfred Chandler's path-breaking work has provided illuminating patterns and persuasive explanations for the rise of big business in the United States. In his work the Du Pont Company and the General Motors Corporation serve as important case studies of the evolution of large, integrated industrial enterprise.[67] Almost simultaneously, they pioneered a strategy of careful diversification by technological and market linkages and a decentralized structure of autonomous product divisions directed by a general office headed by corporate executives.

Carpenter's experience from the inside, however, demonstrated that the landmark changes instituted by both firms in the early 1920s did not end the story and that apparently similar solutions did not always produce harmony between the two giants. He had to fend off Irénée du Pont's personal determination to move his family's firm into steel and rubber in the 1920s. He spent three decades and enormous energy overseeing and defending Pierre's investment of family and chemical company funds in the unrelated automobile industry. Furthermore, despite the parallels in strategy and structure at Du Pont and General Motors, the decade-long battle over reorganization at GM indicated that Walter Carpenter and Alfred Sloan were far more concerned with the nuances and subtle distinctions in the management of their separate enterprises. In addition, though top managers are thought to have focused quickly on long-range planning while coordination and appraisal became standard matters, Walter's continuing struggles with bonus plans at both Du Pont and GM in the 1920s and 1930s suggest that routinization sometimes came far more slowly than expected.

Walter's experiences at Du Pont and GM also remind us that that there is no simple structural panacea for the proper administration of big business. Analysts of later problems at General Motors suggest that he may well have been correct in his concerns about the impact of too powerful executives in a very strong general office. In contrast, at Du Pont Carpenter helped to weaken the development department's role in strategic planning and to place overall control in the executive committee with greater decentralization of responsibility to the industrial departments. His approach proved equally vulnerable after his retirement, when the executive committee subsequently proved unable to guide or control effectively the firm's powerful, autonomous departments, which became virtual fiefdoms. As Walter clearly understood and as his career certainly demonstrated, good management always requires continuous adjustment and sound judgment by strong, able people.

The relevance of Carpenter's career to contemporary American business practice may at first glance seem limited. The rise of conglomerate firms in the past three decades has restricted the opportunity of corporate leaders to direct their often wildly divergent product divisions. Financial formulas and statistical controls have often replaced judgment and decision making. The emergence of large institutional investors such as mutual investment and pension funds has constricted executive power. Indeed, one noted authority has prophesied the decline of the managerial firm before the rise of investor-directed enterprises where equity control would rest in unlisted securities.[68]

Nevertheless, the importance and value of past management practices are rapidly becoming more obvious. The inability of conglomerate concerns to identify economies of scale and scope critical to success has made their parts worth more than the whole. Many such firms have posted poor records and have disappeared or been drastically reorganized by failure, corporate raiders, or leveraged buyouts. Some recent studies have pointed to the urgent need for traditional attention to product-specific skills, market share, and learned managerial routines in large, technologically complex firms in order to maintain organizational capabilities and competitive advantages over the long haul.[69] These scholars now point out what Carpenter long realized: the value-creating ability of such managerial enterprises. Furthermore, the leaders of such companies continue to confront the issues that occupied Walter and his colleagues—the impact of government and public policy on business, the debate over the size and character of executive compensation, the question of guidelines for investment in research and development, and the always vexing problems of where to invest and expand.

Thus, the study of Carpenter's career is valuable because it provides a concrete picture of what a successful executive did and still does. His positions, experiences, and accomplishments in two of the largest industrial enterprises in the United States rank him among the most able businessmen in the nation during the first half of the twentieth century. This professional manager's careful focus on the long-range view is quite striking, especially in light of the much condemned "bottom-line" approach of American firms in the 1970s and 1980s, which has contributed so much to the country's current relative economic decline. Meanwhile our international competitors have been more successful by maintaining the extended, comprehensive outlook so characteristic of Walter Carpenter. The nation's business enterprise as well as its entire economy would benefit from having more people like him.

Notes

Bibliographical Note

Because the secondary sources for this study are cited fully in the notes and because most of the primary materials are located in one archive, there is little need for an elaborate bibliography. Of the numerous works written about the Du Pont Company, many are superficial and lack a solid grounding in the extensive documentation now available. Among the sound, scholarly accounts a few are especially useful and deserve particular mention. Alfred Chandler and Stephen Salsbury's *Pierre S. du Pont and the Making of the Modern Corporation* (New York: Harper & Row, 1971) is a superbly researched and insightful analysis of the company during Walter Carpenter's early years and of the man who helped promote Walter's career and who remained an important factor at Du Pont long after retirement in 1919. Chandler's *Strategy and Structure: Chapters in the History of the Industrial Enterprise* (Cambridge: MIT Press, 1962) includes a valuable chapter on the firm's innovative reorganization between 1919 and 1921, which helped redefine Carpenter's career. A comprehensive analysis of research and development at Du Pont throughout Walter's time there is provided by David Hounshell and John Smith's *Science and Corporate Strategy: Du Pont R&D, 1902–1980* (New York: Cambridge University Press, 1988). Less insightful but still worthwhile for its coverage of the company during the twentieth century is Graham Taylor and Patricia Sudnik's *Du Pont and the International Chemical Industry* (Boston: Twayne, 1984).

The extensive primary data on which this book is based are concentrated at the Hagley Museum and Library in Wilmington, Delaware. The archive contains Walter Carpenter's business and personal papers, which fill more than one hundred boxes and which were the backbone of this study. In addition, Hagley has a number of other large collections of the firm and of key personnel during Walter's era, including the records of Pierre, Irénée, and Lammot du Pont, of the Du Pont Company's administrative operations, of several important antitrust cases, and of such important fellow executives as Donaldson Brown, Jasper Crane, Crawford Greenewalt, Willis Harrington, and John Raskob.

Other useful manuscript sources were the R. G. Dun and Company records at the Baker Library of the Harvard Business School in Boston, Massachusetts; the John Williams papers at the University Library of the University of Delaware in Newark, Delaware; the minutes of the executive committee, the finance committee, and the board of directors of the Du Pont Company at the firm's headquarters in Wilmington, Delaware; and Walter Carpenter's scrapbooks held by his son, Edmund N. Carpenter II of Wilmington, Delaware. Additional material on the General Motors Corporation (though of limited relevance in this study) was located in the papers of John Lee Pratt, Charles F. Kettering, and Charles Stewart Mott in the General Motors Institute Alumni Foundation's Collection of Industrial History at the GMI Engineering and Management Institute in Flint, Michigan.

Key to Abbreviated Citations

The Hagley Museum and Library accession number or source abbreviation is on the left; the name of the collection on the right.

228	Papers of Irénée du Pont
473	Papers of John Raskob
889	Papers of Edmund N. and Donald F. Carpenter
1034	Personal papers of Irénée du Pont
1035	Records of the Christiana Securities Company
1282	Materials gathered by Alfred Chandler and Stephen Salsbury for their study of Pierre du Pont
1334	Papers of Donaldson Brown
1383	Edmund N. Carpenter diaries
1410	Records of the Du Pont Company's public affairs department
1415	Papers of James Q. du Pont
1553	Personal papers of Walter Carpenter
1662	Records of the Du Pont Company, administrative papers of the president's office
1689	Oral history interviews of Du Pont executives
1813	Papers of Willis Harrington
1814	Papers of Crawford Greenewalt
1850	Materials gathered by David Hounshell and John Smith for their study of Du Pont R&D
1889	Crawford Greenewalt's diaries of the Manhattan Project
LMSS	Longwood Manuscripts, Group 10, Pierre S. du Pont Papers
GM Case	*U.S. v. E. I. du Pont de Nemours & Co., General Motors Corporation et al.*, Civil Action No. 49C-1071, District Court for Northern Illinois. Citations include

<table>
<tr><td></td><td>Government Trial Exhibits (GTE) and number; Defendant's Trial Exhibits of the Du Pont Company (DTE-DP) or of the General Motors Corporation (DTE-GM) and number; and printed documents by series and page number.</td></tr>
<tr><td>GM Collection</td><td>Records gathered by the treasurer's and legal departments of the Du Pont Company for the GM Case</td></tr>
<tr><td>II, 1
II, 2
III, 3</td><td>Records of the Du Pont Company, Series II, Part 1 (Firms Absorbed), Part 2 (Administrative Papers since 1902), or Part 3 (Affiliated Companies). Walter Carpenter's business papers are in Part 2, Boxes 817–856.</td></tr>
</table>

Introduction

1. JoAnne Yates, *Control through Communications: The Rise of System in American Management* (Baltimore: Johns Hopkins University Press, 1989); Graham D. Taylor and Patricia E. Sudnik, *Du Pont and the International Chemical Industry* (Boston: Twayne, 1984); David Hounshell and John Smith, *Science and Corporate Strategy: Du Pont R&D, 1902–1980* (New York: Cambridge University Press, 1988); Alfred D. Chandler and Stephen Salsbury, *Pierre S. du Pont and the Making of the Modern Corporation* (New York: Harper & Row, 1971); Alfred D. Chandler, *Strategy and Structure: Chapters in the History of the Industrial Enterprise* (Cambridge: MIT Press, 1962), chap. 2.

2. For discussions of managers' backgrounds and behavior, see Robert and Seon Manley, eds., *The Age of the Manager: A Treasury of Our Times* (New York: Macmillan, 1962); and Francis Sutton, Seymour Harris, Carl Kaysen, and James Tobin, *The American Business Creed* (Cambridge: Harvard University Press, 1956).

3. See, for example, Robert Hayes and William J. Abernathy, "Managing Our Way to Economic Decline," *Harvard Business Review* 58 (July–August 1980): 67–77; and Robert Hayes and David Garvin, "Managing as If Tomorrow Mattered," *Harvard Business Review* 60 (May–June 1982): 70–79. For criticism of the quantitative or "numerative, rationalist" approach, see Thomas J. Peters and Robert H. Waterman, *In Search of Excellence: Lessons from America's Best-Run Companies* (New York: Harper & Row, 1982), pp. 29–54. For a review of this large literature, see Roger L. Adkins, "Competitive Decline: Views of Two Disciplines," *Journal of Economic Issues* 21 (June 1987): 869–76.

4. For the original argument, see Adolf A. Berle and Gardiner C. Means, *The Modern Corporation and Private Property* (New York: Macmillan, 1932). For the current popular view, see John Kenneth Galbraith, *The New Industrial State*, 3d ed. rev. (Boston: Houghton Mifflin, 1978).

5. The best study is Alfred D. Chandler, *The Visible Hand: The Managerial Revolution in American Business* (Cambridge: Harvard University Press, 1977).

Chapter 1   How to Succeed in Business—Quickly

1. For Walter Carpenter's ancestry, see George Valentine Massey II, *The Descendants of the Four Grandfathers of Walter Samuel Jr. and Mary Louise (Wootten) Carpenter* (privately printed, 1970).

2. Ibid., pp. iv–v.

3. Ibid., p. v.

4. For Benjamin Gardner Carpenter, see Massey, *Descendants*, p. iv; and "B. G. Carpenter's Death," an unidentified newspaper clipping dated November 12, 1889, in the first volume of Walter Carpenter's scrapbooks. See also an undated memorandum from Theron Burnet to B. H. Carpenter (Walter's Uncle Harry) in the second volume of scrapbooks, which are in the possession of Walter's son, Edmund N. Carpenter II, of Wilmington, Delaware.

5. The reports on which the subsequent discussion of B. G. Carpenter and Company is based are found in Pennsylvania, vol. 92, p. 91; vol. 93, pp. 685, 744; vol. 96, p. 288; and vol. 97, pp. 64, 67, R. G. Dun & Co. Collection, Baker Library, Harvard University Graduate School of Business Administration (hereafter cited as Pennsylvania).

6. Pennsylvania, vol. 97, p. 67.

7. Ibid., vol. 93, p. 685.

8. Ibid., vol. 97, p. 67.

9. Ibid., vol. 96, p. 288; and Olivier Zunz, *Making America Corporate, 1870–1920* (Chicago: University of Chicago Press, 1990), chap. 1.

10. Pennsylvania, vol. 96, p. 288, and vol. 97, p. 67.

11. Ibid., vol. 97, p. 67; and Massey, *Descendants*, Chart 1.

12. Edmund N. Carpenter diary for 1910–18 (unpaged), entry for September 30, 1910, Acc. 1383.

13. Walter S. Carpenter, "Comments upon Acceptance of the First Annual 'Man of the Year' Award," Wyoming Seminary Association of the Delaware Valley, January 18, 1965, II, 2, Box 856B.

14. For Carpenter's college career, see his scrapbooks, his Cornell University transcript, and "Walter S. Carpenter Jr.," *Cornell Reports* (June 1976): 6–7. The quotation is from Walter Carpenter to John W. Lucas, December 3, 1947, II, 2, Box 829.

15. Walter Carpenter to Alfred Sloan, July 28, 1958, II, 2, Box 849; Walter Carpenter to Mrs. Bennette Germaine, April 27, 1966, Acc. 1553, Box 14.

16. Mable Newcomer, "Professionalization of Leadership in the Big Business Corporation," in James Baughman, ed., *The History of American Management: Selections from the Business History Review* (Englewood Cliffs, N.J.: Prentice-Hall, 1969), pp. 244–52.

17. *Historical Statistics of the United States, Colonial Times to 1970* (Washington, D.C.: U.S. Government Printing Office, 1975), 1:383.

18. Harry M. Pierce to Lammot du Pont, September 23, 1919, Acc. 1662, Box 29.

19. For discussions of the traits of professional managers in Carpenter's

time, see Robert and Seon Manley, eds., *The Age of the Manager: A Treasury of Our Times* (New York: Macmillan, 1962), esp. Herrymon Maurer, "The New Manager," pp. 67–90; Charles E. Summer Jr., "The Managerial Mind," pp. 149–70; and Perrin Stryker, "How to Become an Executive," pp. 329–39. Historical treatments can be found in Thomas C. Cochran, *Business in American Life: A History* (New York: McGraw-Hill, 1972); and Thomas C. Cochran, *Railroad Leaders, 1845–1890: The Business Mind in Action* (Cambridge: Harvard University Press, 1953).

20. Walter Carpenter, "Comments before the Twelfth Annual Dinner Meeting of the Repauno's Foremen's Supervisors' Club," May 16, 1941, II, 2, Box 841.

21. Walter Carpenter, "Comments before the Foremen's Club at the Chambers Works," February 12, 1946, II, 2, Box 831.

22. Walter Carpenter to John Carpenter, August 21, 1939, Acc. 1553, Box 29.

23. Ibid.

24. Ibid.

25. Robert Ruliph Mogan Carpenter file, Acc. 1410, Box 62.

26. Pierre S. du Pont, address book, LMSS, Series A, File 384, Box 343.

27. Pierre S. du Pont to Walter Carpenter, December 16, 1909, in Walter Carpenter's scrapbooks, first volume.

28. Pierre S. du Pont to Elias Ahuja, June 28, 1910, LMSS, Series A, File 507, Box 599.

29. Walter Carpenter's Cornell University transcript.

30. Walter Carpenter, "Comments before Members of the Purchasing Department at the Hotel Du Pont," January 31, 1945, II, 2, Box 841.

31. For the history of the Du Pont Company in the nineteenth century, see Norman B. Wilkinson, *Lammot du Pont and the American Explosives Industry, 1850–1884* (Charlottesville: University Press of Virginia, 1984); Joseph F. Wall, *Alfred I. du Pont: The Man and His Family* (New York: Oxford University Press, 1990), chaps. 1–4; and William S. Dutton, *Du Pont: One Hundred and Forty Years* (New York: Charles Scribner's Sons, 1949). For histories of the chemical industry, see L. F. Haber, *The Chemical Industry during the Nineteenth Century: A Study of the Economic Aspect of Applied Chemistry in Europe and North America* (London: Oxford University Press, 1969) and *The Chemical Industry, 1900–1930: International Growth and Technological Change* (London: Oxford University Press, 1971); Fred Aftalion, *A History of the International Chemical Industry* (Philadelphia: University of Pennsylvania Press, 1991); and Williams Haynes, *American Chemical Industry*, 6 vols. (New York: D. Van Nostrand, 1945–54).

32. For a superb study of the transformation of the Du Pont Company between 1900 and 1920, see Alfred Chandler and Stephen Salsbury, *Pierre S. du Pont and the Making of the Modern Corporation* (New York: Harper & Row, 1971). For an alternative view from Alfred du Pont's perspective, see Wall, *Alfred I. du Pont*, chaps. 5–9.

33. Du Pont Company, *Annual Report*, 1909; and Chandler and Salsbury,

Pierre S. du Pont, p. 324. The subsequent labor figure is for 1910 and is from E. C. James to Miss Sylvanus, April 23, 1953, II, 2, Box 856.

34. For the use of professional managers, see Chandler and Salsbury, *Pierre S. du Pont*, esp. pp. 135–36, 301–21, 428–30. The 1914 figure is from Alfred Chandler, *Strategy and Structure: Chapters in the History of the Industrial Enterprise* (Cambridge: MIT Press, 1962), p. 84. In 1880 the Chicago, Burlington and Quincy Railroad defined middle management jobs as those paying from $1,500 to $4,000. The Consumer Price Index rose from 29 in 1880 to 30.1 in 1914 (1967 = 100). Zunz, *Making America Corporate*, p. 41; *Historical Statistics*, 1:211.

35. The following account of Du Pont's nitrate operations relies heavily on Chandler and Salsbury, *Pierre S. du Pont*, pp. 181–87, 205, 231–37.

36. See the correspondence between Pierre du Pont and Elias Ahuja in LMSS, Series A, File 507, Box 599.

37. Irenee du Pont to T. Coleman du Pont, May 1, 1914, Acc. 1282, Box 4.

38. Pierre du Pont to William du Pont, October 24, 1910, Pierre's documents, vol. 2, LMSS, Series A, File 418-26, Box 424. Pierre's documents are a collection of materials prepared for antitrust litigation and subsequently organized by Pierre du Pont for his historical research on the Du Pont Company.

39. Walter Carpenter, "Comments before the Twelfth Annual Dinner Meeting of Repauno's Foremen's Supervisors' Club," May 16, 1941, II, 2, Box 841.

40. Walter Carpenter to Howard C. Sheperd, August 14, 1958, II, 2, Box 844.

41. Edmund N. Carpenter to Mrs. B. G. Carpenter, May 30, 1910, Acc. 889.

42. For details of Walter's adventures, see Edmund Carpenter's diaries, Acc. 1383.

43. Edmund N. Carpenter to Mrs. B. G. Carpenter, July 6, 1910, Acc. 889.

44. Elias Ahuja to Walter Carpenter, April 26, 1918, and February, 19, 1919, Acc. 1553, Box 1.

45. Edmund N. Carpenter to Mrs. B. G. Carpenter, July 6, 1910, Acc. 889.

46. Chandler and Salsbury, *Pierre S. du Pont*, p. 181.

47. For details of conditions and negotiations, see the diaries and letters of Edmund N. Carpenter in Acc. 889 and Acc. 1383. A general account can be found in Chandler and Salsbury, *Pierre S. du Pont*, pp. 233–37.

48. For Edmund Carpenter's career, see "Travel Record of E. N. Carpenter," n.d., in Acc. 1553, Box 7.

49. Edmund N. Carpenter to Mrs. B. G. Carpenter, April 10, 1910, Acc. 889.

50. Pierre du Pont to Edmund N. Carpenter, March 3, 1911, and Charles Copeland to Edmund N. Carpenter, March 7, 1911, Acc. 889.

51. For an excellent analysis of the growth of big business in the United States and its dependence on the economies of scale, see Alfred D. Chandler, *The Visible Hand: The Managerial Revolution in American Business* (Cambridge: Harvard University Press, 1977), esp. chaps. 9–11.

52. Chandler, *Strategy and Structure*, pp. 71, 60.

53. Irénée du Pont to Coleman du Pont, April 30, 1914, Acc. 228, Box 40, File ID-37.

54. "Transcript: Preliminary Testimony [of Pierre du Pont], April 17–April 25, 1951," p. 96, LMSS, Series A, File 418-26, Box 428.

55. Development committee minutes, July 5, 1912, and executive committee minutes, July 9, 1912, Acc. 1282, Box 4; Walter Carpenter to Edmund Carpenter, March 27 and April 4, 1947, and Edmund Carpenter to Walter Carpenter, March 29, 1947, Acc. 1553, Box 5.

56. Pierre du Pont to Lammot du Pont, October 30, 1942, Acc. 1662, Box 38.

57. For these negotiations, see executive committee minutes, June 8 and 22, 1914, Acc. 1282, Box 4.

58. Walter Carpenter to Ruly Carpenter, July 9, 1914, and Ruly Carpenter to Coleman du Pont, July 9, 1914, II, 3, Box 133.

59. "Notes on Interview with John Lee Pratt, October 2, 1962," Acc. 1689.

60. Walter Carpenter to Edmund Carpenter, April 13, 1916, Document 1106, Acc. 1282, Box 7.

61. Walter Carpenter to the executive committee, December 20, 1916, Acc. 1282, Box 8.

62. For a discussion of British gunpowder orders, see Chandler and Salsbury, *Pierre S. du Pont*, pp. 359–75.

63. Walter Carpenter to executive committee, December 20, 1916, Acc. 1282, Box 8.

64. David Hounshell and John Smith, *Science and Corporate Strategy: Du Pont R&D, 1902–1980* (New York: Cambridge University Press, 1988), pp. 70–71.

65. Ruly Carpenter to Paul Mueller, April 2 and May 28, 1913, Acc. 228, Box 40, File ID-30.

66. Walter Carpenter to Paul Mueller, October 23 and November 18, 1913, and January 20, 1914, and Paul Mueller to Walter Carpenter, March 23, 1914, Acc. 228, Box 40, File ID-30.

67. Walter Carpenter to the executive committee, February 16, 1914, LMSS, Series A, File 418-26, Box 434.

68. Ibid.

69. Ibid., p. 24.

70. Walter Carpenter to Irénée du Pont, April 29, 1914, LMSS, Series A, File 418-26, Box 434. See also Walter Carpenter to Irénée du Pont, April 17, 1914, in ibid.

71. For the definitive study of this innovation, see Chandler, *Strategy and Structure*, esp. chap. 2.

72. Irénée du Pont to Howard Bemis, March 26, 1914, Acc. 228, Box 40, File ID-30. Pierre's later notes indicate that by December 1914 he favored buying a firm instead of starting from scratch. Pierre du Pont's notes in "Memorandum Concerning the Expansion of the Du Pont Company from 1902 to 1920," January 16, 1951, LMSS, Series A, File 418-26, Box 436.

73. Walter Carpenter to Ruly Carpenter, December 11, 1914, Pierre's documents, vol. 2, LMSS, Series A, File 418–26, Box 424.

74. Irénée du Pont to Howard Bemis, March 26, 1914, and Irénée du Pont to the executive committee, April 24, 1914, Acc. 228, Box 40, File ID-30; "Memorandum of Conference . . . ," January 25, 1951, LMSS, Series A, File 418-26, Box 410; Walter Carpenter to Ruly Carpenter, December 11, 1914, Pierre's documents, vol. 2, LMSS, Series A, File 418-26, Box 424.

75. Executive committee minutes, April 14 and 27, 1914, Acc. 1282, Box 2; Irénée du Pont to the executive committee, April 24, 1914, Acc. 228, Box 40, File ID-30.

76. Walter Carpenter to the executive committee, November 11, 1914, LMSS, Series A, File 418-26, Box 428. The quotation is from Walter Carpenter to Irénée du Pont, April 17, 1914, LMSS, Series A, File 418-26, Box 434.

77. Walter Carpenter to the executive committee, November 11, 1914, LMSS, Series A, File 418-26, Box 428. See also executive committee minutes, April 14 and 27, 1914, Acc. 1282, Box 2.

78. Executive committee minutes, November 23 and December 21, 1914, Acc. 1282, Box 4.

79. Jasper E. Crane, *A Short History of the Arlington Company* (n.p., 1945); Jasper E. Crane to F. A. Gudger, July 10, 1918, Acc. 1662, Box 6.

80. Details of the split and Du Pont's negotiation can be found in Walter Carpenter to the executive committee, September 12, 1915, Acc. 1282, Box 8.

81. Ibid.

82. Ibid.

83. Ibid.

84. "E. I. du Pont de Nemours and Company: Acquisitions of Selected Companies or Properties," August 11, 1950, LMSS, Series A, File 418-26, Box 414.

85. Arlington Company, "Treasurer's Report," February 18, 1915, Series II, Part 1, Box 79; Francis Gudger to Walter Carpenter, March 15, 1958, II, 2, Box 844.

86. Chandler and Salsbury, *Pierre S. du Pont*, p. 250.

87. Hounshell and Smith, *Science and Corporate Strategy*, p. 73; "Comparison of Operations," n.d., II, 2, Box 1053.

88. "An American Business Statesman," *Better Living*, January−February 1960, p. 5.

89. Copy of Ruly Carpenter's obituary in the *Wilmington Sunday Star*, June 12, 1949, in Walter Carpenter's scrapbooks, second volume. See also Ruly Carpenter's file in Acc. 1410, Box 62.

90. For accounts of the struggle for control, see Chandler and Salsbury, *Pierre S. du Pont*, pp. 322−58; and Wall, *Alfred du Pont*, pp. 324−55.

91. Chandler and Salsbury, *Pierre S. du Pont*, p. 430.

92. Du Pont Company, *Annual Report*, 1918, pp. 4, 10; Harry M. Pierce to Lammot du Pont, September 23, 1919, Acc. 1662, Box 29; Chandler, *Strategy and Structure*, p. 84.

93. Chandler, *Strategy and Structure*, p. 84.

94. For excellent analyses of Du Pont's diversification, see Chandler, *Strategy*

and Structure, chap. 2; Chandler and Salsbury, *Pierre S. du Pont*, pp. 381–86; and Hounshell and Smith, *Science and Corporate Strategy*, esp. chap. 3.

95. Chandler, *Strategy and Structure*, p. 88.

96. For the best study of Du Pont's investment in General Motors, see Chandler and Salsbury, *Pierre S. du Pont*, chaps. 16–22.

97. John Raskob to the finance committee, December 19, 1917, GM Case, GTE 124. For Pierre's role, see Chandler and Salsbury, *Pierre S. du Pont*, pp. 451–54.

98. See folders labeled "Du Pont Engineering Company" and "Du Pont Engineering Company—Reorganized," in Acc. 1662, Box 23; and folder labeled "Documents on Commercial and Organizational Relations," in LMSS, Series A, File 418-26, Box 440.

99. Irénée du Pont to the executive committee, May 3, 1915, GM Case, DTE-DP 75.

100. Hounshell and Smith, *Science and Corporate Strategy*, esp. pp. 36, 65–67, 77, 96. They label Sparre the "architect of Du Pont's post–World War I diversification strategy" (p. 117).

101. For a full discussion of Du Pont's development of dyes, see ibid., chap. 3.

102. Walter Carpenter to the executive committee, December 29, 1915, GM Case, DTE-DP 85.

103. Ibid.

104. Charles Holloway to Walter Carpenter, July 17, 1918, II, 2, Box 1; Williams Haynes, *American Chemical Industry*, vol. 3: *The World War I Period: 1912–1922* (New York: D. Van Nostrand, 1945), p. 244.

105. Hounshell and Smith, *Science and Corporate Strategy*, pp. 87–96; Walter Carpenter, "Remarks to the Foremen's Meeting at the Dye Works," June 19, 1935, II, 2, Box 856C.

106. Frank MacGregor interview, July 21 and August 8, 1961, Acc. 1689.

107. Ruly Carpenter to the executive committee, January 6, 1917, Acc. 1282, Box 4; Haynes, *American Chemical Industry*, 3:244; Pierre du Pont's notes from executive committee minutes for March 29, 1920, LMSS, Series A, File 418-26, Box 431.

108. For the paint operation, see Frank MacGregor to Ruly Carpenter, April 24, 1918, GM Case, DTE-DP 217; and Frank MacGregor to Walter Carpenter, March 15, 1920, GM Case, GTE 280. For a general discussion, see Chandler, *Strategy and Structure*, pp. 86–88, 92, 100–101.

109. Walter Carpenter to the executive committee, April 7, 1920, p. 1407, in the first of two chronological series of printed documents submitted to the Justice Department in the GM Case.

110. Walter Carpenter to Ruly Carpenter, April 23, 1918, Acc. 1282, Box 8.

111. For the department's wartime operations, see Du Pont Company, *Annual Report*, 1918, pp. 13–14, 16. The personnel count is from Chart A-19, Acc. 1282, Box 7.

112. Walter Beadle interview, June 19, 1961, Acc. 1689.

113. Du Pont Company, *Annual Report*, 1918, p. 14.

114. Pierre du Pont to the board of directors, April 3, 1919, Document 1094, Acc. 1282, Box 7; Irénée du Pont to Lammot du Pont, August 8, 1944, [draft not sent] Acc. 228, Series H, File VC-45.

115. "American Business Statesman," p. 2.

116. Clipping from the *Wilmington Morning News*, June 14, 1914, in Walter Carpenter's scrapbooks, first volume.

117. For details of the transaction, see the correspondence between Irénée du Pont and Walter Carpenter in Acc. 1034, File 240.

118. For Carpenter's income after 1914, see his income tax returns in Acc. 1553, Box 64. For his 1914 income, see Walter Carpenter to John Carpenter, August 21, 1939, Acc. 1553, Box 29.

119. Irénée du Pont to Walter Carpenter, August 2, 1917, and Irénée du Pont to Pierre du Pont, August 2, 1917, Acc. 1034, File 240.

120. Irénée du Pont to the directors of the Christiana Securities Company, September 29, 1919, Acc. 1035, Box 164824.

121. Ibid.

122. Walter S. Carpenter, "Development—The Strategy of Industry," *The Annals of the American Academy of Political and Social Science* 85 (September 1919): 197–201.

123. Donaldson Brown's famous articles include "Centralized Control with Decentralized Responsibilities," *Annual Convention Series*, no. 57 (New York: American Management Association, 1927): 3–24; "Pricing Policy in Relation to Financial Control," *Management and Administration* 7 (February 1924): 195–98 and (March 1924): 283–86; and "Pricing Policy Applies to Financial Control," *Management and Administration* 7 (April 1924): 417–22.

124. This quotation and all of those in the next four paragraphs are from Carpenter, "Development."

125. Alfred D. Chandler, *Scale and Scope: The Dynamics of Industrial Capitalism* (Cambridge: Harvard University Press, 1990), p. 17.

126. Ibid., chaps. 5–6.

127. Chandler, *Strategy and Structure*, pp. 92, 104; Walter Carpenter, "Remarks to the Foremen's Meeting at the Dye Works," June 19, 1935, II, 2, Box 856C.

128. Chandler and Salsbury, *Pierre S. du Pont*, p. 680, note 60.

129. Chandler, *Visible Hand*, chaps. 12–14 and pp. 490–97.

Chapter 2   Top Manager

1. The discussion of Du Pont's reorganization relies heavily on Alfred Chandler, *Strategy and Structure: Chapters in the History of the Industrial Enterprise* (Cambridge: MIT Press, 1962), chap. 2.

2. Crawford H. Greenewalt interview, October 21, 1991.

3. See, for example, Walter Carpenter, "Comments before the Educators' Conference," June 14, 1954," II, 2, Box 852, and "Comments before the

Chemical Engineering Seminar," May 6, 1952, II, 2, Box 852.

4. Crawford Greenewalt to Walter Carpenter, August 20, 1948, II, 2, Box 843.

5. Crawford Greenewalt to Irénée du Pont, June 1, 1944, Acc. 1034, File 244.

6. Lammot du Pont to Edmond Gillet, March 29, 1929, Acc. 1662, Box 8.

7. For top managers' control of large U.S. industrials, see Alfred Chandler, *The Visible Hand: The Managerial Revolution in American Business* (Cambridge: Harvard University Press, 1977), pp. 490–93.

8. David Hounshell and John Smith, *Science and Corporate Strategy: Du Pont R&D, 1902–1980* (New York: Cambridge University Press, 1988), p. 92.

9. Chandler, *Strategy and Structure*, p. 92.

10. Ibid., p. 104.

11. Ibid., pp. 91–112.

12. Ibid., p. 100.

13. Ibid., pp. 94–96.

14. Ibid., pp. 96–99.

15. Executive committee minutes, May 26, June 2, July 21, and September 15, 1919; Chandler, *Strategy and Structure*, pp. 92–93, 412, note 102.

16. Chandler, *Strategy and Structure*, pp. 100–101.

17. Executive committee minutes, June 14, July 13, and September 20, 1920.

18. "Notes on Comments on Organization Made at Meeting of August 8, 1921—E. I. du Pont Co.," LMSS, Series A, File 418, Box 377.

19. Walter Carpenter to Ruly Carpenter, August 6 and 13, 1921, and Ruly Carpenter to Walter Carpenter, August 12, 1921, Acc. 1553, Box 1.

20. Frank MacGregor interview, July 21, 1961, with Alfred Chandler, Norman Wilkinson, and Richmond Williams, Acc. 1689.

21. Executive committee minutes, November 22, 1920.

22. "Notes on Comments on Organization Made at Meeting of August 8, 1921—E. I. du Pont Co.," LMSS, Series A, File 418, Box 377.

23. Ibid.; Walter Carpenter to Ruly Carpenter, August 6 and 13, 1921, Acc. 1553, Box 1; executive committee minutes, July 13, 1920.

24. Executive committee minutes, November 22, 1920.

25. Chandler, *Strategy and Structure*, pp. 105–6.

26. For a discussion of Brown's proposal and its adoption, see ibid., pp. 105–12.

27. Walter Carpenter to C. E. Wilson, April 7, 1944, II, 2, Box 837.

28. For an analysis of the significance and adoption of the change, see Chandler, *Strategy and Structure*, esp. chaps. 6–7.

29. Minutes of the finance committee, March 12, 1919.

30. Irénée du Pont to the directors of the Christiana Securities Company, September 29, 1919, Acc. 1035, Box 164824.

31. Chandler, *Strategy and Structure*, p. 110.

32. For a discussion of the move and of Brown's career, see Alfred Chandler

and Stephen Salsbury, *Pierre S. du Pont and the Making of the Modern Corporation* (New York: Harper & Row, 1971), pp. 493, 496–98; and Donaldson Brown, *Some Reminiscences of an Industrialist* (n.p., n.d.), esp. pp. 19–34.

33. Irénée du Pont to the finance committee, December 21, 1920, Document 1085, Acc. 1282, Box 7.

34. Finance committee minutes, December 27 and 31, 1920 and January 3, 1921; board of directors minutes, January 10, 1921.

35. John Raskob to Irénée du Pont, January 8, 1921, Acc. 1662, Box 78.

36. Irénée du Pont's marginal notes on ibid.

37. Ibid.

38. Board of directors minutes, January 10, 1921.

39. Irénée du Pont to the executive committee, September 12, 1921, Acc. 1662, Box 60. In the same file, see also Lammot du Pont's undated, handwritten sheet headed "Executive Committee" with Irénée's note suggesting Walter Carpenter as a substitute for Donaldson Brown, whom Lammot was proposing but who had already moved to General Motors.

40. Walter Carpenter testimony, GM Case, Transcript, p. 6570; Chandler, *Strategy and Structure*, pp. 60–61.

41. Walter Carpenter to heads of departments, October 4, 1921, Acc. 1662, Box 60.

42. Du Pont Company press release, May 20, 1940, Acc. 1813, Box 31.

43. Walter Carpenter to Irénée du Pont, October 20, 1923, Acc. 1662, Box 78.

44. Du Pont Company, *Annual Report*, 1922, pp. 3–4.

45. Walter Carpenter to Donaldson Brown, April 22, 1925, Acc. 1334, Box 1; Du Pont Company, *Annual Report*, 1925, p. 12.

46. Irénée du Pont to John Raskob, January 27, 1923, Acc. 473, File 677.

47. Du Pont Company, *Annual Report*, 1921, pp. 4, 16. For the depression's national impact, see Peter Temin, *Did Monetary Forces Cause the Great Depression?* (New York: W. W. Norton, 1976), p. 64.

48. William Spruance to Irénée du Pont, August 4, 1921, Acc. 1662, Box 75.

49. Irénée du Pont to Frederick Pickard, August 11, 1921, *U.S. v. Imperial Chemical Industries, Ltd., et al.*, Civil Action No. 24-13, District Court for Southern New York (1944), Defendant's Trial Exhibit 2145. (Hereafter cited as ICI Case, DTE or GTE [Government's Trial Exhibit], and exhibit number.)

50. Walter Carpenter to Frederick Pickard, June 24, 1921, ICI Case, DTE 2143.

51. Du Pont Company, *Annual Report*, 1923, p. 6; Walter Carpenter to Edgar Queeny, n.d. [July 1932], Acc. 1662, Box 78.

52. Edmund N. Carpenter II interview, May 23, 1990.

53. Walter Carpenter to Irénée du Pont, June 29, 1922, Acc. 1662, Box 78; minutes of the finance committee, April 7, 1924. For cash reserves, see Du Pont's annual reports for the 1920s.

54. Pierre du Pont to Elias Ahuja, April 12, 1918, GM Case, Deposition of Pierre S. du Pont, beginning May 21, 1951, Defendants' Exhibit 89, LMSS,

Series A, File 418-26, Box 417. (Hereafter cited as PSduP, DTE or GTE [Government Trial Exhibit], and exhibit number.)

55. Irénée du Pont to Walter Carpenter, May 15 and 18, 1923, Acc. 1662, Box 78. For details of the bond issue, see Chandler and Salsbury, *Pierre S. du Pont*, pp. 507–8.

56. Irénée du Pont to Walter Carpenter, May 18, 1923, Acc. 1662, Box 78. Carpenter's letter presenting his case is missing but his position can be determined from his arguments frequently made elsewhere and from Irénée's response. For later examples of Walter's case, see Walter Carpenter to the finance committee, March 10, 1937, II, 2, Box 824; and Walter Carpenter, "Comments before the Chemical Engineering Seminar," May 6, 1952, II, 2, Box 852. The latter also has data on stock sales.

57. Irénée du Pont to Pierre du Pont, November 4, 1922, and Walter Carpenter to Irénée du Pont, November 4, 1922, LMSS, Series A, File 624, Box 1 (of five).

58. Walter Carpenter to Irénée du Pont, September 7, 1921, Acc. 1553, Box 1; Irénée du Pont to Walter Carpenter, September 8, 1921, Acc. 1662, Box 78; "Administrative Contracts," February 19, 1941, LMSS, Series A, File 418, Box 379.

59. Chandler and Salsbury, *Pierre S. du Pont*, pp. 540–41. They misname the firm the Management Securities Company.

60. Walter Carpenter to Donaldson Brown, July 19, 1923, PSduP, GTE 184, LMSS, Series A, File 418-26, Box 416.

61. Irénée du Pont to Pierre du Pont, July 20, 1923, PSduP, GTE 185, LMSS, Series A, File 418-26, Box 416.

62. Donaldson Brown to Walter Carpenter, July 20, 1923, PSduP, GTE 186, and Irénée du Pont to Pierre du Pont, August 14, 1923, PSduP, GTE 190, LMSS, Series A, File 418-26, Box 416; Chandler and Salsbury, *Pierre S. du Pont*, pp. 541–42. The final plan called for the sale of 2.25 million shares of GM stock for $4.95 million in cash and $28.8 million in the preferred stock of the Managers Securities Company. Alfred Sloan, *My Years with General Motors* (New York: MacFadden Books, 1965), pp. 410–11.

63. Walter Carpenter, "Comments before the Chemical Engineering Seminar," May 6, 1952, II, 2, Box 852.

64. Du Pont Company, *Annual Report*, 1922, p. 12; finance committee minutes, May 22, 1922. For evidence of trading in the unlisted common stock before registration on the NYSE, see Chandler and Salsbury, *Pierre S. du Pont*, pp. 325, 329.

65. "Stockholders: Total Employees & Descendants of Family Stockholders," n.d. [1950] in LMSS, Series A, File 418-26, Box 440A.

66. This story can be found in Walter Carpenter to the board of directors of the E. I. du Pont de Nemours Powder Company, June 17, 1922, II, 3, Box 142. The approvals by Raskob, Irénée, and Lammot are written on the letter. For accounts of the battle for control, see Chandler and Salsbury, *Pierre S. du Pont*,

chap. 12; and Joseph Wall, *Alfred Irénée du Pont: The Man and His Family* (New York: Oxford University Press, 1990), pp. 322–55.

67. For a description, see Du Pont Company, *Annual Report*, 1926, p. 11; and Lammot du Pont to George Harper, August 29, 1923, Acc. 1662, Box 39.

68. Donaldson Brown to Irénée du Pont, January 15, 1921, Acc. 1662, Box 78.

69. Lammot du Pont to Assistant Attorney General William Donovan, October 5, 1928, Acc. 1662, Box 37.

70. B. D. Beyea to Fin Sparre, November 23, 1927, II, 2, Box 823.

71. Walter Carpenter to Thomas Grasselli, September 14, 1928, II, 2, Box 823. Irénée's statement is from Irénée du Pont to B. F. Sherman, August 11, 1921, Acc. 1662, Box 61.

72. Walter Carpenter to Thomas Grasselli, September 14, 1928, II, 2, Box 823.

73. Thomas Grasselli to Walter Carpenter, June 3, 1940, II, 2, Box 839.

74. Walter Carpenter to Elias Ahuja, January 10, 1929, Acc. 1553, Box 2.

75. Hounshell and Smith, *Science and Corporate Strategy*, pp. 162–64, 170–72.

76. Ibid., pp. 164–67, 175–76; Walter Carpenter to W. M. Moore, November 12, 1928, II, 2, Box 818.

77. Walter Carpenter to B. G. Paskus, April 18, 1928, and Walter Carpenter to Albert Blum, November 2, 1928, II, 2, Box 818.

78. Walter Carpenter to Albert Blum, November 2, 1928, II, 2, Box 818.

79. Walter Carpenter to Albert Blum, December 31, 1928, and M. D. Fisher to Walter Carpenter, January 11, 1929, II, 2, Box 818. The final exchange ratios were adjusted for a three and one-half for one split in Du Pont stock on January 21, 1929 (finance committee minutes, January 21 and March 18, 1929).

80. Hounshell and Smith, *Science and Corporate Strategy*, pp. 167, 170, 173, 177, 180; Walter Carpenter to the executive and finance committees, December 10, 1928, II, 2, Box 818.

81. Chandler, *Strategy and Structure*, pp. 112–13; Hounshell and Smith, *Science and Corporate Strategy*, pp. 57, 77, 119.

82. Alfred Chandler, *Scale and Scope: The Dynamics of Industrial Capitalism* (Cambridge: Harvard University Press, 1990), pp. 134–38.

83. Irénée du Pont to Harry B. Rust, April 16, 1927, Acc. 228, Series J, File 218. See also Pierre du Pont to George Baker Jr., February 19, 1924, LMSS, Series A, File 258, Box 203; and Irénée du Pont to John Raskob, March 31, 1926, Acc. 473, File 677.

84. Walter Carpenter to Irénée du Pont, February 14, 1927, II, 2, Box 824. Others have apparently misread the letter. Graham D. Taylor and Patricia E. Sudnik, *Du Pont and the International Chemical Industry* (Boston: Twayne, 1984), p. 88.

85. For an account of the operation, see Walter Carpenter to the finance committee, November 29, 1927, II, 2, Box 824; and U.S. Government: Federal

Trade Commission, "Report of Federal Trade Commission on Du Pont Investments . . . ," February 1, 1929, LMSS, Series A, File 418-26, Box 411.

86. Walter Carpenter to the finance committee, November 29, 1927, II, 2, Box 824.

87. Laird, Bissell and Meeds, "$10,000 Invested in duPont Common" and "$10,000 Invested in U.S. Steel Common," March 10, 1939, LMSS, Series A, File 418, Box 379.

88. Michael J. French, *The U.S. Tire Industry: A History* (Boston: Twayne, 1991), esp. chap. 5; and Glenn D. Babcock, *History of the United States Rubber Company: A Case Study in Corporate Management* (Bloomington: University of Indiana Press, 1966), pp. 146, 148, 154, 171, 248.

89. For an account of the du Ponts' investment in U.S. Rubber, see "Memorandum Concerning the Wilmington Group Investment in U.S. Rubber Stock," April 19, 1951, LMSS, Series A, File 118-26, Box 433.

90. P. D. Laird, Memorandum, August 5, 1927, LMSS, Series A, File 418-26, Box 433.

91. Walter Carpenter to E. N. Carpenter, March 31, 1928, Acc. 1553, Box 1.

92. Walter Carpenter to Irénée du Pont, July 13, 1928, in "Appendixes to Statement of Irénée du Pont," LMSS, Series A, File 418-26, Box 429; and Irénée du Pont to Walter Carpenter, September 14, 1928, II, 2, Box 824.

93. This quotation and those in the following two paragraphs are from Walter Carpenter to the finance committee, September 15, 1928, II, 2, Box 824.

94. Walter Carpenter to C. A. Horsky, May 5, 1953, II, 2, Box 852; Babcock, *United States Rubber Company*, pp. 276, 283, 286.

95. For material on the stock exchange, see File C-49 in II, 2. For the 1937 issue, see Walter Carpenter to A. B. Echols, April 1, 1937, and Walter Carpenter to the finance committee, September 1, 1937, II, 2, Box 824.

96. Walter Carpenter to the finance committee, March 10, 1937, II, 2, Box 824.

97. Walter Carpenter to the finance committee, September 1, 1938, II, 2, Box 824.

98. Walter Carpenter to the finance committee, May 16, 1939, II, 2, Box 824.

99. E. E. Lincoln to Walter Carpenter, August 27, 1938, and Lammot du Pont to Walter Carpenter, October 31, 1938, II, 2, Box 824.

100. For a recent discussion of this approach, see Allen Kaufman and Lawrence Zacharias, "From Trust to Contract: The Legal Language of Managerial Ideology, 1920–1980," *Business History Review* 66 (Autumn 1992): 523–72.

101. Walter Carpenter to E. E. Lincoln, May 17, 1939, II, 2, Box 824.

102. Walter Carpenter to the finance committee, May 16, 1939, Walter Carpenter, Memoranda, October 4 and 5, 1939, and Walter Carpenter to Thomas Parkinson, October 9, 1939, II, 2, Box 824.

103. See correspondence in File C-49, II, 2, Box 824.

104. Lammot du Pont, "Stockholders' Bulletin," December 14, 1939, Acc. 1813, Box 30.

105. Lammot du Pont to A. Felix du Pont, November 1, 1939, and A. Felix du Pont to Lammot du Pont, November 7, 1939, Acc. 1662, Box 40.

106. Walter Carpenter to Harold Stanley, October 30, 1939, II, 2, Box 824.

107. Chandler, *Strategy and Structure*, pp. 136–37.

108. Ibid.; "Administrative Contracts," February 19, 1941, LMSS, Series A, File 418, Box 379; Irénée du Pont to Walter Carpenter, August 2, 1917, Acc. 1034, File 240; "Memorandum of Agreement," June 16, 1923, Acc. 1034, File 199.

109. Walter Carpenter to the finance committee, August 20, 1926, and to the executive committee, August 21, 1926, II, 2, Box 820.

110. Ibid.

111. Finance committee minutes, September 9, 1932; Walter Carpenter to the finance committee, May 12, 1933, II, 2, Box 820.

112. Walter Carpenter to H. H. Preston, April 8, 1947, II, 2, Box 841.

113. H. F. Brown to Walter Carpenter, August 23, 1926, II, 2, Box 820.

114. F. S. Johnson to Lammot du Pont, June 22, 1936, Acc. 1662, Box 79.

115. Pierre du Pont to H. E. Ellsworth, March 8, 1918, GM Case, DTE-DP 60.

116. Walter Carpenter to Lammot du Pont, March 11, 1930, Acc. 1662, Box 46.

117. Ibid.

118. Walter Carpenter to the finance committee, August 16, 1935, Acc. 1662, Box 79.

119. Lammot du Pont to Gerald Nye, November 6, 1934, Acc. 1813, Box 19; Du Pont Company, *Annual Report*, 1934, p. 14.

120. Hounshell and Smith, *Science and Corporate Strategy*, p. 181.

121. For a description of the formula for return on investment, the Chart Room, and the meetings there, see JoAnne Yates, *Control through Communications: The Rise of System in American Management* (Baltimore: Johns Hopkins University Press, 1989), pp. 265–67; and Alfred D. Chandler, "The Functions of the HQ Unit in the Multibusiness Firm," *Strategic Management Journal* 12 (Special Issue, Winter 1991): 45.

122. R. M. Horsey to the executive and finance committees, November 28, 1934, LMSS, Series A, File 418, Box 378; Walter Carpenter to Leonard Yerkes, May 6, 1932, *U.S. v. E. I. du Pont de Nemours and Company*, Civil Action, No. 1216, District Court for Delaware (1947), Defendant's Trial Exhibit 189. (Hereafter cited as Cellophane Case, DTE or GTE [Government's Trial Exhibit], and exhibit number.)

123. Walter Carpenter to W. M. Moore, January 26, 1931, II, 2, Box 818; Walter Carpenter to Leonard Yerkes, December 15, 1928, and August 9, 1932, II, 2, Box 818.

124. Walter Carpenter to Leonard Yerkes, May 12, 1930, and J. E. Hatt to Walter Carpenter, May 14, 1930, Cellophane Case, DTE 5076 and DTE 5077.

125. Walter Carpenter to Leonard Yerkes, September 15, 1936, and Leonard Yerkes to Walter Carpenter, September 17, 1936, Cellophane Case,

GTE 469 and GTE 470; Leonard Yerkes to Walter Carpenter, August 11, 1932 and December 18, 1928, II, 2, Box 818.

126. "Minutes of a Meeting Held in New York on May 6, 1931," ICI Case, GTE 804; Walter Carpenter to the executive committee, November 4, 1927, II, 2, Box 822.

127. Pierre du Pont to the executive committee, September 6, 1916, ICI Case, DTE 1287. For a history of Du Pont's foreign business, see Taylor and Sudnik, *Du Pont.*

128. Walter Carpenter to H. J. Mitchell, April 26, 1934, II, 2, Box 819.

129. Ibid.

130. H. J. Mitchell to Walter Carpenter, May 9, 1934, Walter Carpenter to Réné Bernheim, August 9, 1934, and Walter Carpenter to W. R. Swint, December 2, 1935, II, 2, Box 819. For the final share arrangement, see Richard Fort to John Jenney, April 12, 1939, II, 2, Box 1028.

131. E. J. Barnsley to W. R. Swint, August 12, 1940, II, 2, Box 832; Taylor and Sudnik, *Du Pont*, p. 187.

132. For a discussion, see Alfred Chandler, "Organizational Capabilities and the Economic History of the Industrial Enterprise," *Journal of Economic Perspectives* 6 (Summer 1992), esp. pp. 84–87. The quotation is from p. 84. A more theoretical and extended treatment can be found in Richard R. Nelson and Sidney G. Winter, *An Evolutionary Theory of Economic Change* (Cambridge: The Belknap Press of Harvard University Press, 1982), pp. 14–18 and chap. 5, and a fine historical case study can be found in Steven W. Usselman, "IBM and Its Imitators: Organizational Capabilities and the Emergence of the International Computer Industry," *Business and Economic History* 2d ser., vol. 22 (Winter 1993): 1–35. For the importance of business organization and organizational capabilities in the development and use of productive resources, see William Lazonick, *Business Organization and the Myth of the Market Economy* (New York: Cambridge University Press, 1991).

133. For this subject, I have relied on Hounshell and Smith, *Science and Corporate Strategy*, pp. 311–14, 352–53.

134. Walter Carpenter quoted in ibid., p. 314.

135. Ibid.

136. Walter Carpenter, "Post-War Employment: The Chemical Industry," undated article [July 1945?] apparently written for the *Army-Navy Journal*, II, 2, Box 833.

137. Hounshell and Smith, *Science and Corporate Strategy*, p. 314.

138. Walter Carpenter to Donaldson Brown, March 28, 1938, II, 2, Box 821.

139. Executive committee minutes, January 9 and July 31, 1929, and March 12, 1930. The reports were deferred in 1931 and then apparently stopped.

140. Zachary Phelps to the executive committee, September 11, 1925, pp. 2838–48, in the first of two chronological series of printed documents submitted to the Justice Department in the GM Case. (Hereafter listed as Documents—series number and page numbers.)

141. Walter Carpenter to Fin Sparre, November 24, 1925, Documents, I,

pp. 2584–91. This letter is filed in the 1924 volume, one year out of order. The quotations in the following four paragraphs are from the same document.

142. Hounshell and Smith, *Science and Corporate Strategy*, chap. 9; Du Pont Company, *Annual Report*, 1937, p. 25.

143. Frederick Wardenburg to Walter Carpenter, October 13, 1939, Acc. 1662, Box 5; Willis Harrington to Walter Carpenter, August 30, 1937, II, 2, Box 820; Willis Harrington to Lammot du Pont, December 20, 1939, Acc. 1662, Box 5.

144. See, for example, Deborah Shapley, *Promise and Power: The Life and Times of Robert McNamara* (Boston: Little, Brown, 1993), esp. pp. 65–68; and John A. Byrne, *The Whiz Kids: The Founding Fathers of American Business—and the Legacy They Left Us* (New York: Doubleday, 1993), esp. pp. 7–9, 19–20, 174–76, 364–69, 380–84, 418–22, 486, 515–19.

145. Walter Carpenter to Frederick Wardenburg, October 12, 1939, II, 2, Box 820.

146. "Future Activities of Du Pont Company," August 5, 1949, LMSS, Series A, File 418-26, Box 411; Willard F. Mueller, "Du Pont: A Study in Firm Growth" (Ph.D. diss., Vanderbilt University, 1956), pp. 179–80, 185.

147. For the development of strategic planning in the 1960s and 1970s, see, for example, Charles Cheape, *Family Firm to Modern Multinational: Norton Company, A New England Enterprise* (Cambridge: Harvard University Press, 1985), pp. 305–18.

Chapter 3   Beyond the Firm

1. Alfred Chandler, *The Visible Hand: The Managerial Revolution in American Business* (Cambridge: Harvard University Press, 1977).

2. For informative studies, see Francis Sutton, Seymour Harris, Carl Kaysen, and James Tobin, *The American Business Creed* (Cambridge: Harvard University Press, 1956), esp. pp. 33–36, 57–58, 158–60, 357–58; Thomas Cochran, *Business in American Life: A History* (New York: McGraw-Hill, 1972), esp. pp. 162, 255, 257; Thomas Cochran, *Railroad Leaders, 1845–1890: The Business Mind in Action* (Cambridge: Harvard University Press, 1953); Bennett H. Wall and George S. Gibb, *Teagle of Jersey Standard* (New Orleans: Tulane University, 1974), pp. 111–12, 125–28, 317; and Allen Kaufman and Lawrence Zacharias, "From Trust to Contract: The Legal Language of Managerial Ideology, 1920–1980," *Business History Review* 66 (Autumn 1992): 523–72.

3. Alfred Sloan to Angus Echols, June 28, 1945, II, 2, Box 837.

4. Herrymon Maurer, "The New Manager," in Robert and Seon Manley, eds., *The Age of the Manager: A Treasury of Our Times* (New York: Macmillan, 1962), p. 73.

5. Cochran, *Business in American Life*, p. 160.

6. Ibid.

7. Ibid., p. 253; Sutton et al., *American Business Creed*, pp. 359–60.

8. For Carpenter's income and wealth, see his federal income tax statements in Acc. 1553, Box 64; "Administrative Contracts," February 19, 1941, LMSS, Series A, File 418, Box 379; and executive committee minutes, January 4, 1926, and June 3, 1940.

9. Walter Carpenter quoted in "Walter S. Carpenter, Jr.," *Cornell Reports* (June 1976): 6–7.

10. Cochran, *Railroad Leaders*, pp. 182, 201.

11. Walter Carpenter to Arthur Hays Sulzberger, January 3, 1962, II, 2, Box 845.

12. Walter Carpenter to Alfred Sloan, December 31, 1943, II, 2, Box 837.

13. Edmund N. Carpenter II to the author, June 2, 1993.

14. Walter Carpenter to Alfred Sloan, July 13, 1959, Walter Carpenter's scrapbooks, third volume, now in the possession of Edmund N. Carpenter II.

15. Ibid.

16. "Walter S. Carpenter, Jr.," pp. 6–7; Cochran, *Railroad Leaders*, pp. 79, 216; Chandler, *Visible Hand*, pp. 143–46, 177–87.

17. James Q. du Pont to C. B. Kaufman, September 3, 1959, and James Q. du Pont, "Notes on W.S.C. Jr.," n.d., Acc. 1415, Box 34.

18. Edmund N. Carpenter II interview, May 23, 1990.

19. Walter Carpenter to Lammot du Pont, September 10, 1937, Acc. 1662, Box 80.

20. "Executives Reply to Charge of Excessive Salaries," *Forbes*, February 15, 1948, pp. 25, 40, and March 15, 1948, pp. 21, 40.

21. Cochran, *Business in American Life*, p. 160. See also Maurer, "New Manager," p. 86; and Sutton et al., *American Business Creed*, pp. 158–60.

22. Walter Carpenter to Edmund N. Carpenter II, January 26, 1939, Acc. 1553, Box 31.

23. *Wall Street Journal*, May 21, 1940, p. 1; Crawford Greenewalt interview, June 21, 1991; and James Q. du Pont to C. B. Kaufman, September 3, 1959, Acc. 1415, Box 34.

24. James Q. du Pont, "Notes on W.S.C. Jr. [from an undated interview with George Weth]," Acc. 1415, Box 34. For a sample of such letters, see File C-1, II, 2, Box 817.

25. Walter Carpenter to Lewis Flinn, February 6, 1958, Acc. 1553, Box 11.

26. The story has been told many times. See Edmund N. Carpenter II interview, May 23, 1990; and "An American Business Statesman," *Better Living Magazine*, January–February 1960, p. 7.

27. Cochran, *Railroad Leaders*, pp. 214, 86.

28. James Q. du Pont to C. B. Kaufman, September 3, 1959, Acc. 1415, Box 34.

29. Edmund N. Carpenter II interview, May 23, 1990; "Dynasty Interrupted," *Time*, June 3, 1940, p. 71.

30. The ensuing discussion of Carpenter's family relations, ties to Wilkes-Barre, and philanthropy rests on numerous documents from Walter Carpenter's personal papers in Acc. 1553 and from his three scrapbooks.

31. Walter Carpenter to Walter Carpenter III, November 12, 1934, Acc. 1553, Box 23.

32. Material on Carpenter's philanthropic work can be found in his scrapbooks and personal correspondence, Acc. 1553, Boxes 10–16.

33. John Carpenter to Walter Carpenter, October [n.d.], 1937, and Walter Carpenter to John Carpenter, October 7 and 27, 1937, Acc. 1553, Box 29.

34. Walter Carpenter to Mrs. Walter Carpenter Sr., November 27, 1931, in Walter Carpenter's scrapbooks, first volume.

35. Crawford Greenewalt interview, January 19, 1983, p. 8, Acc. 1850. For Sam's career, see Acc. 1410, Box 62.

36. Untitled note by Kay Smedley, Walter Carpenter's secretary, July 9, 1964, Acc. 1553, Box 32. Material on Ned's career can be found in Acc. 1553, Boxes 31 and 32.

37. Quotations in this paragraph and in the next two paragraphs are from Walter Carpenter to Walter Carpenter Sr., April 28, 1925, in Walter Carpenter's scrapbooks, first volume.

38. For the U.S. Rubber offer, see Walter Carpenter to E. N. Carpenter, March 31, 1928, Acc. 1553, Box 1. For the relationship between John Raskob and Pierre du Pont, see Alfred Chandler and Stephen Salsbury, *Pierre S. du Pont and the Making of the Modern Corporation* (New York: Harper & Row, 1971), esp. pp. 39, 64, 74, 144–45, 435, 584–87.

39. Cochran, *Railroad Leaders*, p. 217. For Sloan's career, see Alfred Sloan, *My Years with General Motors* (New York: McFadden Books, 1965); for Teagle's career, see Wall and Gibb, *Teagle of Jersey Standard*.

40. Chandler, *Visible Hand*, pp. 450–52, 491–92.

41. John Raskob to Lammot du Pont, August 10, 1936, Acc. 473, File 678.

42. "Du Pont Common Stock of Record at December 31, 1948," October 14, 1948, LMSS, Series A, File 418-26, Box 414. For brief descriptions of the two holding companies, see Chandler and Salsbury, *Pierre S. du Pont*, pp. 334–35, 562–63.

43. Donaldson Brown to Alfred Sloan, January 16, 1945, Acc. 1334, Box 1.

44. See, for example, Walter Carpenter's letters to family members in September 1938 preparing them for the exchange in File C-49, II, 2, Box 824.

45. Lammot du Pont to John Raskob, August 29, 1929, Acc. 473, File 678, and June 13, 1930, Acc. 1662, Box 59.

46. John Raskob to John Lee Pratt, December 29, 1930, Acc. 1662, Box 59.

47. Pierre du Pont to John Lee Pratt, December 31, 1930, Acc. 1662, Box 59.

48. Pierre du Pont to John Raskob, January 14, 1931, Acc. 1662, Box 59.

49. Ibid.

50. Alfred Smith to Pierre du Pont, March 30, 1932, LMSS, Series A, File 229-17, Box 188; W. B. Foster to Lammot du Pont, March 16, 1931, Lammot du Pont to the executive committee, March 17, 1931, and Lammot du Pont to Alfred Smith, March 21, 1931, Acc. 1662, Box 59.

51. Irénée du Pont to Pierre du Pont, March 7, 1930, Acc. 1034, File 242.

52. "Du Pont, Part II: An Industrial Empire," *Fortune*, December 1934,

p. 86. See also "Dynasty Interrupted," *Time*, June 3, 1940, p. 71; and *Wall Street Journal*, May 21, 1940, p. 1.

53. Finance committee minutes, December 5, 1927.

54. Walter Carpenter to Lammot du Pont, February 16, 1934, and Irénée du Pont to Lammot du Pont, February 19, 1934, II, 2, Box 817.

55. Walter Carpenter to Lammot du Pont, February 19, 1937, II, 2, Box 817.

56. See, for example, executive committee to finance committee, July 13, 1933, pp. 5093–94, in the first of two chronological series of printed documents submitted to the Justice Department in the GM case (hereafter listed as Documents—series number and page number); and Walter Carpenter to M. D. Fisher, June 11, 1943, II, 2, Box 836.

57. Lee Iacocca with William Novak, *Iacocca: An Autobiography* (New York: Bantam Books, 1984), chaps. 9–11.

58. Cochran, *Railroad Leaders*, pp. 185–203. The quotations are from pp. 190, 192, 199.

59. Walter Carpenter to Crawford Greenewalt, January 24, 1949, II, 2, Box 843.

60. For an alternate view, see Robert F. Burk, *The Corporate State and the Broker State: The Du Ponts and American National Politics, 1925–1940* (Cambridge: Harvard University Press, 1990). Burk argues that Pierre, Irénée, and Lammot du Pont and John Raskob, using their control of "a vast economic empire" with the Du Pont Company at its center, employed a conscious strategy to create a company state, "a single line of political and economic authority to replace the dual, though often interlocking, systems of public and private administration of their day." Whatever the motives of Pierre and Raskob, the description does not fit the actions of Irénée and Lammot and their top managers in their public relationships at Du Pont, and it does not accord with Pierre's earlier behavior. The quotations are from pp. vii and viii. For a more comprehensive assessment of Pierre's approach, see Douglas B. Craig, *After Wilson: The Struggle for the Democratic Party, 1920–1934* (Chapel Hill: University of North Carolina Press, 1992), esp. pp. 6–7, 252–61.

61. Pierre du Pont to R. M. Jones, October 10, 1911, quoted in Chandler and Salsbury, *Pierre S. du Pont*, p. 287. For a discussion of the case, see chap. 10.

62. Ibid., pp. 410–23. The quotation is from pp. 422–23.

63. Irénée du Pont to Coleman du Pont, March 22, 1916, Acc. 1034, File 346, and Irénée du Pont to Pierre du Pont, June 26, 1934, Acc. 1034, File 242.

64. Resolution of the United States Federal Trade Commission, July 29, 1927, II, 2, Box 824. Examples of newspaper coverage can be found in Documents—series II, pp. 1943–58.

65. Undated draft of a letter by Walter Carpenter to William Donovan in II, 2, Box 824. The quotation is from an excerpt of a letter from Irénée du Pont to the Department of Justice quoted in "Report of Federal Trade Commission on Du Pont Investments . . . ," February 1, 1929, p. 7, LMSS, Series A, File 418-26, Box 411.

66. Irénée du Pont to John Raskob, August 26, 1927, Documents—series I, pp. 3477–78.

67. Pierre du Pont to Frank Connable, January 13, 1947, LMSS, Series A, File 384, Box 340; Lord Harry McGowan to Pierre du Pont, July 28, 1952, LMSS, Series A, File 637, Box 1 (of one).

68. "Du Pont, Part I: The Family," *Fortune* November 1934, p. 65.

69. Lammot du Pont to Lord Harry McGowan, January 6, 1944, Acc. 1662, Box 39.

70. George Wolfskill, *The Revolt of the Conservatives: A History of the American Liberty League* (Boston: Houghton Mifflin, 1962), pp. 39–40; finance committee minutes, August 7, 1933.

71. Chandler and Salsbury, *Pierre S. du Pont*, pp. 585–87.

72. Walter Carpenter to Irénée du Pont, August 12, 1928, Acc. 228, Series J, File 261.

73. Ibid.

74. "Hoover Drive Gets Lammot Du Pont's Aid," *New York American*, August 28, 1928, p. 1.

75. Irénée du Pont to Walter Carpenter, August 15, 1928, and Irénée du Pont, untitled memorandum dated August 15, 1928, Acc. 228, Series J, File 261.

76. Arthur Schlesinger Jr., *The Age of Roosevelt: The Crisis of the Old Order, 1919–1933* (Boston: Houghton Mifflin, 1957).

77. Walter Carpenter to E. N. Carpenter, December 27, 1928, Acc. 1553, Box 2; Lammot du Pont to J. L. Whitten, January 22, 1929, Acc. 1662, Box 7.

78. "Weekly Billings as Percent of Same Periods of Average 1928 and 1929," Acc. 1662, Box 78; Salmon L. Wilder to Lammot du Pont, April 24 and October 1, 1930, Acc. 1662, Box 8.

79. Du Pont Company, *Annual Report*, 1932, p. 5, and 1948, pp. 44–45; Walter Carpenter to Frank MacGregor, May 5, 1936, II, 2, Box 817.

80. Maxwell Moore to Lammot du Pont, April 25, 1932, Acc. 1813, Box 12; Du Pont Company, *Annual Report*, 1948, pp. 44–45.

81. Irénée du Pont to U.S. Senator John G. Townsend, May 5, 1933, Acc. 228, Series J, File 261; Irénée du Pont to A. Felix du Pont, August 18, 1934, Acc. 1034, File 238. For opposition, see Pierre du Pont to Irénée du Pont, January 16, 1933, LMSS, Series A, File 1173, Box 1 (of one); E. E. Lincoln to John G. Townsend, May 29, 1933, Acc. 1662, Box 51; and Lammot du Pont's speech to the Chemists' Club, December 10, 1932, Acc. 1662, Box 42.

82. Pierre du Pont to Irénée du Pont, January 16, 1933, LMSS, Series A, File 1173, Box 1 (of one).

83. Pierre du Pont to Alfred Sloan, May 9, 1932, LMSS, Series A, File 1173, Box 1 (of one).

84. Lammot du Pont to David Reed, April 27, 1932, Acc. 1662, Box 34.

85. Lammot du Pont to Salmon Wilder, January 19, 1931, and Lammot du Pont to Charles W. Hawley, March 1, 1932, Acc. 1662, Box 78.

86. Walter Carpenter to Lammot du Pont, February 13, 1934, II, 2, Box 817.

87. Walter Carpenter to Lammot du Pont, February 19, 1931, Acc. 1662, Box 20.

88. The quotations in this and in the preceding two paragraphs are from Walter Carpenter, "Memorandum: Needs of Our Present Position," November 20, 1929, Acc. 1662, Box 8.

89. Pierre du Pont to Lammot du Pont, December 2, 1929, Acc. 1662, Box 8.

90. Du Pont Company, *Annual Report*, 1931, p. 5.

91. Pierre du Pont, "National Recovery Administration," March 5, 1934; Pierre du Pont to Lammot du Pont, November 10, 1932, Acc. 1662, Box 8; Burk, *Corporate State*, pp. 113–18, 124–32.

92. Irénée du Pont to Theodore Roosevelt, June 21, 1934, Acc. 1034, File 274; Irénée du Pont to E. C. Stokes, September 29, 1932, Acc. 228, Series J, File 261; Irénée du Pont to Stephen Raushenbush, October 2, 1934, *Hearings before the Special Committee Investigating the Munitions Industry, United States Senate, Seventy-third Congress, Pursuant to S. Res. 206 (Nye Committee)*, Part 5, p. 1406 (hereafter cited as Nye Committee Investigation).

93. Nye Committee Investigation, Part 5, pp. 1403–11.

94. Lammot du Pont to Robert Lund, November 22, 1933, Acc. 1662, Box 51. See also Lammot du Pont to Alfred Sloan, June 12, 1933, Acc. 1662, Box 51, and Lammot du Pont to L. A. Yerkes, June 26, 1933, and May 21, 1934, Acc. 1662, Box 66.

95. Wolfskill, *Revolt*, pp. 25, 28–30, 60, 63–64, 199.

96. Walter Carpenter to Stephen Raushenbush, October 16, 1934, Nye Committee Investigation, Part 5, p. 1409; Walter Carpenter to B. H. Carpenter, July 20, 1932, Acc. 1553, Box 2; Walter Carpenter to Tom Russell, November 13, 1933, Walter Carpenter to George S. Brown, February 10, 1936, and Walter Carpenter to Francis Cole, January 31, 1935, II, 2, Box 817.

97. Walter Carpenter to Lammot du Pont, July 28, 1933, II, 2, Box 817; Walter Carpenter to E. N. Carpenter, June 15, 1933, and Walter Carpenter to Elias Ahuja, December 8, 1933, Acc. 1553, Box 3.

98. Wolfskill, *Revolt*, pp. ix, viii; Walter Carpenter to George S. Brown, February 10, 1936, and Walter Carpenter to John Raskob, October 10, 1935, II, 2, Box 817; Irénée du Pont to Pierre du Pont, July 7, 1934, Acc. 1034, File 242.

99. Du Pont Company, *Annual Report*, 1931, p. 5, 1932, pp. 5–6, 1936, p. 24, 1937, pp. 24–26, and 1938, pp. 12–14; and finance committee minutes, April 20, 1936, May 17, 1937, July 18 and November 21, 1938, June 5, 1939, and May 6, 1940; Lammot du Pont to Donaldson Brown, June 13, 1934, Acc. 1662, Box 51.

100. For studies of the munitions investigation, see John E. Wiltz, *In Search of Peace: The Senate Munitions Inquiry* (Baton Rouge: Louisiana State University Press, 1963); and Wayne S. Cole, *Senator Gerald P. Nye and American Foreign Relations* (Minneapolis: University of Minnesota Press, 1962). The Nye quotations are from Wiltz, *Search*, p. 224.

101. Jasper Crane to J. Thompson Brown, December 13, 1934, II, 2, Box 1029; Edmund N. Carpenter II interview, May 23, 1990.

102. Pierre du Pont to Elias Ahuja, January 12, 1935, LMSS, Series A, File 507, Box 600.

103. For Carpenter's correspondence about and copies of the statement, see File C-55, II, 2, Box 824.

104. Walter Carpenter to Jasper Crane, n.d. [February 1935], II, 2, Box 1050. My thanks to David Hounshell for pointing out this document.

105. Walter Carpenter, *A Challenge That Was Accepted* (Wilmington: E. I. du Pont de Nemours, 1935).

106. Walter Carpenter, "Comments for the Board of Directors Meeting," September 8, 1937, II, 2, Box 817. The quotations from the next two paragraphs are also from this document.

107. Board of directors minutes, September 8, 1937; Walter Carpenter to Lammot du Pont, March 17, 1939, II, 2, Box 817; executive committee minutes, April 12, 1939.

108. For a study of the Securities Exchange Commission, see Michael Parrish, *Securities Regulation and the New Deal* (New Haven: Yale University Press, 1970).

109. Irénée du Pont to U.S. Senator J. G. Townsend, April 2, 1934, Acc. 228, Series J, File 261.

110. "Memorandum for J. B. Eliason," June 29, 1937, II, 2, Box 824; Walter Carpenter to Thomas Bowers, February 1, 1934, II, 2, Box 817; Louis Schreiber to John T. Smith, August 20, 1935, II, 2, Box 821; Lammot du Pont to Pierre du Pont, February 28, 1934, LMSS, Series A, File 418, Box 378; E. E. Lincoln to Pierre du Pont, March 27, 1934 and Lammot du Pont to Pierre du Pont with attachment by C. R. Mudge, April 13, 1934, LMSS, Series A, File 1068, Box 1 (of two).

111. George Baker to Walter Carpenter, July 25, 1934, and to Carle Conway, September 25, 1934, II, 2, Box 817. For a collection of Carpenter's correspondence on the issue, see File C-56, II, 2, Box 824.

112. Angus Echols to John Raskob, August 15, 1934, LMSS, Series A, File 418, Box 378; Lammot du Pont to Orlando Weber, August 23, 1934, Acc. 1662, Box 79; finance committee minutes, May 17, 1937.

113. Walter Carpenter to John Raskob, August 6, 1935, Acc. 473, File 351.

114. Finance committee minutes, August 20, 1934, and May 20, 1935.

115. Walter Carpenter to Donaldson Brown, July 5, 1938, Acc. 1334, Box 1. For examples of protest against the New Deal, see Walter Carpenter to Lammot du Pont, June 29, 1937, and to Pierre du Pont, March 22, 1938, II, 2, Box 817.

116. Walter Carpenter to Lammot du Pont, June 29, 1937, II, 2, Box 817.

Chapter 4   The Manager as Outsider

1. Walter Carpenter to Ruly Carpenter, January 30, 1942, II, 2, Box 825.

2. Edmund N. Carpenter II to the author, June 2, 1993.

3. Alfred Chandler, ed., *Giant Enterprise: Ford, General Motors, and the Auto-*

mobile Industry (New York: Harcourt, Brace & World, 1964), pp. 5–7.

4. Details of the plan can be found in Alfred Sloan, *My Years with General Motors* (New York: MacFadden Books, 1965), pp. 410–15; and Alfred Chandler and Stephen Salsbury, *Pierre S. du Pont and the Making of the Modern Corporation* (New York: Harper & Row, 1971), pp. 540–43.

5. Sloan, *My Years,* pp. 413–14.

6. For a description of the plan, see ibid., pp. 415–18, and "To the Stockholders of the General Motors Corporation," October 26, 1933 (a draft letter never issued), II, 2, Box 822. File C-22 in the latter entry contains most of Carpenter's material on this episode.

7. Alfred Sloan as quoted in Chandler and Salsbury, *Pierre S. du Pont,* p. 542.

8. Sloan, *My Years,* p. 417.

9. "General Motors Management Corporation," GM Case, GTE 260.

10. For a list of members of General Motors' board of directors and its top committees, see "Members of GM Board and Governing Committees, August 22, 1917 to December 31, 1952," GM Case, DTE-DP 56.

11. GM's 1931 annual report, which appeared as the first default on the principal payment occurred on March 15, 1932, simply reported the shortage and noted that General Motors agreed to continue carrying the bonds. General Motors Corporation, *Annual Report,* 1931, p. 14.

12. "To the Stockholders of General Motors Corporation," draft letter not sent but dated October 1933, II, 2, Box 822. GM common stock prices are conveniently tabulated in "Schedule of Weekly Range of Prices on the New York Stock Exchange of General Motors Corporation . . . from the Week Ending February 9, 1929 through the Week Ending May 29, 1943," in ibid.

13. Donaldson Brown to Walter Carpenter, December 28, 1932, and George Whitney to Walter Carpenter, July 16, 1934, II, 2, Box 822.

14. George Whitney to Walter Carpenter, July 16, 1934, II, 2, Box 822.

15. John Smith to Walter Carpenter, January 3, 1933, II, 2, Box 822.

16. John Smith to Walter Carpenter, December 30, 1932, II, 2, Box 822. See also Donaldson Brown to Walter Carpenter, December 29, 1932, Walter Carpenter memorandum, December 28, 1932, and John Smith to Walter Carpenter, January 3, 1933, in the same box.

17. Donaldson Brown to Walter Carpenter, December 28 and 29, 1932, II, 2, Box 822. The quotation is from the first letter.

18. Walter Carpenter memorandum, December 28, 1932, II, 2, Box 822.

19. Walter Carpenter to George Whitney, January 2, 1933, II, 2, Box 822.

20. Walter Carpenter to Donaldson Brown, May 5, 1933, II, 2, Box 822.

21. Walter Carpenter to George Whitney, May 5, 1933, II, 2, Box 822.

22. George Baker to Donaldson Brown, May 10, 1933, and George Whitney to Donaldson Brown, May 10, 1933, II, 2, Box 822.

23. Donaldson Brown to Walter Carpenter, December 29, 1932, II, 2, Box 822.

24. Walter Carpenter to Donaldson Brown, September 22, 1933, II, 2, Box 822.

25. Alfred Sloan to Walter Carpenter, October 13, 1933, II, 2, Box 822.

26. Ibid.

27. Donaldson Brown to Walter Carpenter, October 18, 1933, II, 2, Box 822.

28. Ibid.

29. Walter Carpenter to Donaldson Brown, September 22, 1933, II, 2, Box 822.

30. "To the Stockholders of General Motors Corporation," draft of letter not sent but dated October 1933, and Walter Carpenter to Donaldson Brown, October 20, 1933, II, 2, Box 822.

31. John Smith to Alfred Sloan, October 27, 1933, II, 2, Box 822.

32. Walter Carpenter to Donaldson Brown, February 20, 1934, and June 26, 1934, II, 2, Box 822.

33. Walter Carpenter to Donaldson Brown, June 6, 1934, II, 2, Box 822.

34. Ibid.

35. Walter Carpenter to Donaldson Brown, June 26, 1934, II, 2, Box 822.

36. George Whitney to Walter Carpenter, July 16, 1934, II, 2, Box 822. Correspondence with others is in the same box.

37. George Baker to Walter Carpenter, August 8 and 20, 1934, and Walter Carpenter to George Baker, August 16, 1934, II, 2, Box 822.

38. Walter Carpenter to Irénée du Pont, September 25, 1934, Acc. 1034, File 208; Sloan, *My Years*, pp. 417–18. For a copy of the amended plan, see "General Motors Management Corporation Plan," Acc. 473, File 278.

39. Chandler, *Giant Enterprise*, p. 7; Owen Young to Donaldson Brown, August 7, 1934, Acc. 473, File 278.

40. Peter Temin, *Did Monetary Forces Cause the Great Depression?* (New York: W. W. Norton, 1976), pp. 75–79. For Du Pont's and General Motors' leadership, see Alfred Chandler, *Strategy and Structure: Chapters in the History of the Industrial Enterprise* (Cambridge: MIT Press, 1962), esp. chaps. 2 and 3.

41. Chandler, *Giant Enterprise*, p. 3.

42. Sloan, *My Years*, pp. 414, 418.

43. Lammot du Pont to the stockholders of General Motors, September 10, 1934, Acc. 473, File 278.

44. For a discussion of the Du Pont bonus plans, see chap. 2, pp. 79–81.

45. "Memorandum Setting Forth Origins and Operations of General Motors Bonus Plans as Revealed by Available Documents," April 12, 1951, LMSS, Series A, File 418-26, Box 433; Chandler and Salsbury, *Pierre du Pont*, p. 542.

46. Chandler, *Strategy and Structure*, chaps. 2 and 3.

47. The story can be found in Chandler and Salsbury, *Pierre du Pont*, pp. 584–87.

48. For a description of Sloan's alterations in the 1930s, see Sloan, *My Years*, pp. 182–86.

49. Ibid., and Alfred Sloan testimony, GM Case, Transcript, pp. 2468–69.

50. Alfred Sloan testimony, GM Case, Transcript, p. 2459; Donaldson

Brown, *Some Reminiscences of an Industrialist* (n.p., n.d.), p. 68; Alfred Sloan deposition in GM Case, April 28–May 9, 1952, p. 89.

51. Alfred Sloan to Donaldson Brown, December 28, 1944, Acc. 1334, Box 1.

52. Alfred Sloan to Donaldson Brown, February 2, 1945, Acc. 1334, Box 1.

53. Ibid.

54. Chandler and Salsbury, *Pierre du Pont*, p. 587; "General Motors Corporation: Members of Board . . . , 1917–1938," LMSS, Series A, File 624-5, Box 5.

55. Lammot du Pont to Alfred Sloan, April 6, 1937, GM Case, GTE 194; Lammot du Pont to Walter Carpenter, April 23, 1937, II, 2, Box 823.

56. Brown, *Reminiscences*, p. 68.

57. Donaldson Brown to Walter Carpenter, September 8, 1938, and Walter Carpenter to Alfred Sloan, February 20, 1939, II, 2, Box 821.

58. Walter Carpenter to Alfred Sloan, June 14, 1943, II, 2, Box 837.

59. Ibid.

60. Alfred Sloan to Walter Carpenter, September 17, 1940, II, 2, Box 833.

61. Walter Carpenter to Alfred Sloan, April 22, 1942, and Alfred Sloan to Walter Carpenter, April 24, 1942, and August 16, 1944, II, 2, Box 837.

62. Walter Carpenter to Alfred Sloan, April 8, 1942, GM Case, GTE 201; Lammot du Pont to Alfred Sloan, April 10, 1942, GM Case, GTE 202.

63. Alfred Sloan to Lammot du Pont, April 13, 1942, GM Case, GTE 203; Alfred Sloan to Walter Carpenter, April 11, 1942, II, 2, Box 837.

64. Alfred Sloan to Walter Carpenter, April 11, 1942, II, 2, Box 837. This letter is the second one from Sloan to Carpenter on that date and is not the one cited in the previous note.

65. Alfred Sloan, Deposition in GM Case, April 28–May 9, 1952, p. 71; Alfred Sloan testimony, GM Case, Transcript, pp. 2470–71; Sloan, *My Years*, p. 186.

66. Alfred Sloan to Donaldson Brown, February 2, 1945, Acc. 1334, Box 1.

67. Ibid.

68. Alfred Sloan to Walter Carpenter, April 25, 1946, II, 2, Box 838.

69. Sloan, *My Years*, p. 186.

70. Brown, *Reminiscences*, pp. 104, 106–8; Lammot du Pont to Walter Carpenter, April 10, 1946, II, 2, Box 838.

71. Walter Carpenter to Alfred Sloan, April 8, 1946, II, 2, Box 838.

72. Walter Carpenter to Lammot du Pont, May 17, 1946, II, 2, Box 838.

73. The bulk of this material can be found in II, 2, Boxes 821, 822, 837, and 838.

74. Alfred Sloan to Walter Carpenter, March 30, 1938, II, 2, Box 821.

75. Alfred Sloan to Walter Carpenter, April 16, 1941, and Walter Carpenter to Alfred Sloan, April 18, 1941, II, 2, Box 837.

76. Walter Carpenter to Alfred Sloan, April 18, 1941, and Alfred Sloan to Walter Carpenter, April 24, 1941, II, 2, Box 837.

77. Walter Carpenter to John Lee Pratt, December 20, 1957, II, 2, Box 849; Alfred Sloan to Walter Carpenter, May 27, 1938, II, 2, Box 821.

78. Walter Carpenter to Alfred Sloan, April 6, 1938, II, 2, Box 821.

79. Alfred Sloan to Walter Carpenter, April 11, 1938, II, 2, Box 821.

80. Walter Carpenter to Alfred Sloan, May 23, 1941, and Alfred Sloan to Walter Carpenter, May 28, 1941, II, 2, Box 837.

81. Walter Carpenter to Charles Stradella, October 4, 1955, II, 2, Box 856D.

82. Ibid., and Charles Stradella to Walter Carpenter, October 18, 1955, II, 2, Box 856D.

83. For a discussion of the associative state, see Louis Galambos and Joseph Pratt, *The Rise of the Corporate Commonwealth: U.S. Business and Public Policy in the Twentieth Century* (New York: Basic Books, 1988), pp. 92–99. The case for a corporate state is found in Robert F. Burk, *The Corporate State and the Broker State: The Du Ponts and American National Politics, 1925–1940* (Cambridge: Harvard University Press, 1990).

84. Donaldson Brown to Alfred Sloan, May 9, and June 22, 1938, and to Lammot du Pont, July 27, 1938, II, 2, Box 821.

85. John Raskob to General Motors Securities Company, August 7, 1929, GM Case, GTE 262.

86. Lammot du Pont to Alfred Sloan, August 20, 1929, GM Case, GTE 264; General Motors Securities Company, minutes, January 6, 1930, GM Case, GTE 265.

87. Lammot du Pont to Walter Carpenter, October 24, 1930, GM Case, GTE 266.

88. Walter Carpenter to Du Pont Company Finance Committee, December 12, 1930, GM Case, GTE 267; General Motors Securities Company, minutes, December 15, 1930, January 17 and February 12, 1932, GTE 268, 269, and 270; H. B. Robinson to A. B. Hull, May 4, 1938, II, 2, Box 822.

89. For material on the 1938 reorganization, see File C-22.3, II, 2, Box 822.

90. Ibid.

91. Proposed Complete Liquidation of General Motors Securities Company, (n.p., n.d.), II, 2, Box 822.

92. *Augusta Winkelman et al. v. General Motors Corporation et al.*, Civil Action No. E 84-221, Consolidated Cause in the U.S. District Court for the Southern District of New York, 44 F. Supp. 960. (1942). See also File 33(b), II, 2, Box 838; and LMSS, Series A, File 624-5, Boxes 1–5.

93. Walter Carpenter to Alfred Sloan, April 8, 1943, p. 8133, in the first of two chronological series of printed documents submitted to the Justice Department in the GM Case (hereafter listed as Documents—series number and page number).

94. Lammot du Pont to Walter Carpenter, September 21, 1950, II, 2, Box 847.

95. The quotations are from Alfred Sloan, "Policy Proposal with Respect to Board of Directors—General Motors Corporation," September 7, 1950, Acc. 1034, File 208. See also Alfred Sloan to Walter Carpenter, June 10, 1943, and July 30, 1945, II, 2, Box 837.

96. George Whitney to Walter Carpenter, December 13, 1946, and Walter Carpenter to George Whitney, January 23, 1947, II, 2, Box 838.

97. Details of this transaction can be found in Acc. 1034, Files 208 and 241, and LMSS, Series A, File 624-4, Box 1 (of one).

98. For Walter Carpenter's efforts on behalf of Frederic Donner, see File 33, II, 2, Box 837.

99. Walter Carpenter to Frederic Donner, February 14 and November 20, 1944, II, 2, Box 837.

100. Chandler, *Giant Enterprise*, pp. 71–72.

101. Walter Carpenter to Donaldson Brown, January 9, 1941, GM Case, Deposition of Pierre S. du Pont, beginning May 21, 1951, Government Trial Exhibit 139, LMSS, Series A, File 418-26, Box 416; Walter Carpenter to Lammot du Pont, December 5, 1944, Documents—series I, pp. 8618–19.

102. Walter Carpenter to Donaldson Brown, September 10, 1946, Acc. 1334, Box 1; Walter Carpenter to Donaldson Brown, August 6, 1947, and to Albert Bradley, June 4, 1947, II, 2, Box 838.

103. Alfred Sloan to Walter Carpenter, June 10, 1947, II, 2, Box 838. For other reactions, see Albert Bradley to Walter Carpenter, June 6, 1947, George Whitney to Walter Carpenter, September 5, 1947, Lammot du Pont to Walter Carpenter, September 5, 1947, and Donaldson Brown to Walter Carpenter, September 9, 1947, II, 2, Box 838.

104. Walter Carpenter to Albert Bradley, June 13, 1947, and Walter Carpenter to Charles Wilson, August 7, 1947, II, 2, Box 838.

105. Walter Carpenter to Albert Bradley, November 4, 1947, II, 2, Box 838; Arthur Kuhn, *GM Passes Ford, 1918–1938: Designing the General Motors Performance-Control System* (University Park, PA.: Pennsylvania State University Press, 1986), p. 323; Alfred Sloan to Charles Wilson, November 14, 1947, II, 2, Box 838.

106. Charles Wilson to Walter Carpenter, August 28, 1947, Acc. 1334, Box 1.

107. Ed Cray, *Chrome Colossus: General Motors and Its Times* (New York: McGraw-Hill, 1980), pp. 343, 352–53.

108. Walter Carpenter to Donaldson Brown, September 22, 1933, II, 2, Box 822.

109. See, for example, Terrence E. Deal and Allan A. Kennedy, *Corporate Cultures: The Rites and Rituals of Corporate Life* (Reading, Mass.: Addison Wesley, 1982). The quotation is from p. 23.

Chapter 5   Chief Executive

1. "Du Pont, Part I: The Family," *Fortune*, November 1934, p. 75.

2. Lammot du Pont to Lord Harry McGowan, May 24, 1940, Acc. 1662, Box 39.

3. "To My Associates," *The Du Pont Magazine*, October 1940, pp. 1–2. The quotations are from p. 2.

4. Ibid.

5. Ruly Carpenter to Willis Harrington, September 25, 1939, Acc. 1813, Box 29; Lammot du Pont to executive committee, September 25, 1939, Acc. 1813, Box 29.

6. Walter Carpenter to Lord Harry McGowan, December 12, 1938, II, 2, Box 820. See also Walter Carpenter to Alfred Sloan, April 18, 1941, II, 2, Box 837.

7. For the role of big business in World War II, see Robert Sobel, *The Age of Giant Corporations: A Microeconomic History of American Business, 1914–1984*, 2d ed. (Westport, Conn.: Greenwood, 1984), pp. 157–75, and John Blum, *V Was for Victory: Politics and American Culture during World War II* (New York: Harcourt Brace Jovanovich, 1976), chap. 4.

8. "Statement of Policy on Foreign Technical and Commercial Relationships," October 24, 1940, Acc. 1813, Box 31. See also executive committee minutes, July 12 and 19, 1939, and August 1 and 21, September 25, and October 9 and 23, 1940.

9. Data on Du Pont's military production during World War II can be found in correspondence in File 5, II, 2, Box 830, and in *The Du Pont Company's Part in the National Security Program, 1940–1945* (Wilmington, Del.: E. I. du Pont de Nemours, 1946).

10. F. W. Broadway to Walter Carpenter, August 5, 1942, II, 2, Box 840; Fred Aftalion, *A History of the International Chemical Industry* (Philadelphia: University of Pennsylvania Press, 1991), p. 209.

11. A. B. Echols to Willis Harrington, March 24, 1942, Acc. 1813, Box 37; David Hounshell and John Smith, *Science and Corporate Strategy: Du Pont R&D, 1902–1980* (New York: Cambridge University Press, 1988), p. 337; *The Du Pont Company's Part*, pp. 20, 30–49.

12. *The Du Pont Company's Part*, pp. 5, 28.

13. Ibid., pp. 22, 24.

14. Walter Carpenter to Lammot du Pont, April 13, 1942, II, 2, Box 828.

15. See, for example, Files 48.2, 48.3, and 48.4, II, 2, Box 840; Walter Carpenter to E. N. Carpenter, January 27, 1942, II, 2, Box 825; and Files 1.3 and 1.4, II, 2, Box 827. For the quotation, see Walter Carpenter to E. N. Carpenter, February 28, 1946, Acc. 1553, Box 5.

16. For the history of Du Pont's part in the Manhattan Project, see Leslie R. Groves, *Now It Can Be Told: The Story of the Manhattan Project* (New York: Harper & Row, 1962); and Thomas Hughes, *American Genesis: A Century of Innovation and Technological Enthusiasm, 1870–1970* (New York: Viking Press, 1989), pp. 381–442. A succinct account from Du Pont's perspective can be found in Hounshell, and Smith, *Science and Corporate Strategy*, pp. 338–45.

17. Groves, *Now*, pp. 42–49. The quotations are from pp. 42 and 43.

18. Ibid., pp. 49–51.

19. Walter Carpenter to E. N. Carpenter, August 8, 1945, Acc. 1553, Box 4.

20. Groves, *Now*, pp. 49–50.

21. William Lawren, *The General and the Bomb: A Biography of Leslie R. Groves, Director of the Manhattan Project* (New York: Dodd, Mead, 1988), p. 92.

22. Crawford Greenewalt diaries, volume II, September 16, 1943, p. 333, Acc. 1889; Crawford Greenewalt interview, December 15, 1982, Acc. 1850; Groves, *Now*, p. 58.

23. Walter Carpenter to Ned Carpenter, August 7, 1945, Acc. 1553, Box 31; Walter Carpenter memorandum, October 26, 1943, II, 2, Box 830; Crawford Greenewalt diaries, volume II, December 21, 1942, p. 4, August 16, 1943, p. 313, September 30, 1943, p. 361, and volume III, January 29, 1944, p. 36, Acc. 1889; Walter Carpenter, "Comments of W. S. Carpenter, Jr. before the Board of Directors at Meeting of October 18, 1943," II, 2, Box 830.

24. Walter Carpenter to Leslie Groves, August 17, 1945, II, 2, Box 830.

25. Walter Carpenter to C. L. Burdick, May 28, 1946, II, 2, Box 826.

26. Walter Carpenter to J. Thompson Brown, February 21, 1946, II, 2, Box 832.

27. B. M. May to Walter Carpenter, August 16, 1944, and Walter Carpenter to Walter Bacon, August 18, 1944, II, 2, Box 831. File 8 in this same box contains a number of other examples.

28. B. M. May to Walter Carpenter, January 16, January 21, and May 10, 1946, and Howard White to B. M. May, January 15, 1946, II, 2, Box 831. For the West Coast plant, see *U.S. v. E. I. du Pont de Nemours and Company*, Civil Action No. 1216, District Court for Delaware (1947), Government's Trial Exhibits 95, 96, 99, 100, and 151. (Hereafter cited as Cellophane Case, GTE or DTE [Defendant's Trial Exhibit], and exhibit number.)

29. Hounshell and Smith, *Science and Corporate Strategy*, pp. 519, 527, 538, 573–75, 586–87.

30. See chap. 2, pp. 88–94.

31. C. H. Biesterfeld to Walter Carpenter, October 1, 1940, and Walter Carpenter to Angus Echols, July 10, 1941, II, 2, Box 833.

32. Walter Carpenter to J. W. McCoy, July 22, 1940, II, 2, Box 841; "Du Pont Price Policy," August 28, 1940, LMSS, Series A, File 418, Box 379.

33. "Du Pont Price Policy," August 28, 1940, LMSS, Series A, File 418, Box 379.

34. Walter Carpenter to Alfred Sloan, September 24, 1941, II, 2, Box 837.

35. Ibid.

36. Ibid. See also Walter Carpenter to Alfred Sloan, December 16, 1943, in II, 2, Box 837; and J. Thompson Brown to Walter Carpenter, September 25, 1943, and Walter Carpenter to executive committee, December 11, 1943, II, 2, Box 834.

37. Walter Carpenter to Angus Echols, January 2, 1941, II, 2, Box 841.

38. Walter Carpenter to Eugene du Pont III, January 28, 1943, II, 2, Box 828.

39. Walter Carpenter to Lammot du Pont, April 13, 1942, II, 2, Box 828.

40. Henrik Shipstead to Walter Carpenter, April 15, 1942, and Walter Car-

penter to Henrik Shipstead, April 22, 1942, II, 2, Box 828; Eugene Meyer to Walter Carpenter, December 28, 1943, II, 2, Box 833.

41. Walter Carpenter to Lammot du Pont, July 31, 1946, II, 2, Box 827.

42. Walter Carpenter to Lammot du Pont, January 2, 1945, II, 2, Box 828.

43. Walter Carpenter to James Byrnes, September 4, 1945, and Walter Carpenter to Adolph Sabath, October 2, 1940, II, 2, Box 833.

44. Walter Carpenter, "Military Preparedness," June 13, 1940, II, 2, Box 828; Walter Carpenter to Lammot du Pont, July 11, 1940, Acc. 1553, Box 41.

45. For the development of public relations at Du Pont and Carpenter's place in it, see Harold Brayman, *Corporate Management in a World of Politics: The Public, Political, and Governmental Problems of Business* (New York: McGraw-Hill, 1967), esp. pp. 43–45, 236–37, 258; and L. L. Golden, *Only by Public Consent: American Corporations' Search for Favorable Opinion* (New York: Hawthorn Books, 1968), esp. pp. 247–57, 274. See also Walter Carpenter to J. W. McCoy, February 10, 1944, II, 2, Box 833.

46. Walter Carpenter, "Comments for Educators' Conference," June 18, 1951, II, 2, Box 852.

47. Walter Carpenter to Harold Brayman, April 3, 1945, II, 2, Box 833.

48. Golden, *Public Consent*, pp. 257, 274.

49. Harold Brayman to Walter Carpenter, October 10 and November 9, 1945, and Walter Carpenter to Harold Brayman, April 3, 1945, II, 2, Box 833; *The Du Pont Company's Part*. The quotations in the next twelve paragraphs are from this book.

50. Golden, *Public Consent*, p. 274; Brayman, *Corporate Management*, p. 45; Lawrence P. Lessing, "The World of Du Pont," *Fortune*, October 1950, pp. 92–93. For a sample of the book's reception, see "Du Pont Tells Its Story," *Time*, March 18, 1946, pp. 80–81.

51. See chap. 2, pp. 91–94.

52. For the changing role of the development department after 1944, see Hounshell and Smith, *Science and Corporate Strategy*, pp. 347–50.

53. Angus Echols to Walter Carpenter, February 3, 1941, Acc. 1813, Box 34.

54. See chap. 2, pp. 93–94.

55. Angus Echols, "The Du Pont Company's Future with Respect to Its Expansion in the Chemical Industry," August 29, 1941, Acc. 1813, Box 36.

56. For correspondence on the debate, see Acc. 1813, Box 36; and W. F. Harrington to Angus Echols, October 8, 1941, Acc. 1813, Box 34.

57. Walter Carpenter to Fin Sparre, December 30, 1940, and January 7, 1941, II, 2, Box 832.

58. Walter Carpenter to C. R. D. Meier, May 26, 1943, II, 2, Box 825; executive committee minutes, October 13, 1943.

59. Walter Carpenter to Elmer Bolton, October 9, 1945, II, 2, Box 832. For an excellent account of the interchange, see Hounshell and Smith, *Science and Corporate Strategy*, pp. 354–55.

60. Elmer Bolton to Walter Carpenter, October 10, 1945, II, 2, Box 832.

61. Executive committee minutes, March 17 and September 8, 1943.

62. Walter Carpenter to E. G. Robinson, November 26, 1945, II, 2, Box 831.

63. Deborah Shapley, *Promise and Power: The Life and Times of Robert McNamara* (Boston: Little, Brown, 1993), pp. 65–68; John A. Byrne, *The Whiz Kids: The Founding Fathers of American Business—and the Legacy They Left Us* (New York: Doubleday, 1993), esp. pp. 7–9, 19–20, 174–76, 364–69, 418–22, 515–19.

64. A. B. King to Walter Carpenter, May 11, 1945, II, 2, Box 833; Du Pont Company, *Annual Report*, 1945, p. 19.

65. Robert Patterson to Walter Carpenter, March 15, 1946, and Leslie Groves to Walter Carpenter, February 27, 1946, II, 2, Box 830.

66. For a discussion of Du Pont's deliberation and withdrawal, see Hounshell and Smith, *Science and Corporate Strategy*, pp. 342–45. For Carpenter's position, see Walter Carpenter to Spencer Brownell, March 27, 1946, II, 2, Box 841; Walter Carpenter to the stockholders of the Du Pont Company, August 13, 1945, and Walter Carpenter to Robert Russell, August 27, 1946, II, 2, Box 842.

67. Executive committee minutes, September 8, 1943; Du Pont Company, *Annual Report*, 1945, p. 19, and 1947, pp. 23–24; Angus Echols to the executive and finance committees, October 3, 1945, LMSS, Series A, File 418, Box 380.

68. Du Pont Company, *Annual Report*, 1948, pp. 13–14. For construction expenditures, see untitled, undated chart of research and building expenses in Acc. 1814, Box 37.

69. Executive committee minutes, December 11, 1946; "Total Dividends as % of Total Earnings," October 20, 1947, LMSS, Series A, File 418-26, Box 411.

70. Angus Echols to Pierre du Pont, December 20, 1946, and M. D. Fisher to Pierre du Pont, April 16, 1947, LMSS, Series A, File 418, Box 380.

71. Walter Carpenter to Thomas Shroyer, August 19, 1947, II, 2, Box 834.

72. Walter Carpenter to E. N. Carpenter, June 12, 1946, and Walter Carpenter to Irving Ives, November 7, 1946, Acc. 1553, Box 5. See also Walter Carpenter to John Piper, June 19, 1946, II, 2, Box 833.

73. Spencer Brownell to Walter Carpenter, March 18, 1946, II, 2, Box 841; Walter Carpenter to Thomas Shroyer, August 19, 1947, II, 2, Box 834.

74. Walter Carpenter to Pierre du Pont, May 13, 1947, LMSS, Series A, File 418, Box 380.

75. Crawford Greenewalt interview, October 2, 1991. For construction expenditures and profitability, see Du Pont's annual reports for 1946–57.

76. For a study of Du Pont's foreign operations, see Graham Taylor and Patricia Sudnik, *Du Pont and the International Chemical Industry* (Boston: Twayne, 1984). For an excellent history of American multinationals in the twentieth century, see Myra Wilkins, *The Maturing of Multinational Enterprise: American Business Abroad from 1914 to 1970* (Cambridge: Harvard University Press, 1974).

77. Taylor and Sudnik, *Du Pont*, pp. 93–94, 123, 127–28, 134–36.

78. Ibid., chaps. 9–10.

79. Walter Carpenter to Philip Reed, April 24, 1945, II, 2, Box 827; Walter Carpenter to J. M. Kaplan, June 13, 1947, II, 2, Box 829; Walter Carpenter to

Lord Harry McGowan, April 7, 1944, II, 2, Box 836; Walter Carpenter to J. Thompson Brown, February 21, 1946, Walter Carpenter to George Messersmith, October 25 and December 3, 1946, and Carpenter's marginal notes on Wendell Swint to Walter Carpenter, December 9, 1946, II, 2, Box 832.

80. Walter Carpenter, "Remarks Regarding Proposed Investment in the Heavy Chemicals Industry in Brazil," November 9, 1942, II, 2, Box 839.

81. Hounshell and Smith, *Science and Corporate Strategy*, pp. 201–2, 204; and William Reader, *Imperial Chemical Industries: A History*, vol. 2: *The First Quarter Century, 1926–1952* (London: Oxford University Press, 1975), p. 432.

82. Hounshell and Smith, *Science and Corporate Strategy*, p. 199; Reader, *Imperical Chemical Industries*, p. 434; Jasper Crane to Walter Carpenter, April 2, 1943, and June 26, 1944, II, 2, Box 836; Patricia Sudnik, "Du Pont Foreign Relations, 1920–1950: A Case Study of Associationism on a Global Scale," paper presented at the conference of the Society for Historians of American Foreign Relations, August 1980, pp. 17–18.

83. Hounshell and Smith, *Science and Corporate Strategy*, pp. 199–200, 480–81; Lord Harry McGowan to Walter Carpenter, September 1941, II, 2, Box 836.

84. For the Carpenter–McGowan correspondence, see File 31, II, 2, Box 836.

85. Walter Carpenter to Jasper Crane, August 31, 1942, II, 2, Box 836.

86. Walter Carpenter to Lord Harry McGowan, October 9, 1941, II, 2, Box 836.

87. E. J. Barnsley to Walter Carpenter, July 30, 1942, and Wendell Swint to E. J. Barnsley, August 6, 1942, II, 2, Box 1043.

88. Wendell Swint and S. P. Leigh to Walter Carpenter and Lord Harry McGowan, October 18, 1945, II, 2, Box 836; Wendell Swint to the general managers of the Du Pont Company, December 20, 1939, Acc. 1813, Box 29; Walter Carpenter's notes on his 1946 European trip in II, 2, Box 842.

89. Walter Carpenter to Angus Echols, January 2, 1941, II, 2, Box 841.

90. "E. I. Du Pont De Nemours and Company: Renegotiation Data—1942," n.d., II, 2, Box 840.

91. Calculations from chart in Du Pont Company, *Annual Report*, 1948, pp. 44–45.

92. Wendell Swint to W. F. Lutyens, December 19, 1941, and Walter Carpenter to Lord Harry McGowan, December 19, 1941, II, 2, Box 836.

93. Lord Harry McGowan to Walter Carpenter, February 23, 1942, and E. A. Bingen and J. L. Armstrong, "ICI/Du Pont Royalties," February 24, 1942, II, 2, Box 836.

94. Walter Carpenter to Lord Harry McGowan, May 7, 1942, and W. F. Jenkins to the Du Pont Company, September 3, 1942, II, 2, Box 836.

95. Walter Carpenter to the Ministry of Air Production, September 17, 1942, II, 2, Box 836.

96. "Antitrust Cases," n.d., II, 2, Box 833; and Simon Whitney, *Antitrust Policies: American Experience in Twenty Industries* (New York: The Twentieth Cen-

tury Fund, 1958), 1:195–225, which includes the precise case citations.

97. Walter Carpenter, "Comments before the Chemical Engineering Seminar," May 6, 1952, II, 2, Box 852.

98. Walter Carpenter to E. N. Carpenter, June 11, 1942, and to Walter Carpenter III, January 10, 1944, Acc. 1553, Boxes 3 and 24.

99. Whitney, *Antitrust Policies*, 1:195. For the political background to antitrust in this period, see also Neil Fligstein, *The Transformation of Corporate Control* (Cambridge: Harvard University Press, 1990), pp. 170, 173–77.

100. Ellis Hawley, "Antitrust," in Glenn Porter, ed., *Encyclopedia of American Economic History: Studies of the Principal Movements and Ideas* (New York: Charles Scribner's Sons, 1980), 2:780–81; Tony Freyer, *Regulating Big Business: Antitrust in Great Britain and America, 1880–1990* (New York: Cambridge University Press, 1992), chap. 6; Alan Brinkley, "The Antimonopoly Ideal and the Liberal State: The Case of Thurman Arnold," *Journal of American History* 80 (September 1993): 557–79; and Fligstein, *Transformation*, chap. 5. For a discussion of the shifting focus of New Deal economic policy, see Alan Brinkley, "The New Deal and the Idea of the State," in Steve Fraser and Gary Gerstle, eds., *The Rise and Fall of the New Deal Order, 1930–1980* (Princeton: Princeton University Press, 1989), pp. 85–121.

101. Hawley, "Antitrust," pp. 780–81; John McDonald, "Businessmen and the Sherman Act," *Fortune*, January 1950, pp. 104–14.

102. Walter Carpenter to Frederick Bidwell, May 21, 1942, II, 2, Box 828; Walter Carpenter to Walter Carpenter III, January 10, 1944, Acc. 1553, Box 24.

103. For Arnold's practice of industry-wide prosecutions, see Brinkley, "Antimonopoly Ideal," p. 565.

104. For examples of the scorecards (usually labeled "Anti-Trust Cases" or "Box Score on Antitrust Suits"), see II, 2, Boxes 833 and 852.

105. For the requested delay, see J. Thompson Brown to Henry L. Stimson, March 12, 1942, II, 2, Box 830; and Henry L. Stimson to Francis Biddle, May 25, 1942 and Francis Biddle to Henry L. Stimson, June 3, 1942, Acc. 1662, Box 39; and Blum, *V Was for Victory*, pp. 134–35. For the paint case and the tax code, see Whitney, *Antitrust Policies*, 1:224.

106. Walter Carpenter to Thomas Russell, April 25, 1946, Acc. 1553, Box 5; Whitney, *Antitrust Policies*, 1:195–225.

107. *U.S. v. E. I. du Pont de Nemours and Company*, Civil Action No. 1216, District Court for Delaware (1947). The quotation is from Findings of Fact, Conclusion of Law and Opinion of Chief Judge Paul Leahy, December 14, 1953, p. 381. See also *U.S. v. E. I. du Pont de Nemours and Company*, 351 U.S. 377 (1956).

108. *U.S. v. Imperial Chemical Industries, Ltd., et al.*, Civil Action No. 24-13, District Court for the Southern District of New York (1944). (Hereafter cited as ICI Case.)

109. For material on Carpenter's work on the ICI case, see Files 31 and 31.1, II, 2, Box 836.

110. Ibid.; Walter Carpenter to Lord Harry McGowan, October 17, 1947, II, 2, Box 842; Reader, *Imperial Chemical Industries*, 2:435–38.

111. ICI Case, Final Judgment. The quotation is from p. 207.

112. Ibid., p. 192.

113. Reader, *Imperial Chemical Industries*, 2:438, 441–42.

114. See, for example, Crawford Greenewalt to Walter Carpenter, July 24, 1947, Acc. 1814, Box 6.

115. Walter Carpenter to Crawford Greenewalt, May 29, 1947, II, 2, Box 829. For examples of such negotiation, see "Summary of Cellophane Process Sale Negotiations," December 14, 1949, Cellophane Case, GTE 594; and Crawford Greenewalt to Walter Carpenter, February 4, 1949 and March 10, 1950, II, 2, Box 843.

116. Walter Carpenter, "Remarks to Be Made before the Meeting of the Chemical Directors on May 9, 1941," II, 2, Box 856C.

117. Crawford Greenewalt, "Development Department Functions," n.d. [1945], Acc. 1814, Box 5. For the impact of Du Pont's focus on fundamental research after World War II, see Hounshell and Smith, *Science and Corporate Strategy*, pp. 360–64, 527, 532–34, 538–39, 573–75.

118. Walter Carpenter to Sir John Nicholson, July 19, 1948, II, 2, Box 847. For Carpenter's chart on the presidents, see "Tenure of Presidents, E. I. Du Pont De Nemours and Co.," n.d., II, 2, Box 829.

119. Walter Carpenter to Ruly Carpenter, January 30, 1942, II, 2, Box 825.

120. Ibid.; Walter Carpenter to E. G. Nourse, October 18, 1945, II, 2, Box 829.

121. Walter Carpenter to Ruly Carpenter, January 30, 1942, II, 2, Box 825.

122. E. K. Bolton, "Crawford Greenewalt," November 16, 1939, in Ruly Carpenter to Pierre du Pont, December 18, 1939, LMSS, Series A, File 418-14, Box 400. For Greenewalt's career, see Hounshell and Smith, *Science and Corporate Strategy*, pp. 358–59.

123. Walter Carpenter to E. G. Robinson, May 16, 1946, II, 2, Box 826.

124. Walter Carpenter to Lammot du Pont, April 29, 1947, Acc. 1553, Box 5; and Crawford Greenewalt to Walter Carpenter, May 27, 1947, II, 2, Box 829.

125. Data on sales and return on operating investment are from Du Pont Company, *Annual Report*, 1948, pp. 44–45. Data on assets are from untitled, undated table of assets, 1909–52 in Acc. 1410, Box 45. For an excellent source on the company's cash position and sources of funds, see Angus Echols to the finance committee, October 16, 1947, Acc. 1814, Box 2. Sales figures for new products are from "Du Pont: After 146 Years, Still Growing," *Businessweek*, May 15, 1948, p. 104.

126. "Ages of Executive Committee Members," n.d. [1952], LMSS, Series A, File 418, Box 383; "Growth in Net Sales," GM Case, DTE-DP 443.

127. For data on sales and net income between 1946 and 1955, see charts in File CO-21, II, 2, Box 856. For the changing membership of the executive committee, see the chart cited in the previous note.

Chapter 6   *The Manager in Active Retirement*

1. Walter Carpenter to William Gray, January 20, 1948, and Sir John Nicholson to Walter Carpenter, July 4, 1948, II, 2, Box 847.

2. "Du Pont Circle Cleveland: Comments of W. S. Carpenter, Jr., April 28, 1958," and Walter Carpenter to Victor Emanuel, May 5, 1953, II, 2, Box 852; Walter Carpenter to E. N. Carpenter, April 4, 1947, Acc. 1553, Box 5.

3. David Hounshell and John Smith, *Science and Corporate Strategy: Du Pont R&D, 1902–1980* (New York: Cambridge University Press, 1988), pp. 345, 377.

4. Ibid., pp. 474–80.

5. Untitled table for income tax returns, 1955–1971, Acc. 1553, Box 64. Accounts of individual donations can be found in Walter Carpenter's scrapbooks, third volume.

6. GM Case, Complaint, June 30, 1949.

7. Crawford Greenewalt to Walter Carpenter, August 27, 1948, II, 2, Box 843; Walter Carpenter to Edmund Carpenter II, October 28 and November 5, 1948, Acc. 1553, Box 32.

8. Attorney General Clark quoted in *New York Times*, November 20, 1952, p. 47; Willis Hotchkiss quoted in *Detroit Free Press*, November 19, 1952, pp. 1–2; and Theodore Kovaleff, "Divorce American-Style: The Du Pont–General Motors Case," *Delaware History* 18 (Spring–Summer 1978): 42. See also *New York Times*, September 25, 1948, p. 1, October 1, 1948, p. 37, and July 1, 1949, p. 1. For other studies of the GM case, see Charles Hackman, "The Du Pont–General Motors Divestiture" (M.S. thesis, Rutgers University, 1965), and Arthur Lloyd Welsh, "The Du Pont–General Motors Case" (Ph.D. diss., University of Illinois, 1963).

9. Kovaleff, "Divorce," pp. 28–30; and Tony Freyer, *Regulating Big Business: Antitrust in Great Britain and America, 1880–1990* (New York: Cambridge University Press, 1992), pp. 221–22, 298–99. For an earlier discussion of antitrust, see chap. 5, pp. 219–20.

10. See Ellsworth Alvord to Angus Echols, January 28, 1945, and related correspondence in GM Collection, Box 62527.

11. See, for example, Walter Carpenter to Pierre du Pont, January 21, 1947, II, 2, Box 833; and Angus Echols, "Du Pont Company's Investment in General Motors," March 25, 1946, GM Collection, Box 62527.

12. Walter Carpenter to the finance committee, September 1, 1938, II, 2, Box 824; Walter Carpenter to Pierre du Pont, January 21, 1947, II, 2, Box 833; and Walter Carpenter to Angus Echols, July 28, 1950, GM Collection, Box 62527.

13. Walter Carpenter to Angus Echols, July 28, 1950, GM Collection, Box 62527; Pierre du Pont to Walter Carpenter, January 23, 1947, II, 2, Box 833; Irénée du Pont [to Walter Carpenter], September 22, 1950 (misdated 1930), II, 2, Box 847; and Lammot du Pont to R. P. Vanderpoel, April 3, 1946, Acc. 1662, Box 50.

14. "Transcript: Preliminary Testimony [of Pierre du Pont]," Volume II, May 9–11, 1951, p. 423, LMSS, Series A, File 418-26, Box 428.

15. Irving Shapiro interview, August 13, 1991.

16. Ibid. See also Alfred Chandler and Stephen Salsbury, *Pierre S. du Pont and the Making of the Modern Corporation* (New York: Harper & Row, 1971), pp. 287–88, 414, 419–20, 422.

17. Irving Shapiro interview, August 13, 1991.

18. See, for example, Donaldson Brown to Walter Carpenter, February 16, 1952, Walter Carpenter to Donaldson Brown, February 16, 1952, to Harry Haas, November 25, 1952, to Baxter Jackson, November 26, 1952, and to Oscar Prevost, November 5, 1952, II, 2, Box 852.

19. Walter Carpenter to Francis Gudger, February 24, 1954, II, 2, Box 843.

20. GM Case, Decision of Judge Walter LaBuy, December 3, 1954. The quotations are from pp. 89, 39, 33.

21. Pierre du Pont to Clarence Woolley, September 9, 1952, LMSS, Series A, File 418, Box 381; Walter Carpenter to Lord Harry McGowan, December 14, 1954, Acc. 1553, Box 9.

22. Kovaleff, "Divorce," pp. 30, 36. See also Theodore Kovaleff, *Business and Government during the Eisenhower Administration: A Study of the Antitrust Policy of the Justice Department* (Athens, Ohio: Ohio University Press, 1980), pp. 3, 155–56.

23. *U.S. v. E. I. du Pont de Nemours and Company, et al.*, 353 U.S. 586 (1957). See also Kovaleff, "Divorce," pp. 36–37.

24. Walter Carpenter to the Du Pont finance committee, July 12, 1957, II, 2, Box 852.

25. National Analysts, Inc., *Survey of Du Pont Stockholders, July 1959*, GM Collection, Box 105011. For the various plans, see GM Collection, Box 82584.

26. Examples of Carpenter's work are scattered throughout the GM Collection. See, for example, Walter Carpenter to R. R. Pippen, August 23, 1957, Box 82854, and G. W. Morris to Walter Carpenter, September 12, 1957, Box 62529.

27. Walter Carpenter to Robert Anderson, March 14, 1958, and Walter Carpenter, "Meeting with Attorney General Rogers," January 14, 1959, II, 2, Box 848; Walter Carpenter to Du Pont finance committee, July 12, 1957, II, 2, Box 852.

28. GM Case, Final Judgment, November 17, 1959.

29. Opinion of Judge LaBuy, October 2, 1959, p. 99; Walter Carpenter, "Memorandum [for Charles Rittenhouse]," March 9, 1959, GM Collection, Box 62455.

30. R. R. Pippen to the House Ways and Means Committee, August 17, 1961, GM Collection, Box 62527; Kovaleff, "Divorce," p. 39.

31. "Memorandum of Conference: Department of Justice," October 22, 1959, GM Case, Box 62451.

32. Ibid.

33. Walter Carpenter, "Comments Regarding Memorandum of Conference

with the Department of Justice, October 22, 1959," October 26, 1959, II, 2, Box 852.

34. Ibid. See also Walter Carpenter, "General Motors Suit," October 22, 1958, II, 2, Box 852.

35. Du Pont finance committee, Advice of Action, October 27, 1959, GM Collection, Box 62451.

36. *U.S. v. E. I. du Pont de Nemours and Company, et al.*, 366 U.S. 316 (1961).

37. Crawford Greenewalt to the stockholders of the Du Pont Company, August 14, 1961, GM Collection, Box 62186.

38. Allen Frear to Crawford Greenewalt, August 1958, Acc. 1814, Box 15; "Memorandum of Telephone Conversation with Senator Kerr . . . August 7, 1961," GM Collection, Box 105015.

39. For the bill's legislative odyssey, see Walter Carpenter to R. R. Pippen, October 2, 1959, GM Collection, Box 105014; "Address of United States Senator J. Allen Frear before the Wilmington Rotary Club," October 22, 1959, GM Collection, Box 62451.

40. Ibid.

41. For the positions of Byrd and Williams, see U.S. Senate, "Report of Proceeding: Hearings Held before Committee on Finance, Executive Session, September 5, 1959," esp. pp. 49, 55, 112, in Box 11, File 625 of the John J. Williams Papers, University of Delaware, Newark, Delaware. The transcript of Allen Frear's oral interview with Charles Morrissey, May 12, 1979, which is in the same archive, is not very informative.

42. Ibid.; John Williams, untitled memoranda, January 28 and April 6, 1959, Williams Papers, Box 11, File 625.

43. John Williams, untitled memoranda, August 8–31, 1960, and Louis Schreiber, "Comments on Senator Williams' Letter to Stockholders, August 25, 1960," Williams Papers, Box 11, Files 635 and 638 respectively; Walter Carpenter, "Memorandum," December 7, 1960, II, 2, Box 848. Newspaper clippings of the Greenewalt–Williams battle are in GM Collection, Box 62451.

44. John Williams, untitled memoranda, August 8–31, 1960, Williams Papers, Box 11, File 635.

45. GM Case, Opinion of Judge Walter LaBuy, March 1, 1962. The bill became Public Law 87-403.

46. Charles Hackman, "The Du Pont–General Motors Divestiture" (M.A. thesis, Rutgers University, 1965), p. 42. Trial costs at the end of 1953 were over $6.8 million. "Expense of Antitrust Suits (Since 1939) Through December 31, 1953," GM Collection, Box 62527.

47. C. A. Rittenhouse to Walter Carpenter, July 24, 1961, and T. E. Clough to Walter Carpenter, September 8, 1961, GM Collection, Box 62457. See also *Edward Shenker and David Shenker v. E. I. du Pont de Nemours & Co., et al.*, July 5, 1962, in GM Collection, Box 62184.

48. Ellis Hawley, "Antitrust," in Glenn Porter, ed., *Encyclopedia of American Economic History: Studies of the Principal Movements and Ideas* (New York: Charles Scribners Sons, 1980), 2:783; Kovaleff, "Divorce," p. 37; Irving Shapiro inter-

view, August 13, 1991; Hounshell and Smith, *Science and Corporate Strategy*, pp. 527, 538–39; Walter Carpenter, "Du Pont Circle Cleveland: Comments of Walter S. Carpenter, Jr.," August 15, 1958, II, 2, Box 852.

49. "Resolution Adopted by the Board of Directors, E. I. Du Pont De Nemours & Company," August 20, 1962, II, 2, Box 845.

50. Walter Carpenter to Catherine Irving, February 17, 1958, II, 2, Box 844; Irving Shapiro interview, August 13, 1991.

51. T. C. Davis interview with Alfred Chandler, June 20, 1962, Acc. 1689.

52. Irving Shapiro interview, August 13, 1991.

53. Walter Carpenter to Crawford Greenewalt, September 21, 1966, Acc. 1553, Box 14; Edmund N. Carpenter II interview, May 23, 1990. For Carpenter's obituary, see *New York Times*, February 3, 1976, p. 34.

54. Pierre du Pont to Ruly Carpenter, March 27, 1944, LMSS, Series A, File 418, Box 380.

55. For entrepreneurial activity in modern big business, see Harold Livesay, "Entrepreneurial Persistence through the Bureaucratic Age," *Business History Review* 51 (Winter 1977): 415–43.

56. For the general picture, see, for example, Mabel Newcomer, "Professionalization of Leadership in the Big Business Corporation," in James Baughman, ed., *The History of American Management* (Englewood Cliffs, N.J.: Prentice-Hall, 1969), pp. 244–52; Herrymon Maurer, "The New Manager," in Robert and Seon Manley, eds., *The Age of the Manager: A Treasury of Our Times* (New York: Macmillan, 1962), pp. 67–89; and Francis Sutton, Seymour Harris, Carl Kaysen, and James Tobin, *The American Business Creed* (Cambridge, Mass.: Harvard University Press, 1956).

57. Irving Shapiro interview, August 13, 1991. For a more general treatment of the transition among white-collar workers, see Olivier Zunz, *Making America Corporate, 1870–1920* (Chicago: University of Chicago Press, 1990).

58. Herrymon Maurer, "Who Are the Executives—II," in Editors of *Fortune, The Executive Life* (New York: Doubleday, 1956), p. 36.

59. Chandler and Salsbury, *Pierre S. du Pont*, pp. 592, 602–3.

60. John Garraty, *Right-Hand Man: The Life of George W. Perkins* (New York: Harper & Brothers, 1960); Robert Hessen, *Steel Titan: The Life of Charles M. Schwab* (New York: Oxford University Press, 1975).

61. See William Lazonick, "Financial Commitment and Economic Performance: Ownership and Control in the American Industrial Corporation," *Business and Economic History*, 2d ser., vol. 17 (1988): 115–28.

62. "Ages of Executive Committee Members," LMSS, Series A, File 418, Box 383.

63. Chandler and Salsbury, *Pierre S. du Pont*; Alfred Chandler, *Strategy and Structure: Chapters in the History of the Industrial Enterprise* (Cambridge: MIT Press, 1962), esp. chap. 2; Alfred Chandler, *The Visible Hand: The Managerial Revolution in American Business* (Cambridge: Harvard University Press, 1977).

64. Pierre du Pont to Lord Harry McGowan, December 9, 1949, LMSS, Series A, File 637, Box 1 (of one). For a recent analysis of the federal govern-

ment's role in the evolution of big business in the United States, see Neil Fligstein, *The Transformation of Corporate Control* (Cambridge: Harvard University Press, 1990).

65. See, for example, B. Joseph Monsen, "The American Business View," *Daedalus* 98 (Winter 1969): 159–73; and Sutton et al., *American Business Creed*, pp. 216–17.

66. For studies demonstrating more traditional or differentiated views, see Howell Harris, *The Right To Manage: Industrial Relations Policies of American Business in the 1940s* (Madison, Wisc.: University of Wisconsin Press, 1982); and Jacqueline McGlade's forthcoming dissertation tentatively titled "The Illusion of Consensus: American Business, European Recovery, and the Making of Cold War Aid, 1948–1958" (from George Washington University).

67. Chandler, *Strategy and Structure*, chaps. 2 and 3, and *Visible Hand*, pp. 438–50, 457–62.

68. Michael C. Jensen, "Eclipse of the Public Corporation," *Harvard Business Review* 67 (September–October 1989): 61–74. See also Allen Kaufman and Ernest J. Englander, "Kohlberg Kravis Roberts & Co. and the Restructuring of American Capitalism," *Business History Review* 67 (Spring 1993): 52–97.

69. Lazonick, "Financial Commitment"; William Lazonick, "Organizational Capabilities in American Industry: The Rise and Decline of Managerial Capitalism," *Business and Economic History*, 2d ser., vol. 19 (1990): 35–54; Alfred Chandler, "Managerial Enterprise and Competitive Capabilities," *Business History* 34 (January 1992): 11–41.

Index

Ahuja, Elias, 12, 59, 67, 105, 130; and
 Du Pont nitrate operations, 12–14;
 sponsors Walter Carpenter, 13, 32–
 33
Allied Chemical and Dye Corporation,
 66, 67
Alvord and Alvord, 174, 235
American Liberty League, 129, 130, 135
American Viscose Company, 85
antitrust policy, of U.S. government,
 218–20, 234–35; and General
 Motors–Du Pont antitrust case, 234–
 35, 239–40, 241–44, 249
Arlington Company, 20, 22, 23, 203; acquisition of, by Du Pont, 23–25; performance of, 23, 25
Arnold, Thurman, 219, 220

Baker, George F., Jr., 70, 135; and crisis
 in General Motors bonus plan, 145–
 46, 148–49, 151, 153
Barksdale, Hamilton, 34, 138
Barton, Bruce, 132
Beadle, Walter, 15, 79
Bicks, Robert, 243, 244, 250
big business, xvi, 39, 81, 96; assessment
 of, 259–60; economies of, 22, 36, 49,
 59, 88, 259; external audiences and,
 96–97, 257; learned routines of, 59,
 88; management in, 100–101, 103,
 158–59, 181, 255; structure of, xvi,
 40–42, 49, 158, 258–59. See also professional management
Blum, Albert, 30, 68, 69
Blum, Henry, 30, 68
Bolton, Elmer, 207, 209, 232
bonus plan, 81. See also General Motors
 Corporation; Du Pont Company

Bradley, Albert, 139, 162, 166, 177, 179
Brayman, Harold, 199–200
Brennan, Justice William, 240, 244
Brown, Donaldson, 35, 110; criticism of
 Charles Wilson, 178, 179; Du Pont
 career of, 34, 44, 50, 64, 114; and
 General Motors bonus plan (1923),
 61–62, 156, 172; and General Motors
 bonus plan (1930), 144, 147, 150,
 153, 155–56; General Motors career
 of, 50, 138, 161–62, 167; opposition
 of, to Walter Carpenter, 51, 52, 62;
 public relations and, 132, 171; and
 reorganization at General Motors,
 159–60, 165
Brown, Harry Fletcher: opposition of,
 to Walter Carpenter, 51, 81; and reorganization at Du Pont, 47, 49
Brown, J. Thompson, 34, 196
Bunge and Bourne, 88
Burdick, C. Lalor, 193
Burton, Justice Harold, 240
Byrd, Sen. Harry, 245, 246–47, 248

Canadian Industries Limited (CIL) 86,
 222, 226
Carpenter, Benjamin Gardner, 2–3
Carpenter, Benjamin H. (Uncle Harry),
 3, 104
Carpenter, Edmund N. (Uncle Ed), 3;
 career of, 13, 18; correspondence of,
 with Walter Carpenter, 104, 129, 189,
 190, 211; and nitrate search in South
 America, 13–14, 34; sponsors Walter
 Carpenter, 13–14, 32, 33
Carpenter, Edmund N., II (Ned), 33,
 101, 107, 234
Carpenter, Isabella Morgan, 3, 106

Library of Congress Cataloging-in-Publication Data

Cheape, Charles W., 1945–
    Strictly business : Walter Carpenter at Du Pont and
General Motors / Charles W. Cheape.
        p.   cm. — (Studies in industry and society) ; 6)
    Includes bibliographical references and index.
    ISBN 0-8018-4941-1 (hc : alk. paper)
        1. Carpenter, Walter Samuel, 1888–1976.   2. Exec-
utives—United States—Biography.   3. E. I. du Pont
de Nemours & Company—History.   4. Chemical industry—United States—   Management—History.
5. General Motors Corporation—History.   6. Automobile industry and   trade—United States—Management—History.   I. Title.   II. Series.
HD9651.95.C37C48   1995
658.4'0092—dc20
[B]   94-22652
                                                  CIP